Robert Southwell

Robert Southwell

Snow in Arcadia:
redrawing the English lyric
landscape, 1586–95

ANNE SWEENEY

Manchester
University Press
Manchester and New York

distributed exclusively in the USA by Palgrave

Copyright © Anne Sweeney 2006

The right of Anne Sweeney to be identified as the author of this work has been asserted by her in accordance with the Copyright, Designs and Patents Act 1988.

Published by Manchester University Press
Oxford Road, Manchester M13 9NR, UK
and Room 400, 175 Fifth Avenue, New York, NY 10010, USA
www.manchesteruniversitypress.co.uk

Distributed exclusively in the USA by
Palgrave, 175 Fifth Avenue, New York, NY 10010, USA

Distributed exclusively in Canada by
UBC Press, University of British Columbia, 2029 West Mall, Vancouver, BC, Canada V6T 1Z2

British Library Cataloguing-in-Publication Data
A catalogue record for this book is available from the British Library

Library of Congress Cataloging-in-Publication Data applied for

ISBN *0-7190-8567-5 hardback*
EAN *978-0-7190-8567-3*

First published 2006

15 14 13 12 11 10 09 08 07 06   10 9 8 7 6 5 4 3 2 1

Typeset in Scala with Pastonchi display
by Koinonia Ltd, Manchester
Printed in Great Britain
by CPI, Bath

To live at peace among ... those who oppose us, is a great grace, and a most commendable and manly achievement.

> (from Thomas à Kempis, *The Imitation of Christ*, translated and introduction by Leo Sherley-Price (Harmondsworth; Penguin, 1952, repr. 1979), p. 71)

Contents

Preface and acknowledgements   *page* ix

Introduction   Ben Jonson's Admiration for Southwell's 'burning Babe   1
    A different Englishness   4
    Hatching butterflies: the Jesuit approach to writing   8
    The Englishness of Southwell's art   11
    Southwell's authorial identity   14
    Performing deeds: Southwell's poetic purposes   18
    Grace and the individual talent   21

1   Rome: the discernment of angels
    'Sacra paradisi in sede locavit': Southwell's Roman life   38
    Schooling the eye of the heart: learning to read beauty   42
    Painting by numbers: Southwell's new poetic vision   45
    Learning to do violence to the self   50
    English College: cross-purposes   53
    Painful subjects: the new English martyrs   57

2   The *Spiritual Exercises*: the 'inward eie'
    Raphael and the refining of the sight   71
    Learning to read the emotions: resolving in tears   77
    Reading and learning the self   80
    The end of training: hidden motivations   84

3   Hidden ways and secret veins: into England
    In His service: England's metaphorical martyrdom   93
    Authority and writing: the virtual church   96
    Needing a new sort of English   99
    The Catholic cultural network: songs among swords   105
    Southwell's contacts: public voices, hidden selves   109

4   The flight of angels: England's altered confidence
    'Joseph's Amazement'   123
    Caesar's or God's? Law versus love   129
    Waking Christ's sleeping friends: Magdalen and the passionate imagination   135

Contents

A golden distraction: metaphorising the Real	140
Hamartolos: redirecting love	146
A new voice: the femaled soul	151
The English Bethany	155

5 Snow in Arcadia: rewriting the English lyric landscape

Disordered order	164
In an English garden	170
Mapping the new Albion	178
'Astonish't dread': Lazarus in Parnassus	184
Cold comforts: a Breton and a Southwell Christmas	186

6 Southwell's war of words

Dies irae	194
Two queens and an orphaned State	199
Emblems and idolatrous images	205
Deathly loves: Southwell's pointed poetry	213
Battle lines	219

7 The 'performing Word': Southwell's sacralised poetic

The cross-action of grace	228
Hearts and thorns: Sidney's and Southwell's poetic vision	235
Southwell's poetic sacrament	240
Southwell and Spenser: truth and beauty	243
Love songs to the soul: the priest-poet	246
God's numbered universe: Southwell's divine symmetry	251
Last lines: Southwell's first and last public sermon	254

8 Conclusion

'A sharp sword, yet as I suppose well sheathed'	269
Terrible semblances: love's violence	272
Torn and fretted velvet: the pattern of a poet	274
The burning Babe	279

Bibliography	293
Index	309

Preface and acknowledgements

This work began as a duty and quickly developed into a passion. Professor Richard Wilson suggested that I might find something of interest in Robert Southwell and, as I had always been intrigued by 'The burning Babe', I had a little look. Six years of labour later, some funded by the Arts and Humanities Research Board and under the inestimably patient eye of Professors Richard Dutton and Alison Findlay and Dr Hilary Hinds at Lancaster University, and, most especially, Professor Peter Davidson (who put fire into the work even from the cold North), I have gained a deeper understanding of a part of my nation's history that has been all but 'disappeared', and learned to respect the young Jesuit priest-poet. I undertook this work for the love of the man and his words, and I hope this book will be read in that same spirit. As a poet Robert Southwell has much to say to this age, bloodied as it is, and with voices striving to be heard. Many, many thanks to Manchester University Press for undertaking to offer it to a wider readership.

More personally, when I began the research Southwell's insights into human evanescence were antique theoretical positions from an age all too well acquainted with death; but unfortunate circumstances meant that I came to need, and have gained, courage from one who could look so steadily upon his own mortality. Having 'lost' six months at the start of the year, much of the book was written up in hospital, fuelled by regular NHS cuppas and the sterling companionship and support of NHS staff and volunteers, with the deadline drawing near; the term never sounded so resonant. Deepest thanks to all at Lancaster, Liverpool, and Clatterbridge Hospitals, and to all those other chance companions along this strange road.

But the greatest debt is due to my husband Michael, whose generosity and intelligence helped my work immensely; he, my dear sons, and wider family have been wonderfully encouraging and tolerant of the inevitable effects of such a project upon our lives. Thanks also to untold friends and supporters who have shown kindness or interest at key moments, and, in too many ways to detail, have made a difference. Stonyhurst College kindly made its Library available to my studies, its late Librarian, Father Turner, S.J., and the late Bishop Foley, contributing much at the outset to a project that I was so very less well qualified than they to embark upon. I am also very grateful that Father Thomas McCoog, S.J., of Mount Street, took the time to look over and comment on aspects of the work, which has, in any case, called much upon

Preface and acknowledgements

his expertise in this area. If I have committed any solecisms against the belief systems of the bodies represented by these gentlemen, it is unintentional, and regretted. I have been acutely aware from the outset that, in discussing a saint from outside the boundaries of religious studies, I was on the thinnest of ice. I hope it is evident that I am addressing discoursal and literary issues only; St Robert Southwell is beyond all comment spiritually, but as a poet and an Englishman he earned his garlands, I believe. 'Muse not', as he said, 'to see some mud in cleerest brooke, | They once were brittle mould, that now are Saintes.'

Dr Anne Sweeney
Lancaster

Introduction

Ben Jonson's admiration for Southwell's 'Burning Babe'

Southwell was hanged, yet so he had written that piece of his *The burning babe* [Ben Jonson] would have been content to destroy many of his.[1]

> As I in hoarie Winters night
>   Stoode shivering in the snow,
> Surpris'd I was with sodaine heate,
>   Which made my hart to glow;
>
> And lifting up a fearefull eye   5
>   To view what fire was neare,
> A pretty Babe all burning bright
>   Did in the ayre appeare;
>
> Who scorched with excessive heate,
>   Such floods of teares did shed,   10
> As though his floods should quench his flames,
>   Which with his teares were fed:
>
> Alas (quoth he) but newly borne,
>   In fiery heates I frie,
> Yet none approach to warme their harts,   15
>   Or feele my fire, but I;
>
> My faultlesse breast the furnace is,
>   The fuell wounding thornes:
> Love is the fire, and sighs the smoake,
>   The ashes, shames and scornes;   20
>
> The fewell Justice layeth on,
>   And Mercie blowes the coales,
> The metall in this furnace wrought,
>   Are mens defiled soules:

> For which, as now on fire I am 25
>   To worke them to their good,
> So will I melt into a bath,
>   To wash them in my blood.
>
> With this he vanisht out of sight,
>   And swiftly shrunk away, 30
> And straight I called unto minde,
>   That it was Christmasse day.[2]

'The burning Babe' is probably the only poem most readers will know of Robert Southwell's. I recall reading it as a child; it seemed pleasantly atmospheric to a childish imagination, the holy Babe appearing like a bright bauble against the dark of a snowy English Christmas evening. It is homely, yet cryptic in the Elizabethan style, and blessedly short, a silly sentimental thing that manages, apparently on these merits, to make its way into most anthologies of the English poetic canon. It came as something of a shock to me as an undergraduate to learn that Ben Jonson, with his reputation as a hard man of letters, had singled out this bagatelle for admiration – indeed, he wished he himself had written it; there can be no greater possible encomium from a great ego. What did he admire in it? In the nineteenth century a minister of the Reformed church, Alexander Grosart, considered Southwell's writing to be 'more potential in our Literature than appears on the surface'; his edition, generous as it is to his brother in Christ, does not elaborate upon his estimation of Southwell's poetry.[3] There have been some fine commentaries on Robert Southwell's life and work, but none of them has explained to my satisfaction why a man like Jonson would have admired this poem so. This book is an attempt to answer that question.

St Robert Southwell, S.J. (1561?–95), was a third son, born to Norfolk gentry enriched by the Henrician dissolutions; his home was part of an old Benedictine priory at Horsham St Faith, not far from the celebrated medieval shrine of Our Lady of Walsingham, which had been reduced to ruins only twenty-three years before his birth. Walsingham was a site of considerable significance to English Christian piety, a place of pilgrimage replicating the Holy House of Nazareth, built on the strength of a dream of the Mother of God. This ancient link with the Holy Land and the affairs of the Holy Family was twenty-one miles – a day's journey – from the Southwells' home; one can only guess at the shock of many of the local families at its destruction and the burning of the wooden statue of the Virgin in 1538.[4] The ruins themselves achieved an iconic significance for those who feared for England's spiritual health as the sixteenth century drew towards a close, reflected not only in melancholy poetry but in Southwell's later lyrics, where he metaphorises an English courtier's spiritual dereliction as a ruined building.[5]

Southwell's own church, St Faith's, contains a near-miraculous preservation of religious decoration, a rich medieval parade of painted saints and bishops. Eight of the eleven on the choir screens are female, and St Bridget of Sweden, shown at her desk busily writing down her vision of Christ, could be an exemplar for Southwell's mother Bridget (Copley), an educated gentlewoman attendant on Queen Elizabeth.[6] The Catholicism of his mother, which, like that of a large part of the English population, persisted despite increasingly harsh attempts by the Elizabethan administration to suppress it, must have existed somewhat uncomfortably in the house built on confiscated priory land amongst the very ruins of the old English Church.[7]

Southwell had been born into an inheritance that epitomised the entanglements and confusions of a century of dissolution and reformation. His childhood nickname perhaps betrays a nostalgia for the old religion: 'Even from my earliest infancy', Robert wrote to his father much later, 'you were wont in merriment to call me *Father Robert*.'[8] Southwell's family appears to have maintained Catholic sympathies in private, while struggling to conform to royal wishes and laws in public, a nervous, precarious existence. Robert's connections included significant Catholic families: another reference to this nickname, to 'Mr Southwell, otherwise known as Father Robert, [who, with others] desire their commendations', occurs in a letter from a Roman student, Robert Middlemore, to his cousin Robin Throckmorton of Coughton.[9] The Throckmorton family included some celebrated recusants; they were connected to Vauxes and to that celebrated builder and gardener Sir Thomas Tresham, both of whom were to be of consequence to Southwell's poetic production. Southwell was close to the Copley family, too, on his mother's side, and William Cecil was also a relative.[10]

Many coteries of boyish resistance were built up in the shires by interrelated groups of youngsters such as these in the late 1500s. 'Father Robert', sent to his mother's relatives between the South Downs and the coast, found a thriving Catholic community connected to the exiled Catholics of the Continent, centred on such noblemen as Henry Wriothesley, second Earl of Southampton. Robert stayed with the Copleys, then the Cottons, mixing also with Shelleys and Gages.[11] Thus, Southwell's early adolescence was spent in an atmosphere of gallant resistance and wild enterprise which coloured his responses to Catholicism. While the heads of Catholic households endured an increasingly complicated situation of compromise, dissembling, and anxiety, those groups of adolescents busy making a minor nuisance of themselves in the shires may well have looked upon the attempts of their parents to preserve their family fortunes as at best weakness, and at worst culpable betrayal of their faith. Southwell was later to write some sharp attacks on English Court trimmers, one, perhaps, his own father; and was it with his mother in mind that he directed a few poetic hints towards ladies in positions of influence with the Queen and their duty to their proper faith?[12]

A DIFFERENT ENGLISHNESS

On 10 June 1576, aged fourteen, Robert left his Catholic coterie for the nearest Catholic school, the English College set up by William (later Cardinal) Allen at Douai in Flanders. This cannot have been mere family habit on the part of his parents, in fact it seems a peculiarly risky act: the Pope had declared Elizabeth excommunicate six years earlier, and given English Catholics permission to consider her overthrow.[13] It therefore might be expected that those hoping for preferment at Court would be more than usually anxious to dissemble any family Catholicism. Despite this, and despite even the fact that his father was at that moment in Marshalsea prison accused of speaking against the Queen, Robert was sent across the water for a Catholic schooling. He travelled with John Cotton, under whose surname he was later to go during his English mission.[14]

Lodging at the English College, it was while studying at the university college run by the Society of Jesus nearby that he encountered the Jesuit intellectual Leonard Lessius.[15] Lessius, only seven years Southwell's senior, was developing ideas on free will and the limits and duties of secular power that were to have profound effects upon European thought.[16]

Edmund Campion had been at Douai three years previously. The celebrated Oxford scholar left a strong impression, his conversion to Catholicism feeding English Catholic hopes of a revival and stiffening the resolve of the exiles for a more active engagement in England's affairs.[17] A college man, Cuthbert Mayne, had left for England less than two months before Southwell's arrival.

Southwell had determined to go into orders, first considering the contemplative Carthusians; but, after much struggle, and perhaps in response to Mayne's heroic endeavour, he decided instead to aim for the Society of Jesus. This radical, new Order taught a Tridentine Catholicism unfamiliar, even inimical, to the more conservative Catholics in England. From the moment that he settled on the Society, nothing could ever be the same for Southwell at home in an English State increasingly hardening its heart against confrontational Catholicism.

Local, English-aided struggles to throw off Spanish Catholic domination meant that Southwell's first stay in Douai lasted only about six months, and he is next noticed attending classes in Paris, under the English Jesuit Thomas Derbyshire, probably returning to Douai in June 1577, only to hear of the execution of Mayne in England.[18]

As a result of all these events, Continental encounters with Southwell's own countrymen were more strongly polarised than those at home, and his training in language use reflected this. English was the language of contestation with English Protestants, vying for the hearts and minds of ordinary English men and women; Latin was the language of the angels,[19] while the vernacular was a weapon of war, whether propaganda or direct assault; Allen by now believed that Catholicism in England would not survive without missionaries trained in active disputation.[20]

Southwell's ingestion of Latin and English was therefore driven by both the circumstances of his induction into a cadre of religious brothers, and the practical needs of controversy and refutation. Allen made sure the students were 'acquainted "with the chief impieties, blasphemies, absurdities, cheats and trickeries of the English heretics, as well as their ridiculous writings, sayings and doings"', an atmosphere in which Southwell was immersed from waking to retiring.[21] In order to achieve 'greater power and grace in the use of the vulgar tongue, a thing on which the heretics plume themselves exceedingly, and by which they do great injury to the simple folk', the College boys were trained in controversialism and English, as well as Latin, rhetoric.[22] Southwell was learning a new language of oppositional English along with his scholarly Latin.[23] His choice of English for much of his mission writing can thus be seen to be primarily a means to an end, not a matter of habit; discussion of his work must be founded on this understanding. Southwell was not an English poet, but one who sometimes chose English as part of his rhetorical arsenal.

This would seem sufficient to explain Southwell's later poetic critique of some of his countrymen, an assault which more reverent studies of Southwell prefer not to notice. But even the swiftest vocabulaic trawl through his lyrics produces lexis such as this in the short 'Saint Peters Complaynte' (p. 29), where he describes a 'pastor' who is 'craven', full of 'Untrewth', 'pride' and 'servile feare'; a 'disloyall wretch', who 'could with cursinge othes forsweare [his] kinge' (lines 9–10, 25, 29, 60). 'Pastor' is a technical term for a minister in charge of a church and congregation: Jesuits operated outside such church structures; Southwell is addressing ministers of the English Church here. In his assault on those dancing attendance on Elizabeth such as Dyer (and his father) he is equally harsh about 'one that lives in shewe', yet 'Whose knowledge is a bloody field, | Where vertue slaine doth lie' ('[Dyer's] Phansie turned to a sinners complaint', p. 36, lines 25–8); Southwell is here writing as Allen's pupil, taking the fight to the opposition in the semi-public arena of vernacular lyric poetry.

But it is not quite that simple: although weaned on Allen's anti-Protestant programme, Southwell moved somewhat away from it once he decided to enter the Jesuit novitiate; a novice's perceived usefulness as a simple counter to Protestantism altered and refined as he rose through the levels of study. Allen's agenda was not that of the Society; his attitudes seemed clear in regard of the place of the generality of his students: 'Our students, being intended for the English harvest, are not required to excel or be great proficients in theological science, though their teachers ought to be as learned and prudent as possible.'[24] Jesuits were not being groomed by the Society for front-line conflict in Protestant states. Campion's vigorous anti-Protestant labours in Prague were interrupted (and ultimately terminated) by the requirement to go to England. Allen's English College was founded to train men for the English mission. The foot-soldiers took an oath to return, while those considered 'learned and prudent' enough to supply teaching and other roles in the Society, as Southwell clearly was, did not. This, too, was to affect Southwell's relationship with his writing.[25] Even when the missionary oath conceived by Robert Persons was ratified by Pope Gregory XIII in 1579, it was required only of those who were supported by the college's foundation. It was not customarily taken by those funded by parents or relatives; nor was it taken by Jesuits, who did not study at the English College.[26] Southwell's subtlety and prudence, prized Jesuit assets, may have altered the ways in which he later responded to the pressures of his mission. Historicist scholarship has tended to argue convincingly that any early tendency towards polemic which he had was modified by actual contact with English Catholics struggling with their awful dilemma during Southwell's English mission, people such as his own family, who wished to remain faithful to Rome yet not to ruin themselves in the process.[27]

Southwell's determination to join the Society, once back in Douai in 1577, appears to have alarmed his family – they dropped correspondence with him at around this time.[28] His family's lay tradition of Christian church going was very different from the new, strongly Iberian order he was vanishing into. Douai was supported with Spanish funds, and the Jesuits themselves had very close (some believed too close) affinities with the Spanish Court towards the close of the century.[29] Southwell's national identity was therefore under scrutiny in his English writings, and this can be seen in the letter he wrote to Robert Cecil from prison after his capture in 1592 (see p. 14 below). His English writings were inevitably harnessed to the cause of Rome, with all the problems and implications that this carried in England.

The reintroduction of Protestant worship in Elizabeth's reign was at first accompanied by public disputations staged between Protestant churchmen and Catholic apologists, who were dependent on books sourced on the Continent and soon to be proscribed in England; the churchman's right of public disputation was, therefore, simultaneously offered and rendered impossible, contumacious, disloyal.[30] Recent historicist approaches to literature have allowed us to unlock such contexts for Southwell's writing, especially the extra burdens it carried in England of communication and engagement, and the consequent sensitivity about nationalist concerns.[31]

Southwell, immersed in the excitements of his youthful coterie, could not have anticipated (and possibly would not have cared about) the rising suspicion with which the Society was viewed by the English State, or its eventual criminalisation. Even so, for Southwell (and other young radicals) to veer off into this new, still largely non-English order of the Roman Catholic Church

Introduction

was something of a departure from the normality of a university education followed by a pastoral or clerical appointment, or a post at a court, English or otherwise. We know from his own writing that the results of his decision to enter an order which had not taken part in England's return to Catholicism during Mary's reign, by way of a schooling bent on disputation with the existing English Church, caused some self-searching. He was, by dint of Allen's and Robert Persons's training and influence, a recusant recusant, resistance or resolve doubled, and all of this becomes condensed in his writing (including his poetry) into a new ideal of self-identification, an agonistic, yet deeply personal response to God which he redeployed to help souls in his English ministry.

The few writings from Southwell's years in school show a sensitive, somewhat fragile personality sometimes tormented by doubts. In the way he expresses his indecisions and anxieties we see a young man of passionate convictions with both the ability and the need to enlarge upon his spiritual dilemmas in affective writing.[32] Almost from the start, presumably because of the emphasis put on this very issue by Allen and Jesuits such as Thomas Derbyshire, he seemed to see poetry as a potentially persuasive amplification of his normal voice, and, more than that, as a specific form of expression for the non-rational, the felt; in this sort of work he was closer to the Ignatian emphasis on inner experience than to Allen's rhetorical pragmatism, although he never lost sight of either. His close friend John Deckers having been accepted into the Society, Southwell turned to elegiac poetry in English to express his own feelings on being rejected: his *Querimonia*.[33]

Perhaps 'The prodigall childs soule wracke' (p. 43) was written up from a meditation of that time. 'Disankered from a blisfull shore' of homely certainties, and 'lancht into the maine of cares', he finds himself 'on every side | Enwrapped in the waves of woe'. He is isolated, lost in a stormy sea, and can 'to no port for refuge go' (lines 1–8). His preoccupation with the confession of human frailty and isolation is as clear here as in his letter to his friend. The ship/soul emblem is commonplace enough as a means of showing the frailty of the spiritual vehicle, but Southwell does more than borrow its illustrative potential, translating moody confusion into the metaphorised emblem, using it as a means of expressing what ordinary language could not convey. When 'Denide the Planets guiding light' (l. 17), he resorts to the recreational magic of metaphor, as if ordinary language could not cope with the chaos of his disordered feelings.

On being at last accepted by the Society, Southwell wrote a sort of autobiographical retrospective to Deckers, describing how he had felt torn between Ignatius's 'bark' and that of the Carthusians, drowning, as a result, in waves of temptation; it is as if lack of interest from either authority was somehow to blame for his floundering in disaffection. In the margin there is a little metrical prayer to the Virgin.[34]

There can be no doubt that Southwell saw such imagery in terms of personal confession: the language of his *Querimonia* is founded on the same imagery of being adrift on storm-tossed, wintry seas; we see him lost 'amid the billows of carnal desires, [...] dashed on the reefs of sinful occasions. [...] o wretched me, who would forbid my tears?'[35] But added to it is a new imagery, informed by his new Jesuit schooling in the powers of memory and imagination: Ignatius privileged emotional response as a legitimate way to experience God, and the recollected memory of that response as a methodology for Jesuit witness and ministry. Poetry becomes communication and movement through memory to Southwell, supplying an escape, a means of self-expression (witness) and a methodology of communicating with certain people (ministry). Here, then, we see the sound beginnings of a strategy in which the language of metaphor is considered not only generally influential, but also handmaid to individual response, to self-expression. Here, too, we see his first acknowledgement of the 'winter' that threatened to overcome his spirits throughout his life.[36]

HATCHING BUTTERFLIES: THE JESUIT APPROACH TO WRITING

As a result of engaging in that altered course of the Jesuit novitiate, Southwell becomes, in historical terms, more than a poet. At the same time, by the standards of post-Arnoldian criticism, he is less than one, because as a Jesuit he was a trained rhetorician with a didactic brief: the creation of poetry for its own sake was not his end; helping souls was. But that Jesuit training is integral to an understanding of his writing. It was, by the standards of his day, unusual, and, as it focused to an unusual degree on creative arts and the uses to which they can be put, it is relevant to Southwell's development as a writer. In answering my own question about Jonson's estimation of 'The burning Babe', therefore, it becomes necessary to inquire into aspects of the life, training, and various agendas of the man who wrote it. The first part of this book is the product of those enquiries. More than most, Southwell's purposes are his poetry and vice versa, and one cannot be understood without the other.

The Jesuits were not just churchmen who happened to write, and their innovative attitudes to the uses of visual image are vital to an understanding of Southwell's work. The dream of their founder Ignatius of Loyola was of thriving city churches that could accommodate both sacraments and arts, the sacred alongside the beautiful, masses, sermons, lectures, music, and drama all working to the greater glory of God. The great Gesù in Rome had figured hangings that obscured the sanctuary to provide backdrops to religious dramas and pageants.[37]

As a novice in Rome, Southwell was to be entirely surrounded, from rising to sleeping, with the imagery of Christian heroism. In the churches the altars were overlooked by the first tentative expressions of the baroque, combining affective mystical realism with dramatic action, human bodies in extremis thrusting forward out of enigmatically shadowed depths, seizing the attention of the viewer, drawing him into their drama. This artistic vision was to inform Southwell's poetic expression in turn; the imagery of his shorter English lyrics is highly visual as a rule, his language clearer of allegory and argument than was usual in Elizabethan poetry, as if his primary intention was to replicate the pictures rather than engage in rhetoric about texts or subject matter.

Southwell's English poetic diction, too, is remarkably succinct, his metaphors used largely with restraint, a product, I would suggest, of his Continental seminary education, in which he was unused to any English but the most restrained and focused, and very used to seeing a message condensed into emblem and imagery on the walls of his colleges (often with concise, even pithy, inscriptions).

He was being trained in theories of artistic response: the baroque vision being developed in Europe was addressing the theory of the visual and its connection with the immanent, making the imagined as real, and as potent, as possible. Where *rhetorical* manifestations of the baroque, generally represented in English poetry by the thematic multiplicity developed by Crashaw, failed to excite the English, Southwell's poetic descriptions of the super-real human drama of baroque visual imagery leaped the boundary into English letters. The drama of his ventriloquisations of Biblical penitents such as Sts Peter and Mary Magdalen are clearly related to the new early baroque imagery of near-photographic realism which showed biblical persons caught in the middle of spiritual crises, a portrayal far more immediate than the impassive medieval saints of his home church. Such realism allowed a new engagement, opening up a private space to be filled by the observer with his or her personal response to the affective scene. But the idea carries through into Southwell's shorter works of praise or exhortation, works where the imagery occasionally outshines the message, so that one has to dig deeper to exposes the layers of meaning.

The Jesuits saw a close relationship between the image and the action of viewing it, developing programmes of related, revelatory image and inscription through which a viewer could be led, arriving at a better spiritual understanding as if on a spiritual progress. There is a telling interconnectedness between the techniques of revelation in Jesuit art and drama and Southwell's use of imagery. His ideal is to turn the beauties of art, as he has experienced them, to the greater glory of God, in order to teach the soul to look skyward to the new baroque heaven, into azure vistas piled with sun-glazed clouds and divinely beautiful beings. His 'Seeke flowers of heaven' (p. 52), for instance, paints a vivid picture of the illuminated treasures of the Church as the fittest food for a refined sensibility, flowers 'staind in beauties die', 'inameld with delight, | And limbde with glorious gleames' (lines 9, 11–12). The imagery is as sensually rich as the Catholic Church believed was necessary to encourage a closer approach to God; the 'glorious gleames' of this garden are the like the gorgeous and uplifting images surrounding Southwell and the others in the churches of Rome. The soul, admonished to shake off that part of itself that feeds on earthly weeds and sip instead heavenly nectar, is clearly word-painted as a butterfly, though this is never explicit. The imagery is allowed to float free of words into a clearer metaphysical space; an informed reader would fit the picture to a memory-store of imagery, recalling the classical tale of Psyche, the mortal female who captured the heart of Cupid, and who (often depicted as a butterfly) is taken as a symbol of the elevated human soul, and the possibility of its immortality through love of God.[38]

Unlike contemporary English poetic structures, even Spenserian ones, this is almost the opposite of allegory, suggesting a partnership in Southwell's mind between image and understanding that seems to exist in part outside language. That dizzying trompe l'oeil manipulation of the imaginary space between God's heaven and viewer's earth seen in baroque decoration is here co-opted: Southwell collapses the distance and difference between his reader and God, the airy gulfs of blue sky replaced by the internal spaces, comprehension and affection of the reader, directed upwards by Southwell towards his desired heavenly point.

This understanding of the connections between, and uses of, different artistic genres was not Southwell's alone, although he was one of the first to import it into English poetry. To illustrate this point, his Psyche imagery may be linked to a particular Jesuit use of it in the Continental colleges, in a college drama about Psyche which theatricalises the dereliction of England; if this undated play was contemporary with Southwell's schooling, then Southwell is offering an extra layer of meaning in his poem, a more pointed, embedded message yet to any reader who had shared his education, and who would associate Psyche not just with the human soul but with the *Catholic* soul. Plays were produced extensively in Jesuit schools from 1554, part of the Jesuits' programmes for reform.[39] This play, written in Latin for production in the Continental English colleges, comments on the Elizabethan situation through an imaginary sequel to the Psyche story in which an older Psyche and her sons negotiate worldly evils. In the interrelationship between play, poem, and readership, one has the beginnings of an argument linking Southwell's artistic surroundings at college, his poetic imagination and his artistic methodology. 'You have seen the tears of Psyche!' the Chorus to Act II tells the audience; 'They have a mystery: a mystery that may be better taught by means of tears than by tongue [...] Oh, England, England.'[40] In Southwell's version, the English speaker, no longer sharing the safety of Latin, or of a Continental Catholic college, prefers to leave such specific identifications free for his reader

Introduction

to apprehend. The play *Psyche* is unusually inscrutable. Without its prologue, epilogue, and chorus it becomes, like Southwell's poem, an engaging puzzle, a charade of strange imagery, sensual effects, and rich costumes.[41]

The didactic intentions of these dramas were unmistakable. In one of the earliest extant plays from the English College at St Omer a 'Weeping Anglia' wrings the scholars' emotions as she recounts her griefs, in order to arouse 'their manly spirits to re-enact Thomas' virtue'. In the cases of both Becket and More, 'Thomas' virtue' was to refuse, to the death, to relinquish papal to royal law; and this is what the boys were being exhorted to imitate. The language is inescapably martial and nationalistic, although reflecting the inevitable discontinuities in English Catholic nationalism; the 'English battle-lines', though 'glowing in opposition' to heresy, like Southwell's childhood coterie, are, like many of his fellows, 'scattered across the globe'. All that unites the 'followers of Thomas' is that virtuous resistance to the English Crown.[42]

THE ENGLISHNESS OF SOUTHWELL'S ART

The last two decades of the sixteenth century (the time of Southwell's English mission and the poetry that was such an important part of it) saw the emergence of a new artistic and literary vision in England, the appearance of a new sort of visual realism to replace the flat, surface-rich style preferred by Elizabeth throughout her reign, and the translation of that realism into new characterisations in literature, via Shakespeare and others. Southwell's almost unique translation of Continental early baroque imagery into poetic imagery has a central place in the discussion of that new artistic and literary vision.

Strangely, although surrounded by popular and modish Italian baroque poetry in Rome, Southwell was not to repeat the baroque literary style in his shorter English poetry, despite early translations of such works.[43] The emotional drama of baroque poetry is a drama rhetorically constructed, a quivering extravaganza of repetitions on an emotional theme perhaps too hectic for English literary tastes, at least as the English prefer to define them; there is an English critical tendency to dislike its 'foreignness' in Crashaw, while admiring its richness in Milton.[44] But there is a difference: Milton's poetic vision is what we might now call 'cinematic' – visually constructed, with a character-led dramatic narrative, like that Jesuit play – while Crashaw's is more often structured rhetorically, through repetition of closely linked elements, more pattern-embroidery than moving picture.

Southwell's Latin poetry displays even more his responsiveness to the dramatic and visual, rather than the rhetorical, possibilities of the baroque. In his 'Poema de Assumptione B.V.M.' ('On the Assumption of the Blessed Virgin Mary'), he describes Paradisial idyll and furious Stygian debate with all of the visual power Milton was later to bring to his *Paradise Lost*. Southwell's

Stygian lords are painted in strong lines, passionately eloquent in their umbrage, where his God is plain, curt, rational, just.[45]

Southwell's use of poetry for religious matters was attacked by the Puritan and Calvinist Joseph Hall as trivialising,[46] but Milton clearly did not agree. It seems that it was Southwell's pedagogically directed, simplified baroque vision that was the model seen as the more useful by Milton, who later possibly visited Southwell's English College in Rome,[47] and who experienced Rome's baroque art in all its glory, complete with those succinct Jesuit glosses and captions.

The pedagogic and dialogic possibilities of such a vision will have been immediately apparent to him, as it no doubt was to Southwell. Southwell's poetry was intended not simply to proselytise on doctrinal subjects but to bring fire to the heart of the reader, in the hope of raising his or her spiritual sensibilities. This new foregrounding of sensual apprehension of the divine allowed a more emotional relationship with God,[48] Southwell developing Tridentine ritualism into a poetically narrated, scriptural passion-play that he suited to the English cultural climate. A new self-consciousness about what constituted proper, heartfelt Englishness, a religious sensibility, and the proper attributes of the professional writer therefore came into being almost simultaneously in Southwell's English lyrics.

While Southwell's 'Saint Peters Complaint' is constructed along more typically baroque rhetorical lines, his short English lyrics are, for the most part, designed to engage the reader through a combination of limpid 'visual' imagery (most sumptuous in his version of Psyche), and almost impenetrably mystical shadows, as in 'The burning Babe'.

The closer one looks at 'The burning Babe', the more it reveals itself as the strangest of all Southwell's lyrics; critical commentary on it has varied widely, and although it retains a readable rhetorical structure, it is one that seems to break down under close scrutiny. But if one approaches it in terms of one of those altarpieces, an example realised in the mind of the dramatic effects of contrasted light and dark, it begins to make more sense: the sudden radiance in the gloom, with the tragic-heroic person of the Man-Babe occupying the centre of the composition, surrounded in baroque style by lesser but more obviously emblematic personifications such as Justice, Mercy and Love, and faint reminders of the Passion. This is the immediacy of painting or theatricals, not mere description: the pace and reception of the imagery is played with as in a drama, the peripheral characters opposed in their busyness to the dramatic, compelling posture of the Babe and the utter stillness of the narrator, standing outside the vision, yet caught within the twilight-shadowed framework of the poem itself, like one undergoing a vision in a baroque altarpiece. We, in turn, view (and identify with?) the frightened wanderer, in the moment that he recalls a central liturgical moment of the Christian Calendar, just as Southwell would have done in his Roman church, before real altarpieces designed to produce such effects. In England that church did not exist outside of the minds of his congregation – they were wanderers in the wintry night indeed: Southwell was offering them the encouragement of an imaginary Rome.

One of the most important paintings in the Novitiate was *Ignatius's Vision at La Storta*.[49] Christ with his Cross appears with the Father in a great burst of light as the pilgrim, Ignatius, having turned aside from his journey to Rome to visit a rustic chapel and ask guidance, kneels, amazed. Here, surely, is 'The burning Babe' in its first incarnation, with a wanderer in doubt seeing a fiery, affirming vision in the twilight, the whole scene reproduced to edify the viewer, and sited at the very foundation of Southwell's Order, at the moment of God's acknowledgement of the Society and its relationship not just with Christ, but with Christ Crucified.

These two, the poem and the painting, exemplify the relationship between Southwell's poetic vision and the works he encountered in Rome. In reproducing that visual immediacy, he was revolutionising the nature of English poetry. Southwell formed part of a crossing-point from artistic visual imagery to creative literature that empowered the English creative writer and provided a fruitful stylistic, and occasionally spiritual, template for the work of later writers.

This was not just a matter of new approaches to rhetoric or ornamentation. As O'Malley has demonstrated, the Jesuits' idea of ministry was itself so closely connected with creativity that central to its ideal of ministry was the concept of 'spiritu, corde, practice' ('in the Spirit, from the heart, practically'). This articulates their attitude to reaching souls in ways that took sermonising and rhetoric beyond older approaches to it into a ministry of affectivity, 'heart to heart'. A Jesuit scholar like Southwell, then, was brought up *ab initio* in an environment which put a strong emphasis on creative, affective literary production, which in fact defined its own difference and purposes by it; it was not 'simply conforming to the received wisdom of the day, but a pursuit that correlated with their deepest pastoral impulses'.[50]

The approach encouraged emotionalism; a change of heart was to be signalled and accompanied by signs of 'consolation' – usually tears.[51] Much recent work has focused on the importance of tears in the literature of the English Catholic exiles, and how it helped to establish their identity as exiles, and emphasise their difference from the Protestants, left in possession of Jerusalem. The medieval Magdalen as the tearfully repentant sinner is a central feature of such discussion. Southwell certainly carried an idea of Magdalen with him from Rome to England, and there is, therefore, a tendency to fit Southwell's religious poetry into this canon of tears, repentance, and exile, but I think it more useful here to investigate the clear differences between

Southwell's poetry and that penitential tendency. He was himself neither exile, nor stay-at-home Catholic, nor, once he had returned as a priest, simply a recusant; his Magdalen did far more than teach England how to weep, whatever use English writers subsequently made of her.

SOUTHWELL'S AUTHORIAL IDENTITY

Who was writing the poetry? What did Southwell see himself as, once in England again: exile, or English Catholic priest in hiding, or English youth not in hiding who was also, sometimes, to fulfil secretly his functions as an ordained priest? Which was writing, and for whom?

A letter later written from prison to Robert Cecil, his relative and his captor, to explain his unlawful presence in England, may be taken as Southwell's own mission-statement; in imagery that refers to the god-directed Aeneas unjustly accused, he defines himself as the son of a Christian parent first, with a son's duties: 'I was the childe of a Christian woman and not the whelpe of a tygar; I could not feare, and foresee, and not forewarne'; he was simply afraid for their souls. How could I, he asks Cecil, 'despise their bodies and soules, by whome I received myne'? Only a 'damned caytiffe', he adds, heatedly, could have ignored such duties. It is England that has changed, not Southwell; he remains constant: Christian Englishman, dutiful son, loyal subject. England has made her ancient faith unlawful, 'an inveigled zeale, a blinde, and now abolished faithe; a zeale notwithstanding, and a faithe yt was. And god allmightie is my wittnes I came with no other intention into the realme.'[52]

This robust, almost aggressively disappointed, statement of self is from the same pen as the gentle 'burning Babe', and both were written during his six years in England, the letter after torture and long incarceration. Southwell is clearly a man with a complex and multi-layered understanding of himself, and his writings bear witness to it in their varied, sometimes apparently conflicting natures. His concerns were domestic ones, his English writings for domestic, not overseas, consumption, a very different sort of discourse from that of the exiles addressed in his Latin works. His lyrics were no doubt intended to be pleasing to members of the exile communities on the Continent, but most, it seems likely, were for immediate and intimate consumption by those around him, readers he felt to be in need more of consolation than of polemic.

Southwell's poetry can be seen, too, in the light of the pleasant conversation, encouraged by the Society to draw less devout minds in towards a higher understanding of their soul. Southwell made many journeys about England, some in lively company of the sort he had known in his days with the Copleys and Cottons; it is likely that some of his lighter poetry was written during such occasions.[53] If Southwell's college habit of sharing poetry as part of an expression of collegiate feeling was now being exercised amongst English

Introduction

companions, then Southwell's lyric poetry was not necessarily linked directly with his Catholicism or his priestly status: these journeys were not always made in Catholic company, as Southwell himself has told us.[54]

This six years of tripping to and fro across an invisible but deadly front line problematises the usual modern breakdown of the English Catholic community and Southwell's place in it. The relationship between his literary production and the controversialist writings of his predecessors, especially Persons, is similarly problematised. Southwell did engage in such writing, but his co-missioner and superior Henry Garnet was less combative than Persons, and seemed inclined towards accommodation with aspects of Elizabeth's rule. A distinction must here be drawn between attacks on heresy, which Southwell continued to produce in various forms when in England, and attacks on the monarch, which, arguably, appear only in the heaviest disguise as medieval diatribes against fickle females such as False Love and Fortuna, as will be discussed later. The only surviving letter of Southwell's from the difficult years just after his ordination in 1584 is to tell Persons that he wishes that Campion's 'conciliatory position regarding the Queen's supremacy in temporal matters' should be continued by missioners.[55] This emphasis on dissuading missioners from expressing hostility to the English Crown was arguably no more than strategy, but recent scholarship shows that Southwell's rhetorical mission work reached beyond the earlier policy of engaging in controversy with the Protestants.[56]

It is this body of works of piety and affective force produced on the Garnet–Southwell mission that interests me here, works that, by Persons's own admission, were different from those produced in exile, as they could not be expected to support Persons's continuing wish to challenge England's authority. So different and complex were the circumstances of the 1586 English mission, even compared with those of Persons's earlier mission in England, that Southwell was being urged by him to seek, through encouragement and instruction, to 'formulate the kind of life possible for Catholics living in the midst of an alien society'.[57] Southwell did this in part by offering his distressed flock possibilities of sympathetic identification, creating models of biblical characters in similarly complex positions, characters such as Magdalen and Joseph, whose crises are worked through in his shorter lyrics.

If his poetry is read in the light of his mission, Southwell clearly took his authorship very seriously indeed, even that of his lighter poetry. He could so easily have carried on where the admired Campion had left off, trying to continue the strategy of rational appeals to scholarship in a forensic rhetoric of legal proof,[58] but Southwell also chose to borrow the newer energy of Elizabeth's courtly language, thereby gaining the attention of the young men who themselves were immersed in it: a far more deliberative, persuasive (and still thoroughly Jesuit) poetic. He was responding to eroticism in English poetry by turning it towards heaven rather than eschewing it altogether, setting out to demonstrate a Christianised mastery over many poetic forms, some satirical, some almost approaching the burlesque, a variety of tone and genre that seems to have caused some unease in Southwell scholarship.[59] But why should not a priest have a sense of humour? Southwell could be playful even with religious themes, as in 'New heaven new warre' (p. 13), where, perhaps in sly reference to the secrecies imposed on priests by their mission work, he reverses the process common in religious plays of the period of casting ordinary people as biblical characters, instead casting divine characters as ordinary ones: Gabriel, for instance, is a 'groome', the man employed, in part, to arrange accommodation for travelling gentry; Raphael is the cook; and the Seraphim constitute a warming fire (lines 13, 11, 8), characterisations calculated to bring a smile to a reader's face.

I believe that a point has been missed about the importance of Southwell's lighter poetry, a point which has been made available to scholarship through new critical approaches, especially those that allow for the historical contexts of a piece of work to be discussed. In their wider context, it is actually the lighter pieces that tell us most about Southwell's sense of who he was and what he wanted to say, at least as missioner. The traditional English critical approach to poetry that argues that the aesthetics of it are the only consideration might say that an underlying didactic agenda makes a man less of a poet, but Jonson clearly did not think so, and in this discussion of Southwell's poetry I address the contemporary interests of that moment in the history of literature which has been so taken over by the memory of Shakespeare, and the whole Romantic/Arnoldian vision of individual, inspired, aesthetically driven creativity. Jonson praised 'our Shakespeare', but I do not know that he ever wished he had authored any of Shakespeare's poetry.

Ironically, Southwell's work might have been fitted into that traditional canon in several ways, and some of his editors or biographers have tried to do so.[60] He was a distant relative of Shakespeare; there were even pathways by which to follow Sidney: a shared cousin, Richard Shelley, met Sidney on his arrival in Venice in 1573, and an Anglo-Italian poet travelled with him across the Alps, marking the trip 'through many a hill and dale, | Through pleasant woods ... | Along the banks of many silver streams'.[61] Cousin Southwell was soon to follow them through the mountain passes, but Southwell saw it with a different eye, rejecting that modishly pastoral interpretation of a benign, generic nature: his craggy and uncompromising version of the passage of the mountains, 'vale of teares', is an evocation of a real and frightening landscape as well as a metaphorised soul-state, full of that emotional immanence that seems to us to be the sole province of the Romantics. His trope has theological roots, evoking the exile of the children of Eve described as 'this vale of tears' in the 'Salve Regina', the prayer for intercession to the Virgin, upon which

Southwell based that little poem in the margin of his letter to John Deckers.⁶²
Here, though, Southwell has hidden the liturgical signifiers, foregrounding
the abstract imagery of the prayer, bringing it to life by the sheer realism of his
observation, with a descriptive integrity most unusual in English vernacular
poetry of this time. A later Shelley preferred the storm-bedevilled Southwell
version of Mont Blanc to the silver streams of his Sidneian poetic forbear.

It is Shakespeare's realism that is studied as an innovation, though, not
Southwell's. In choosing the Roman Catholic way in opposition to the major
national/Protestant urges of that particular moment Southwell has, perhaps,
been judged to have made himself a stranger to the Englishness that Sidney
and Shakespeare have come to represent.⁶³ Even though his work is demon-
strably full of political cross-currents, it is Shakespeare who is made to speak
for Albion: '*Hamlet* is very much of its moment, in London, on Bankside',
says Frank Kermode, acknowledging the references to both the Globe and to
its Hercules sign in the play.⁶⁴ Southwell's work was none the less important
in that 'moment' itself, judging by the many reissues of it, and by Jonson's
praise; 'The burning Babe', despite its apparent rusticity, was absolutely of
its moment and place in London too. The language of *Hamlet* does not exist
in a vacuum, and neither does that of the Rome-trained Englishman Robert
Southwell.

Southwell cannot address an English national agenda of the sort recognis-
able to modern criticism – an autonomous Englishness that probably did not
exist outside the minds of a few around the Queen at the time. Despite the
nationalistic efforts of Puttenham, Spenser and other Englishers of literature,
the Continent was generally seen as the source of new skills and knowledge,
the Catholic diaspora serving only to increase that impression.⁶⁵

The turn of the century offered all sorts of violence to those who stuck
their necks out in doctrine or politics; even Southwell obscured elements of
his meaning and mission in his poetry, and his early publishers were discreet
in their selections. Despite – or because of – this discretion, he was at the
forefront of the new interest in religious poetry in 1595, the year his collection
of lyrics with the long *St Peters Complaint* was published for the first time,
immediately after his execution.⁶⁶ Southwell engaged with evident relish in
contemporary debates about national agendas and the nature of creativity;
and he was read and appreciated. Later canon-makers may have lost sight
of the relative importance of Southwell compared to Sidney or Jonson but
his immediate posterity treasured his work: John Bodenham's *Belvedere, or
the Garden of the Muses* (1600) contains seventy-five quotations from South-
well; only Drayton, Spenser, Shakespeare, and Lodge are better represented.
Jonson appears seven times, Sidney six.⁶⁷ Although before his capture and
death Southwell's Roman Catholicism was known to few, and was explicit only
in some of his manuscripts, the notoriety of his death ensured that it became

public knowledge before the first publication of his poetry. Released and much rereleased for many years after his execution (and increasingly identified with the Jesuit himself through the Continental editions), Southwell's writings, thanks in part to the discretion of Southwell and his editors, clearly attracted widespread general popular favour regardless of any underlying doctrinal agenda. Southwell is included in John Pitts's 1619 *De illustris Angliae scriptoribus* (*On the Illustrious Writers of England*).[68] Whatever the English authorities thought about Robert Southwell's activities, whatever literary critics have since thought about his poetry, it was highly regarded at the time by people who knew who and what he was.

PERFORMING DEEDS: SOUTHWELL'S POETIC PURPOSES

Sir Philip Sidney's death in the Low Countries, his 'mantle of Protestant exemplarity', as Shell puts it, and the circulation of his manuscripts, ensured that England was a place of opposing poetics when Southwell arrived in 1586; Sidney's *Defence of Poesie* appeared virtually alongside Southwell's poetry in the year of his execution, 1595.[69]

The affective artistic Muse born at the Council of Trent was by now hard beset by non-Catholic poetic successes, such as du Bartas's Protestant *Muse Chrétienne*, Urania, accessible to the English in Sylvester's 1590–92 translations. Gabriel Harvey praised du Bartas's 'colours of astonishing Rhetorique' and 'amazing devises' in 1593.[70] In 1595, the year of Southwell's first poetic publication, the collection titled *Saint Peters Complaint*, two different publishers produced versions of the du Bartas. Southwell was clearly near the centre of things poetical, despite later unease at his religious agenda.[71]

But the religious is political as well as personal; and, in the case of the Jesuits at least, psychological. Southwell's poetic was informed by the peculiarly flexible approach of Jesuitism to the identification of those in need of help (and the methods devised to help them), rather than the effects of Catholic recusancy, and the resistance poetics of the exiled English Catholic community. It was this more positive, less doctrinally inflected element that escaped into a wider imaginative poetic construct of 'hidden' or obscured meanings, in opposition to the wish for exegesis of previous generations of poets. A poem with a kernel of personal witness hidden at its core, especially one written by a recognised author as deeply committed to a life-and-death cause as Southwell, clearly had a glamorising and galvanising effect upon contemporary authors and their sense of self-importance, quite beyond any devotional importance. Manuscripts circulating amongst private groups could carry more than face meanings. In tune with the habits of his day, Southwell's shorter lyrics (including, of course, 'The burning Babe') certainly did so. I am not merely arguing the now commonplace point that Elizabethan poetry had hidden meanings, available to a select coterie, under wider meanings available to the generality; nor do I make the mistake of seeing secret 'codes' in every emblem or allegory, which were far too widely and flexibly used to allow for such a reductive analysis. I am suggesting that Southwell's layers of meaning were so complex in their various implications and stratifications, amongst (or in spite of) all the various companies that he kept, that they almost override the idea of meaning at all, becoming, as it were, spaces for meaning to be realised by the reader, but ultimately transcending full interrogation by any but the author himself.

Southwell had a unique methodological precedent for this in one of the most important aspect of his training as a Jesuit: the Ignatian *Spiritual Exercises*, a carefully planned system of internal meditations on aspects of the individual's relationship with God, including extensive visualisations of the Passion of Christ.[72] It is each individual reader's memory store that supplies contexts and personal meaning; the occlusions in Southwell's poetry, as in the hidden classical referents, such as Psyche, can be seen to appeal to and interrogate the reader's own imaginative capabilities in a similar way.

His position relative to his work was not fully transparent until his death, and thus some of his embedded meanings would have become generally clear only when his Jesuitism became known, as if the revelation itself would contribute to the impact and meaning of his words. The idea that the author's intention cannot be recovered comes as no surprise to a modern critic, but that an early modern author might have included the concept of authorial elusivity – not disappearance as such – as a strategic element, or as integral to the unfolding of meaning in his work, seems worthy of investigation.[73] Southwell himself acknowledged in print that 'in fables are often figured moral truths, and that covertly uttered to a common good which without mask would not find so free a passage';[74] a recent editor acknowledges, at least, that Southwell disguised missionary agendas in his lyrics, that 'beneath the musical cadences of the lyrics lies an undeviating didactic intention; the conventional diction is given a new relevance, and traditional motifs a deeper significance'.[75] But Jesuit ideas of 'deeper significance', not to mention those significances particularly relevant to Southwell, are not necessarily those commonly ascribed to the Catholic recusant community, nor do such significances sit in polar opposition to English interests.

Southwell's near-invisibility in literary studies to date may encourage the belief that he was writing against the national literary project, and therefore unfit to sit alongside the poets of England's early modern flowering, but this is not the case: Englishness was to Southwell a good, and one bound up in his mind with an admirable, ancient habit of piety to which he wanted to add one that was clearer and more contemporary. Southwell's lyric 'From Fortunes reach' (p. 66) challenges aspects of the English national literary project. It can be read as a poetic as well as a spiritual manifesto in that it answers his poetic contemporaries as well as those of his countrymen who had fallen from faith. In this poem it is possible to detect a direct challenge to the self-reflexive Shakespearean or Danielan sonnet on the immemoriality of poetry; his very language seems to echo and deride them. 'I settled have an unremoved mind' he insists, echoing the note of anxiety over altered fortunes and broken promises creeping into contemporary poetry. The 'choyse' of a man firm in his faith is 'guided by fore-sightfull heede', not, as at the English Court, 'the game of phancies chase, | [...] vaine to shew the chaunge of every winde'. His life-choice (or choice of love, synonymous in Jesuit eyes) was 'averred with approving will', and should be 'followed with performing deed', Southwell's lyric insists (lines 1–9).

The phrase 'performing deed' is immanent in all of Southwell's work, and central to both his ministry and his poetics. It is the moment where his poetics and his ministry meet, the pivot around which turns his entire mission, and it will appear throughout this book. Philosophically, it is Aristotle's proper fruit of teaching, *praxis*, rather than *gnosis* alone. Doctrinally, it is both the self-sacrifice of Christ and the only possible conclusion, in Catholic terms, to confession or prayer, which are effectively negated without it. Talking about doing the right thing is not doing it, and cannot attract divine grace. Theologically, this engaged with contemporary controversies over the access of divine grace, highlighting a perceived weakness of Calvinism: 'performing deed' seemed irrelevant to a 'Saved' soul already destined heavenward; and if a soul were denied such heavenly election from birth, what difference would a good deed make? Poetically, it was a rejection of the Petrarchan ideal that was thriving in Elizabeth's neo-chivalric Court, with its potential locked into fascinating contrarieties. Politically, it was by implication a call for Catholic resistance, even to death (although not in itself necessarily a call to arms). All of these socio-religio-political elements met in Southwell's poetry, but only each individual reader knew which seemed the most significant.

It can be seen, then, that Southwell's poetry was part of a project far sterner than its lyric simplicity would suggest. That project was centred upon the idea of authority, expressed through authorship, upon the very Jesuit understanding of writing as ministry, of reader as soul, as the death of the author as a way of understanding the text most fully. The London air was full of the reek of execution, and part of the reason for such annihilations was the issue of authorship itself, something that no contemporary author could have overlooked.[76] Southwell's last prose work, *An Humble Supplication to Her Majesty*, was in part a plea for rights of individual autonomy – soul rights[77] – to be recognised; it was a major reason for his imprisonment and execution, according to many of his editors and biographers.[78] How could the lightweight 'burning Babe' have fitted in to such a grim agenda to the extent of attracting Jonson's admiration? *An Humble Supplication* will be addressed in brief later; the issue here is

Introduction

that Southwell addressed the whole concept and sacred context of his ideal of authorship, produced both poetry and prose designed to express his views of it and, having stated his right to be the author of his own internal reality, as well as an authority in his own right as a priest, stood by it through many torturings, and died for it. No personal authority can be more profoundly held than that of one ready to die to maintain it. No public act of authorship could have taken place without the acknowledgement of State anxieties, and no private act of authorship is likely to have been made outside the influence of such anxieties and debates.

Certainly Southwell's lyrics, in their less overtly Catholic form, were popular enough to require many editions, and elicit many responses and citations. Perhaps it was the deep, yet sometimes almost childlike, appeal to ancient traditions of devotion and feeling, a Christian England, a Jerusalem, not Rome, nor yet a pagan classical landscape. For some – Jonson perhaps – it may have been the raw simplicity of the educated but (necessarily) sparse English.[79] Other poetic voices were calling for an elegant spareness in English, but perhaps it was the Jesuit-trained Southwell who made the first examples in it that were more than delicate essays in the technique. I would suggest that it was Southwell's clear, Christian Englishness and its appeal to popular feeling that made him a threat to a State project that sought to alter and own that very tradition.

GRACE AND THE INDIVIDUAL TALENT

A god might reconnect a dismembered Osiris or Orpheus, but the reclamation of Southwell by critical posterity is a Frankensteinian work, an unsatisfactory patching and stitching of scavenged things. The various names, pseudonyms and identities by which he was known are as good an illustration as any of this process of piecemeal composition. Southwell, for long on his English mission incognito, and going under various pseudonyms or misnomers, was effectively a written construct. At the start (from 1586), the name 'Robert Southwell, S.J.' could not be attached to the person of the poetic young gentleman, apparently a Cotton, residing in London; Southwell was still known to the Council only as '*Robertus*' in 1591. He was eventually described – a good-looking, auburn-haired, beardless man – then in 1591 a name was found: 'Mr. Southwell, a Jesuit about London, apparelled in black rash' (a fine wool cloth), both items of intelligence coming from an ex-colleague (John Cecil) and a priest.[80] 'Mr Cuthwell' next appears, courtesy of a spy (Chomley) on official records; Southwell's identity was finally out of his control.[81]

He also wrote himself, cannily and deliberately. His writings were designed to conform themselves to circumstances, and the variations within his canon make an interesting study. Letters, reported conversations, reminiscences, poetic and literary meditations on his condition exist, put together in certain ways by himself (in his first, unrecoverable selection of poems, for instance), though later rearranged according to the intentions of his biographers. Janelle, Devlin, McDonald and Brown, Caraman, Brownlow, and Pilarz have all described Southwell's origins, college life, and English mission from the sparse textual evidence available. This general reconstruction has been enlivened by some of Southwell's own letters discovered in the archives in Rome.[82]

Southwell is most easily reclaimed through the nature of the memories to which he drew attention at a later date, such as his babyhood abduction by a gypsy woman from his Norfolk home, which later became the foundation of pious meditations: pure youth rescued from the clutches of a pagan, female erotic lust, Samuel saved for marriage to God.[83]

That sensual thief was always to distract and tear at Southwell: his was a fragile, passionate sense of self, judging by his record of spiritual development. This remarkable document has been well preserved, due to the Ignatian habit of keeping a developmental diary for self-assessment and correction, as Southwell's *Spiritual Exercises and Devotions*.[84] It is perhaps as close to the real Southwell as it is possible to approach.

Terminology itself contributes to the identity problem: Southwell was an English gentleman, a Catholic, and in due time a member of the order called the Society of Jesus; he is therefore likely to be thought of as an English Catholic by modern commentators. This may, in fixing meaning to modern ideas of Catholic identity, mislead: the term 'English Catholic' was a less meaningful distinction in sixteenth-century England, after all, so soon after the lay Christian world had need to distinguish mainly between Christian and non-Christian, and at a time when a considerable part of England's population was still more-or-less Catholic.

Protestants might see national advantages in the break from Rome, and consider Protestantism the best for England; at the same time, those Catholic Englishmen who, in the 1580s and 1590s, had been driven overseas for continuing in their traditional religious observances (especially those who had thrived in Mary Tudor's Catholic State) considered themselves to be the continuation of England's true national religion, steadfast Christian Englishmen; the English Protestant party were to them scoff-laws and heretics, infected by the religious and social disturbances of Germany. Pockets of strongly articulated religious self-definition of all kinds existed alongside much larger areas either where a general obedience to the prevailing law obtained, or where laissez-faire officers allowed private preferences to continue unmolested, at least until the anti-Catholic laws began to harden in the 1580s. Parts of the North and West were never wholly or substantially persuaded to alter ancient traditions of worship.

Introduction

Distinctions, as Peter Lake has pointed out, tend to grow in response to problems, and have tended to become associated with those problems retrospectively.[85] I will not try to reproduce the various arguments here, merely stress that the prime function of the Roman Catholic missions of the 1580s and 1590s was demonstrably pastoral, whatever constructions have become attached to them as a result of other plans and actions. 'I am determined', Southwell was later to write to Claudio Acquaviva, the father general of the Society, six months after his arrival in England, 'never to desist from the works of my calling, though the works, when done, cannot long escape their notice'; this was written after Southwell had just escaped arrest by the skin of his teeth twice while ministering to Catholics in their houses and prisons.[86] When is a Catholic not a Catholic? Even the contemporary terminology was unable to contain the variety, range, and depth of shades of religious conformity or otherwise in late Elizabethan England, and Southwell's life was entirely bound up in that deadly tangle.

The Jesuits were foot-soldiers for the Pope, but in England they were primarily concerned with those who were slipping away from religious observance of any sort, regarding these, whether 'pagan, Muslim, heretic, or Catholic', as 'lost sheep'; they saw it as their prime work to search for them wherever they were to be found and return them to Christian piety. Southwell called Protestant churchmen 'heretics'; some courtiers he considered 'atheists'; the rest were 'souls'. His poetry, which dwells mostly on helping souls, was part of this latter work, a distinctive feature of Jesuit ministry of this period.[87] Whilst this is a far from complete picture, it sketches the position as Southwell himself described it.

Vital, too, to an understanding of how Southwell's authorship related to his vocation and mission is an understanding of the peculiar nature of the Jesuit priests' situation as missioners in England (as in other countries). Because of the Jesuit insistence that no beneficed curacy should be taken up – that their priests could not become established as 'pastors of parishes' – they were never in a position to compel, only to attract and persuade those they wished to help to approach their way of proceeding; they could hope to attract only by seeming more effective or more special; they had perforce to become expert fundraisers, if no more.[88] This alters the authorial imperative upon Southwell: he was primarily there to woo, not to condemn, and this difference of texture is reflected in much of his lyrical writing, in its lightness of touch, a spirituality offering 'dymm glymses to the light' of a universal brightness beyond its lines ('Of the Blessed Sacrament of the Aulter', p. 26).

Southwell was surrounded on the post-Tridentine Continent by a new interest in theories of religious imagery, and he adapted its strategies for his poetry.[89] Peter Bruegel's novel synthesis of the realistic and the poetic, and his transposition of renaissance humanist ideals on to the quotidian experience of the peasant, had made him highly influential in the northern Netherlands in the 1560s, just prior to Southwell's arrival there. Southwell's later use of realistically rustic surroundings in his Nativity poems (and the theological point he was trying to make thereby), can be related directly back to Bruegel's artistic innovations. Bruegel's Flemish realism was bringing Gospel narratives and proverbs closer to his northern audience, as in his translation of the Census of Bethlehem to the snow and mud of a Flanders village. In the same way, Southwell later drew on his muddy winter travels in England to form the backdrop to 'New heaven new warre' (p. 13), 'The burning Babe' (p. 15), and 'New Prince, new pompe' (p. 16), all of which set the infant protagonist in the 'chilling cold' of a 'freesing Winter night', a pearl dropped 'In depth of dirty mire' ('New heaven', l. 7, 'New Prince', lines 2, 12).

As parts of Europe were experiencing this newly impassioned flowering of devotional expression, at Douai the fourteen-year-old Southwell encountered William Allen's belief in the power of plain words.

That Jesuit habit of producing school plays in the vernacular as well as in Latin, in order to reach lay audiences, also encouraged clarity and immediacy.[90] The debate in his Latin 'Poema de Assumptione B.V.M.' between the powers of 'Erebus' and Gabriel (speaking for the Virgin) shows the effects such dramatic productions had on Southwell's creativity; its rich physical effects and plangent language engage, as an unfolding drama can engage, even when one knows the outcome.[91] His English characterisations were later to echo that dramatic grandeur and immediacy, although the other half of the debate was there by implication only.

Southwell's earliest artistic vision can therefore be seen to be very much a product of this particular sort of schooling. Into a poetic field long deserted by Wyatt and Surrey and overgrown with weeds had come the spare new style of Southwell's English prose and poetry, informed by Allen's interest in the classical humanities. Allen had believed that pagan art-forms could be harnessed for the benefit of the church: this 'profane lore', as another Catholic educationalist, Gregory Martin, called it, in the hands of able men, formed the basis of a new expression that was productive beyond all expectation, catching the attention of many, able to pluck grapes from bramble-bushes 'almost', as Martin told Campion, 'against the words of the Saviour'.[92]

Southwell's vision of England and the ideal English poet was conceived on the basis of a new emphasis on individual responsibility. He was no doubt inspired by the new ideas of Leonard Lessius in this, and in any case his chosen Order enshrined such an individualism in their 'way of proceeding', a 'way' that included poetry and the arts along with the sacraments, as we have seen. Whatever may make Southwell's poetry 'potential' in English letters, therefore, is to be found in the ideals of the Society of Jesus as he knew it.

Members of the Society had worked from the start to give theological expression to such new attitudes, via men like Jerome Nadal, Luis de Molina, and Francisco Suárez. Considered the Jesuits' foremost theologian and central to the development of modern systems of thought, Suárez was teaching at Roman College during Southwell's time there.[93] He steered the concept of subjective circumstances into the choppy scholastic debates about the tension between God's foreknowledge and human free will, proposing, with Molina, a reconciliatory position: 'middle knowledge' (*scientia media*), a concept that proposed a systematic flexibility in our reception of divine grace that allowed God's foreknowledge to exist alongside an uncompromised human free will. Grace was, through God's special foreknowledge, always suited to the circumstances of a particular case. But although we accepted or rejected this *gratia congrua* through free will, we were not able to alter the efficacy of a grace sent by God, who knew beforehand the limits of our capacities. This concept was to be pure gold to Southwell on mission in 'heretic' England, improving upon or modifying considerably the rather unforgiving Calvinist conception of predestination. The canon that critics such as Barbara Lewalski have treated as a separate and self-contained Protestant devotional poetic might never have developed without the injection, largely via Southwell to begin with, of poetic theories based on Suárez's more flexible concept of free will. Southwell did not invent meditative literature, of course, nor did he have the sole rights over Suárez's new theories; his English phrase 'soul rights' was innovative, however, and his transmission of such concepts into poetry was unique at the time in England.

The Jesuit view of grace was revolutionary.[94] Southwell, pupil in Rome both of Suárez and of his pupil Lessius,[95] was exposed to lively debates on the subject which later grew acrimonious. Father general Acquaviva, seeing the dangers of seeming to allow too much agency to free will at the expense of grace, was later moved to require Jesuit teachers to moderate their position. Southwell's views therefore appear to reflect the earlier, unmoderated concept, which tended to privilege human free will.

The early baroque artistic vision was an expression of these new theories in two dimensions, creating newly accessible visual spaces into which the individual could float his imagination, freed from the more prescriptive allegorical formulae of earlier art, as free will was freed a little from medieval theories of premotional grace. What was on offer was the possibility of autonomic emotional response leading to willed spiritual interaction. Similarly, what Suárez offered was the possibility that God knew what a person would have *chosen* to do in any given contingency, introducing a new flexibility into the interaction between divine grace and free will. Concepts of individuation and singularity became discussable within scholastic precedent; the possibility of holding one and the same truth by both science and faith gave new space and importance to individual apprehension. The affectivity of those glorious gleams of the early baroque was part of a new room for theological manoeuvre, and Southwell was to take full advantage of its flexibility to reach the widest possible flock in Protestantised England, appearing to reconcile, whilst never compromising his own religious ideals.

Rome was alight with discussions of this new elevation of human autonomy – it was theology taken quite legitimately and systematically into the realms of the imagination. Jesuit thinkers had also developed a modified attitude to the effects of Original Sin: our will was weakened but not annihilated by it, allowing for grace-fuelled effort; indeed, 'grace, always the primary factor, allowed the will to "cooperate" with it, so that in some mysterious way human responsibility played its part in the process of salvation'. This is a constant underlying thesis in Southwell's poetry, and it gave comfort, as well as a dignity to human enterprise that was, for the moment, denied in Protestantism.[96]

Exposing as they did weaknesses in reformed theology, the promotion and dissemination of such ideas were integral to Southwell's mission; one can expect to see them promulgated in his writing therefore, and indeed they are. 'At home in Heaven' (p. 55) presents grace as part of a co-operative act, a dynamic matter of active choice and spiritual guidance: the soul must be persuaded not to spoil its spiritual circumstances through regard for things undivine, 'Not valewing right the worth of Ghostly grace' (l. 34); clearly the soul has responsibilities along with the rights. 'Of finest workes wit better could the state,' he says in 'Looke home' (p. 57), but only 'If force of wit had equall power of will' (lines 9–10). In 'Of the Blessed Sacrament of the Aulter' (p. 26), he insists that the grace of the Holy Communion pours out regardless, but if it is not received it is because the 'men' are inefficient, not the grace; even though 'blynde men see no light, the sunne doth shyne' (lines 41–3). 'All ghostly dynts that grace at me did dart, | Like stubborne rocke I forced to recoyle', says the narrator of 'Mary Magdalens blush' (p. 32), taking full soul-responsibility for her own circumstances, circumstances which, in the mission context, meant that Catholics, in an England divorced from the source of Roman Catholic power, were to be pitied rather than condemned. Power and its doctrinally correct transmission was Suárez's argument.

Southwell's task in England was to find a means of transmitting the power of the Roman Church where the doors of legitimate debate were now barred against it. Concepts that had begun as doctrinal issues later found acceptable literary expression in Southwell's lyric poetry. The opening words of the *Spiritual Exercises*, the Jesuits' central text, and their stated purpose of 'seeking and finding God's will', might suggest that one could gain access to God's will alone. Grace certainly was accessible, in Tridentine Catholic doctrine, as the 'fruits of good works' but only because of the supremacy of Christ's power to offer it, not because we ourselves had power to attract it. Southwell's marriage in 'At home in Heaven' (p. 55) of Christ and the human soul is interesting in the light of this proviso; it is the soul that seems to do the attracting; indeed, its 'ghostly beautie offred *force* to God', chaining him, albeit in 'the lynckes of tender love' (lines 6–7; my emphasis).

Southwell's Jesuit-founded Reformation poetry was reflecting a new, sacred near-autonomy: by Suárez's concept of theology the poems are moments of received grace in themselves, as, although pagan things in form, they are, through the authority of the priest and martyr, a will toward grace in their author's, and, it is to be hoped, their reader's, intention. Whatever their lacks, they are sacralised by the purpose of their priestly creator in allowing God access to his own native skills, for the greater glory of God, and energised by his execution. Sacred poetry might appear in due time from Protestant pens, but no such actively *sacralised* or grace-visited poetic could have been consciously created by even the best Protestant poet, look in his heart as he might.[97] Whether he intended it to empower an individual poet or not, this is the nature of what Southwell was importing into England, and discussion of it should range beyond its artistic qualities alone; it is far more than just poetry.

Southwell, once in the Society, was being trained not only in the concept of *gratia congrua* but in the process of feeling its affects: his Jesuit training therefore prepared him for his poetic project in many ways. As their core principle was the individual response to God's direct action on one's heart and soul, the principle of emotionally revealing autobiography was a central element of Jesuit witness. Supporting this new vision was Ignatius's programme of psychological self-apprehension; Ignatius's own experiences were formulised into the *Spiritual Exercises*. A poet sensitive to the possibilities of such emotional honesty and imaginative efficacy could be a powerful poet indeed.

Southwell was also being trained to see the benefits of simplified pedagogical strategies to involve hearts and minds as widely as possible in this new vision of Christian piety, to accommodate himself to his actual audience. Catechesis, an interactive teaching tool of ancient pedigree, was being further developed on far-flung missions in part to overcome cultural and language problems, and, in attempting to overcome such barriers, could even be expressed as lyrics; Southwell's own lyrics must be read in light of this missionary practice.[98]

Even more importantly, from the point of view of this book, Ignatius insisted that such catechistical teaching was founded on the 'accommodation of the teacher and lesson to the audience'.[99] Southwell's poetic vision is entirely informed by such theories. His 'light' lyrics, and even more so his 'St Peters Complaint', can therefore be seen as a pastoral initiative designed for a mission to a land where Catholic teaching was forbidden, and where many were beginning to fall away through lack of teaching from sound Christian understanding across the range of doctrines. Southwell's own later, Jesuit-trained understanding of the needs of a more secular and disaffected audience is therefore reflected in his poetry, especially the lighter sort.[100] Southwell's English poetry, though not in itself overtly catechetical, can none the less therefore be seen to fit into a lively, flexible and creative pedagogical tradition. Faithful to Jesuit principles, he was addressing responsive not doctrinal issues using the best means at his disposal, according to his native skills, the rhetorical often replacing the catechistical question. For lack of teachers in England, he was effectively trusting his reader to come up with the right response using their own 'native light' and wit.[101] Here the division between his fourteen 'Virgin Sequence' poems (largely unpublished in the mainstream book trade until the nineteenth century) and the rest, especially 'Saint Peters Complaint' itself, becomes most clear: the poems of the Virgin Sequence contain no questions; all are as if part of one overarching programme portraying the condition, state and nature of the Virgin's holiness, sites for meditation, not education. But twelve out of the thirty-eight poems in the *Saint Peter* collection of short lyrics use question as part of their rhetorical strategy, those (such as the Peter and Magdalen complaints) inspired by or borrowed from Continental versions being the more likely to use the device, and 'Saint Peters Complaint' itself (including its shorter version) being virtually an extended self-catechism from the first line:

> How can I live, that have my life deny'de?   1
> What can I hope, that lost my hope in feare?
> What trust to one that trewth it self defyde?
> What good in him that did his god forsweare?

The questioning, which also reflects the 'dialogical reasoning process with the inner self' of the *Exercises*,[102] elicits harder questions that were bound to cause disquiet in any who had abandoned the Catholic sacraments:

> Was life so deare and Christ become so base,   31
> I of so greate, god of so smalle accounte:
> That Peter nedes must followe Judas race,
> And all the Jewes in Crueltye surmounte?

This is answered by 'Yett Judas deemed thirtye pence his price: | I, worse then he, for nought deny'd him thrice' (lines 35–6). Or sharper still, given the situation under the female monarch in England:

> Where was the hart that did so little feare
> The armed troupes that him did apprehende?
> Where was the sworde that strooke off Malchus eare?
> Where was the faith of Christes professed frende?   40
> O Adams childe, it was a selye Eve
> That thee of faith and force did thus bereave.

Introduction

Some questions are clearly rhetorical: 'O who would live so many deathes to trye?' ('What joy to live?', p. 53, l. 25). Some poems, as in 'Josephs Amazement' (p. 21), use question dramatically, offering readers one half of a catechism to which they, but not the protagonist Joseph, have the answers, involving them in the unfolding of a moment in the drama of the lives of the Virgin and Christ, as well as in deeper questions about the irrational, hidden nature of belief; an object-lesson in the faithful nature of the loving heart, or in Suárezian *scientia media*. Others are closer to the pedagogical function of catechesis, such as 'Life is but Losse' (p. 50), where there is a series of questions:

> Who would not die to kill all murdring greeves,   7
>   Or who would live in never dying feares?
> Who would not wish his treasure safe from theeves,
>   And quit his hart from pangues, his eyes from teares?

These are answered, or countered, by the by now commonplace: 'Death parteth but two ever fighting foes, | Whose civill strife doth worke our endlesse woes' (lines 11–12); while the histrionic 'Come cruell death why lingrest thou so long, | What doth withholde thy dint from fatall stroake?' is answered by the doctrinally foundational and rhetorically powerful: 'There is a God that over-rules thy force, ... | I on his mercie, not thy might relye, | To him I live, for him I hope to dye', the culmination of all these questions (lines 38, 41–2). Similarly, 'I die alive' (p. 52), has the rhetorical-sounding question 'O life what lets thee from a quicke decease? | O death what drawes thee from a present pray?' (lines 1–2) answered by something closer to Christian doctrine: 'Grace more than nature keepes my hart alive, | Whose Idle hopes and vaine desires are dead' (lines 11–12).

'At home in Heaven' (p. 55) takes the device to its logical extreme, catechising the soul itself: 'Faire soule, how long shall veyles thy graces shroud? | How long shall this exile with-hold thy right?' (lines 1–2), while 'A Phansie turned to a sinners complaint' (p. 36), a parody of fashionable courtly verses in praise of a quiet life, sharpens the rhetorical questions typical of such work by the unmistakable lexis of catechism: 'grace', 'torment', 'sinne', 'blisse' (lines 81–8), leaving the unanswered questions to hang in the air, that clear blue Southwellian space between the reader and heaven that only he or she, in the privacy of their own conscience, could fill.

All Jesuits were encouraged to write, setting 'an ideal of frequent and frank communication', mostly in their own vernacular, designed for information, edification and support both from and back to base.[103] The Jesuits existed outside traditional church hierarchies, but elected their superior general for life, which lent them a centralised, courtly, almost feudal air. Southwell's and Garnet's mission letters to their father general in Rome fully reflect that dependence and attachment. Writing was their ministry: not just an adjunct to it, but part of the living, multi-faceted thing itself.[104] Southwell was therefore being trained in an order that valued initiative and flexibility and saw itself as belonging in the world: the Jesuits were technically mendicant clerks regular; from the outset their energetic founder had insisted on freedom from the site-dependent daily offices of prayer to which the older orders were tied. Differences from the medieval orders, such as freedom from the requirement to sing the divine offices throughout the day, were defended vigorously: 'We are not monks ... The world is our house' was the ultimate expression of that difference, and of the Jesuits' profound sense of the importance and scope of their ministry.[105] Society men worked out in the world in an invisible matrix of internalised rituals and disciplines, freed to launch missions to the Americas, India, Japan and China. Missions to those European homelands given over to 'heresy' fitted somewhat uncomfortably into this more global outlook. The name of the Society itself described their pastoral vision: Nadal pointed out that 'being members of the "Company of Jesus" meant being "companions of Christ Jesus" – *socii Christi Jesu*"' too.[106] This energetic self-definition with Christ's Apostles enthused youths such as Southwell, but caused problems amongst other orders and hostile laity, who saw in it a claim to some special proximity to Christ. It is an identification which inevitably becomes more exaggerated by martyrdom.

The teenaged Southwell, forming and hardening his immature communicative skills in the forge of the Continental seminary and the exile community, was learning a new language: passionate but never self-regarding or disproportionate; a global vision, but refined to the uses of the moment; and he was finding men who could use it. He was learning about the relationship between suffering and ministry as well; not only was the language of the colleges inflected with that brand of anti-heretic polemic expressed through rehearsals of Protestant cruelty, but his own sufferings, inseparable from his sense of his own piety, it seems, were crystallising out into a new language of emotionalised poetic metaphor.

In 1578, Allen moved his college to the safety of French Rheims, while Southwell, mind at last made up, remained in Tournai with the Jesuits, where in October 1578 he was finally admitted to the novitiate of the Society of Jesus. He was about seventeen. When the troubles came too close to the Jesuit door, the college was disbanded and the students dispersed; Southwell might have returned home, as his family and his colleagues appear to have desired.[107]

Instead, he set off for Rome.

NOTES

1 Ben Jonson, quoted by William Drummond, in Ben Jonson, *Works*, ed. C. H. Herford and P. and E. Simpson, 8 vols (Oxford: Clarendon Press, 1925–52), I, p. 137.

2 Robert Southwell, 'The burning Babe', from Cawood's 1602 edition of *Saint Peters*

Complaint, With other Poemes 'newlie augmented'; see A. F. Pollard and G. R. Redgrave (eds), *A Short-title Catalogue of Books Printed in England, Scotland, and Ireland, and of English Books Printed Abroad, 1475–1640* (London: Bibliographical Society, 1926), 22960a; references to titles from this catalogue are hereafter cited by number, prefixed *STC*; in James H. McDonald and Nancy Pollard Brown (eds), *The Poems of Robert Southwell, S.J.* (Oxford: Clarendon Press, 1967), p. 15; this being the most recent edition of Southwell's poetry to date, I use it throughout, cited as M&B; further references to this edition are given as page/line numbers after quotations in the text. A new edition of Southwell's poetry, including the Latin, is in preparation. See also Brown's comments on Cawood's inclusion of 'The burning Babe' into his revised edition, p. lxv.

3 Alexander B. Grosart, *The Complete Poems of Robert Southwell, S.J.* (London: Robson, Fuller Worthies' Library, 1872), p. lxxxi; hereafter cited in the text.

4 See www.walsingham.org.

5 'A Phansie turned to a sinners complaint' (p. 36), lines 37–40. For a discussion of priestly attitudes to perennial superstition, see Alexandra Walsham, 'Miracles and the Counter-Reformation Mission to England', *The Humanities Journal*, 46 (2003), 779–815.

6 See Eamon Duffy, *The Stripping of the Altars: Traditional Religion in England c. 1400–1580* (New Haven: Yale University Press, 1992), p. 86; hereafter cited in the text.

7 For discussions of the persistence of the old faith, see John Bossy, *The English Catholic Community 1570–1850* (London: Darton, Longman & Todd, 1975); Eamon Duffy; Christopher Haigh, 'The Continuity of Catholicism in the English Reformation', in Christopher Haigh (ed.), *The English Reformation Revised* (Cambridge: Cambridge University Press, 1987), pp. 176–215; all hereafter cited in the text.

8 *The Triumphs over Death*, ed. J. W. Trotman (London, Manresa Press, 1914), p. 43.

9 Letter of April 1582, intercepted; *Calendar of State Papers, Domestic, 1581–1590*, ed. Mary Anne Everett Green (London: Longmans, 1865), hereafter *CSP, Dom., 1581–1590*; see Christopher Devlin, *The Life of Robert Southwell Poet and Martyr* (London: Longmans, Green, 1956), pp. 6, 58, 52; hereafter cited in the text.

10 Information on family connections and histories can be found on www.tudorplace.com.

11 See Devlin, p. 11, and Scott Pilarz, S.J., *Robert Southwell and the Mission of Literature 1561–1595: Writing Reconciliation* (Aldershot: Ashgate, 2004), pp. 41–2; hereafter cited in the text. Pilarz characterises the fervour of Southwell and his friends as 'romantic enthusiasm' fired by accounts of Jesuit missionary works (p. 42).

12 See a brief account of Southwell's early years (and the politicking of Southwell's grandfather), in Pilarz, pp. 41–2, 6–13.

13 James McConica, 'The Catholic Experience in Tudor Oxford', in Thomas M. McCoog, S.J. (ed.), *The Reckoned Expense: Edmund Campion and the Early English Jesuits* (Woodbridge: Boydell, 1996), pp. 39–66 (p. 56); hereafter cited in the text.

14 Pilarz, p. 42; Southwell was entered on the register along with John and his brother, as 'nobilium filii', Pierre Janelle, *Robert Southwell the Writer: A Study in Religious Inspiration* (London: Sheed and Ward, 1935), p. 17; hereafter cited in the text.

15 Janelle, p. 7; M&B, p. xvi; see also F. W. Brownlow, *Robert Southwell*, Twayne's English Authors Series, 516 (New York: Simon & Schuster Macmillan, 1996), p. 2; hereafter cited in the text.

16 Lessius's *De justitia et jure* was published in 1605, proving popular in Europe.
17 See Michael E. Williams, 'Campion and the English Continental Seminaries', in McCoog (ed.), *Reckoned Expense*, pp. 285–99 (p. 285); hereafter 'Campion'.
18 Brownlow, p. 2; Williams, 'Campion', p. 285.
19 See Pilarz, note 9, p. 150; Pilarz cites Walter Ong, *Fighting for Life: Contest, Sexuality and Consciousness* (Ithaca: Cornell University Press, 1981), p. 130; Bruce Smith, *Homosexual Desire in Shakespeare's England* (Chicago: University of Chicago Press, 1991), pp. 83–4; the Latin works offered in Peter Davidson's edition currently in preparation illustrate this special usage.
20 Thomas M. McCoog, S.J., '"Playing the Champion": the role of disputation in the Jesuit mission', in McCoog (ed.), *Reckoned Expense*, pp. 119–41 (pp. 121–2); hereafter cited in the text.
21 Letter of Allen to Vandeville, 16 September 1578 or 1580, quoted in *The First and Second Diaries of the English College, Douay*, trans. Thomas Francis Knox (London: Nutt, 1878; repr. Farnborough: Gregg, 1969), pp. xxxviii–xliii; see McCoog (ed.), *Reckoned Expense*, p. 122.
22 Letter of Allen to Vandeville, 16 September 1578, quoted in Janelle, p. 9; for teaching in Latin, see Janelle, pp. 22–3; M&B, p. xix; for Southwell's comments, see Brownlow, p. 11.
23 McCoog (ed.), *Reckoned Expense*, pp. 121–2; his Latin poetry is notably more 'treasonable' than his vernacular, and more eloquent.
24 Michael E. Williams, *The Venerable English College Rome: A History 1579–1979* (London: Associated Catholic Publications (on behalf of the College), 1979), p. 28; hereafter *English College*.
25 Williams, *English College*, pp. 10–11.
26 At his trial in 1581 Campion referred to a perceived difference between the mature university men who came from England to complete their studies on the Continent, and 'young striplings that be under tuition' at the seminaries, who were expected to take the missionary oath; see Williams, 'Campion', fn. 6, pp. 286–7.
27 See Brownlow, Chapter 3, pp. 50–72, especially 'An Humble Supplication to her Majesty', pp. 64–72; also see Pilarz, whose work on Southwell is subtitled 'Writing Reconciliation'. Both in my view tend to overstate the case for Southwell's irenicism; he rather accommodates *to* than reconciles *with* other positions, in accordance with the precepts of his training, I would argue; his habit of trusting his reader to draw their own conclusions (up to a point) seems to lessen the didactic impact. The reconciliation theory begs the question in regard to Southwell's own attitude, and tends to leave unaddressed some of his more awkward poems. Both works illustrate the highly complex relationship between Southwell and his authorship, however.
28 Janelle, pp. 14, 30–1; Brownlow, p. 46; Pilarz, pp. 2–3, 16.
29 Williams, *English College*, pp. 10–11. Even in the days of Catholic reinstatement under Mary Tudor, the foremost English churchman, Pole, had kept the Jesuits at arm's length, never accepting Ignatius's offers of help in the reconciliation of England; see Thomas F. Mayer, 'A Test of Wills: Cardinal Pole, Ignatius Loyola, and the Jesuits in England', in McCoog (ed.), *Reckoned Expense*, pp. 21–38 (p. 21).
30 McCoog, '"Playing the Champion"', p. 121.

Introduction

31 The Society was inevitably enmeshed in European politics whether it acted politically or not. The Jesuit *Constitutions* allowed the striking of alliances with princes, but 'alliance' began to be interpreted as permanent residence, and proximity to certain courts led to the appearance of political support. There was a lack of long-term political insight about the compromising effects of an alliance with one magnate upon dealings with another; see John W. O'Malley, *The First Jesuits* (Cambridge, MA: Harvard University Press, 1993), pp. 72, 287, 308.

32 The letter outlining his motives and aims, as demanded by the Ignatian Exercises, is in MS 5618 Bibliothèque Royale de Belgique, *Exercitia et Devotiones R. P. Roberti Sotwelli*, fol. 43b. (p. 11); see also Publications of the Catholic Record Society Series, 5 ([London]: Catholic Record Society, 1908), pp. 294–300; in M&B, pp. xvii–xix.

33 Devlin, p. 32; M&B, p. xix. Southwell's *Querimonia* is preserved only in Henry More's Latin translation in his history of the Jesuit English Mission, *Historia Missionis Anglicanae Societatis Jesu* (St Omer: 1660), p. 173; Janelle, p. 23; Brownlow describes the *Querimonia* as a 'verbose' and highly idealised view of a 'privileged cadre, united against the world, secure in the service of a perfect master' (p. 3). See Pilarz's discussion of Southwell's crises of 'personal relationship' and 'vocational discernment' in chapter 4, pp. 117–37; Pilarz's account crystallises recent opinion that immaturity delayed Southwell's acceptance into the Society, pp. 133–7.

34 Southwell's letter is of October 1580, see Southwell, 'Letters to various Persons', in John Hungerford Pollen, S.J. (ed.), *Unpublished Documents Relating to the English Martyrs*, I (1584–1603), CRS, 5, pp. 293–333, p. 298. Southwell was replying to a letter of Deckers's, preserved as Stonyhurst MS A.vii.1, now at the Jesuit Archives, Mount St, London; see Henry Foley, S.J., *Records of the English Province of the Society of Jesus*, 7 vols (London: Burns and Oates, 1877, I, 301–87 (pp. 307–8); Pilarz, note 1, p. 149. It may also be seen in Peter Davidson and Anne Sweeney (ed. and intro.) *The Collected Poems of S. Robert Southwell S.J.* (Manchester: Carcanet, forthcoming).

35 See Janelle, p. 24.

36 See Fr Nathaniel Southwell, *Catalogus primorum patrum*, Stonyhurst MSS A.iv.3, p. 17; cited in Janelle, p. 23.

37 See www.sjweb.info/articles/rometour_all.cfm.

38 Thomas Bulfinch, *Mythology* (New York: Avenel, 1978), pp. 80–91.

39 See O'Malley, p. 367. Peter Davidson, discussing the amount of material providing evidence of literary creativity in the archives of the early Jesuits, also argues that such cultural production defined Jesuit culture itself, observing that the classrooms were called 'play-rooms'; on speech and feast days students were encouraged to write poems and picture-poems which were displayed for the edification of visitors; Peter Davidson, 'Archives of the British Province of the Society of Jesus', unpublished conference paper, *Recusant Archives and Remains from the Three Kingdoms 1560–1789: Catholics in Exile at Home and Abroad* (Downside Abbey, 23–4 June 2004).

40 Alison Shell, *Catholicism, Controversy and the English Literary Imagination 1558–1660* (Cambridge: Cambridge University Press, 1999), pp. 191–2; hereafter cited in the text. Shell discusses the pedagogical function of Jesuit dramas in general and their task of 'stimulating the reader, or the audience, to provide extra-textual hope' by determining to make good the damages to Catholicism demonstrated in the plays, p. 182.

41 See Karel Portemann, Dirk Sacré et al., *Emblematic Exhibitions at the Brussels Jesuit*

College: A Study of Commemorative Manuscripts (Brussels: Royal Library, 1996); see also Shell's discussion of Jesuit uses of *ornatus*, p. 192.
42 See Shell, p. 183.
43 'Saint Peters Complaint' began as a translation of *Le Lagrime di San Pietro*, by Luigi Tansillo, a popular writer whose works were often set to music (see Pilarz, p. 255). Southwell's later reworkings owed little to the original however, less narrative and more a protracted self-dissection of a guilty conscience. It is his nearest poem to the baroque *literary* style, however. For a discussion of the remarkable Jesuit contribution to the emergence of baroque religious art in the commissions they made for their colleges and churches, including those attended by Southwell, see Gauvin Alexander Bailey, *Between Renaissance and Baroque: Jesuit Art in Rome, 1565–1610* (Toronto: University of Toronto Press, 2003); hereafter cited in the text.
44 See Shell, pp. 56–7.
45 After a magnificent, painterly description of Tartarus and its loquacious denizens, God's first words are: 'Esto, ait, aequus ero, causa exagitetur utrinque | Cui ratio cui jura favent victoria cedat.' (lines 177–8) (Be it so. I will be fair. Let the cause be considered on both sides: the victory shall be given to whichever side reason and law favour); from 'Poema de Assumptione B.V.M.', Stonyhurst MS A.v.4, lines 177–8, translation from Davidson and Sweeney.
46 See Pilarz, pp. xvii–xx, for a discussion of Hall's satires on the subject.
47 Shell, p. 172.
48 Ibid., p. 97. Shell compares Crashavian and Southwellian visions of the baroque: '[Southwell's] audaciousness', as Shell puts it, is in 'doing away with neo-platonic machinery and other transitional figures between human and divine; his poetry seeks an apprehension of God with which even a heavenly muse would interfere', p. 67.
49 Bailey, fig. 21.
50 O'Malley, pp. 371, 373.
51 Ibid., pp. 19–20.
52 Letter to Sir Robert Cecil, quoted in Nancy Pollard Brown, 'Robert Southwell: The Mission of the Written Word', in McCoog (ed.), *Reckoned Expense*, pp. 193–214 (p. 197); hereafter 'Mission'; there is a modern-spelling version in Nancy Pollard Brown (ed.), *Robert Southwell, S.J.: Two Letters and Short Rules of a Good Life* (Charlottesville: University Press of Virginia, for the Folger Shakespeare Library, 1973), p. 81. A decade earlier, Southwell had written to Persons in the same vein in the aftermath of the Campion mission; in Pollen, pp. 301–3; also see Pilarz, pp. 2–4.
53 Nancy Pollard Brown has proposed this in 'Mission', p. 198.
54 Letter, 28 December 1588, quoted in Devlin, p. 182.
55 See Pilarz, p. 214.
56 Brown, 'Mission', p. 196; Pilarz argues throughout that Southwell was a reconciler; see Chapter 7 especially.
57 Brown, 'Mission', p. 198.
58 See Thomas M. McCoog, S.J., 'Sir Philip Sidney's Debt to Edmund Campion', in McCoog (ed.), *Reckoned Expense*, pp. 85–102, (p. 96); also see E. E. Reynolds, *Campion and Parsons: The Jesuit Mission of 1580* (London: Sheed and Ward, 1980), p. 105, for a

Introduction

discussion of what Reynolds calls Campion's 'naïve' belief in academic disputation.

59 Of major commentators, only Brown and Brownlow have, in my view, paid sufficient attention to the religio-political aspects of Southwell's activity to unlock the wider implications of his poetry, and then mainly with reference to the more 'important' (i.e. longer, more refined, or more pious) pieces (but see Pilarz's exploration of some of Southwell's shorter pieces); 'scholarship has tended to concentrate upon the influence of Southwell's short poems upon the *religious* lyricists of the next generation' (Shell, p. 61; my emphasis). Shell herself makes an invaluable contribution in this neglected area, describing the 'sudden large-scale reaction from both elite and non-elite poets' to the publication and 'immediate, sustained popular success' of the collection *Saint Peters Complaint* after Southwell's martyrdom in 1595, but still the focus is upon Catholicism and its imaginative constructions, p. 59.

60 See Grosart, p. lxxxi. Devlin and Brown have also argued for greater attention to Southwell's poetry.

61 Part of a poem by Ludovic Bryskett quoted in A. L. Rowse, *The Elizabethan Renaissance: The Life of the Society* (Harmondsworth: Penguin, 2000), p. 27.

62 See a version of this eleventh-century prayer on www.catholic-forum.com/saints/pray0055.htm. Its expression of the pain of exile no doubt resonated with some notable English Catholics at Southwell's time.

63 See Shell, pp. 97–103; Shell also notes the lack of attention paid to Fr Herbert Thurston's essays in the Jesuit *Month*, 1895, which define Southwell's 'importance, popularity and influence', p. 103.

64 Frank Kermode, *Shakespeare's Language* (Harmondsworth: Penguin, 2000), p. 112.

65 George Puttenham, *The Arte of English Poesie*, ed. Gladys Doidge Willcock and Alice Walker (London: Cambridge University Press, 1970).

66 See Shell's discussion of this in *Catholicism*, p. 59.

67 Clifford Davidson, 'Robert Southwell: Lyric Poetry, the Restoration of Images, and Martyrdom', *Ben Jonson Journal*, 7 (2000), 157–8 (n. 4, pp. 177–8).

68 See Shell, chapter 2, 'Catholic Poetics and the Protestant Canon' especially. Pitts claimed to know Southwell at college, and said that he was 'a good student in philosophy and theology' and 'wooed with considerable eagerness the graces of the mother tongue both in prose and verse'; see Devlin, p. 58; also Brownlow, p. 7.

69 See Shell, *Catholicism*, pp. 72, 67.

70 Gabriel Harvey, *new letter of notable contents*, 1593, in C. S. Lewis, *English Literature in the Sixteenth Century excluding Drama* (Oxford: Clarendon Press, 1944), p. 538; hereafter cited in the text.

71 See Shell, p. 66.

72 See St Ignatius of Loyola, S.J., *The Spiritual Exercises and Selected Works*, ed. George E. Ganss (New York: Paulist Press, c.1991); see also O'Malley, p. 37.

73 Such an idea was alien to scholastic humanism and to most pastoral ministry alike, and, appearing at the cultural moment identified by recent criticism as the birth of the self-fashioning self, surely requires more attention. See Stephen Greenblatt, *Renaissance Self-Fashioning: From More to Shakespeare* (Chicago: University of Chicago Press, 1980); also see his *Hamlet in Purgatory* (Princeton, NJ: Princeton University Press, 2001).

74 From Southwell's preface to *Marie Magdalens Funeral Teares* (1591), in Devlin, pp. 268–9.

75 M&B, p. xv.

76 When looking at Shakespeare *Comedy of Errors*, say, it is of note that, in writing about judicial execution, he locates the gallows with unusual meticulousness by the ditches of an old abbey; such a site existed near the Theatre at Shoreditch, where Fr William Gunter was executed as part of the bloody Armada backlash of 1588, the killings taking place before certain houses, as a warning to Catholic sympathisers.

77 He defines them as 'ghostly rights' in 'Of the Blessed Sacrament of the Aulter', M&B, p. 26, l. 56.

78 Brownlow, pp. 64–72.

79 Brownlow quotes A. C. Partridge on 'the purity of Southwell's un-Latinized English'; 'the language is so clear and precise that it seldom needs glossing'; from A. C. Partridge (ed.), *The Tribe of Ben: Pre-Augustan Classical Verse in English* (Columbia: University of South Carolina Press, 1970), p. 170; cited in Brownlow, p. 79.

80 Devlin, pp. 228–30.

81 This reference to Southwell is in a report by Chomley, *Calendar of State Papers, Domestic, 1591–1594*, ed. Mary Anne Everett Green (London: HMSO, 1867; repr. Liechtenstein: Kraus, 1967), vol. 241, no. 35 (?January 1592), p. 176; hereafter *CSP, Dom., 1591–1594*; cited in M&B, p. xxx. For John Cecil's report to the government see *CSP, Dom., 1591–1594*, vol. 238, n. 62, and for his report to Persons, see Pollen, pp. 199–203.

82 Southwell's and his co-missioner Henry Garnet's correspondence is detailed and discussed in Philip Caraman, S.J., *A Study in Friendship: Saint Robert Southwell and Henry Garnet* (Saint Louis, MO: The Institute of Jesuit Sources, 1995).

83 See Janelle, p. 6.

84 J. M. de Buck, S.J. (ed.), *The Spiritual Exercises and Devotions of Blessed Robert Southwell, S.J.*, trans. P. E. Hallett (London: Sheed and Ward, 1931); hereafter *SE&D*. Southwell's biographers have followed his spiritual progress through its study; Janelle finds traces of it in Southwell's English works (chapter iv); Brown sees it as a record of 'inner suffering' and of the step-changes by which the 'sensitive and rebellious spirit' was subdued to service (M&B, p. xviii); 'its influence on Southwell's future works is profound', as Pilarz says, agreeing with Martz and others; Pilarz sees in the entries Southwell maturing as he 'wrestles with conflicting desires, thoughts and emotions'; pp. 144–9 (p. 144).

85 Discussed throughout Peter Lake's 'Religious Identities in Shakespeare's England', in David Scott Kastan (ed.), *A Companion to Shakespeare* (Oxford: Blackwell, 1999), pp. 57–84.

86 Southwell to Aquaviva, 21 December 1586, in Caraman, pp. 38–9.

87 O'Malley, pp. 18, 73. See Brown, 'Mission', for a discussion of the odd inclusion of half of Southwell's reproving *Epistle to his Father* with Ralegh's *Instructions to his Sonne* (1632), which Brown says highlights Ralegh's alleged atheism; pp. 206–7.

88 The embargo on beneficed curacies meant that Jesuits could not exert influence, as could pastors, via 'canonical penalties', the 'pastoral prerogative' strengthened by Trent. Jesuits 'could not by virtue of office or jurisdictional status oblige anybody to accept their ministrations', O'Malley, pp. 73–4.

89 The contribution of the Jesuits to late sixteenth-century artistic theories and practice developed after the Council of Trent 'can hardly be exaggerated'; Bailey, pp. 3, 5.

90 Bailey, p. 224; Shell, pp. 173–4.

91 From the "Waldegrave" manuscript (Stonyhurst MS A.v.27, now at the Jesuit Archives, Mount Street, London). See also in Davidson and Sweeney.

92 Martin to Campion, 20 December 1575, quoted in Janelle, pp. 9–10; see also Bailey, pp. 210–11, 221.

93 See Francisco Suárez, *Of Laws and God the Lawgiver* (*De legibus ac deo legislatore*) (New York: Wiley, 1964); also see, for instance, Bernice Hamilton, *Political Thought in Sixteenth Century Spain: A Study of the Political Ideas of Vitoria, De Solo, Suárez and Molina* (Oxford: Clarendon Press, 1963).

94 See O'Malley, pp. 37, 68, 293.

95 See Pilarz, p. 150, n. 8. in his lectures Suárez was developing the basis of his *Disputationes Metaphysicae*, which Caraman and Pilarz call the textbook for modern philosophers such as Descartes, Leibniz, and Schopenhauer; Williams, *English College*, n. 9, p. 40; Caraman, p. 25; Pilarz, p. 160.

96 O'Malley, pp. 108–9, 249; Trent 'had asserted that grace was operative and that it enabled the human co-operation that was also essential in the process [...] Thus was established the deepest foundation of human dignity, a dignity that Lutheran teaching denied', p. 282.

97 Background information on Suárez and Molina is available from the informative website www,newadvent.org/cathen.htm.

98 'Juan de Avila, a reformer influenced by Erasmus, had perhaps as early as 1527 published his catechism, written in verse and meant to be set to tunes – *Doctrina cristiana que se canta*' (O'Malley, p. 116).

99 Ibid., p. 116.

100 The Jesuit Francis Xavier, on mission in India and China, often taught without a text, using 'verse, song, dialogue and "lesson" as occasion seemed to suggest' (O'Malley, pp. 118–19). His use of such varied means was shared by his relative Jerónimo and Claudio Acquaviva, the linchpin of the new Jesuit artistic programme encountered by Southwell in Rome (Bailey, 'Mirror', p. 388).

101 'Looke home', p. 57, l. 16.

102 O'Malley, p. 41.

103 Ibid., pp. 2, 62–3.

104 Ibid., pp. 4–5, 18–19.

105 Ibid., pp. 247, 6, 68.

106 Ibid., p. 69.

107 See Pilarz's account of this, pp. 137–8.

Chapter 1

Rome: the discernment of angels

I, who in a looke, | Learnd more by rote, then all the scribes by booke.[1]

'SACRA PARADISI IN SEDE LOCAVIT': SOUTHWELL'S ROMAN LIFE[2]

Rome was the centre of Southwell's world. Here his writing matured and took on its colours and textures; but, whatever his immature expectations, he soon found that Rome was not Paradise. Beauties it may have owned, but angers and enmities abounded, too, in the city built among the ruins of an earthly empire whose language was its most lasting monument, and the lingua of Southwell's college years. Southwell's Latin poetry has had little airing to date, but it expresses the texture and tone of that whole experience. Latin, or the experience of Rome itself, formed Southwell's idiolect, his personal dialect, in these years, and his poetic expression is founded upon it.

A supervising member of the elite Sodality of the Virgin, and therefore honour-bound to engage in Marian apologetics,[3] Southwell has poeticised a debate between heaven and hell on the vexed question of her Assumption, the bodily progress into heaven, that Catholics believed to be rejected by Protestants and that became symbolic of the post-Reformation battle in which Southwell was to engage in Rome. Death is given the Protestant's supposed part:

> Atra cohors, nostris semper fidissima sceptris,
> Olim quanta fuit Lethei gloria regni
> Qua Phoebus, qua luna suos agit aurea currus,
> Quas bello edidimus strages, quot funere reges
> Mersimus, et totum quoties consumpsimus orbem
> Non latet, et vestris cecidit pars maxima telis.
> [...]
> Nunquid tanta ruet virtus ingloria, et uni

> Noster cedet honos, sic formidabile numen
> Imperiumque ruet, sic nostris hostia templis
> Deficiet, tantique cadent fastigia regni?[4]

(Dark company, ever most faithful to our ruling power, how great was formerly the glory of the realm of Lethe, wherever Phoebus, wherever the golden moon, drive their chariots, what massacres we brought about by war, how many kings we submerged in violent death, and how many times we devoured the entire world: this is no secret, and the majority fell to your weapons. [...] Surely such great virtue will not be cast down inglorious, nor our honour yield to a single individual? Is formidable authority and command so to topple? Is sacrifice to become absent from our temples? Are the pinnacles of so great an empire to collapse?)

After this affecting loquacity, and as if to embody the plainer rhetoric learned under Allen, Southwell's impassive Gabriel delivers his message without embellishment (God, the arbiter, is more succinct yet; the model that Milton was later to adopt in *Paradise Lost*). Points are made with lawyer-like lucidity: first, all agree upon the Virgin's immaculacy, second, God does not punish the innocent; ergo: Adam and Eve's punishment – death – cannot apply to her. Southwell's dramatic evocation of that debate, although directed against 'heresy', also reflects the contrasts exposed in Rome, the angelic appeals and Stygian antipathies that almost overwhelmed him while there, and which were the indirect cause of his death.

Angelic majesty and busyness must have been his first impression, however. The Norfolk youth, brought up amongst the effaced shrines and ruins of the ancient English church, was, on arrival in 1578, thrust into the middle of a visual explosion of new artworks, angel-sent inspirations and theories of perceiving and feeling, new processes of transmitting God's missionary messages, Gabriel-like, to human minds.[5] But he also arrived in the middle of an intractable and deadly turmoil over ways of proceeding and mission agendas, and not all the paintings he saw appearing on his college walls were angelic: some showed tortured and twisted bodies, including those of men he had known; at some point in Rome he was to decide that his path lay that way. In Rome he learned to write into that dichotomy, to reconcile violence with beauty. The regular spiritual report required of every Jesuit novice was, in Southwell's case, a testament to his painful struggles towards maturity, while his early poetry seems to reflect both the horrors and the felicities of the visual splendour of Rome as if he is never really able to tear his eyes from them, even in England.[6]

On arrival, not at the Novitiate on its airy hill but at the *Venerabile*, the English College in the busy streets down on the Tiberine levels, he met with disappointments and disruptions. Sir Richard Shelley, a relative of Southwell's influential in the exile community, was involved in a bitter dispute with the Welsh Archdeacon of the English College, Owen Lewis. An invasion of Ireland was being pressed by Thomas Stucley and Shelley objected, only the intervention of Robert Persons saving him from the Inquisition.[7] The resulting turmoils simmered on, to erupt again with dreadful effect later in Southwell's time there.

It is hard to ascertain Southwell's movements at this time, but it seems clear that he was not immediately accepted into the novitiate, but set to further study, remaining at the English College, the Society still unsure, perhaps, of his maturity and motivation. He will none the less have been required to work in the kitchens and do other chores, as well as studying hard, among all the grand or sordid distractions Rome had to offer.[8]

He and his companions, let loose for an afternoon, looked up at ceilings beginning to pulse with the early baroque, glimpsing beings of light among the gilded mouldings of the twilit, scented churches. Angels were central to Jesuit theology. Jesuit methodology, with its emphasis on accurate discernment of personal motivations and feelings, had resulted in the development what we would now consider a theory of psychology, based on 'angelic' action on the inner landscape. This discernment of spirits and the theories of perception and depiction of divine action met in the person of the angel. Southwell's experience of these new perceptive and depictive theories can be explored both through the spiritual record he made during his novitiate and through the paintings he saw in Rome; and, more importantly, through his lively, innovative poetic response to them.

Although the cult of angels really took flight only after Southwell's time in Rome, guardian and assistant angels were becoming a Jesuit preoccupation. By 1600 the Gesù was thronged with angels, but even in 1584 some of the first of them were trying their wings in the ceiling decorations above the young priest's head.[9] In Circignani's *Heavenly Celebration of the Birth of Christ*, a miracle of mirrored symmetry and restrained movement, angels in their orders and ranks are still peripheral to the central sunburst of light; none the less they are there, singing, playing lutes and viols in support and imitation of God's orderly and rhythmic creativity. They embody and enact a baroque quasi-reality transcending older, more literal, depictive limitations, appearing to occupy actual, not pictorial space, their divine gaze vaulting the limits of their painting as they look beyond its frame towards the Christ-Child above the Nativity Chapel altar.[10]

As Southwell's more mature writing was to insist, this was not art for pleasure's sake, but art serving God. England was debating whether decoration and imagery had any place at all in God's house, but the spiritual atmosphere Southwell encountered in Rome was highly visually charged; painting was an integral part of a mystical journey towards God.[11] As Gauvin Bailey puts it, '"the activation of the sacred was embodied in the process of the experience and interiorization of the sacred narrative"'. None of the new artistic initiatives celebrating this difference was as carefully co-ordinated and scripted as the

Rome: the discernment of angels

programme of the Jesuits in Rome.[12] Southwell's later poetic mission can be seen in the light of this new thinking: the carrying into England of internalised shrines and relics, replacing sacred object and pilgrimage with internal mediation, the emphasis being on perception, rather than poetry. To that different emphasis was added the fact that where the novices of other orders spent much time training for choir and ceremonial, Jesuit novices trained solely for ministry in the wider world from the start. Other orders lived with beauty as sacrament, but the Jesuit youths lived with beauty as message.[13] Southwell's vision of his future ministry was therefore entirely bound up with the depictions of that greater ministry of image and its apprehension surrounding him in Rome.

Novices and probationers were required to take moral instruction, listen to homilies and attend vespers on Sundays and feast days, the paintings among which they sat or moved enhancing the lesson. The altarpiece that dominated the Jesuit Novitiate chapel on the Quirinal Hill was not a painting of Christ but of one of his celebrated imitators, St Andrew, pictured alive in the process of crucifixion, surrounded by crowds. The message was graphically clear: the *living* example of self-sacrifice and mass-communication in the service of God, these, not death, were the desiderata. The martyrdom expected of the Jesuit was not necessarily to be literal.

This theme of self-martyrdom through ministry and missionary zeal was repeated throughout the novitiate in paintings, frescos and emblems, and meditation on the message was a central method of developing the novices for their own ministry.[14] Ignatius stressed this view, insisting on an obedience of 'execution, will, and understanding'. While other orders practised Christian self-denial in prodigious austerities or periods of prayer, a Jesuit's way of showing self-sacrifice was 'through the abnegation implied in obedience to their superiors'.[15] This was to cause Southwell considerable anguish as his stay in Rome drew to an end.

As Bailey observes, the very ahistoricity of the generic St Andrew landscape painted by Durante Alberti demonstrates this wider understanding of martyrdom, something seen in the rest of the collegiate chapels and the Jesuits' great Gesù, and designed to guide the viewer, lay or otherwise, into the same path as that of the Ignatian *Exercises*, with their 'composition of place': the supplying by the viewer of the context and emotional impact of the action, thereby replacing being told with experiencing for oneself.[16] In the facial expressions of Andrew's followers, Alberti supplies a range of emotional responses with which a viewer might be in sympathy, just as Southwell later was to paint word-pictures of grief, despair, or anger for his English readers, to help them to site themselves at an imaginary Calvary, and to contextualise their own losses.

The Jesuits taught through image. The chapel of the Collegio Romano was one of the first in Italy to feature textualised mural images, using letters with a key below.[17] Southwell was being trained to see imagery and word as an interactive, interdependent resource for passing on information that could not be contained in words alone. In England he developed this into a potent poetic that melded metaphoric picture and biblical shorthand to the same end.

SCHOOLING THE EYE OF THE HEART: LEARNING TO READ BEAUTY

The influence of the new father general of the Society, Claudio Acquaviva, cannot be overstated; he was central to the artistic project in Rome, directing, fundraising for, and possibly even designing, many programmes of religious painting.[18] Southwell's fight to be sent, against Acquaviva's wishes, to near-certain death on the English mission, was, paradoxically, tightly bound up with such visual stimulation. The preponderance of imagined visualisation in his poetry, though founded in the emotional arena of the Ignatian *Spiritual Exercises*, was stimulated further by his special proximity to this vast artistic project and its imagery of passion and crisis.[19]

The progressive series of paintings planned for the Jesuits' Roman churches reflected the progression of thought and awareness of the *Exercises*. It opened the viewer gradually to ever-heightened responses to, and understandings of, God's action on the soul.[20] It is clear, though, that not only were the Jesuits involved in the promotion of such high culture, but that their concept of the impact of religious art included its written expression, in the form of spiritual exercises, meditations, drama, and poetry. The novices were required to undergo the full Ignatian *Spiritual Exercises* during their two years; the process was central to their education and development.[21] The iconography of the College and Novitiate was clearly designed to contribute to this experience, the visual and the spiritual effectively inseparable. Recent scholarship has shown how close this relationship was.[22] Southwell's attitude to his own metaphoric programme and its pastoral purposes must be viewed in the light of this interdependence.

Such beauties were a double-edged sword though: Calvinist rejection of the relationship between sensual beauty and spirituality meant that the arts programmes of Rome were inevitably implicated in Catholic apologetics (as employed by Bellarmine, for instance). Beauty worked both to draw the soul Godwards and to drive heresy back. And living in Rome, as even their Catholic masters admitted, could have undesirable effects on English students, many from simple backgrounds, and accustomed to stripped altars. Southwell's spiritual record stresses the dangers of being distracted by physical beauty. His second preparation prior to making his Exercises includes a passage which is interesting in the way it conflates the physical altar at which the novice assists and church depictions of crucifixion, trying to reveal the real altar under the gilding and flowered cloth, covered in the blood of the sacrifice:

> Day by day He has come down from heaven to earth and like a suppliant lain before thee upon the altar. He continues to beg of thee the same boon, and to beseech thee by His own body and blood offered for thee upon the altar of the cross, that thou wouldst unite thyself perfectly to Him and never leave Him by thy sins. But thou like a deaf man hast not listened, thou hast barred the entry into thy heart, thou hast broken faith, and after promising love thou hast transferred it from the Creator to the creature. (13, p. 16)

Southwell was surrounded by 'creature' magnificence in Rome, and was commanded to regard it with indifference, except in that it spoke with the voice of God. Later he was to describe such a struggle for the benefit of others: 'Mans civill warre' (p. 49) is an extended commentary on the hindrances to perfection that Southwell's own director was trying to make him address: 'Faine would my ship in vertues shore | Without remove at anchor lie', he says; it would be so easy never to go out into the world and have to face its temptations; 'But mounting thoughts are hailed downe | With heavie poise [or counterweight] of mortall load' (lines 3–6):

> Fond fancie traines to pleasures lure,
> Though reason stiffely do repine.
> Though wisdome wooe me to the saint, 15
> Yet sense would win me to the shrine

This could almost be a Calvinist's concern over the uses of beauty; but the constant dichotomy of needing to be in the world – at the Catholic centre of it in Rome, indeed – and not be seduced by its physical beauties, was a source of tension for any Jesuit, and Southwell's diary explores these tensions and dislocations.[23]

Southwell was, in keeping this confessional diary, extending his understanding of the work words can do in managing feelings and situations; his poetic interior monologues are founded on the interrogative sensitivity it encouraged in analysing and expressing emotional states and motivations. The *Devotions* provide, according to de Buck, an 'introspective analysis' almost unsurpassed in the picture it gives of 'the formation of a martyr's soul', exposing 'the real reasons, the motives deep in [Southwell's] soul, which led him to take the step of going back to England'.[24] Vocation aside, it also allows glimpses into Southwell's emotional and psychological life, the self-analyses, the hopes and fears implied by various entries, the bitterly self-excoriating, almost self-destructive, tone that seems to emerge, even in his resignation.[25] Both the resulting self-awareness and the habit of self-analysis in itself contributed to the emotional realism of his poetry, and the impact it later had on other English authors. This does not make the poetry confessional in itself, of course, but his experience of the *Exercises* and keeping the diaries gave him a new, deeply felt language of personal emotional response.

Southwell brought to the Society a level of inspired creativity, as suggested by one of the diary entries which notes certain 'natural gifts and aptitudes' of his, useful in the saving of souls: expressive skills, and a passionate nature to help him envision the way to salvation, which caused him to 'burn with more ardent desires than others towards God and divine things'.[26] This ardour, judging by diary entries, could sometimes run over into impulsiveness in the immature Southwell. John Deckers, too, characterised his friend's precipitate rush towards a Jesuit novitiate in Rome as 'trampl[ing] underfoot all those values which cause worldly men to hesitate, oblivious of your homeland, your parents, your colleagues, not to mention your costly property';[27] Southwell seems prone to self-dramatise, seeing himself as 'singled out from all my family and kindred' in his vocation, succumbing to the 'temptation to "singularity"', 'wanting to be special and knowing that his manner should be ordinary', as Pilarz puts it.[28]

Nothing illustrates this sense of a special voice better perhaps than one of his entries, written as the words of the ultimate head of the Society, Christ – perhaps the first and most signal of Southwell's biblical ventriloquisations (27, p. 38). He never repeats this Christly ventriloquising in his short English poetry, apart from Nativity baby-noises and the words spoken by the enigmatic Burning Babe, although he does in his prose-poem or sermon, *Marie Magdalens Funeral Teares*, albeit preceded carefully by '[it is] as if thou haddest said ...'.[29]

The effects of the intense self-searching carried out through the diary entries is clearly visible in later English work like *Mary Magdalen*. This reconstruction of a 'real' interiority was brought new to England by Southwell in the shape of his expansions of Gospel characters; complaint poetry had existed in English, but nothing like this extended and psychologically insightful dramatic personation. Every sort of English writing now considered 'good', all the soliloquies, dramatic monologues, the poetry and novels full of emotional immediacy and integrity, has developed in part out of Southwell's literary experiments in English, all those, in their turn, derived from the response of an imaginative mind to Jesuit diary and confessional practices learned in Rome.

Nothing in the whole diary so clearly demonstrates the effects of the *Exercises* on Southwell, the indivisibility of the products of the imagination from the experience of the divine, than this imaginary encounter with the living Lord. In this entry more than any other, perhaps, we are witnessing the force behind his formation as an adult, a writer, and a Jesuit priest. Later he would see no reason not to call up similar visions for others via his poetry in support of his mission to help souls. The Thomistic urge to find harmony wherever possible between 'nature and grace', a theme repeated in the Jesuit *Constitu-*

tions, combined with the Jesuits' understanding, via Thomistic theology, that it was desirable to harness all 'human means' at their disposal, again a theme of the *Constitutions*,[30] combined to produce Southwell's poetic ministry just as much as Suárez's or Nadal's tracts on the part played by the individual in the accessing of divine love.

But Rome was far more than private spaces. It was undergoing a public revolution, from below ground to the skies, revealing ancient Rome and the frescos of its first Christian martyrs under their feet and working architectural wonders high above their heads, as new buildings and churches rose among the ruins. The message of this sumptuous vision could not have been lost on Southwell, schooled in its uses by Acquaviva (as his younger colleagues were to be by Acquaviva's friend, the art theorist Louis Richeôme).[31] It seems clear that Southwell's English poetry was full of its visual richness and clarity, 'staind', 'inameld' and 'limbde with [its] glorious gleames'.[32] It was, primarily, to be the visual impact of Southwell's Roman experience that was borrowed and translated into poetic metaphor for his English enterprise.

PAINTING BY NUMBERS: SOUTHWELL'S NEW POETIC VISION

In the Collegio Romano, Southwell had arrived at what was 'an international institution and the pre-eminent college' of an already exemplary educational order, at a time of great expansion and change. He was no doubt delighted by his first experience of the Collegio Romano's eight-day spectaculars of erudition in rhetoric and emblematics that advertised the opening of each academic year to the 'Roman intelligentsia'.[33] His already sharpened interest in poetry would have been further excited by the importance placed upon poetry in the vernaculars as well as in Latin, where the students' efforts were pinned up alongside emblems and their captions – a rich training ground in the uses of imagery and metaphor.[34]

Received at last into the novitiate at San Andrea al Quirinale, Southwell's life was now immersed in the issues of the Roman College and the Novitiate, very much global and headquarters concerns. He shared his space with lay students and men training for the diocesan priesthood, not just Jesuits; his daily preoccupations were with his studies and his Jesuit development and any possible future career; they were no longer those of England, as they had been at William Allen's school in Douai. As in Paris, he was part of the European network of Catholicism, with its wide concerns about European Protestantism and the missions to the Indies, Japan, and the Americas, and Latin its international language. Letters from these exotic outposts arrived during Southwell's novitiate, sometimes with news of deaths but always with intriguing details of newly encountered cultures.[35]

As if in poetic response to these new artistic theories, Southwell's poetry in English seems to reproduce visual moments, rather than telling stories, as if he is quoting the painting itself. It is these new cycles of paintings, and the effects that they had on a viewer such as himself, that he reproduced in his English poetry, rather than narratives taken directly from the Bible, as if he is trying to recapture and import into England their glossy, almost photographic affectivity without freighting his poetry with the original text. In England they had Bible texts in profusion, but they did not have this astounding visual proliferation.

Southwell quotes the imagery, rather than the text, even in his Gospel poems. His Virgin Sequence poem 'His circumcision', for instance, refers to knives piercing the Madonna's heart: 'No blow that hit the sonne the mother mist' (p. 7, lines 15, 18). His model for this image may have been an iconic depiction of the Seven Sorrows of the Virgin, in which the circumcision of the eight-day-old Christ-Child figures. It is shown in Tempesta's S. Stefano *Madonna* of the early 1580s, which depicts each sorrow as a roundel in the pommel of a series of long thin blades centred upon the breast of the Virgin, fanned like an array of throwing-knives.[36] The sword that pierces Mary's heart is mentioned in the Gospel only at the presentation of Christ in the temple, by old Simeon, who thus prefigures her heartbreak at the crucifixion (the Presentation also appears among Tempesta's stilettos).[37] Southwell's poem therefore addresses the mystic iconography he has seen, not just the underlying texts.

The presentation of Christ occurs also in Southwell's Virgin Sequence, but without mention of the sword of the Gospel narrative, as if he is thinking of a different account, pictorial, rather than biblical, preferring to separate it from the element most central to his 'circumcision' poem, the shedding of Christ's blood. Circignani's *Presentation of Christ at the Temple* was in the Nativity Chapel at the Jesuits' great church, the Gesù, and this may have been in Southwell's memory as he conjured up his poetic images.

The rest of his Virgin Sequence echoes the light, unemphatic mysticism of the programme of paintings in the Madonna Chapel of the Gesù, which was a small, essentially round chapel approached by a decorated corridor from the apse, the whole containing seven paintings. Bailey describes its 'gilded stuccoes and frescoes' and 'lavish coloured marbles'; 'Few places in the early Gesù so closely resembled a jewel box' he adds, 'or an extravagantly decorated reliquary': the chapel was in actuality a great reliquary.[38] A Jesuit of the Sodality of the Blessed Virgin, as Southwell was, would have regarded the chapel and its imagery with special reverence. The sequence of paintings was: *The Immaculate Conception, Birth of the Virgin, Presentation of the Virgin, Marriage of the Virgin, Annunciation, Visitation,* and *Assumption of the Virgin*. Bailey comments on the fact that the Jesuits forwent the opportunity to use the seven panels to present the Seven Joys or Seven Sorrows: this programme was probably incidental to the more general 'Life of the Virgin' theme celebrated in the chapel as a whole.³⁹

Southwell's sequence is doubled to fourteen. He has the 'Conception'; 'Her Nativity'; 'Her Spousals'; but misses out her presentation at the temple (replacing it with the presentation of Jesus); the Annunciation, which, in Southwell's version (called 'The Virgins Salutation', p. 3), seems to be informed by visual elements of the Gesù painting.⁴⁰ Where the yielding, sweet-faced Virgin in the painting points to her breast, and is being bowed to or gazed up at adoringly by the cloud of cherub faces that support Gabriel, Southwell has 'O virgin breast the heavens to thee incline, | In thee their joy and soveraigne they agnize,' (lines 7–8). He has his 'Visitation' (p. 5), adding after it the 'Nativitie of Christ' (p. 6), 'His circumcision' (p. 7), 'The Epiphanie' (p. 8), 'The Presentation' (p. 9), 'The flight into Egypt' (p. 9), 'Christs returne out of Egypt' (p. 10), 'Christs Childhoode' (p. 11), and 'The death of our Ladie' (p. 11), before returning to match the cycle of the Gesù with his last, 'The Assumption of our Lady' (p. 12), that element so important to Catholics in the aftermath of the Reformation. Just as the artist of the Gesù *Assumption* has washed out all the customary background scenery of this event, including the Virgin's tomb and the apostolic mourners, so Southwell's 'Assumption' boasts 'No tombe but throne', because 'Tombe prison is for sinners that decease,' (lines 4, 3). As in the painting, Southwell describes his Virgin's eyes fixed, undazzled, on the brilliant sky above; 'Our Princely Eagle' (l. 12) is borne away by heavenly hosts. In the gauzy background of the painting, before which a queenly Virgin, in flowing silks, her arms outstretched as if to greet a lover, is borne up upon a cloud studded like a plum pudding with cherub heads, almost overwhelming its cherubic bearers like rising dough, can be dimly seen in the dazzle a great crowd of attendant figures, some playing musical instruments. There is the faintest suggestion of palatial colonnades. With this painted scene compare Southwell's metaphoric one:

> Gemm to her worth, spouse to her love ascendes,
> Prince to her throne, Queene to her heavenly kinge,
> Whose court with solemne pompe on her attends,   15
> And Quires of Saintes with greeting notes do singe.
> Earth rendreth upp her undeserved praye,
> Heaven claymes the right and beares the prize away.

He is not descanting upon the idea of the Assumption, as he does in his complex and fluid Latin 'Poema de Assumptione'; he is reproducing this, or a similar painting, in English words. The new vision is entirely connected with the 'astonishing results' realized by the Society at the end of the sixteenth century, 'results gained by the triumph of a reasoning so perfect and brilliant as to mark the superimposition of Utopia on reality'.⁴¹ No doubt the artist responsible for the main sequence of paintings in the Madonna Chapel, the

Jesuit Giuseppe Valeriano, was perfectly aware of the novelty of his vision; and the same combination of elements that he introduced was later to inform Southwell's English poetry: a restrained classicism, a new realism. Southwell, influenced by this new mood of universality and accessibility, had transcribed it into English poetry.

Southwell's new understanding of the intimate connections between music and the divine order expressed into human history through Mary and Christ would have resonated deeply with his experience of this chapel, and especially with the way in which it was tailored for the public, who had long visited relics of the Madonna della Strada on this site.[42] Southwell, perhaps in response to this element of the chapel decorations, has presented a Life of the Virgin of his own, very much in the mystic but accessible spirit of this cycle (some of which he can have seen only just before he left Rome for England), perhaps intending it as a condensed virtual tour of this and the Nativity Chapels for his countrymen, now bereft of their own.[43] The metaphorical carrying away of the images of the reliquary chapel was Southwell's way of bringing these forbidden things into England, safe in the special reality of his and his reader's imagination.

He drew the extra elements from other cycles, it would appear, as if trying to engage the Marian cycle with metaphors of mission and martyrdom, although he does not include a Calvary scene, as if trying to emphasise Mary's, rather than Christ's, place in the history of man's redemption, and her special relationship with the missioners and martyrs; Mary was the Queen of Martyrs, after all.[44] His Virgin Sequence includes 'The flight into Egypt' (p. 9), in which he takes the opportunity to describe the Massacre of the Innocents, frescoes of which appeared in the German College's S. Stefano Rotondo in 1583, and in the Gesù in 1584.[45]

The Holy Innocents clearly had an important place in Jesuit iconography: the first painting of the celebrated S. Stefano sequence showed two of the Holy Innocents standing at the foot of a Crucifixion, amongst male and female martyrs, an almost unprecedented usage.[46] The connection of the Innocents with the Martyrs and Christ crucified links them to the sacrament of Holy Communion, but Southwell seems to have absorbed more than the theological implications of the imagery. In his description of the Innocents in 'The flight into Egypt' (p. 9), they are static, framed by martyrs' garlands and singing Christ's praises. It is as if he has in mind the christological triumphalism of the Tempesta painting rather than the dramatic, distressing scenes of the frescos actually dedicated to their slaughter, although elements of the massacre are there: 'Who though untimely cropt faire garlands frame, | With open throats and silent mouths you sing | His praise' (lines 14–16).

This penultimate phrase connects his poem even more closely to the church cycles, with their elucidatory inscriptions: *The Massacre of the Innocents* was in the Nativity Chapel of the Gesù, but in the Martyr's Chapel, under a *Martyrdom of St Lawrence*, the inscription ubiquitous in Jesuit painting cycles includes part of a sermon attributed to St Ambrose: 'and if the holy martyrs are silent in their voices they teach us by their virtue, and if their tongues are silent they persuade us by their suffering' (p. 237). Southwell seems to have had a portfolio of this powerful imagery and text in his head, and to have accessed that, rather than his biblical, store, when composing his pious English lyrics. As so often in his devotional poetry, he finishes on a musical theme, adapting St Ambrose: 'Your tunes are teares, your instruments are swords, | Your ditty death, and blood in lieu of wordes' (lines 17–18).

'The virgin Mary to Christ on the Crosse' (p. 71), from the collection printed after *Saint Peters Complaint*, the *Moeoniae*, has the same odd collocations; again, it appears as one of Mary's Seven Sorrows in the S. Stefano painting. In the poem, she views her son on the cross, heartbroken, and yet the theme of music appears in the background: she demands why the angels are not singing sorrowful symphonies, and ends by crying 'Let sorrow string my heavy lute' (l. 28), as if music is to be the inevitable finale to this scene.

It is equally important to note that the inscriptions that were so central to the didactic point of these pictures used the vernacular – Italian – as well as Latin, something that would not have been lost on Southwell as he observed their pedagogical and didactic impact on the less educated Roman commons – they were for the laity as much as anybody, the crowds that flocked to view them being ample justification of the method. His decision to reproduce these powerful images in poetry in the vernacular must be seen in the light of such all-inclusive pedagogic projects.

Southwell's training actively encouraged this cross-over. The underlying idea of the *Exercises*, the 'composition of place', which sought to recreate actual experiences in the imagination in order to lend immediacy to meditation, was a powerful conceptual driver for Jesuit uses of imagery. Nadal realised what was probably Ignatius's dream, a richly illustrated and captioned series of engravings based on the Gospels, in order to provide a portable pilgrimage of the mind.[47] Francisco Borgia used visual images in his preaching, likening them to spices in food; Robert Bellarmine stressed the necessity of accurate observation including the knowledge of anatomy, perspective, and optics, to inform art with truths about God's creation. Antonio Possevino, by 1595, was able to argue that 'painting was a mute form of poetry [...] capable of moving the emotions more quickly than words'.[48]

Is it perhaps this natural, honest, non-allegorical focus upon imagery – foundational and psychologically suggestive poetic imagery – that attracted the demanding Jonson to the young priest's work?

Robert Southwell

LEARNING TO DO VIOLENCE TO THE SELF

At first Southwell was no doubt hoping, like many of his peers, for one of the missions to the courts of Europe or the New World. Such diplomatic postings called for men innocent of guile and appetite, yet skilful in the policy and refinement of courts. In pursuit of such subtle skills, Southwell's Roman training was becoming increasingly complex: he was learning controversialism alongside his confessional skills, developing that curious alchemy of compromise which only practical experience can teach. One of Southwell's earliest diary entries emphasises the requirement to the young novice that he must work to attract, not repel, souls, using the Jesuit desideratum of the 'devout conversation', the facility to engage likely minds in pleasant speech, encouraging them towards a higher spiritual engagement. Southwell's poems can be seen in the light of such 'conversations', each tailored, perhaps, to one or two special minds in Rome or in his literary circle in London, in the mould of his pre-Continental recusant companionship. The 'conversations' were considered a special application of the ministry of preaching God's Word, the more effective for being delivered into the individual heart; poetry written by a Jesuit can therefore be seen as sacred, even when it is profane, providing it brings minds towards God and the Society.[49]

As importantly for a developing poet, Southwell's wordcraft was becoming sophisticated and lissom: the Jesuits worked words hard, driving them like soldiers into the post-Reformation battle or casting them lightly like salmon flies: the sparkling attractions of the 'devout conversation' were set into a steely carapace of controversialism and confessional rigour. These are the twin skills which meet and coalesce in Southwell's poetry, the necessary condition for its existence. Diary entries describing the parlous condition of European Christianity illustrate the complexities he was expected to absorb and to reflect in his ministry, and the burden that his new skills were to bear. Poetry for poetry's sake would have seemed a trivial distraction in these circumstances; Southwell's training should warn his critics to look for more in it than art, even in the little 'burning Babe'.[50]

'The burning Babe', after all, is a pain-filled piece; violence is being done; the babe is not sermonising but sobbing. Violence was also part of the Jesuit 'way', and Southwell's life in Rome bears witness to its effects. In 'Some Hindrances to Perfection' (*SE&D*, p. 28), his meditation has thrown up an exacting self-analysis, identifying avoidance of frequent talk with his superior and failure to ask his advice; a habit of trusting himself and his own opinions; failure to root out wrong passions at the beginning, so that they build up. The whole is summed up as refraining from doing violence to oneself in order to offer resistance to the passions. 'The kingdom of heaven suffers violence and the violent bear it away', the entry adds: heaven permits violence to be done to the animal self in order to bring its passions under control; one must hurt one's personal inclinations as hard as one can, to get to heaven. Here is the dichotomous nature of the Jesuit approach to the battle in a nutshell: violence to achieve serenity and heaven's bliss.

This was to have difficult resonances in his mission life: intended to be an interior violence done by the self to the self, for Southwell and his companions on the English mission, the same text could so easily attach itself to the actual violence inherent in the recusant experience and impending Spanish invasions, and that worthy dichotomy would become externalised and uncontrollable. Southwell would have to fit his own authorial activities into strategies for invasion developing in some corners of the exile community; issues of violence were to become a serious distraction. 'Refer to meditation book', the entry ends, sharply. There was a remedial formula for his inner conflicts; the wider battle was to have no such clear way through for Southwell.

The matter of judgement in moderating the behaviour of oneself and others was a foundation of the Jesuit ministry – a good Jesuit needed to be 'a person of sound judgement' above all, trained as they were to go far from 'brethren and superiors, in strange and difficult situations'.[51] The application of good judgement and prudence necessitated the vital Jesuit characteristic of flexibility. It was not a new notion as a general principle but, as O'Malley says, a young Jesuit learned it explicitly and emphatically from its constant reiteration in the *Exercises*; 'in practice, of course,' O'Malley adds with some delicacy, 'it might be separated by only a hair's breadth, or less, from opportunism'.[52]

A Jesuit confessor was generally exhorted to be kind, gentle and infinitely approachable, and in the diary we see Southwell learning that kindness at the unflinching hands of an expert seeker-out of his personal failings: his spiritual director, and, ultimately, himself. Pierre Favre had asked his brothers of the early Society to be, as confessors, 'vicars of the mild Christ', but for all that they were sharp psychologists in pursuit of character flaws, insisting not only on the traditional ritual of sins listed and repented but on something much harder, especially for the young – a conscious effort to locate 'their most characteristic sin that gives rise to the others', that actual character flaw in themselves which caused the repetition of a particular sin, with a view to self-knowledge and self-reform, as in Southwell's diary.[53] He was, as a Tridentine priest, to prove to the world *in his own person* the essentially elevating, beautifying and perfecting nature of Catholicism.

That curious, almost paradoxical, poetic image of the mild but incandescent Babe calling up the conscience of the viewer to join him in the midst of fires blown hot by justice and mercy now begins to coalesce: the caller-up of conscience, in the Jesuit model, must be attractive and of childlike purity, while at the same time having at his command a world of pain and self-examination for himself and those that approach him, for the good of their souls.

The burning Babe is as much about the peculiarly Jesuit vision of the Father become the Son, of the painful, purifying sacrament of Penance and its effects, as Christmas Day.

Along with the messages about angelic apprehension of the divine, Southwell was learning a subtler skill that in turn informed his poetry. Casuistry, the management of perceptions and conscience, was a core Jesuit preoccupation; Southwell was being trained to manage the perceptions of others, and the diary reflects this training. Exchanges between the enthusiastic writer of polemic and the reprover of an overzealous manner expose a complex set of requirements in the response to sin. Resulting in part from their need to be sensitive to those who came to them for guidance, casuistry – 'cases of conscience' – was an investigation into the modifications of criminality due to individual circumstances that greatly refined Jesuit ministries of confession and penance. Injustice is a bad teacher: the only proper end of penance was, to a Jesuit, a genuine change of heart and life – not merely a show of tears, but a promise of change and a concrete plan for it, which could come only from detailed and starkly realistic self-interrogation.[54]

Southwell seems to have absorbed the lesson; his English poetry touches upon tearful repentance, of course, but does not often dwell on it, minimising tears in favour of analyses of how that sin arose, or a particularised promise of change and improvement. The question of why a sin had been committed by that person at that moment, the *anatomy* of sin, to paraphrase Southwell himself,[55] became so central to Jesuit thinking that students were encouraged to attend regular discussion groups dedicated to its study, even suggesting their own 'cases' for dissection: was a killing murder or self-defence? Premeditated or a crime of passion?[56] O'Malley's insight that casuistry, in its change of focus away from 'abstraction' and 'moral absolutes' to a 'more lowly human reality of "times, places, and circumstances"', owes as much to the classical discipline of rhetoric as to medieval scholasticism, is of particular relevance.[57]

A connection between the function of rhetoric and pastoral practice fixes Southwell's English poetic agenda clearly and completely to his Jesuit ministry. In learning the hard lesson about the importance of a flexible and sensitive response to others' failings, he was learning compromise: first how to apply the rules of rhetoric to his small ministry as a prefect of studies with preternatural delicacy, then, matching his poetic utterance to times, places, and persons in England, translating that rhetorical consideration into his relationship with his various addressees the better to attract their attention to the mending of their lives.

His efforts to find the apt and appropriate way forward for himself can be seen as a parallel to his authorial responsibility to offer the exactly appropriate remedies in his poetry. 'Davids Peccavi' (p. 35), for instance, makes the link between conscience and rhetoric explicit, arguing the toss as if in a college 'cases' debate about the nature and depth of a particular man's sin, in the guise of a quasi-biblical apostrophe. The princely 'David', having chosen the life of earthly luxury over that of godliness, wrestles with the exact nature of his crime, wriggling on the fine barbs of casuistic definitions:

> If wiles of wit had over-wrought my will,
>   Or subtle traines misled my steppes awrie,   20
> My foile had found excuse in want of skill,
>   Ill deede I might, though not ill doome denie:
> But wit and will must now confesse with shame,
> Both deede and doome, to have deserved blame.

'David' finds himself wanting, despite his wish to show that he might have had an excuse through 'want of skill' or experience, because he had known better and still elected the way of sin; the punishment must therefore acknowledge that he committed his sin intentionally with no mitigating circumstances: it was not merely bad luck, but a conscious decision. Whatever Southwell's particular intention in writing this piece, which did not appear in print until Cawood's augmented edition of 1602, the impact of his training and pastoral preoccupations clearly informs it. Southwell here offers to the English poetic scene a new mood of tautly-realised confession, a grand, tragic self-consciousness.

If the final promise of a change of heart and life seems a little pat, it is very much in keeping with the Jesuit agenda for the sacrament of Penance: 'But now sith fansie did with folly end, | Wit bought with losse, will taught by wit, will mend' (lines 29–30).

ENGLISH COLLEGE: CROSS-PURPOSES

His own will now under at least rudimentary control, Southwell was ready to move on in his work. 'Moved, as I hope, by no inordinate passion', he writes in his record of his final vows, 'but burning with a desire to save my soul and to fulfil God's purpose in myself', I now commit myself to the Society (69, p. 83). His commitment is to be total: if the whole world and the angels were to be damned and annihilated unless he left the Society, he still would not leave. Even if everybody else left, he would not leave (p. 84). The very angels must bow to the authority of his Society now. The discernment of angelic inspirations he had learned as a novice is either less liberating than it might seem, or so empowering that he now requires considerable control.

This potentialising new training technique was designed to work in specific circumstances; Southwell's position as an English Jesuit actually presented him with rather different ones. The vow to obey the superior in the face even of God's messengers assumes that there is a single superior with a single set of objectives, and up on the Quirinal Hill, in the world of masters and scholars, that was no doubt the case. Southwell, however, was becoming an English Jesuit at a time of crisis in the Catholic enterprise of England. Sent down the hill to teach in the English College, he arrived just before the celebrated English mission of Robert Persons and Edmund Campion collapsed, as new cracks were appearing in the increasingly frail English Catholic ship.

The energetic and strategically minded Persons had clashed with a Jesuit co-missioner, Jasper Heywood, an Oxford intellectual of good standing at Court; Heywood now refused to engage with Persons at all, threatening the safety of what was left of the mission, and inviting division amongst English Jesuits and other parties when they most needed unity.[58] Too complex to enter into here, the problem boils down to one of agendas: the notion of quietly negotiating with the Queen and her Council for missions to comfort English Catholics was typical of the approach of Heywood and many English Catholics. In pursuit of this, Heywood maintained a magnanimous profile among his courtly peers, travelling in a coach with full pomp when visiting Oxford to raise support amongst his old colleagues, for instance, while Persons's agenda, touching powers less friendly to the Court, required some level of secrecy.[59] By 1582, after Campion was dead and Persons virtually in hiding in France amongst the powerful men who were later to form the Catholic League, Heywood in England was busy amongst the very aristocratic Catholics who, in having, in Persons's view, allowed their faith to be cut down, ran counter to his vision of the way forward in England.[60] The mission was seriously affected as a result, causing great consternation in the *Venerabile*. Southwell, sent to teach there, ran full-tilt down the hill and into the wreckage.

The nationalist ill-feeling already mentioned led to violent demonstrations.[61] Jesuits had been put in charge of the College, to bring some measure of perspective and control to the situation, and Alfonsus Agazzari became the new rector.[62] This was the mistrustful and cross-purposed atmosphere where Southwell began teaching, aged twenty, in 1581.

Just as the unhealthy summer miasmas that rose from the Tiber caused bodily sickness, the ferment of the state of exile itself provoked feverish, unbalanced views. In 1582 even Allen condemned 'this exile' as a breeding ground of 'murmurings, complaining, contradictions and discontent'.[63] The exile community in general was free to engage more hotly and overtly with the English problem than would be possible for any Catholic who had remained in England, or any Jesuit who returned on mission.[64] This was an issue that was to concern the English Jesuits greatly once they were back in England, living and working among Catholics who were under great pressure to offer public assurances of loyalty, and whose private consciences were increasingly under scrutiny.

Southwell's writing talents were put to work at English College in support of the battle against Protestantism. He seems to have become a secretary

Rome: the discernment of angels

to Agazzari, preparing the Annual Letters and news reports, and no doubt contributing other writings to the life of the College. Here he was once again encouraged to write occasionally in English. Surviving papers of his time at English College include a translation of a medieval meditation on Mary Magdalene and part of Luigi Tansillo's 'Lagrime di San Pietro'.[65] These and his newsletters describing English Protestant outrages are his first essays in the English language for some time, possibly since his *Querimonia* in 1577. The troubled, penitent characterisations of Peter and Magdalen are therefore connected to Southwell's concept of a ministry of words in English, the idea of the sinner who betrays or loses Christ being fixed by these translations on to his idea of the English and their general fall from piety, not to mention the intransigency he witnessed in some of the exiles about the English College. He had been surrounded by the imagery of ancient Christian piety in the Novitiate, and the triumphs and common purpose of his Order; now he was surrounded by evidence of schisms even within the English Catholic community, and was, almost certainly, translating these works in order to offer them as lessons in remorse and true love to that community. Peter and Magdalen beat their *own* breasts: they are not anti-heretical personations as Southwell presents them.

At the Roman College, the Chair in controversial theology was Robert Bellarmine, powerful in his defences of Catholic teaching but notably less aggressive in his polemic than was usual at the time.[66] In the English College, however, Southwell was surrounded by a newly focused antipathy. The older images of early Christian martyrs in their antique, unruffled piety were joined, in the English and German College artistic programmes, by harsher, darker imagery, emphasising (as did the reports he wrote) the oppressive cruelty of their heretical enemies. His Jesuit vow of obedience to the Pope now had to live alongside the words of Pope Gregory XIII's 'Bull of Foundation of the Venerable English College in the City: 1 May 1579' (which was drawn up in favour of the Jesuits in response to the troubles of that year).[67] As well as aiming to counter the spread of heresy by giving Catholic youth a firm educational foundation, the Bull turned directly to the subject of England, naming Gregory I, the first pope to send missionaries to pagan England, in order to emphasise the historical links between the English and the papal authority of Rome (and to link Gregory XIII's innovative projects to those of his illustrious predecessor), deploring England's fall into heresy and praising her martyrs, including those of the previous generation, the most celebrated being Sir Thomas More and John Fisher:

> We turned Our loving attention to the Kingdom of England: this once flourished with great wealth and concern for the Catholic Faith, but it is now devastated by the dreadful taint of heresy which has seized almost the whole Kingdom. We took pity on this calamity, as We have often in other cases, and We remembered

that the English people have always excelled in faithfulness, reverence and obedience towards the Roman Pontiffs and the Holy Apostolic See ever since they were brought to the Faith of Christ by Blessed Pope Gregory. Even in the darkness of Our times she has shone in the lives of distinguished and renowned men who have not hesitated to pour out their life's blood for the authority of this See and the truth of the orthodox Faith.[68]

Having covered the history of the connections between England and the papacy from the beginning up to Henry VIII and his daughter Elizabeth, Gregory then returns to present-day scholars and concerns, and formalises the educational and missionary purposes of the College. Here we see papal ratification of the extra missionary oath, the promise to return to England that Robert Persons had designed and had been pressing the *Venerabile* to adopt:

> Moreover there appear frequently before Our eyes young men who have fled hither from that wretched Kingdom, and have been led by the Holy Spirit to abandon their country, their families and their possessions, and have sorrowfully offered themselves to Us to be instructed in the Catholic religion in which they were born, with the aim primarily of assuring their own salvation, but also so that once instructed in the knowledge of theology they might return to England to enlighten others who had fallen away from the way of truth.[69]

Southwell had made no such commitment to return, of course; but perhaps this highly gratifying attention from God's vice-gerent on Earth caused him to question his remaining in Rome.

The wording and drift of Gregory's Bull was to be echoed in the gruesome painting cycle put up in the College chapel in the next couple of years, the only difference being the addition of Campion and the rest, as if to stress Gregory's support of the English enterprise and its brand-new martyrs.

Southwell was now part of this irregularly constructed, more autonomous, Anglocentric system, back, in a sense, to the intense programmes and preoccupations of Douai. He listened to and disseminated the dreadful reports from England, and participated in hard, probably somewhat rancorous, debates that set out the Protestant arguments; he perhaps even took the Protestant side for argument's sake in order to be strong in refutation, an English College habit echoed in the debate in his 'Poema de Assumptione B.V.M.'.[70]

He was also surrounded by that newly agonistic interpretation of mission that seemed peculiarly Personian. Up in the Novitiate there was the semi-classical ideal of the early Christian martyrs, painted in serene detachment with their coveted palms, victims of a Christian/pagan battle line that was distant in time. Down at the English College it was personal – family, even. The mission of Southwell's countrymen Edmund Campion, Robert Persons, English College man Ralph Sherwin and others coincided with the front line of the battle against heresy. Where the martyrs and saints of old were remembered

Rome: the discernment of angels

in the litanies, their living colleagues had become the subject of daily prayers and anxious enquiries as to their progress.

Southwell may now have desired to go himself: Michael Williams quotes Persons's account describing the charismatic Campion's fifteen days in Rome preparing for the mission, during which time he 'put great desire in some many priests of the College' to follow his example; Southwell's diary shows that he was, at some point, one of those 'some many', and the self-will of his desire causes him much soul-searching.[71]

Working, writing, or in devout conversation with English visitors to Rome, Southwell was now actively engaged in the Allen/Persons enterprise of England. His own letters to the European network concerning the cruel treatment of Catholics in England had done much to engage the College youths with the tradition of the early Christian martyrs, so much so that Burghley complained that he was the writer most responsible for England's bad name abroad.[72] Whatever his later feelings once in England, here amongst exiled Catholics and the missioners of the English College, Southwell at this time identified with their endeavour 'with a youthful eagerness that had sometimes to be subdued by his superiors'.[73] Even Persons was moved to tell Southwell to stop writing such things and get on with his studies.[74]

PAINFUL SUBJECTS: THE NEW ENGLISH MARTYRS

Much of Southwell's manuscript poetry in English depicts moments from the Gospels, elements of Catholic Mariology or sacramental belief, but some of it seems bloodier and more visceral, and his spiritual diary contains a passage in which the subject of torture is painfully explicit. What had engendered such images?

The martyr images in the Novitiate were, as I have said, a celebration of the triumph of steadfast faith, and were accompanied by pictures that emphasised the 'identity, esprit de corps, and missionary work' of the Society, highlighting devotion, as much as death, in ministry.[75] The Novitiate programme, part of the Palaeochristian revival, favoured the established saints of the early church. Only in the private spaces of the Society, such as the recreation rooms of the Novitiate, could Jesuit heroes, men not yet saints, have been lauded and revered without scandal.[76] The new martyr cycle at the English College was to change all that, and Southwell was at the centre of that change.

The placid martyrs with their palms and guardian angels which Southwell saw appearing in the recreation rooms of the Novitiate were 'quite different in spirit' to the even newer images of the German and English College cycles with their focus on anti-heresy.[77] Southwell and his companions must have been excited by the whole project, the gruesome fascination of each new depiction of cruelty no doubt a main subject of conversation.[78]

Southwell's spiritual diary records an alteration in the attitude to martyrdom, from references to a general imitation of Christ in the earlier sections to an impassioned self-identification with the more intimate aspects of martyrdom and its relationship with himself and with salvation in later passages: 'Happy ye who are now safe from all danger of sin! Happy ye whose love of God is unfailing, who love and are loved. It is noble indeed, glorious and praiseworthy to suffer for the love of God toil, pain, torture and agony', he writes, as if in a sort of blurted threnody to men he knew personally (63, p. 72). He questions his own worth and his ability to survive in a life so full of hate and endless opportunities for sin, yet fears his desire for death as a desire to 'shirk toil' or avoid 'torment and agony'; then he begs for death again, and pleads with God to tell him if he is loved or hated, because he can no longer tell for himself (p. 73).

Whatever his intention in writing this remarkable piece of self-exposure, there is no doubt of the altered connections it makes with martyrdom. Those images of ancient killings seem suddenly to spring to life for him here, and in the new context of a highly charged, impassioned, but apocalyptic love. He adopts an extreme chivalric position towards God as Ideal Lover: 'True love can never suffer the loved one to be grieved, either in small things or in great. A love which could endure it would not be true love, but a deceit.' But this love asks for much, indeed, all. Southwell's distress about his ability to resist sinful occasions are written into the context of the martyrologies, as he places himself into the centre of the pictures he had seen, taking the place of the saint or martyr:

> An ardent desire for a timely and speedy death is most fitting in one who knows that he cannot remain in life without offending the God he loves. But yet if God who knows man's misery, still wishes to lengthen my life (although He knows that it cannot be without at least venial sin), and to exercise me still further in this valley of tears, then let toil come, let come chains, imprisonment, torture, the cross of Peter and Andrew, the gridiron of Lawrence, the flayer of Bartholomew, the lions of Ignatius, all things in a word which can possibly come. Indeed, I pray from my heart that they may come. (63, p. 73)

'For Thy sake allow me to be tortured, mutilated, scourged, slain and butchered', he goes on, as if desperate to share in the cleansing bloodshed (p. 74). Although the general positions set out in this entry are not unusual, his sometimes barely articulate delivery is near-unique in the diary, an outpouring whose repetitions are almost anti-rhetoric, so little do they resemble the progress of any rational argument: 'I wish to be torn by penance in this life and if not, let me die soon – so that by dying soon I cease to sin or living I offer thee a holocaust in my own blood', he cries; 'may I then die soon, O good Jesus' (63, p. 72).

This may have been written in response not only to his first close encounter with the living horrors of martyrdom in the shape of the collapsed Campion mission but also to his first view of one of the earliest and the most dreadful of all the martyr cycles, the new series at S. Stefano Rotondo, the two events separated by only a few months. The awful potency of the martyr spectacle is demonstrated by the responses to those who saw the cycle of the German-Hungarian College chapel, S. Stefano, a series of martyr paintings on a scale that stunned Rome.

The S. Apollinaire and S. Stefano cycles of Niccolò Circignani marked the crossover from older attempts to recreate that stilted primitive Christian imagery of the Catacombs to more modern, vital and extensive depictions, contextualised by contemporary elements such as recognisably Roman buildings, contemporary fashions, or even known faces.[79] Martyrdom as an artistic, dramatic act now dominated Roman church decoration. Southwell will have joined multitudes making their way to the circular martyrium of S. Stefano for one of the great unveilings in the early 1580s, to absorb its captioned depictions of early Christian fidelity; it was the site, as Bailey says, 'of some of the most horrifying and moving pictures of the age'.[80] It was completed between March (a matter of weeks after news of Campion's death arrived) and August 1582. And it was the direct antecedent for the martyrdom cycles in S. Tommaso di Canterbury, the English College chapel.[81]

These new depictions were a gruelling spectacle in the round, the dreadful vista being absorbed in one relentless gyration, the gasps and sobs elicited by the images no doubt part of the drama. It has had a profound effect over the years. Bailey offers Charles Dickens's description of:

> grey-bearded men being boiled, fried, grilled, crimped, singed, eaten by wild beasts, worried by dogs, buried alive, torn asunder by horses, [...] women having their breasts torn with iron pincers, their tongues cut out, their ears screwed off, their jaws broken, their bodies stretched upon the rack, or skinned upon the stake, or crackled up and melted in the fire.[82]

These, says Dickens, are the mildest of the scenes; if, as Bailey notes, even the Marquis de Sade was frightened by the spectacle, what were the young men of the Jesuit colleges to make of it?

Southwell's own response to the imagery of these ancient martyrs was galvanised horribly, late in 1581, when Campion, Ralph Sherwin, and Alexander Briant were butchered at Tyburn.[83] The first great English College project of Allen and Persons had collapsed, and controversial theology had been crushed by violence.

The graphic depiction of cruelty was nothing new in early modern society, and not only in church, but to a young man still absorbing the shock of torture, mutilation, and butchery inflicted on men known to, and admired by, him, to stand at the centre of such a display will have had a more profound effect, and one can read traces of such an effect in his diary. One image depicted St Peter on his cross, with St Paul in the distance, in a very Roman cityscape (fig. 40); this composite connected themes of martyrdom, the papacy, and the missionary Apostle, linked in Jesuit minds with their own contemporary missionaries (p. 142). The connection of the cross of St Andrew with that of the papal referent, St Peter, seen in Southwell's diary entry therefore includes the patron saint of the Novitiate chapel in the landscape of the celebrated martyrs, as if celebrating the Jesuit martyrs and would-be martyrs of his novitiate. The diary entry can be seen in the light of an attempt to reconcile the dreadful imagery of S. Stefano (or of Christian martyrdom in general) with his personal experience of the martyrdom of Jesuits. His response seems to flee rationality, one minute pleading to be allowed to follow them, the next trying to explain why he cannot live in any case, as a repeat sinner; a death wish battling with a plea for martyrdom, all beaten back again by the remembrance of his promise to serve Christ however and wherever he is asked, and all somewhat against the grain of teachings against singularity and his vows of total obedience, as subsequent entries show.

He had recently been pleading to follow his spiritual director Persons and the others, as some of the diary entries suggest. But he is told over and over again to stop having ambitions for himself, or trying to carry out wishes or projects of his own, and to accept that doing as he is told by superiors is the only martyrdom proper to a Jesuit.

Southwell's new and fervent engagement with martyrdom as a way to Christ cannot be divorced from the new imagery surrounding him or from the new circumstances of the collapsed mission. He was not permitted to see these things as distant or of only incidentally pious relevance. Contemporaries were clearly recognizable in at least one of the frescos. Did Southwell think of the body parts of his friends and colleagues, lying in a heap as in a shambles, boiling in vats, or spiked on Tower Bridge? 'To Die Soon would be a Safe Thing and to Live Long in Pain for Christ a Holy Thing' is the text: he had clearly decided on the immediacy of the 'Safe' rather than the 'Holy' long view; but who had given him this text to meditate upon, and why?

His apparent desire for England may have been provoked by anxiety for his family in the wake of the collapse of the Campion mission. Campion had fled into Norfolk at one point, and Southwell may have been half-hoping, half-fearing to hear that they had given him aid, because it seemed that Campion, under his interrogation, had given names of some of those who had protected him. But if his family had not been involved, then why not? If they had fallen away from the faith then he would be in fear for their souls. Unable to maintain holy indifference, he found another sort of employment for symbolic imagery than the immediately edifying, using the jewel-merchant code typical of letters exchanged during the Campion mission: 'one request I particularly make', he begged Persons; 'it is that you would contrive by all possible means to dispose of some of [your goods] to the relatives of your friend Robert S., for I remember that at one time they were very keen about that particular quality of goods, and kept a factor who was occupied solely in searching for such gems'.[84] The goods included Catholic texts and devotional aids, banned in England, Persons being responsible for their import and dissemination;[85] 'factor' meant 'business agent', or estate manager, among other things, but it was also used in coded messages between Catholics in England and Catholics on the Continent to describe more precise roles; metaphor is not exclusively an artistic effect in Southwell's writing.[86] Southwell begs Persons to persuade his people 'not to lose heart because of any small loss that may happen'. 'A strong suspicion for fearing that they may have withdrawn from this line of business', the young man continues, 'is occasioned by my never hearing of their having the same success as others have had'. 'Success' here must be read alongside the outcome of the Campion mission.

The death of Campion brought an agonistic immediacy to an already martyr-minded Rome, stimulating fervid excitement amongst the scholastics. But the new martyr cycle of S. Stefano included no Jesuits. Heroes of a relatively new order as yet unblessed with saints, the dead Jesuits would not normally have been considered suitable candidates for the walls of churches.[87] But they had martyrdoms of their own now, and could enter into the spirit of the martyr cycles with pride. Martyr imagery acted as a measure of religious quality, the bodily locus for the rightness of a religious position. 'Bloody' Mary Tudor had already given Protestantism a respectable body count, celebrated in Foxe's *Acts and Monuments of These Latter and Perilous Days* (London, 1563; reprinted 1583). Persons and Allen, disturbed by the popular success of Foxe's book with its accusations of Catholic barbarity, had both responded in kind on behalf of their Church.[88] The programme of frescos of English and Welsh martyrdoms begun in the church of the English College in 1583 was founded upon, and in support of, that response.[89]

The sending of men was a blow in the face of the Protestant ascendancy, designed to undermine their implied claim to represent an enlightened, willing populace in a State that embodied the proper rule of law, but it was not a demand for self-annihilation. The mere presence of such men in England compromised the State's claims, as well as preparing the way amongst the populace for the hoped-for reconciliation with Rome. It was the numbers of those who *went* that represented the triumph, not the numbers of those who died, although the imagery of courageous deaths reinforced the message of the rightness of their cause. Southwell's writing skills were therefore being employed by the Society to promulgate the message of that rightness amongst the English exile community in Europe, not to cry for more blood. Much has been written about 'martyr fever' in Rome, but it must be remembered that the sacrifice was inherent in the going, rather than the dying.

Southwell had just arrived in Rome in 1579 when the first English College alumni were sent back to England. By Southwell's last year in Rome forty-two of the English College boys had 'made the perilous trip', but Ralph Sherwin was the first of them to die, alongside Campion. The deaths caused a deep unease in some hearts, and there was a growing division of opinion between some of the English exiles and the new father general, Acquaviva, which seems to be echoed in the martyr paintings and those writings of Southwell connected with them.[90] Acquaviva continued to insist that seminary men were not to be wasted in heroic last stands, but to be spiritual doctors and consolers, to keep a communion of the English with Rome for as long as possible, for the good of their souls.

Acquaviva's was a courageous stance, given the English College preoccupations. This less literal attitude to martyrdom is supported by Acquaviva's new painting cycles in the Novitiate: created from 1582, at about the same time as those of the English College, they showed Jesuit martyrdoms, but only in the private rooms; such martyrdoms were celebrations of Jesuit heroism and a reminder to the novices of their daily duty to do violence to their wilful inclinations and passions, not to end their lives in direct imitation. Acquaviva's later partner in the artistic enterprise, Richeôme, made the point clear in 1611: 'You are in the premier academy of this Society, where one learns how to handle arms, to stab and subdue the body, to give the death blow to vice, and vanquish the passions'.[91]

But down at the English College, attitudes were somewhat altered. The new *Venerabile* cycle was not quite the same as that of S. Stefano. For the first time, the paintings in their St Thomas Chapel celebrated the engagement in Christian history of contemporary men, alongside the ancient British martyrs. The English College men in Rome now had an almost mystic significance as they prepared themselves for their missions. The chapel of St Thomas became a pilgrimage site 'devoted to present-day and future martyrs', where 'students were revered as walking relics with the greeting "Salvete Flores Martyrum"', the living martyrs drawing a crush of Romans into the church; reflecting this new mood, the paintings of S. Tommaso were, unlike the S. Stefano murals, decidedly anti-heresy in conception.[92] Instead of offering a model for the killing of self-will, martyrdom itself was shown in the English College programme to be central to the battle against heresy – blood was now their argument. The deaths of Campion and his followers, dealt with in detail in the martyr books of Persons and Allen and on the walls of the chapel, were presented both as palms for the Catholic faith and a deep stain on the character of the Protestant English State, and the memorialising of them brought the iniquities of the English anti-Catholics to a wide and receptive audience in Rome, linking the ancient imagery of martyrs to the contemporary political emergency, and to the activities of a particular establishment, and even particular personalities.[93]

The College already contained relics of former saints and martyrs, but now it could revivify their force with the relics of brand-new martyrs, honouring them in the company of their living brothers. As if to consecrate the link between the present and the past, Gregory XIII 'made a number of concessions' between 1580 and 1585, which permitted the use of these new non-saints' relics in the consecration of altars, the singing of Te Deums on each new death, and the commemoration of the as yet non-sainted martyrs upon the walls of the church.[94] In elevating these still unsainted heroes to places normally reserved for the established saints and martyrs of church history, Gregory was crossing a Rubicon, virtually pre-empting the formal church processes as regarded the making of saints, and, by celebrating the executed ones, elevating bloody sacrifice in the process of canonisation.

Southwell, as a College tutor, prefect and secretary to Agazzari, was at the very heart of these developments. Stonyhurst College owns a corporal used by some of the imprisoned missioners at their last Mass before their executions in 1582, which was subsequently embroidered with their names (Kirby, Jonson, Briant, Shirt, and Cottam) by a fellow priest and prisoner who escaped execution. He sent the relic to English College, Rome, maintaining the College tradition of commemorating martyrs for the edification of the students. Shirt, Cottam, and Kirby were English College men (Cottam being the brother of Shakespeare's schoolmaster). The accompanying Latin inscription in ink explaining this relic for the benefit of viewers is in the hand of Southwell, writing to remind the scholars of these new English Christian martyrs.[95] The galvanising effects of these fresh martyrdoms cannot be overestimated. They were taken up with avidity and fitted into the revivalist mood, upping the ante yet further in the streets down by the Tiber.[96]

At around this point, despite rigorous opposition, reflected in repeated stern reminders in his diary to obey the wishes of his superiors,[97] Southwell appears to have decided to go home. This may have been in response to intolerable strains; his diary suggests that new responsibilities had brought new pressures, exposed new frailties. Some factions at the English College were attacking the Prefect of Studies personally, yet the expectations of superiors continued.[98] Rivalries and conflicted agendas abounded. One diary entry hints at the hindrances peculiar to Southwell that might cause trouble in his interactions with colleagues and 'those who live in the world' ('Rules for Intercourse with Others', p. 54). He has, it seems, been over-familiar, giving someone the idea, by word or gesture (possibly with the intention of being amusing), that the young Prefect considered himself his better (p. 49).

But the arrival of his nephew Anthony Copley in September 1584 probably offered Southwell a rare glimpse of the lighter side of English recalcitrancy, and a welcome reminder of freer days on the South Downs. If even the Queen's dread torturer Topcliffe described Anthony Copley as 'the most desperayt yowthe that lyvethe' (he had allegedly thrown a dagger at the

Horsham parish clerk, amongst other outrages), what could have been his impact on the austere Roman Jesuits?[99] Southwell, mindful of his aunt's feelings, helped to extricate Copley from multiple scrapes at college.[100] He seems to have been well-liked if disruptive, and attractively quick-witted, picking up on and making merry with the motifs and emblems beloved of the Jesuits, perhaps carrying his youthful uncle along with the hilarity.[101] Copley shared Southwell's interest in English poetry; his *A Fig for Fortune* has the semi-autobiographical hero return from 'Sion' (Rome) to 'Elizium' with his lap full of roses, suggestive of the response of an English youth to the rich affective principle blooming on the Continent.[102]

Southwell was an iron in the harsh, hot fire of a demanding, intensive training that tempered him and yet caused him to be twisted by intolerable tensions in his attempts to carry out his vocation, as we shall see. Many hands wished to draw him from the fire to their own purposes. He had desired to go back to England – but was it still 'home'? and what did he carry in his lap back to Elizium?

NOTES

1. Robert Southwell, 'Saint Peters Complaint', lines 389–90; in James H. McDonald and Nancy Pollard Brown (eds), *The Poems of Robert Southwell, S.J.* (Oxford: Clarendon Press, 1967); hereafter M&B; further references to Southwell's poetry are from this edition, given as page/line numbers in the text.

2. 'Hos orbis statuit dominos, atque omnibus ornans | Delitiis, sacra paradisi in sede locavit' (He appointed them as rulers of the world and, adorning them with all delights, placed them in the sacred abode of Paradise), from Robert Southwell, 'Poema de Assumptione B.V.M.', lines 7–8; from Stonyhurst MS A.v.4, at Stonyhurst College, Clitheroe, Lancashire. Translation from Peter Davidson and Anne Sweeney (ed. and intro.), *The Collected Poems of S. Robert Southwell, S.J.* (Manchester: Carcanet, forthcoming).

3. The Sodality set up by the Society in Rome, based on older models designed to foster spirituality, illustrates the mixed nature of Southwell's Roman experience, inspiring his fine Marian sequence of poems yet attracting accusations of spying and preferment from English College students; see a careful discussion in Scott Pilarz, S.J., *Robert Southwell and the Mission of Literature 1561–1595: Writing Reconciliation* (Aldershot: Ashgate, 2004). pp. 219–21.

4. 'Poema de Assumptione B.V.M.', lines 91–103. Translation from Davidson and Sweeney.

5. For a comprehensive discussion of the contribution of the Society to this artistic explosion, see Gauvin Alexander Bailey, *Between Renaissance and Baroque: Jesuit Art in Rome, 1565–1610* (Toronto: University of Toronto Press, 2003); hereafter referred to by page or figure numbers in the text.

6. For the diary, see Robert Southwell, *Spiritual Exercises and Devotions*, ed. J. M. de Buck and trans. P. E. Hallett (London: Sheed and Ward, 1931); hereafter SE&D. For a discussion of the relationship between the SE&D and Southwell's later writing, see Pierre Janelle, *Robert Southwell the Writer: A Study in Religious Inspiration* (London: Sheed and

Ward, 1935), especially ch. 4; hereafter cited in the text.

7 The turmoils at the English College are described meticulously in Michael E. Williams, *The Venerable English College Rome: A History 1579–1979* (London: Associated Catholic Publications (on behalf of the College), 1979); hereafter cited in the text. See also Christopher Devlin, *The Life of Robert Southwell Poet and Martyr* (London: Longmans, Green, 1956), especially ch. 4; hereafter cited in the text. See Pilarz, p. 138.

8 See Pilarz, n. 35, p. 152.

9 See Bailey for a detailed discussion of artworks appearing at this time

10 Bailey, p. 231, fig. 89.

11 See Randi Klebanoff, 'The *Vita* and the *Morte*: Making the Sacred in Renaissance Bologna'; paper delivered at the Sixteenth Century Studies Conference, Toronto, 24 October 1998 (n. 5, p. 283), in Bailey, p. 40. Reformation arguments over the value of the concrete imagery of the Church were readily translatable into debates over the value of metaphorical imagery in poetry. Du Bellay said that without ornamentation poetry was naked ('[sans] ornemens [...] toute oraison et poëme sont nuds, manques et debiles'; *Défence* (I, v)). In 1631 John Weever said the same about the Church, stripped of 'hangings, and all other ornaments whereupon the story, or pourtraiture, of Christe himselfe, or of any Saint or Martyr, was delineated, wrought, or embroidered; leaving Religion naked, bare, and unclad'; quoted in Clifford Davidson, 'Robert Southwell: Lyric Poetry, the Restoration of Images, and Martyrdom', *Ben Jonson Journal*, 7 (2000), 157–86 (p. 165).

12 Bailey, p. 195.

13 See John W. O'Malley, *The First Jesuits* (Cambridge, MA: Harvard University Press, 1993), p. 80; hereafter cited in the text.

14 See Bailey, p. 53.

15 O'Malley, pp. 351–2.

16 Bailey, p. 53.

17 Bailey, p. 108. For a discussion on uses of visual symbol, see Michael Bath, *Speaking Pictures: English Emblem Books and Renaissance Culture* (London: Longman, 1994).

18 Bailey, p. 12.

19 In fact, the two may be connected even more directly: it was Acquaviva's version of the *Spiritual Exercises*, 'a work that draws heavily on Ignatius's "composition of place"', that Southwell will have used in Rome, as it was designed for 'the express use of novices'; Bailey, p. 12.

20 Bailey discusses this connection in great detail in relation to the works in the Gesù church, p. 195.

21 Bailey, p. 110.

22 See Bailey's detailed discussion of the relationship between the Passion Chapel and the Third Week of the Ignatian *Exercises*, which shows a direct relationship, one which was no doubt recognizable and stimulating to those who knew their *Exercises*. Perhaps it also led others to wish to make the retreat that lay behind the imagery. Certainly it will have allowed lay persons to feel some level of emotional engagement with the central moment of their faith, its intensity depending upon their own capacity for feeling. But the main point of the *Exercises* was that the exercisant should supply the imagery from within himself, thereby 'owning' it. Jeffrey Chipps Smith gives an even more detailed account

of the experience of such a programme, stressing the individual's own responsibility in the manner and pace of it; Jeffrey Chipps Smith, 'The Art of Salvation in Bavaria', in John W. O'Malley, S.J., and Gauvin Alexander Bailey, et al., *The Jesuits: Cultures, Sciences, and the Arts 1540–1773* (Toronto: University of Toronto Press, 1999), pp. 568–99 (p. 581); hereafter *Cultures*. See also Jeffrey Chipps Smith, *Sensuous Worship: Jesuits and the Art of the Early Catholic Reformation in Germany* (Princeton, NJ, Oxford: Princeton University Press, 2002).

23 See Devlin, especially ch. 4.

24 De Buck, pp. v–vi; Brown notes that the entries are only datable circumstantially, if at all, M&B, p. xvii. Pilarz explores them in greater detail, finding evidence in some entries of Southwell's maturing ability to reconcile tensions, pp. 144–9.

25 Apart from its importance as a pointer to his 'psychology and his literary method', it acts as 'a commentary on the *Spiritual Exercises* of Ignatius', p. vi.

26 56, p. 63; de Buck has assigned various entries to particular episodes in the life of the novice Southwell, especially to the vow-taking and to the crises that have been so well documented elsewhere, as in Williams's *English College*, pp. 12–16.

27 John Deckers to Southwell, 29 September 1580, Stonyhurst MS A.vii.1, now in the Jesuit Archives at Mount St, London; see Devlin, p. 34.

28 Pilarz, p. 145.

29 From the edition of 1591, printed by John Wolfe for Gabriel Cawood, London, full text version found in www.eebo.chadwyck.home, doc. 69, p. 6ır; hereafter *Teares*. It is numbered 29950 in A. F. Pollard and G. R. Redgrave (eds), *A Short-title Catalogue of Books Printed in England, Scotland, and Ireland, and of English Books Printed Abroad, 1475–1640* (London: Bibliographical Society, 1926); hereafter *STC*.

30 O'Malley, pp. 242, 249–50.

31 Richeôme's understanding of how the artworks related to the purposes of the place and to the viewer provide us with insights about how Southwell and the other novices were expected to view and use them. Bailey discusses the contribution to theories of art and appreciation made by this Jesuit teacher at length in chapter 2, p. 51 especially.

32 'Seeke flowers of heaven', p. 52, lines 9–12.

33 Bailey, pp. 111, 110.

34 See Louise Rice, 'Jesuit Thesis Prints and the Festive Academic Defence at the Collegio Romano', in O'Malley, et al., *Cultures*, pp. 148–69.

35 See Bailey for a description of the sumptuous painting celebrating the meeting between Francis Xavier and the Daimyo of Bungo in Japan in 1549, p. 64.

36 Bailey, fig. 59.

37 Luke 2.35.

38 Bailey, pp. 247–8.

39 Ibid., p. 248.

40 See Bailey, fig. 108. The feast of the Presentation of the Virgin was reintroduced into the Roman calendar only in 1585; it may have occurred too late for inclusion, or seemed a step too far in Southwell's project of reminding the English of their traditional habit of worship; see M&B, n. 1, p. lxxxiii.

Rome: the discernment of angels

41 Federico Zeri, *Pittura e controriforma: l'arte senza tempo di Scipione da Gaeta*, repr. (Vicenza: Neri Pozzone, c.1997), p. 54, Bailey's translation.

42 Bailey, p. 251.

43 Ibid., pp. 248, 251.

44 Pilarz, p. 222. The painting celebrating this in the Gesù did not appear until after Southwell's time, it would seem; Bailey, p. 237.

45 Bailey, figs 60, 88.

46 Ibid., pp. 141–2.

47 www.faculty.fairfield.edu/jmac/nadal/nadalintro.htm.

48 Bailey, pp. 9–12.

49 One diary entry reminds him that the days of being the recipient of such sweet attentions are past; he is a member of the Society now, the attracter, not the attractee: 'As thou wert strengthened in thy vocation by the example of the religious conversation of other brothers of the Society, so now in the same way those who are drawn by the desire that then moved thee may be helped by thy modesty, thy kindness, thy love, thy charity' (9, 'Incentive', p. 8).

50 See O'Malley, *First Jesuits*, p. 303.

51 Ibid., p. 81.

52 Ibid., p. 81.

53 Ibid., p. 142.

54 Ibid., p. 140.

55 'Saint Peters Complaint', p. 76, l. 665.

56 O'Malley, pp. 147, 144.

57 O'Malley cites in support a recent study which has observed that '"Rhetoric and casuistry were mutual allies. It is not surprising to find the Jesuits, who were dedicated to teaching classical rhetoric in their colleges, become the leading exponents of casuistry"'; see Albert R. Jonsen and Stephen Toulmin, *The Abuses of Casuistry: A History of Moral Theology* (Berkeley and Los Angeles: University of California Press, 1988), p. 88; O'Malley, n. 40, p. 406.

58 See Dennis Flynn '"Out of Step": Six Supplementary Notes on Jasper Heywood', in Thomas M. McCoog, S.J. (ed.), *The Reckoned Expense: Edmund Campion and the Early English Jesuits* (Woodbridge: Boydell, 1996), pp. 179–92.

59 Flynn, pp. 184, 180.

60 Ibid., p. 184; Devlin, pp. 68–9.

61 An English student writes of a meal in the refectory where, without provocation (he insists), knives were drawn on the English by Welsh students, at the instigation of the Welsh rector; 'judge you, what time we had to look unto ourselves', he writes indignantly; but 'if it had not been for the common cause and for God's especially, we had been sure to have payed [them] for it', he adds, with a most un-Christian regret. See Bailey, p. 154, and n. 7, p. 321.

62 Williams, p. 6; Bailey, p. 154.

63 Williams, p. 17.

64 See Alison Shell, *Catholicism, Controversy and the English Literary Imagination 1558–1660* (Cambridge: Cambridge University Press, 1999), p. 109; hereafter cited in the text.
65 See Nancy Pollard Brown, 'Robert Southwell: The Mission of the Written Word', in McCoog (ed.), *Reckoned Expense*, pp. 193–214 (p. 197); hereafter 'Mission'.
66 Elizabeth was, during Southwell's mission, to devote much thought to countering Bellarmine's *Controversies* (1588); Southwell may, as Pilarz argues, have learned a less hateful expression of anti-'heresy' from Bellarmine, but it was no less strongly held for all that; Pilarz, pp. 165–6.
67 See Williams, p. 210.
68 Ibid., pp. 211–12.
69 Ibid., pp. 211–12.
70 Bailey, p. 154.
71 Michael E. Williams, 'Campion and the English Continental Seminaries', in McCoog (ed.), *Reckoned Expense*, pp. 285–98 (pp. 289, 290); hereafter cited in the text.
72 See Devlin, p. 51; the *Annual Letters* of the English College, 1581–84, contain most of his accounts of this nature.
73 M&B, p. xvi.
74 Devlin, pp. 52, 44–5.
75 Bailey, p. 62. Some scholars date the cycle of Jesuit martyrs to the 1570s; Bailey dismisses this, noting that one depicts a martyr of 1583; but there were almost certainly murals of an edifying nature there in Southwell's time, as Jesuits such as Nadal had been very keen on such exemplary works; see Bailey, n. 134, p. 292, for scholars against whom he argues.
76 Bailey, p. 66.
77 Ibid., p. 62.
78 Ibid., pp. 124–6, 16, 132, 144.
79 Ibid., pp. 126, 132, 144.
80 Ibid., p. 135.
81 An Annual Letter of 1582 'is typical of Jesuit enthusiasm' in response to the S. Stefano cycle, and the importance the Jesuits attached to its effects upon the viewers; the Pope was very satisfied with the work; Bailey, pp. 128–9.
82 Ibid., p. 123.
83 McCoog (ed.), *Reckoned Expense*, pp. xxi–xxii.
84 Southwell to Persons, early 1582, in John Hungerford Pollen, S.J. (ed.), *Unpublished Documents Relating to the English Martyrs*, Publications of the Catholic Record Society Series, 5 (London: Catholic Record Society, 1908), pp. 301–3; hereafter CRS; quoted in Janelle, p. 31.
85 See J. B. Black, *The Reign of Elizabeth 1558–1603* (Oxford: Clarendon Press, 1959), p. 183.
86 This use of 'factor' still obtained in the 1590s: Patrick H. Martin and John Finnis quote a selection of correspondence between one of the chief Catholic exiles, Thomas Fitzherbert, and William Sterrell, another Oxford man and a vital component in London of the

Catholic intelligence network later run by Persons, Allen, and Verstegan from across the Channel, according to Martin and Finnis. Fitzherbert describes Sterrell frankly as a 'general factor' in their enterprise; Verstegan, more cautious perhaps, disguises his report on the setting-up of the intelligence network by using the language of commerce when he writes to Sterrell that 'we have signified to the merchants here what commodities you have to sell'. The 'merchants' (Persons and Allen, mainly) wish to know 'for what merchants in particular [Sterrell] is the factor' (or, what party was he with? He was secretary to the loyalist Catholic Edward Somerset, fourth Earl of Worcester; his relationship with Southwell requires further study); Patrick H. Martin and John Finnis, 'Thomas Thorpe, "W.S.," and the Catholic Intelligencers', *English Literary Renaissance*, 33 (2003), 3–43 (pp. 17, 25, 4).

87 Older saints stood for them in the Jesuits' public buildings, as in S. Stefano, where Francis of Assisi was a diplomatic nod to Francis Xavier, Ignatius of Antioch to Loyola, as Bailey shows (p. 66). The recognisable Roman buildings around Ignatius of Antioch may have been suggestive, but the Jesuits kept depictions of Jesuit figureheads for their private rooms, as in the Novitiate.

88 Bailey, p. 155. The college decorations can, he argues, be seen as a rhetorical refutation of Foxe, with illustrations to give weight to the argument, part of the wider effort that included Persons's *Epistle of the Persecution of Catholics in England* (Douai, 1582), and Allen's *A Briefe Historie of the Glorious Martyrdom of Twelve Reverend Priests* (1583), translated into Italian and published under the patronage of the Venerable English College as *Historia del glorioso martirio di sedici sacerdoti* (Macerata, 1583).

89 Williams calls these 'gruesome' (p. 293), which they are, but I agree with Bailey when he resists Williams's account of a fixation upon agony and death, suggesting that the main point of such decorations was to urge a selfless engagement with the assault upon heresy, rather than a crude exhortation to fall upon heretic swords, p. 155.

90 John Bossy's account of the period demonstrates a fundamental (though not vast) division in the attitudes to the mission of Acquaviva and Persons, identifying a far more subtle 'inwardness' in Acquaviva's belief that martyrdom was arguably something approaching a self-willed end, in certain circumstances; he insisted 'that their task was not to edify the Church in general but to bring help and comfort to souls in England'. Acquaviva's was a gentle criticism of Campion's careless courage. Of course 'martyrdom', Acquaviva told Allen, 'was more meritorious than a life of toil, and Campion would have his reward'; Bossy offers us his interpretation of Acquaviva's between-the-lines view: 'that the salvation of the missioner's soul was not the purpose of his mission' (p. 147). Bailey notes that Acquaviva's own nephew Rodolfo had been among the Jesuit Mughal missioners killed in May 1583 (p. 65); it is possible that the tendency demonstrated by some of the English exiles of regarding martyrdom as a weapon of war rather than a pattern to live by seemed especially wasteful of Society resources in the light of this sort of death. Certainly Acquaviva became increasingly clipped in his dealings with Persons over the 'enterprise of England' at this time, as Bossy shows (pp. 149–50).

91 Bailey, p. 68.

92 Ibid., pp. 156–7.

93 The probable model for the English College cycle with its frank anti-heresy message was the series of six engravings, each with Latin inscription, probably cut for Persons's *Persecution*, and recycled for Allen's *Twelve Reverend Priests*. The engravings used by Persons and Allen were very similar to the paintings of the College chapel of S. Tommaso di Canterbury, Bailey notes, pp. 155–6.

94 Ibid., p. 156.

95 At the time of writing, the relic had returned briefly to the Tower of London as part of an exhibition, but its home is in Stonyhurst College, Lancashire, via Robert Persons and St Omer College; my thanks are due to Jan Graffius, Stonyhurst's archivist, for the information about Southwell's handwriting.

96 See Devlin, p. 51.

97 53, p. 57, names England for the first time as a place of mission, but reminds Southwell that 'mission' and 'martyrdom' are obedience to God, not to one's own wishes, however strongly held.

98 F. W. Brownlow, *Robert Southwell*, Twayne's English Author Series, 516 (New York: Simon & Schuster Macmillan, 1996), p. 6.

99 Devlin, p. 257; Janelle, p. 55; Pilarz discusses the diary and Southwell's interpersonal problems (pp. 142, 144–9); he also describes Southwell's chequered relationship with 'my Anthony' Copley (pp. 16–25); see Brownlow, pp. 81–3.

100 See Devlin, p. 257.

101 See a discussion of such associations in Anne Dillon, 'Praying by Number: The Confraternity of the Rosary and the English Catholic Community, c.1580–1700', *History*, 88 (July 2003), 451–71.

102 Devlin, p. 257; Brownlow, pp. 81–2; Alison Shell argues that Copley became 'fervently anti-Jesuit', p. 135; she and Brownlow argue for this poem being a Catholic riposte to the first book of Spenser's (Protestant) *Faerie Queene*.

Chapter 2

The *Spiritual Exercises*: the 'inward eie'[1]

RAPHAEL AND THE REFINING OF THE SIGHT

In Southwell's Latin poem on the Assumption of the Virgin, Gabriel appears in the court presided over by God to speak for the Virgin against the powers of the Underworld. The counsel for the prosecution, Death, enraged by Christ's usurpation of her rule over humanity, is described in horrid detail, her mellifluous speech in stark contrast to her physical foulness. Gabriel, on the other hand, is only message: his words speak for him, he is little else but Word.[2] Hidden or obscured within Southwell's poem are truths about Truth, about his Church, and about Southwell himself. If the nature of this classic/Christian, legalistic debate perhaps has its roots in some college drama, the richness and suggestiveness of the word-painting relates directly to the unique training in visions that he encountered in Rome, an invisible, angelic potentiality which he carried with him to England.

Angels were the symbolic site of difference between Protestantism and Catholicism at this time. A Protestant could not look for God's daily agency in earthly things, a Catholic could, and did, especially in the metaphoric or divine form of angelic activity. Southwell's training sensitised him to the presence of the angelic, and his poetry expressed it accordingly, as if transporting angels in metaphor to England could ease the soul-plight of his countrymen. His writing is full of that special training in secret or hidden forces; its veiled potency informs his poetry and indeed his mission in its entirety: there is an element of sacred immanence new to English poetry in Southwell's metaphorical word-store. Nothing could be further from the sententious 'Drab', with its anxiety to lay bare the truth by endless exposition. In his poetry Southwell refers again and again to this hidden truth, a thing beyond words, the undefinable potency that he metaphorises variously as: 'Angells giftes'; 'Strange effects'; 'Unwonted workes'. These mysterious effects arrive by 'secret waies', or out of 'secret vaine'.[3] English literary creativity may have dropped the angelic element of this immanence, but it never lost its potency, and it learned that language first from Southwell.

He is talking about a two-way stream: both an inner human force, meditative, but directed always towards God, an 'inward eie' that 'to heavenly sights | Doth draw my longing harts desire'; and a streaming of perfect forms, graces and inspirations from God which we must try to capture and comprehend. He is trying to find a language to express the inexpressible, the mysterious colloquy with God understood in the concept of prayer, of moments of supranatural significance like transubstantiation.

He is also trying to find words to describe, in layman's English and in secular poetry, something once the province of the most esoteric of devotional communities: the capacity to open an interior channel to and from God through meditation upon the concrete or mental image, as reclaimed and redirected by his own Jesuit order. He is metaphorising the near-angelic action and the performative experience of the Ignatian *Spiritual Exercises*, the programme of directed mental effort designed to bring on that strange state of heightened and focused imagination where the eye of reason is blind but 'Where thought can see', a state which encounters God outside the realms of 'sence or reason'.[4] Southwell's poetry, even the lightest, is built upon the new creative framework of the *Exercises*: this new emphasis on psychological self-awareness was part of what he imported into England that was entirely new. The established form of English poetry foregrounded rhetoric through repetitions and rhymes; it was technically athletic and persuasive, as is the Death in Southwell's 'Poema de Assumptione'; Southwell's new poetry was to foreground the message itself, like Gabriel. It was his experience of the *Exercises* that helped Southwell, steeped in Roman beauty, to discern the difference between technique and message.

Jesuits were trained to conform their own appearance to the circumstances in which they found themselves, and not only the artistic vision that sprang from them, but the *Exercises* themselves were notably flexible in application.[5] This flexibility translated into artistic and creative theory: there was systematic differentiation between the pictures that surrounded Southwell in the privacy of the Novitiate and the more public ones of the colleges.[6] Through such methodological differentiations, Southwell became as alert to the uses of hidden meaning as to the divine implications of their revelation, and applied both these understandings to the creation of his English poetry, learning to stratify, veil, or pique meanings for different audiences. In his poetry we see the same covert transferrals of meaning (and spiritual value) as those of the Roman painting cycles, of easy access to all, but full of code-letters and elucidatory keys targeted on particular readerships or ideoloects.

In just this way, external angelic agency in Southwell's writing began to be replaced by internal psychological self-awareness as he matured in his studies,

The Spiritual Exercises*: the 'inward eie'*

and angelic intervention was suppressed or disguised in his English poetry. His angels do not offer guidance, appearing mostly in the role of assistants at those great moments of the life of Christ where it enacts or refers to his sacrifice; this more Catholic angelology has been suppressed either by his own or his editor's intent: the Mass is mentioned directly in only two poems, neither of which appears in the early editions of *Saint Peters Complaint*. Again, the angels merely sing at the Nativity in 'A childe my Choyce' (p. 13, l. 14), which appears in the first edition in 1595, while in 'New heaven new warre' (p. 13), absent until Cawood's augmented 1602 edition,[7] the 'heavenly quires' are more active in the Nativity scene, with specific roles appropriate to their type, a theory of hierarchic angelic agency rejected by Protestantism. Despite its distinct Counter-Reformation importance, this angelology is treated with some humour by Southwell, as if to soften the doctrinal implications.

For Southwell's humour veils a hard position: 'Raphaell' brings 'meate' to 'our little Tobie' (the Christ-Child, here depicted in a pitiful and neglected state); this parallels the Bible story of the boy whose father was cured of blindness with Raphael's help, at once portraying English Christians as neglectful of their Lord, and in need of spiritual assistance, and prefiguring Christ's restorative role (lines 11–12). The book of Tobias prefigured several features of Catholic doctrine, including exorcism, prayers for the dead, and God's reward for those who remain steadfast, elements of Roman Catholicism rejected by Luther; reference to Tobias was therefore a challenge to the Lutheran canon, which considered Tobias, and several other books, apocryphal and not to be held as articles of faith (although they were not actually banned from church services until the next century). Far from offering just a pretty Christmas lyric, Southwell is here acting as a poetical Bellarmine, to those readers up to speed with post-Reformation controversies, attacking Luther at a weak point, Catholic apologists regularly demanding to know by what right he set aside those parts of the Bible that he did not like. Its narrative of practical support for a mission to an alien land is even more germane to the Catholic situation in England, as is the vexed question of the dissembling by the agent of God of his true identity. Tobias could almost be the narrative of the Catholic mission itself. Closer still to Jesuit interests perhaps is Raphael's statement that he is one of the seven angels of apocryphal revelation, a particularly Jesuit study a reminder of which appeared in the privacy of the Novitiate Dormitory.[8] Once again Southwell's imagery can be seen to be multi-layered, and with different meanings residing at different levels.

His archangel 'Gabriell', the announcer and groom, also seeks accommodation in the reader's heart, as if another disguised version of a mission priest (lines 13–14). This secret message of enterprise and hope was part of what Southwell was importing into England, himself having to play the angels' part, pleading for funds and constancy. But not all the angels correspond to priestly activities: the knight-archangel Michael stands guard over the helpless baby, and, while angels sing a lullaby, they also sound trumpets to warn of coming battle; the readers must seek deep inside themselves to decide which side they will be on (lines 15, 18, 42).

Bringing the debate to the English was impossible if not hidden in such involved metaphysical metaphors. How might Southwell have offered his private community of Catholics an image of the Mass to meditate upon when he was not to refer to it directly in public, and could only offer its bare bones even in those hurried secret Masses in Catholic households? But he had been trained in the hidden and the implicit: the Roman painting cycles of his order were created with layers of such implication and suggestion in mind, fleshing out the bones of Gospel truths with special references and underlying implications.[9]

An example of such an embedded meaning in his poetry can be seen in 'His circumcision', one of the Virgin Sequence (p. 7). The Circumcision is clearly a metaphor for the Cross, but also, less obviously, for the Mass. To suggest the link, Southwell describes angels gathering up the blood of the Christ-Child as if assisting at the Mass (l. 11); but embedded within this imagery is an address to an even smaller group: his Jesuit brothers. The Circumcision being also the moment of the naming of Jesus, there is a link with the naming of the Society itself, as in the SS Annunziata *Circumcision* painting, which was linked to the naming of Jesus and thereby to the Society.[10] In a poem written by a Jesuit, one would expect to find mention of the first link between the shedding of Jesus's blood and his name, but Southwell acknowledges this only indirectly, through the fact that the name 'Jesus' appears in this poem for the first time in the Sequence; the Child has been named somewhere in the virtual space between poems, and in the private arena of comprehension of the reader. A Jesuit would see a deeper significance yet, a direct identification with Jesus that would have disturbed some readers.[11] As in their public chapels, Jesuits would recognise the great idea behind the simple depiction, drawing extra spiritual strength from it. Thus the drama of the chapel imagery seems to be repeated by Southwell in his own occluded depictions, glinting out of the metaphoric shadows: the ubiquitous sunbursts, the beautiful human forms frozen in their moment of crisis, and above all that cerulean space dotted with the mysterious, all-containing Marian cloud out of which sprang Christ, just as out of meditations upon these images sprang divine understanding. In his training in the uses of hidden meaning, therefore, Southwell had gained a double-edged weapon in his war of words. His training as a Jesuit had honed his rhetorical skills in debate and sermon; and his experience of the Ignatian *Exercises* had given him access to an imaginative inner world, and taught him how to express it in words, or to hide its deeper meanings for others to grow into as their understanding ripened.[12] How much of either can be seen in his

The Spiritual Exercises: the 'inward eie'

poetry is an important consideration, then, not for any spiritual reason but for the insight it gives into his poetic vision and rhetorical strategy.[13]

The Ignatian *Spiritual Exercises* were fundamental to the important new ideas brought by Southwell to England, less in their systematic detail than in their effects upon the imaginative self-confidence of the individual. They were the informing principle behind all the Jesuit theories of art, uses of imagery, application of the senses, and explorations of motivation, emotional response, and psychological state. Anything that Southwell learned in terms of looking with the inner eye came primarily from the *Exercises*, the brainchild of the founder of the Society, Ignatius of Loyola, a meditational and confessional programme based on medieval monastic models adapted for delivery to the early modern lay person. They constituted a month of carefully directed fasting, vigil-keeping, and programmed thought founded on Augustine's 'three powers of the soul' (memory, understanding, and will, from his treatise *De Trinitate*). Dry medieval scholasticism, in Ignatius's view, had hindered Church thinking; it seemed useless in enabling good decision-making out in the busy world beyond the monastery walls. He had wanted lay people to be trained as active, engaged Christian public servants, not scholars.[14] More to the point of this book, his idea of education insisted on the power of literature to mould the ideal moral citizen, with daily classes in letters, and only weekly classes in Christian doctrine. He himself had empathised with the saints most when he pictured them as contemporary and familiar – knights busy in the service of the Spanish Court, but with Christ, not a Lord or Lady, as the object of their chivalry; warriors gathering around the banner of God in the face of Satan's armies.[15] Here the roots of Southwell's adoption and adaptation of chivalric and courtly genres of writing are plain: Christ as ideal lover or helpless child in need of protection informs much of his poetry.[16]

Ignatius's vision rested on an act of recreative magic, combining the immediacy of personal memory with Christian narrative. His emphasis upon visualisation and the use of personal experience in giving immediacy to spiritual experience informed the Jesuits' visual programmes, just as it produced the *Exercises*. It also informs Southwell's colloquial St Peter, or his David as Renaissance courtier.

The core principle of this new model of thinking, and its audacity, was the precedence it gave to personal inner experience, the individual's response to the cosmos in all its divine complexity, demonstrated by Ignatius's insistence on the keeping of diaries recording the results of such interior pilgrimages. Southwell's devotional diaries and self-reflexive habit are the direct descendants of this principle. In making the Exercises, memory was put before intellect in importance (after the Neoplatonic model: 'the intellect acts on principles, the imagination on origins');[17] Ignatius insisted on the importance of the personal. What originated inside the self had become in certain respects more important than what was being told from the outside, a far cry from the standard schoolroom experience of training through *imitatio*. The use of illustration was no longer merely a prop for the illiterate or the unengaged Christian but a complex, highly theorised iconographics, a method of reaching deeper into already informed minds, aiding their own mental and cognitive processes: 'a knowledgeable Christian is far less likely to be lured astray by Lucifer', after all.[18]

It can be readily seen how this means of accessing, projecting, and applying self-recovered memories and feelings could inform the imagination of a man looking for engaging imagery, and how it would be of use in turn to other poets in the search for emotional/moral integrity, and for more expressive ways of delivering the new artistic affectivity.

Southwell's 'The prodigall childs soule wracke' (p. 43) takes the form of a (dis-gendered) dramatic monologue founded on the confession to his father of the Prodigal Son of the Gospel. This idea is never defined by any external narrator, however, apart from in the title itself: readers make their own connections; the poem thus detaches itself from the Gospel original and begins to be a metaphor for the relationship between an exercisant and the spiritual director designed to stimulate, in its turn, a colloquy between sinful Self and God the Father.[19] The speaker, through the same process of self-exposure as in the *Exercises*, achieves that state of highly felt remorse without which he could not have made the journey home, or even begun to find forgiveness:

> I plunged in this heavie plight, 25
> Found in my faults just cause of feares:
> By darkenes taught to know my light,
> The losse thereof enforced teares.

Only by an honest acknowledgement of (and experience of) his own 'darkenes' could he understand himself sufficiently to know himself (and, by Southwell's Christianised Neoplatonic model, to know God/'light' in himself). A director would have encouraged an exercisant to dwell upon these things, tears being rather the yardstick than an affecting image here; they are not dwelt upon. Sympathetic readers, especially those who had, through lost hope, renounced their faith, might well supply their own to complete the effect. The delivery, by an unnamed agency, of the means to repair the deficits of sin is the point of this poem, not the anguish of the protagonist's recognition of it: 'mercy' and 'grace', although not doctrinally defined here, are more readily seen to be in the gift of the Catholic confessor, and are the hoped-for fruits of the tearful experience of the Exercises.

The poems therefore extend, through the dissemination of the manuscripts, the *effects* of the *Exercises*, not the process itself. Nor are they personal confessions. Southwell the poet's aim in 'uplifting' the reader's imaginative faculty and spirit is similar to that of Ignatius the director. The end result of

The Spiritual Exercises: the 'inward eie'

all this upset was not, according to Ignatius, to be a man trained to follow the suggestions of others – his will was not to be broken but to be made highly responsive to the will of God, or to the more abstract 'goodness', directly communicated rather than interpreted by any other authority (*Exercises*, nos 23, 15). Confessional poetry would defeat its own object here, as would any sign of personal urging by the writer. 'The lack of personal detail, meant to open space for readers to enter into Southwell's poems, is consistent with advice given at the start of the Ignatian *Exercises*. A spiritual director should never let himself get between God and the person making the Exercises.'[20] It was to be empowerment, not brainwashing, just as Southwell's poetry, as he said himself, was to offer better targets for creativity, not to prescribe patterns for poetry – perhaps this is why he uses so many of the different styles and tones already in existence:

> The best course to let them see the errour of their workes, is to weave a new webbe in their owne loome; I have here layd a few course threds together, to invite some skilfuller wits to goe forward in the same, or to begin some finer peece, wherein it may be seene, how well verse and vertue sute together ..., neither Arte nor invention, giving it any credite.[21]

It is not intended to destroy old patterns, but to improve their quality, to lay down better warp-links between earth and heaven into which they might weave their own designs. More than the parallels between the building in the exercisant of sensitivity to 'good' and the creative sensitivity required by Southwell of the good poet, there are wider implications for English poetry, I would argue. Not only was Southwell's sensitivity informed and given a language for expression by the *Exercises* but his uttering of that information in his poetry reproduces, and makes accessible to other poets, these emotionally powerful effects.

LEARNING TO READ THE EMOTIONS: RESOLVING IN TEARS

The next stage of the *Exercises* could have been designed to give poetic voice to such inner turmoils. It was to learn how to 'read' the affects brought on by the first stage, carefully guided by the director through a gentle elenchic cross-examination, towards spiritually useful interpretations and away from self-indulgence or pointless despair. This explored the psychology of response in depth – how does a certain thought make the retreatant feel, and why? How to tell if a thought is good or bad? The response of the individual to his or her interior feeling was all; it was about feeling, certainly not idea, and barely even language; words could be singled out for meditation until they lost their accustomed associations. This giving up of previous certainties while 'one cannot anticipate that the empty spaces are going to be filled' is an almost eleusian going into the dark, a self-erasure requiring great faith.[22] The process deconstructed the links between language and thought, to turn instead to the frightening, unruly pre-language of psychological state; then teaching, in turn, the translation of newly affective responses into new words. The language register of the *Exercises* includes the exclamations of amazement as one's emotional state heightens; 'By the time the will becomes habituated to those exercises there will no longer be room for external and familiar languages', as de Nicolás puts it.[23]

It is this encouragement to articulate and interrogate personal feeling that makes the Ignatian *Exercises* so useful to an investigation of the creation in English poetry of a new psychological realism and emotional integrity, I would suggest. I agree with Frank Brownlow's point that poetry is not meditation, and that affective devotion *per se* was a central feature of the Counter-Reformation developed, rather than initiated, by the *Exercises*.[24] Ignatius did not invent strong response; he created a lay methodology, and a new emotional language capable of transference across boundaries – again: 'multiplex est modus tradendi exercitia'.[25]

Southwell then transposed it into poetic English. The tone of self-interrogation in so many of Southwell's poems, new to English lyric poetry in this colloquial, highly psychologised style, reflects this. 'Saint Peters Complaynte' (p. 29) is an articulation of inner turmoil. In 'S. Peters afflicted minde' (p. 31), the 'heart consumde with care' utters 'signes of paine' as if in the throes of such an exercise (lines 5–6). 'Mary Magdalens blush' (p. 32) also describes this state of heightened anxiety – remorse teaches 'guiltie thoughts' to comprehend the scope of personal failure; 'Faults long unfelt doth conscience now bewraye' (lines 9, 11). The first stanza of 'S. Peters remorse' (p. 33) describes the same state:

> Remorse upbraids my faults,
>   Selfe blaming conscience cries,
> Sinne claimes the hoast of humbled thoughtes,
>   And streames of weeping eies.

The 'hoast' of thoughts is there assaulting the penitent, as in the retreat, and of course the central feature is 'selfe blaming' – coming to know one's failings. The result is, as it would be in the retreat, tears: a total collapse of self-confidence, ready to be recreated differently, more morally aware and insightful than before.

Ignatius's full programme demanded four gruelling weeks of retreat, fasting and prayer, using the effects of sleep-deprivation and disorientation to facilitate the deconstruction of the self. Even access to light was to be controlled and manipulated to have its effects upon the retreatant, in a rigorous programme very different from the modern version, harsher, yet more intimately focused, because always tailored to an individual.[26]

The Spiritual Exercises: the 'inward eie'

The central purpose was a collapse in self-confidence; only after this could the restorative programme begin. Many of the Jesuit and other orders were, as a result of this emphasis upon contrition, focusing on tears as a sign of God's action in their hearts, a sign of consolation in a heart moved by love or contrition.[27] Southwell, despite reminding his readers of their wretchedness, was popular in part because being made to cry was popular, Harvey famously fearing that an onion was more often the cause than any genuine repentance.[28]

In importing a Continental fashion for lachrimosity, Southwell fed 'a common devotional need which, in Protestant circles, was only just beginning to be acknowledged again'; Southwell's poetry provided a populist, yet highly disciplined, entry point into this richly emotional arena, still so new to the English Protestant laity, amongst whom the Christian poetry of Protestants like du Bartas was only just beginning to circulate in English.[29]

But this focus on the imagery and implication of tears is perhaps unfortunate: in Ignatian thinking, what counted was the internal integrity of the penitent, not external manifestations. Literature that focused on tears could therefore be seen to be describing the measure, not the thing measured, to some extent. Crashaw's exhaustive exploration of Magdalen's tears in 'The Weeper' seems to give their copiousness priority above all else, a tendency quickly seized upon by Protestant critics as evidence of idolatry and excess. Nevertheless, tears literature, resonating as it did with the need for signs of true repentance, was popular in Protestant circles. Bellarmine's *De Gemitu columbae* was to become widely read after Southwell's time, despite being by a formidable Catholic apologist.[30] It may be that Southwell moderated the lachrimosity of his English lyrics in order to make them more generally accessible; it may be, equally, that as a trained exercisant and confessor, he was closer to the kernel of the process than those who saw it primarily as an issue of copious tears. That penitential vein could too readily become a glib alternative to the real effects sought by the *Exercises* – a livelier relationship with God, a change of life, a positive movement into the future.

The long 'Saint Peters Complaint' opens this penitential vein as if to bleed away the sickness of apostasy; the short 'Saint Peters Complaynte' (p. 29) is a tightly condensed rehearsal of the same failings, also dramatised as Peter's soliloquised confession of his betrayal of Christ. It does not mention tears during the self-accusatory first eleven stanzas, in which the Apostle catechises himself at length; only in the twelfth and last stanza are tears mentioned, and then at distance, not as part of the affective burden of the poem. The *reader* is to be the site of the tears, in self-recognition of Peter's anguish at his failure; the reader is being taught to feel tears, not merely shown them in the protagonist. The reader *is* the protagonist, in a Southwell poem, always; like a spiritual director trained in catechesis, he is asking his readers for a response, not telling them what to feel.

Robert Southwell

Finishing on a prayer for forgiveness and a promise of better actions, as did the *Exercises* themselves, the ventriloquised Apostle asks Jesus to measure his offence by the penitent's own levels of remorse – 'Lett teares appeace when trespas doth incense' (l. 69). The tears are there almost in the abstract within the poem, a means of valuing the depth of repentance. If the reader himself is moved to weep, he has become part of the drama of Saint Peter, and central to the Gospel narrative: his tears are offered up with Peter's in the final stanza, as a director giving the *Exercises* would hope to see.

READING AND LEARNING THE SELF

The core experience of the Ignatian *Exercises* was the reading and learning of the hidden self, the exercisant learning to define his responses according to a Christian morality that would then moderate his behaviour. After a powerfully imagined involvement in, say, Christ's birth, he was required to withdraw the mind's eye from the scene before him and redirect it into himself to analyse with care the feelings thereby aroused. 'Saint Peters Complaint' could be said to be an extended description of the effects of this part of the exercise as it was experienced by the exercisant. As in those Netherlandish or Italian paintings that showed Christ scourged by men recognisably contemporary with the viewer of the time, provoking a sense of recognition, participation, even guilt, the process of reflection was not to be abstract musing; it was to be a painful self-interrogation, involving the giving over of the wilful self to the surgeon, as if a cancer in need of excision:

> My sight was vaild till I my selfe confounded,
> Then did I see the dissenchanted charmes.
> Then could I cut th'anotomy of sinne, 665
> And search with *Linxes* eyes what lay within.

There was a painting in the Novitiate Infirmary (a building that was, in its first modest years, known to Southwell), based no doubt upon those engravings that Nadal produced to energise his novices. It depicted a youth 'surrounded by surgeons ready with scalpels and razors to cut him open for an anatomy lesson'. The old man shown nearby rejecting the assistance of the doctors is the Self with sight veiled, unaware of the extent of its sickness, while the brave youth presents himself to the surgeons for spiritual curettage.[31] This was a powerful exhortation to expose the workings of the self to scrutiny, via an image almost certain to stick in the memory of any young person who had seen it (especially in the painful context of an early modern infirmary).

This rigorous self-interrogation, this insistence upon an integrity that could be articulated and read, lent itself to the exposure of the 'real', unmasked self that we now associate with 'real' poetic creativity or inspiration. In the hands

The Spiritual Exercises: the 'inward eie'

of Southwell that interiority gives a psychological realism to his writing of exactly the sort noticed recently by Kermode as new in Shakespeare's writing at a slightly later date.[32] Southwell was instrumental, for whatever reason, in introducing such realism of personation into English letters, at the same time as Sidney's Astrophil, and, arguably, to better purpose.

This new Southwellian poet/exercisant had done more than desire; he had, in all but the most actual sense, shared in the Nativity of Christ, assisting, indeed almost helping to bring it about, engaging with the chief participants (with due humility and sensitivity) through the magic of human memory and creativity. Now he was to explore how it had felt to do so, through long hours of sensory deprivation, circumstances almost designed to make the 'experience' seem more real than details of the life he had lived outside his place of retreat: indoctrination, certainly, but training in imagination and response-management too.

This breaking of the boundaries between the imaginary, the historical, and the 'now' was deliberate, as can be seen from its reproduction in the Jesuit (and other) painting programmes: the *Holy Trinity* altarpiece of the English College, which Southwell knew, begins to show this blurring-together of different spheres, with the churchmen and the dead Christ portrayed with near-photographic naturalism in a dramatic 'now', backed by architecture echoing the real church interior, with the boundaries between the heavenly and the earthly shadowed out.[33] Many of the Gesù paintings show magical realities, the Virgin on a cloud, mystical lights in mundane landscapes. The martyr cycles were not required to imitate reality; only one or two of these actually broke through the frame of their medium to invade apparently, the viewer's real space. Both Nadal and Bellarmine encouraged pictorial experimentation; such new pictorial effects as perspective and the meta-framing of scenes-within- (or -without-) scenes could leave a viewer unsure where the divine moment depicted in the painting ended and the objective reality outside it began.[34] This breaking of boundaries can clearly be seen developing in Southwell's 'painted' scenes: he includes the Ignatian visualisation of the place, but also the implication in the *Exercises* that, if done properly, the imagined and the real places become one in the mind of the imaginer. That realisation was as fundamental to the action of the Exercises as it was to Southwell's later poems about bloody self-sacrifice.

Lastly, then, the exercisant, having experienced an invasion of his life-space by divine figures, would be steered towards converting the new insights gained into action, the performing deed, the making of actual day-to-day decisions. Southwell's 'remorse' poems usually close with a promise of a better life or at least a prayer for mercy, as if in deference to the process and logic of the *Exercises*. The persona of 'Sinnes heavie loade' (p. 17), after a six-stanza meditation on the pain inflicted upon Christ by the sins of the speaker (and reader), prays

'O prostrate Christ, erect my crooked minde' (l. 37). This was no abstraction of piety: life-changing actions were to be taken.

He was being taught to self-monitor; his director, in turn, was taught to maintain a distance, thus the exercisant would 'own' the new conception of himself, instead of merely accepting it at second hand. It was an almost organic view of the subjectification of the self to higher authority, which, taught to self-interpellate, could continue to self-subjectify in any circumstance, no matter how far from the central controlling authority. Whilst this might not have been, in modern terms, necessarily a 'good' thing, it was certainly a new one: autonomy of sorts. The purpose was to enable an exercisant to develop a plan for a modern life lived outside the Church in an increasingly secular society: a decision-making system, a method of self-appraisal that emphasised the importance of the (right-thinking) self in autonomous acts of discernment.

Its strength and its weakness lay in the fact that it was a model that could be effective to any Christian in a secularising world, though; subsequent Protestant interest in medieval and even contemporary Catholic meditational texts shows how far this was the case. Deconstructing a congregation into its component parts and teaching each to respond directly to God was a necessity in a land deprived of its priests, but it might also undercut the authority of church hierarchies. Despite the reservations of authority, though, Ignatius's *Spiritual Exercises* was taken up first by other orders, then by lay members of the European Catholic congregation. Jesuit and other devotional tracts were imported into Britain towards the end of the sixteenth century and 'borrowed', even those by Jesuit authors, and even by Puritan communities.[35] Southwell was making a translation of Fr Diego de Estella's *A Hundred Meditations on the Love of God* in 1589, despite a heavy workload.[36] These works were clearly very special.

Part of their impact rested on the way a well-directed retreatant of any denomination could be helped to feel that he was engaging personally with the central dramas of Christian history. The dramatic resiting of self that characterised the *Exercises* (say, into a shepherd at the Nativity, or even a despairing Peter or Magdalen) is also central to the creation of believable situations in literature (in the exercisant's case it was to be lived, not merely impersonated, of course). This parallels the presenting of historical characters in a play in the costumes and props of the players' own lives and times: Christ as a 'modern' knight or gentleman, his tormentors as contemporaries of the exercisant, angry Moorish or Netherlandish soldiers, a Lutheran mob, London apprentices on the rampage, whatever was in the individual's consciousness. To many pious but nonconforming people in England, including Puritans, this identification with the dispossessed of the Bible, and the nearness to the primitive Christian community it synthesised, was a potent antidote to the sense of isolation brought about by loss of community acceptability.[37] This placed the imaginer and his or her own social or ideological preoccupations amidst the prime authority of a Biblical epic, with the added immediacy of modernity and personal involvement. But in this it could also be seen to be borrowing the Gospel's emotional and authoritative capital for current political or religious ends. It seems that not all those who requested the *Exercises* did so for godly motives. The discerning of angelic agencies could be misunderstood, or even harmful. Even its creator saw its potential dangers, Ignatius warning directors not to proceed with conversation on the subject of spirits if the exercisant seemed unversed in such matters, or made crude objections to the advancement of the service of God, which from the Jesuit's perspective was the Roman Catholic, even the Jesuit, cause. 'This matter [of discerning spirits] is too subtle and too advanced for him to comprehend, and the rules of the second week are as likely to do him harm as the rules of the first week are likely to be of assistance to him' (*Exercises*, 'Annotations', nos 4, 8, 9, p. 106).

Southwell, in his biblical ventriloquisations of Peter, David or Magdalen, borrows the dramatic effects of the *Exercises*, employing the Bible's authorised 'Truth' to present characters that move between their original narrative and contemporary ones; he introduces elements that have inescapably political overtones. 'St Peter' draws the reader out of the Gospel into contemporary politics, using the modern trimmings of the Court anachronistically to draw attention to his contemporary target; a discussion of the evils of a corrupt and tainted court does not appear in the Bible narrative (l. 243). Peter cries out against this 'court' and its corrupting influence in lines 230 and 245:

> O *John* my guide into this earthly hell,
> Too well acquainted in so ill a court, 230
> Where rayling mouthes with blasphemies did swell,
> With taynted breath infecting all resort.
> Why didst thou lead me to this hell of evils:
> To shew my selfe a feind among the divels?

Southwell adds a warning, embedded in his biblical narrative and yet separated from it by anachronism again. He has his Peter seem to excuse himself by showing how sheep-like the courtiers are, blindly following each other into the rejection of the true site of faith as Southwell sees it, and dragging Peter, almost without his realising it, along with them (p. 83):

> It seemes no fault to doe that all have done:
> The nomber of offenders hides the sinne:
> Coatch drawne with many horse doth easely runne.
> Soone followeth one where multitudes begin.
> O, had I in that court much stronger bene: 245
> Or not so strong as first to enter in.

There is a contemporary hint of plague in the 'taynted breath' infecting all who gather together at Court (it was visiting London in the 1590s), and the coach and horses is a particularly modish sixteenth-century addition to the Bible version: Southwell was asking his reader to recreate the experience of the *Exercises* and find those hidden realities, via the 'secret waies' he hints at in 'vale of teares'.³⁸

THE END OF TRAINING: HIDDEN MOTIVATIONS

Ignatius's way shows that although he makes no bones about a human being subject to the entreaties and influences of good and bad angels, the way he included them into the methodology displayed an understanding of the psychological processes involved in self-analysis. He had created a cognitive structure for 'going forward', as a modern counsellor might put it, and of assessing the various tensions and responsibilities to which the individual is subject.

What would be most stimulating to any alert mind was the global scope of the imagining envisaged by Ignatius. Where the First Week focused on recognition of one's sins, the Second Week involved a global vision, with the armies of God and Satan ranged across the map. The imaginative personation of evil, not to mention the permission implicit in Ignatius's instructions to imagine what the panoptic Holy Trinity might be saying about it all, are sufficient reasons for Ignatius's caution about the proposed exercisant. Ignatius's discriminatory mechanism is perhaps his own acknowledgement of the potency and potential of his method.³⁹

Perhaps the danger, from the point of view of containment, resides in the sheer vision of the *Exercises*, in the Second Week especially. The exercisant was not only encouraged to inhabit and realise the biblical narrative, a spear-carrier in a Gospel play, but from this homely close-up the eye of the imagination was directed to pull back like some sky-borne camera to take in the vast panorama of 'the whole expanse or roundness of the earth [...] all the different people on the face of the earth, so varied in dress and in behaviour' (1st Day, 2nd Week, pars 101–6, p. 124). This was not the medieval Dream of Scipio, no philosophic diagram of a Ptolemaic onion-world dependent on the Chain of Being, but a virtually real vision of the globe with its modern multi-racial masses and their living preoccupations. The director sets the scene: 'Some are white and others black, some at peace and others at war; some weeping and others laughing; some well and others sick; some being born and others dying' (par. 106). The exercisant was thus directed to reach in the course of a few hours from the most intimate corners of his self to a dizzying God's-eye view of the world, a soaring new perspective for the individual imagination; in imagining the Trinity he was even required to 'hear what they are saying, *or what they might say*', an option that effectively allows the exercisant to put words generated in his own head into the mouth of God (pars 121–5; my emphasis).

Scipio's Dream had furnished medieval minds with philosophical possibilities, but only now perhaps, in an age of printing, vernacular literature, and travel, was the lay imagination sufficiently fed with detail of the real world's variety and scope to make the picture real, and apply its great principles to their individual circumstances.[40] The structure for training a new mobility and power for the 'I' was being created, in part, through the Ignatian *Exercises*. An English exercisant was being enabled to open his 'I' on, and to, the world.

Southwell's vocation was founded on this global mindset, but he was trapped, as it were, in a nationalistic bind that foregrounded local issues, and called for local and severe solutions.

In 1583 and 1584 Allen, overwhelmed in Rheims by the numbers of men coming out of English universities to avoid the oaths of loyalty now being forced upon them, had sent some of them to the *Venerabile* in Rome.

Southwell's new skills of casuistry and confessional meekness were stretched to the limit. Some of the later diary entries may be Southwell's own exhortations, and one (58, p. 66) may be a copy of a letter he is known to have written to Persons in the Netherlands complaining (prophetically) about Dr Bagshaw and the others. Persons dismissed his fears; he was busy fighting off another anti-Jesuit faction.[41] It was perhaps this College antipathy that later led John Cecil to go to the English authorities with a description of Southwell in 1591, making his arrest inevitable.[42]

Southwell's diary entries show a struggle going on between his desire to return to England and his Roman superiors' wish that he should not. Southwell might have escaped that struggle by being moved to another institution in Europe, as Campion had been ten years before, but something clearly happened that changed everything utterly.

We can only speculate, but we do know of one change that occurred in the months before his return to England. Persons had fallen out with Jasper Heywood over his courtly contact-making and accommodations with the Crown, and had now lost his vital courtly contact on the English mission, possibly alienating the Elizabethan Catholic nobility to boot.[43] Too many forces pulling in outward directions meant that the whole enterprise of England was in danger of tearing itself apart.

Amongst all this other business, Persons had news of two things that will have given him particular concern regarding the English mission. In September 1584 he had dispatched William Weston from Paris to replace the now imprisoned Jasper Heywood. Through letters and, later, a 'family' Christmas visit to the Tower (for which Weston borrowed Heywood's nephew John Donne), Weston learned that Burghley's wish to de-legalise incoming Catholic priests had at last prevailed over the appetites of Leicester and Walsingham for bloody public executions. Instead of adding further flowers of martyrdom to his opponents' bouquet, Burghley now planned to defame, weed out, and deport all existing Catholic priests, and create new laws against further incursion.

Heywood and twenty other priests were to be deported in January 1585.[44] The new laws were to be created during the Parliament of 1584–85; Persons may therefore have applied in some urgency for replacement priests to be inserted before the legislation came into being. Southwell's courtly contacts and cultural attributes would have recommended him as a missioner in the mould of Campion and Heywood.

Certainly, Persons was now painfully aware that the original plan of the Campion mission to engage the Catholic ruling classes had all but collapsed, and the possibility of continuing to attempt to do so was vanishingly small. Weston and his friend Garnet were more populist in their approach, Weston preaching widely and performing exorcisms, and Garnet, through his theories of the uses of the rosary, promising to engage the English, even if illiterate, in the basics of religious observation, whether or not they had access to a church or a priest.[45] Southwell, perhaps responding in turn to Persons's urgency, wrote to Acquaviva in January and February 1585 to be allowed to go to England.[46] The diary entries chiding him for questioning his orders are almost certainly from this period.

The second thing that Persons had learned concerned a project in line with Heywood's view of the mission as a means of reconciliation between the Catholic nobility and the Queen, through compromises and tolerations. William Lord Vaux and other Catholic nobles meant to petition the Queen to ask for toleration in exchange for certain concessions about her status. Persons had instructed Weston to learn more, hence Weston's dangerous visit to the Tower. John Donne later recalled an important part of the long day spent in the Tower cell with the two priests: 'at a consultation of *Jesuits* in the *Tower* in the late Queene's time, I saw it resolved, that in a Petition to bee exhibited to her, shee might not be stiled *Sacred*'.[47] These debates were not over whether but over how far to move towards reconciliation with the English Crown, and how far her legality could, in return, be recognised by Catholics. This new brand of English Catholic loyalism was preparing to debate the issue of papal authority over princes. This would compromise 'the whole political design of the mission',[48] and Persons seems to have set up the new mission structure to address the problem. Garnet and Southwell later made their first English home with various Vauxes,[49] who were to figure largely in support of their mission.

There was, demonstrably, a major fault-line in the English mission. If it held here, it was only to give way catastrophically there. When the clubbable Heywood's work at the universities had begun to bear fruit in 1582, and a great many students had reconciled to Catholicism and fled across the water to Rheims, many of them noblemen's sons, Persons had chosen to bypass the Heywood mission structure completely, sending over pamphlets which aroused severe reactions from the Council, which insisted from then on that the universities administer the Oath of Supremacy to certain twelve- to fourteen-year-old students. The flow of noble defectors faltered, and Heywood complained to Acquaviva.[50] It was at the very period of Heywood's attempted reconciliation that Allen's and Persons's campaigns of martyr engravings and descriptions of English Protestant cruelty were at their height, and the martyr cycles at the German and English Colleges in Rome appeared. Two increasingly irreconcilable strands had developed in the concept of the proper structure of the English mission, the Jesuit notion of ways of proceeding that adapted to every circumstance seemed to be buried under personal visions of what was right for England. Southwell and Garnet therefore were to minister to an England at once inhabited by quiet Catholic gentlemen like Vaux and assaulted by Catholic gentlemen like the Duke of Parma. At one time or another over these few years his immediate superiors had been furthering the designs of both, making the Society rules of total, unquestioning obedience to superiors somewhat problematic: Acquaviva was their Roman superior, Allen and Persons were ultimately their English mission superiors, a situation that was awkward in terms of vows to obey one's superior, if no more.

Persons's request that Southwell be released for the English mission in 1584 was refused by Acquaviva.[51] But Southwell, convinced that he could do some good there and perhaps worried about the soul-state of his family, or unable to meet the eye of those of his English scholars bound to the mission, wrote to Acquaviva a little more insistently than his rule of obedience allowed:

> About myself I will add only one thing: nothing is more in my prayers, and nothing more welcome could ever happen to me, than this. It is Your Paternity's decision that I devote myself to the English here in Rome. May it also be your decision, by God's inspiration, that I do the same for England herself, with the supreme goal of martyrdom in view. I will not cease to strive with God in prayer that he may grant me this in his mercy, and that he may keep Your Paternity long years to rule over us. X Cal. Feb. 1585.[52]

Heywood had been recalled to Rome by Acquaviva in April 1585, Acquaviva insisting that the English mission could work only if all on it were prepared to 'advance by the same paths'.[53] Letters from Persons at this time may have relieved the mind of the father general, who had been watching almost helplessly as the Society became more and more deeply involved with Catholic League and other western European power-politics.[54]

Southwell, his regular correspondence showing him to be very much in step with Persons, who called him 'my dearest Robert',[55] may now have become indispensable to the mission to make up for the loss of Persons and to replace the courtly, well-connected Heywood. The death in 1585 of Gregory XIII, the pope responsible for blessing the painted images of the English martyrs and renewing the excommunication of Elizabeth,[56] also signalled a change in the way the English enterprise was to be regarded, and perhaps explains why

Acquaviva could be persuaded to allow Southwell to go on mission at last, hoping that the enterprise would return to its original pastoral agenda.

Sickness, always stalking the halls of the College, came close to Southwell at this crucial point, threatening his return to England. His diary shows agonised self-catechisms warning him not to desire anything different from that given by God. Perhaps God knows that he is not strong enough to endure 'the torments of martyrdom', that he is not 'fit to win souls'. In his anguish, he tries to quiet himself with the words, 'if we live, we live to the Lord, or if we die, we die to the Lord. Whether we live or whether we die we are the Lord's', the words he was to repeat, also in Latin, a decade later as he stood on the platform at Tyburn.[57]

Persons clearly had a new mission in mind, one that acknowledged the need for the inclusion of the Catholic nobility, yet remained separate and free to operate along Society lines; one, equally important, that would keep him well informed about the younger Catholic nobility. Philip Howard, thirteenth Earl of Arundel, a relative and favourite of Elizabeth, had reconciled himself to Catholicism in this year (1584). He was a great prize for the missioners, and it was of vital importance that the example to the more accommodating aristocracy of his overt constancy be maintained. Persons could have chosen no better men to persuade the English Catholic nobility and commons alike of their peaceful intent than Garnet and Southwell, Garnet a yeoman's son mild enough to be nicknamed *pecorella* – 'little sheep' – by Robert Bellarmine, and Southwell, a charming, cultured, poetically minded youth, related to both the Cecils and the Howards.[58] When Arundel was taken to the Tower in the spring of 1585, the need to have men on the ground in London grew even greater. The whole network of safe houses and secret presses relied on such patronage.

In the winter of 1585, Persons and Allen finally journeyed to Rome, and in March or April 1586 Persons made his Exercises in the Novitiate of S. Andrea,[59] at about the same time that Southwell and Garnet left for England. He was able to ride out with them to the Milvian Gate to say goodbye in late May.[60] Acquaviva, clearly unhappy and never fully reconciled to the idea, called them 'lambs to the slaughter'.[61]

NOTES

1 'Mans civill warre', p. 49, lines 9–10; in James H. McDonald and Nancy Pollard Brown (eds), *The Poems of Robert Southwell, S.J.* (Oxford: Clarendon Press, 1967), hereafter M&B; further references to Southwell's poetry are from this edition, given as page/line numbers in the text.

2 Robert Southwell, 'Poema de Assumptione B.V.M.', lines 180–205, from Stonyhurst MS A.v.4, at Stonyhurst College, Clitheroe, Lancashire. Translation from Peter Davidson and Anne Sweeney (ed. and intro.), *The Collected Poems of S. Robert Southwell, S.J.* (Manchester: Carcanet, forthcoming).

The Spiritual Exercises: the 'inward eie'

3 'Of the Blessed Sacrament of the Aulter', p. 26, l. 84; 'A holy Hymme', p. 23, l. 36; 'Her Spousals', p. 4, l. 6; 'The Epiphanie', p. 8, l. 10; 'A vale of teares', p. 41, l. 49.

4 'Josephs Amazement', p. 21, l. 77; 'Of the Blessed Sacrament of the Aulter', p. 26, l. 52.

5 Jerome Nadal, S.J.: 'multiplex est modus tradendi exercitia'; see John O'Malley, *The First Jesuits* (Cambridge, MA: Harvard University Press, 1993), p. 127, and n. 232; hereafter cited in the text.

6 See Gauvin Alexander Bailey, *Between Renaissance and Baroque: Jesuit Art in Rome, 1565–1610* (Toronto: University of Toronto Press, 2003), p. 106, hereafter cited in the text.

7 STC 22960a.

8 The cult had had some undesirable effects in the early days of the Society; later Jesuits such as Bellarmine preferred the four apocryphal angels to remain nameless, but they continued to appear alongside Michael, Gabriel and Raphael; Bailey, pp. 68–70. I am indebted to Peter Davidson for encouraging a closer look at Tobias.

9 Bailey, p. 66.

10 Ibid., p. 117.

11 See Bailey on the importance of the naming aspect of the Circumcision in relation to the Gesù painting cycle, pp. 196–7.

12 See St Ignatius of Loyola, S.J., *The Spiritual Exercises and Selected Works*, ed. George E. Ganss (New York: Paulist Press, c.1991); material on the Ignatian *Spiritual Exercises* is based on Antonio T. de Nicolás, *Ignatius de Loyola: Powers of Imagining* (Albany: State University of New York Press, 1986); information on Ignatius's educational vision comes from George E. Ganss, *Saint Ignatius' Idea of a Jesuit University* (Milwaukee: Marquette University Press, 1956); also from Thomas Hughes, S.J., *The Educational System of the Jesuits* (London: Heinemann, 1904); all hereafter cited in the text.

13 Louis L. Martz, in proposing that the *Exercises* are functionally reflected in Southwell's poetry, began a line of questioning that, valuable as it was in opening out the arena of debate around Southwell's writing, polarised aspects of it in what now appear to be artificial and overly linear ways. Via commentators such as Barbara Lewalski, it has become locked into a discourse that seems more to do with Reformation/Counter Reformation arguments than poetry *per se*, to the detriment of studies of Southwell's contribution to English literature. See Louis L. Martz, *The Poetry of Meditation* (New Haven: Yale University Press, 1954); hereafter cited in the text; also see Barbara Kiefer Lewalski, *Protestant Poetics and the Seventeenth Century Religious Lyric* (Princeton, NJ: Princeton University Press, 1979). Scott Pilarz presents an overview of this debate in his prologue, pp. xxvi–xxviii; I agree with his view that 'Loyola's *Spiritual Exercises* is not the last word in understanding Southwell', especially as he 'faced ministerial contexts that are highly unusual even by Jesuit standards' (p. xxviii). Pilarz presents a thoughtful discussion of Ignatian *Exercises* in relation to Southwell's *Short Rules of Good Life* (pp. 99–116); see Scott Pilarz, S.J., *Robert Southwell and the Mission of Literature 1561–1595: Writing Reconciliation* (Aldershot: Ashgate, 2004); hereafter cited in the text.

14 De Nicolás, p. 16. See *The Autobiography of St. Ignatius Loyola*, ed. John C. Olin, trans. J. F. O'Callaghan (New York: Harper and Row, 1974); *Letters of St. Ignatius of Loyola*, ed. and trans. William J. Young, S.J. (Chicago, IL: Loyola University Press, 1959).

15 O'Malley, pp. 44–5.

16 Pilarz, pp. 98–9.

17 De Nicolás, pp. 13–14, 102.

18 See Jeffrey Chipps Smith, 'The Art of Salvation in Bavaria', in John W. O'Malley, S.J., Gauvin Alexander Bailey, et al. (eds), *The Jesuits: Cultures, Sciences, and the Arts 1540–1773* (Toronto: University of Toronto Press, 1999), pp. 568–99 (p. 593); hereafter cited in the text.

19 A Latin poem on the same subject by Southwell explores the inner experience of a repentant sinner more closely yet; from Stonyhurst MS A.v.4. It may be seen also in Davidson and Sweeney.

20 See Pilarz, p. 223.

21 'The Author to his loving Cosen', prefatory letter to *Saint Peters Complaint* (Ca, 1595), in M&B, p. lvii.

22 De Nicolás, pp. 38–9.

23 Ibid., pp. 37–8.

24 F. W. Brownlow, *Robert Southwell*, Twayne's English Authors Series, 516 (New York: Simon & Schuster Macmillan, 1996), pp. 127–8; hereafter cited in the text.

25 O'Malley, p. 127.

26 For a discussion of the problems inherent in modern delivery of the *Exercises*, see Gerard W. Hughes S.J., *In Search of a Way: Two Journeys of Spiritual Discovery* (London: Darton Longman and Todd, 1986, repr. 1998). Hughes's attempt to recreate the circumstances of the original form helps to emphasise the differences, and to show the potential of Ignatius's conception; his self-imposed isolation has parallels with that of Southwell in England; see especially pp. 27–8.

27 O'Malley, p. 19. An exercisant, directed in his retreat by his spiritual teacher, was encouraged to open himself out to the flood of feelings that would naturally follow such sensory deprivations as fasting and sleeplessness. He was led towards a profound realisation of his failings; tears and deep anxiety were to be expected, and if not apparent, the director was to check with the exercisant that he was fully engaged (*Exercises*, 'Annotations', no. 6, p. 106). Tears become the obvious emblem of such a state, and the tears literature so prevalent on the Catholic Continent became its formalised expression. There has been much written on this subject recently, especially on how the theme of tears was taken up by various communities, Puritan as much as Catholic, becoming the sign of proper penance. Alison Shell's discussion of this looks in part at Southwell's place amongst the poetic weepers. see Alison Shell, *Catholicism, Controversy and the English Literary Imagination 1558–1660* (Cambridge: Cambridge University Press, 1999), ch. 2 especially; hereafter cited in the text.

28 Christopher Devlin, *The Life of Robert Southwell Poet and Martyr* (London: Longmans, Green, 1956), p. 266; hereafter cited in the text.

29 Shell, pp. 61, 65.

30 *De gemitu columbae, siue, De bono lacrymarum*, 3 vols (Antwerp, 1617). Shell shows a Protestant poet describing copious tears as 'carnall sorrowinge', a sin of sensuality and self-love; he recommends that those of his readers in search of spiritual communion 'looke up & cheere thy harte' instead, pp. 86–7.

31 Bailey, pp. 84–5.

32 See Frank Kermode, *Shakespeare's Language* (Harmondsworth: Penguin, 2000).

33 See Bailey, fig. 64.

34 See the magnificently meta-depictional painting of *The Vision of St Thomas Aquinas*, S. Marco, Florence, and Bailey's discussion, p. 29; fig. 7.

35 A devotional work by de Piñeda of the Inquisition appeared in the town library of Puritan Ipswich, for instance; see Anthony Milton, 'Qualified Intolerance: the Limits and Ambiguities of Early Stuart Anti-Catholicism', in Arthur F. Marotti (ed.), *Catholicism and Anti-Catholicism in Early Modern English Texts* (Basingstoke: Macmillan, 1999), pp. 85–109 (p. 85).

36 M&B, p. xxiv.

37 The initial preparatory period of fasting and praying was, in any case, carried out in total isolation from normal life; the Christian memory of Christ's life was to be the methodology and the structure that replaced that more familiar and problematic to the exercisant. First came the Life, then the Passion of Christ, those traditional images brought – literally conjured – to 'life' by the wizardry of memory, fleshed out and augmented from the exercisant's own memory-stores of family, acquaintance, enemies – whoever they were; Ignatius, whose interest in meditational pictures probably underlay Nadal's *Evangelicae historiae imagines* of 1593, and therefore the painting cycles in Rome, meditated before paintings every day in his rooms in Rome; '"Le style jésuite n'existe pas": Jesuit Corporate Culture and the Visual Arts', in John W. O'Malley, S.J., Gauvin Alexander Bailey, et al., *The Jesuits: Cultures, Sciences, and the Arts*, pp. 38–89 (p. 38); hereafter 'Style'. Ignatius's *Holy Family*, one of that collection, survives today, Bailey, p. 7.

38 I am unable to agree with Pilarz's proposal that Southwell felt nothing but respect for Elizabeth (based on his reading of *Humble Supplication*), because of the existence of such suggestive and reproving passages in his poetry. In criticising the body of the Court, Southwell reproves its head, Elizabeth, however covertly; see Pilarz, pp. 228–39.

39 See *Exercises*, pars 121–5; Bailey, pp. 99, 52.

40 Abraham Ortelius's important atlas, the emphatically post-Ptolemaic *Theatrum Orbis Terrarum* (Antwerp: Coppenium Diesth, 1571), had appeared five years before Southwell arrived at Douai; an update was published two years before his arrival in England (Antwerp: Plantin, 1584); it was itself a 'global' work, collected from many other sources; see Marcel P. R. van den Broecke, *Ortelius Atlas Maps: An Illustrated Guide* ('t-Goy: HES Publishers, 1996), pp. 39–289.

41 Devlin, p. 62.

42 For John Cecil's report to the government see *CSP, Dom., 1591–1594*, vol. 238, n. 62.

43 See Dennis Flynn, '"Out of Step": Six Supplementary Notes on Jasper Heywood', in Thomas M. McCoog, S.J. (ed.), *The Reckoned Expense: Edmund Campion and the Early English Jesuits* (Woodbridge: Boydell, 1996), pp. 179–92 (p. 184); hereafter cited in the text.

44 Flynn, pp. 188–9.

45 Fr Weston's picture was placed alongside those of college martyrs in the English College set up by Persons at Valladolid in 1620, with a book of exorcisms and an exorcism scene in the background; see Williams, 'Campion', p. 298; see also O'Malley, p. 267; Garnet's use of the rosary in addressed in depth by Anne Dillon, in 'Praying by Number: The Confraternity of the Rosary and the English Catholic Community, c.1580–1700', *History*, 88 (July 2003), 451–71; hereafter cited in the text.

46 Brownlow, p. 7, and n. 12, p. 137.
47 John Donne, *Pseudo-Martyr* (London, 1610), STC 7048, p. 46; quoted in Flynn, p. 190.
48 Flynn, p. 189; in 1590 the first volume of Bellarmine's *Controversies* narrowly escaped the *Index Expurgatorius* due to his proposal of a less direct, less immediate papal authority in secular matters; Robert Bellarmine, S.J., *De controversiis christianae fidei adversus huius temporis haereticos* (Cologne, 1620); see www.newadvent.org for general material concerning Bellarmine's life and works.
49 Philip Caraman, S.J., *A Study in Friendship: Saint Robert Southwell and Henry Garnet* (Saint Louis, MO: The Institute of Jesuit Sources, 1995), pp. 28–9; hereafter cited in the text.
50 See Flynn, pp. 185, 187.
51 Devlin, p. 69.
52 Ibid., pp. 76, 344, n. 19. Ignatius had allowed for a certain amount of 'feedback' during 'manifestations of conscience', the superior and subject discussing whether or not the subject was really fitted for a particular post, and where their natural inclinations and strengths lay; the subjects might 'impress their viewpoint upon their superiors' with 'modesty but firmness' on such occasions, O'Malley, p. 355; also see Pilarz's discussion of Southwell's self-doubts, pp. 147–8.
53 Flynn, p. 191.
54 Flynn, p. 153. Persons, complained of by exiles and local churchmen for his various activities, and seemingly suffering from exhaustion, ignored several calls by his general to return to Rome, finally asking to return to make his third year in the novitiate in order to 'recollect [himself]' in February 1585: 'for I feel myself extremely debilitated by these daily dealings with the world, and even though I were never more keen to perform them, the importunity of these affairs [*negotiorum*] does not allow me to find any satisfaction in them. The passions of my disposition [*passions animi*] have greatly grown and strengthened, and unless I get time to attend carefully and undistracted to *this* business I do not see how I shall be able to subjugate them.' He asks not to be offered a job concerning England for the time being; Bossy, 'Persons', p. 152.
55 Devlin, pp. 45, 47.
56 Ibid., p. 77.
57 Brownlow, p. 21.
58 Caraman, pp. 4, 5.
59 Bossy, 'Persons', pp. 146, 155.
60 Brown, 'Mission', p. 196.
61 Caraman, p. 1.

Chapter 3

Hidden ways and secret veins: into England

> O Pleasant port, O place of rest,
>   O royall rifte, O worthy wound,
> Come harbour me a weary guest,
>   That in the world no ease have found.
>
> I lie lamenting at thy gate,   5
>   Yet dare I not adventure in:
> I beare with me a troublous mate,
>   And combred am, with heape of sinne.
>
> Discharge me of this heavy load,
>   That easier passage I may finde,   10
> Within this bowre to make aboade,
>   And in this glorious tombe be shrin'd.
>
> Heere must I live, heere must I die,
>   Heere would I utter all my griefe:
> Heere would I all those paines descrie,   15
>   Which here did meete for my releefe.[1]

IN HIS SERVICE: ENGLAND'S METAPHORICAL MARTYRDOM

The opening prayer of the Ignatian *Spiritual Exercises* began 'O good Jesus hear me; Within thy wounds hide me'.[2] Southwell's training had been designed to fit him for a vocation that promised to realise to the full the imaginary sharing of Christ's agonies encouraged in the *Exercises*. After 1586, Southwell's writing is full of that new understanding. In the days immediately before entry into England, he had written of his fears about what lay ahead. He acknowledged Acquaviva's comparison between the missioners and sacrificial lambs, going open-eyed to his death, and asking for prayers to help him 'play His part' – take over the role of Christ. 'It is true', he had told his father general, 'that I am being sent "among wolves", and likely enough to be led to the slaughter. I only wish it were "as a lamb" for his name's sake who sent me.' 'The flesh is weak', he had added, 'and even now revolts from what is proposed.'[3] He saw himself as representing 'the cause of the whole Church', a burden above and beyond his own fears. This letter and the crossing of the Channel mark the point of departure from any normal strategy of self-protection.

His understanding of the physical enormity of what was proposed is demonstrated in the poem quoted above, part of the impact of which for English readers was its pan-Christian integrity. For a Catholic reader, the meditation upon the crucifix was contained within the metaphor, without denying access to the most Puritan of readers through any overt iconographical reference. 'Man to the wound in Christs side' works through the Christian meditation on the wounded body of Christ, seeing the gaping wound made in his side by the 'spitefull speare' of human iniquity (l. 18) as a portal through which the human soul enters, by the redeeming self-sacrifice of Christ, to share divinity.

Southwell and Garnet, having dwelt upon this ideal daily since entering the Society, were trained to see it as an actual, not a metaphorical ideal. It makes an apt image for the English mission, both in the metaphor it provides for the Eucharist, linked as it is in this image to loss and sorrow, and in the scope of the pitiful injury and the response of the penitent to it: the wound is 'the mirror of al mourning wights', as it sheds drops of water as well as blood (l. 22), and the penitent is to repay or match it with tears of regret before re-entry to the body of the divine can be achieved. Whatever politicking was happening in the English, Spanish or French Courts, or in Rome, the English mission was to Garnet and Southwell a separate, part-metaphysical space, a way into the wounds of Christ, through that metaphysical inversion described in the poem that precedes 'Man to the Wound' in Southwell's *Moeoniae*, 'The virgin Mary to Christ on the Crosse' (p. 71). In this poem Mary Mother of God is herself meditating upon the wounds of her son: 'Come helpe me now to cleave my heart,' she begs Gabriel, who had cleaved her heart for the entry of the Son of God some thirty years before, 'That there I may my sonne intombe' (lines 15–16). To gain entry to those royal ports, one must risk everything, taking them into oneself.

The Catholic rising in the North had marched under the banner of the Five Wounds of Christ earlier in the century, but, as the drift of Southwell's poem indicates, his own sacrifice was to be more than emblematic. This was his training and his vocation – his church was not now requiring his congregation to enter into Christ's wounds quite so literally, despite the reflections upon martyrdom in so many of the poems, and the apparent preoccupation with it in Rome. Agazzari had assured Acquaviva that the fresco cycle of S. Tommaso was conceived mainly 'to show the world the glory and splendour of the English church, but also so that when the students in this college should see the example of these predecessors of theirs they might also be stirred toward martyrdom'. A wider purpose is added, however: 'that with the images of our new martyrdoms the miserable state of [the benefactor's] fatherland would be placed before the eyes of Rome and of all the world'.[4]

The overarching theme of the decorations at S. Tommaso was that of English Christian history and its double relationship with Rome as oppressor and rescuer. Realistic portrayal of the martyrdoms was not the main point, as much as the accusations against the English State implicit in them. Some of the recent torturers appeared in contemporary dress, complete with Tudor rose emblems, although many of the older ones were in generic costume. Becket was being killed by a Roman, yet one of the assistants at his altar was clearly a College student in contemporary dress (including rosary), fixing the impact and implications of the martyrdom in contemporary minds. Campion and the others, recognisable in their contemporary clerical garb, were being tortured by men in a costume more Roman than Renaissance; but, to emphasise the State's culpability, the Council members viewing the spectacle were also in contemporary dress, inviting comparisons between Elizabeth's ministers and the torturers of Christ and the early martyrs. The contemporary imagery reattached the ancient meanings to modern circumstances; it was a 'battle cry', though, not a suicide note.[5]

The artwork therefore made useful political as well as spiritual points, as Agazzari suggested: the modern martyrdoms were actually in part legal examinations (from the point of view of the examiners), their legality actively undermined by the imagery, an effect repeated in Southwell's poems. But it was primarily the ancient drama of persistence and dogged piety that the paintings were attempting to recreate for the viewer, and the unusually long period of Southwell's and Garnet's days of freedom on the English mission suggests that they understood that difference well enough.

As if to make explicit the unreality of the world they were about to enter, Southwell and Garnet arrived in a time that did not quite exist, an English time-warp. They had departed from Boulogne on 16 July 1586. On 7 July Southwell and Garnet landed at sunrise between Folkestone and Dover, the feast day of St Thomas Becket, priestly challenger of the rights of English kings.[6] The world had turned upside-down. Garnet the mathematician was interested in the logical oddity of their situation: 'I remember that we said the first Vespers of St Alexis [in Boulogne] but on the following morning, as the sun was rising, we landed on the feast of St. Thomas – ten days earlier.' England was dragging its feet in calendar reform, as well as in reform of piety, and this anomaly in the count of days and the liturgical cycle itself was an elegant demonstration of its unnatural and backward state.[7]

To this temporal discontinuity was added a sort of miracle: Garnet adds that owing to the negligence of their ship's captain they had been landed on an unknown stretch of shore and were actually in the diocese of the saint whose feast day it was, St Thomas of Canterbury, between Dover and Folkestone.[8] This was certainly a lucky chance – it was easier to move about at a time of fairs, feasts and pilgrimage; random wandering was becoming a criminal activity, and even gentlemen were coming under scrutiny. Not only had they had the unprecedented opportunity of celebrating his feast day twice, but St Thomas, the patron of the English community in Rome, had covered them in the protection of his cloak, it seemed.

It was a very necessary protection, no doubt. False friends, spies, and counterspies being everywhere, the arrival of two 'very young' Jesuits was quickly known to Burghley.[9] Indeed, information on their departure for England had already been relayed to Burghley by Thomas Phelippes. News of Southwell's arrival would therefore have reached him at about the same time as the Jesuits arrived in London, on 8 July 1586.[10] Burghley might have raised an eyebrow at first: young William Cecil had just been given a guided tour of Rome by his relative, Robert Southwell, with no suggestion of an imminent departure.[11] It would be interesting to know what William reported of the new frescos of the Campion martyrdom in S. Tommaso, with the capped and bearded Elizabethan court gentlemen presiding over the racking of men of God, exposed to the eyes of Rome and the visiting world. Six or so years later, the rack was notably absent from examinations of Southwell, replaced by something harder to portray, but equally hard to endure; this may have been in some measure a response to the martyr paintings of S. Tommaso and the odium with which, as Burghley himself admitted, England's name was now widely regarded in Europe; he had already had reason to note down Southwell's name in respect of England's spoiled reputation,[12] and now Southwell had arrived on his doorstep.

The young writer was now committed to an almost uncontrollable course in a deadly and unpredictable place, but what made it dangerous also made it special in terms of his authorship: more than one curious chance associated with the peculiarities of the English mission brought the developing authorship of the young priest into an unprecedented arena of near-uncontrolled literary production.

AUTHORITY AND WRITING: THE VIRTUAL CHURCH

Bellarmine and other post-Reformation theorists were making great waves on the Continent, with their new rhetorical and visual approaches, public lectures and exhibitions, church building programmes. The full panoply of the Counter-Reformation was not accessible in England, and nor were its effects of regaining holy ground lost to the reformers. Southwell and Garnet would have to build their own virtual church and pulpit, and create a reader-

Hidden ways and secret veins: into England

ship-congregation that, as a group, existed in the imagination as much as in reality.

In pursuit of this, the mission was officially to concern itself with the issue of holy texts and catechisms to support faith, and other scholarly works countering Protestant propaganda. They would certainly have been sent copies of Bellarmine's *Controversies* as soon as they became available in 1586.

The printing of books without prior ecclesiastical approval was by now extremely difficult in England. It was not permitted under papal law either, and it is of great importance to this book that Garnet and Southwell (following on from the Campion mission, and unlike other clerics or commons) had special papal permission to write and to print material at their own discretion, after the capture of Weston, and to disseminate it as circumstances allowed. Hard times, hard measures: Jesuit pastoral flexibility combined, in Southwell and Garnet's mission, with the rare opportunity to disseminate what was considered *by themselves alone* to be useful in the helping of souls. This was an almost unprecedented sort of authority and authorship in a time of increasing surveillance and suppression.

Garnet lost no time on arrival in setting up the secret press which was to print catechisms and other texts for ten years, a risk-fraught achievement that implies a considerable level of support at many levels.[13] The Catholic Church in late sixteenth-century England was formed of words and arguments alone; its congregation and clerisy could be grown only through sufficiently persuasive rhetoric. Writers had now the same significance as the early saints and church-builders, not least in that they could become martyrs through their authorship. Sermons and pamphlets by Campion and Persons had had 'dramatic effects' in 1580–81,[14] and Southwell, armed and equipped by Suárez and Bellarmine, was another such specialist in the making.

Here another chance intervenes: such works were under the scrutiny of the Society as transmitted through the local superior, in this case, initially, William Weston, who answered to his superiors in turn; but who was Weston's superior, and what was his agenda? This was becoming a confused picture. Cardinal Allen, the only senior Englishman in episcopal orders now able to speak for the English Catholics in Rome, was given faculties as 'Prefect of the English Mission', in 1581. Although subject to the Cardinal Protector in Rome, he was effectively the ecclesiastical superior until his death in 1594.[15] As an exiled priest, Allen was, like Robert Persons, closely involved in exile agendas, and regarded controversial works as useful in helping England's souls.[16] Persons was now chaplain superior to the English troops fighting in the Spanish Army, a post that could hardly claim to be neutral in these terms.[17] Two years into the Southwell–Garnet mission, on 5 November 1588, after the collapse of that year's Armada invasion, Persons was given charge of the Jesuits living in England too; Southwell was therefore struggling to hold a neutral course in England while his superior Persons was increasingly identified with Spain.[18]

Even without such confusing inward pressures, written production on mission was not a single, homogenous project, it is clear; Southwell, given the options of print or manuscript, wrote in various ways to fit messages to particular minds in particular circumstances.[19] Understanding this helps to explain the curious shifts in texture and quality of some of Southwell's poetry, elements that have made it seem puzzling, inconsistent, and even amateurish to the modern reader. This, an internal pressure of his own to conform a particular piece to a particular understanding and set of expectations is modified by an external pressure on the sort of author that Southwell was supposed to be – polemicist and reprover, or attractor and reconciler, or both at once. But whatever he was to his immediate readership was always mediated through whatever the Society seemed to be doing on the Continent. It would become increasingly difficult to separate the local pastoral agenda of, say, Southwell from the wider European agendas of, say, Persons, especially when the Spaniards finally set sail for England. Southwell's writing, even his lightest poetry, cannot be looked in isolation from such considerations: all choices of genre and style stand in relationship to these concerns. Southwell's printed English prose works, taking the form of pastoral letters to his virtual congregation, seem to flow between the two poles, without ever losing their basic pedagogic point. And though a printing press allowed access to a wider audience than that afforded by a spoken sermon, print was controlled by law, while poetry was not; and manuscript dissemination could allow confidences to be exchanged amongst sympathisers alert to subtextual meanings.

Southwell's manuscript production is in a less obviously confrontational register than his printed works; some poems seem to stand outside the parameters of Church discourse altogether. Despite Garnet's enthusiasm for 'numbers', when Southwell's poems finally appeared in print, it was not on Garnet's press, and it was with Catholic doctrine edited down to a minimum.

Southwell's professional output required the permission of his superior prior to going to press, but how much did his superior know of his manuscript poetry? Garnet became Southwell's superior soon after their arrival; he was keen to report their achievements in other things, yet never mentioned Southwell's poetry in his letters 'home' until after Southwell's execution, six years later.[20] When Garnet finally mentioned the poetry, one suspects that circumstances had forced his hand: his letter is of 1 May 1595, after Southwell's execution, and after the first appearance in print of his poetry. Wolfe's first, doctrinally neutral, edition of Southwell's poems had appeared in March, followed by a fuller version on 5 April.[21] Garnet's letter reads almost as a defence of Southwell's lightest lyrics, suddenly (and unexpectedly?) appearing in public alongside more devout ones; but Rome may have been surprised even by these, in their apparent doctrinal caution. Some of the lyrics are palpable hits on well-known courtiers, others play with the forms of amorous poetry, losing little of its fashionable eroticism. Just as the trend for satirical poetry was beginning, perhaps Southwell was writing such things to attract certain minds, in the Jesuit style of devout conversation, drawing them towards a place where they could be taught, rather than teaching *per se*. That casuistic hair's breadth between adaptability and opportunism was being explored by Southwell to the full in his poetry, it seems. Garnet, in his letter, insisted that Southwell had 'surpassed many profane authors and poets', demonstrating 'how they might turn their talent from lascivious to religious and serious subjects', as if anxious to emphasise the way the poetry fitted into accepted Jesuit pastoral methodology, despite its apparently unorthodox manner.[22]

The Jesuit press of St Omer eventually put out an 'official' posthumous edition of his poems (1616, and another in 1620), now altered towards more obviously Catholic doctrinal themes, arranged to emphasise their religious content. Although based in general on the 1602 text, the first part is based on 'St Peters Complaint', the second on the prose work, here called *Saint Mary Magdalens Funerall Teares*, with a selection of the shorter poems following each. Some titles are altered to clarify the plan ('Looke home' is retitled 'S. Peters Returne home'), and, twice, two poems are presented as one ('Scorne not the least' and 'Times goe by turnes', now titled 'Saint Peters Comfort'); 'Life is but Losse' becomes 'Saint Peters Wish'. The courtier-reproving poems, 'Lewd Love is Losse' and 'From Fortunes reach', become 'S. Mary Magdalens Traunce' and 'S. Mary Magdalens farewell' respectively.[23] These changes seem rather inappropriate to Southwell's own Magdalenic vision. One is an admonition to a sinner, reflecting a medieval Magdalen that Southwell left aside in favour of the warm lover; the other boasts a constant heart, but in rational tones inimical to Southwell's passionate personation. His poetic vision seems to sit oddly alongside this more official literary version, as if he had learned to utter his Catholicism in a slightly different language.

NEEDING A NEW SORT OF ENGLISH

There is no doubt that Southwell would need a new language register to reach into the English psyche, in the troubled circumstances of the English mission. When he was composing his text, what language did he think in? In the globally minded world of the Novitiate and the Roman College, he was forbidden anything but the universal language of Latin, even in his private daily intercourse.[24] He inhabited, for the best part of a decade, a world – a cosmos – defined and described in Latin, despite the occasional venture into the vernacular at Douai and the *Venerabile*. Poetry may be an emotional shorthand, but it is built of a vocabulaic abundance; a reduced vocabulary would not offer the refinements of choice necessary for the best building of imagery and structure; Herbert's English is pared to the bone, but it is not scant; and what complex articulations he achieves with it. Southwell, apparently aware of this necessity, practised in Rome to achieve an adult vocabulary and poetic fluency in his mother tongue, translating Latin and Italian passages into English. Although to-and-fro translation was standard practice in schools, there is a preponderance of simplified forms in Southwell's English unusual even for this period, when phonetic spelling was not uncommon. Single consonants and vowels appear in words where they are more commonly doubled; single vowels replace diphthongs; unpronounced letters are elided; there is the occasional loss of a final 'e', the alteration of 'i' and 'e' and sometimes 'o' and 'u'.[25] Southwell's little English was well taught; his regular writing and digesting of newsletters may also have given him a taste for elision and contraction. In an age which often admired *copie* for its own sake, he had been trained in especially concise communication, after all. The oddly condensed nature of Southwell's English, its quotidian vocabulary, and the decorous, alert simplicity that was so attractive to critics like Jonson and C. S. Lewis, might suggest that full adult fluency in English in the elaborate Sidneian style was never fully achieved by the youth who had last conversed freely in English at fourteen, and never attended an English university, and was therefore innocent of 'inkhorn' or university English. His reasons for using a contracted and plain English were therefore connected as much to his formation as an English user as to his agenda, that of reaching as many English souls as possible. So much for writing; but what language did he think in?

If he ever did think in English, it would be inflected with the controversialism of Allen's schools. Alexander Grosart, discussing fluency as an aesthetic issue, notes that the changes Southwell made to his 'Peeter Playnt', the earliest known version of his 'Saint Peters Complaint', translated from an Italian original, show a tendency to Anglicise and simplify the vocabulary and to improve the rhymes, changing 'avowe' to 'did boast' to rhyme with 'ghoast', or 'gryping griefe' to 'angry smart' to rhyme with 'hart'.[26] These changes actually serve to increase the muscularity and vehemence of the imagery, as if with the studied intention of emphasising its accusatory tone; the original, *Lagrime di San Pietro*, by Luigi Tansillo, was in part a meditation upon the failings of the Catholic Church and its ministers, and applicable to anyone tempted by apostasy, while a version in English had a more suggestive edge, as if addressing English churchmen who had rejected Roman Catholicism completely; or, in English, attacking the pastor who had most famously broken from the old faith, Luther – either way, a poeticised confrontation as much as a confession. It illustrates an intersection of Southwell's new Jesuit concept of pedagogical literature with robust controversialism, reflecting something of Southwell's understanding of the peculiarity of circumstances in England

Hidden ways and secret veins: into England

compared to other Jesuit missions, and an Allen-like belief in the efficacy of muscular vernacular debate: he had last used English as part of Allen's confrontational project, and it was in the English Colleges where he found the strongest feeling and the most robust polemic. If he thought in English, perhaps it was at first in confrontational mood. Southwell had written to Agazzari, Rector of the English College, after only a few months in England, asking that he send men fluent in English and trained in controversy rather than in theology.[27]

Croft's transcription, copied below, shows the poet struggling to pull the material round to his way of thinking. An elided 'n' is shown by a line over the preceding vowel; items in brackets represent material that has been erased; pointed brackets mark words caught in the later binding of the page:

     once to a minion bold   face
Thre seuerall tymes [twy]se by two hãdmades voyce
Next [once]to a mã last to that reuyl rout
[and last by meanes of that accursed crue]
 voucht   [adherent] he was not of the fold
he sed and swore [that he nere folower was] made his choise
    adherents never
of Chrysts whome he [denyed that he] knew
[to folowe Ch^ryst a man he neuer knew]
⟨But⟩ when
The cocke had blased out this [stubborne] brall
   in as thing
and brought [the] day for witnes of the cryme
        stubborn
[When as] the [wh] wretch scarse markying yet his fall
Did with his eies meete th'eies of Christ his king.[28]

The facsimile shows a crabbed and painful few verses of translation and adaptation into English; he used a 'mixed' hand in his Continental Latin poems and letters.[29]

These alterations in vocabulary speak of a new attitude to English, but the alterations he made to the narrative emphasis of the poem reveal something going on at a more fundamental level. Apart from showing that Southwell's poetry was deeply thought through, and not the outpouring of feeling that it is given, in some accounts, to be, this work-in-progress also shows his sensitivity to the uses of language that his Jesuit training had given him. Whatever language difficulties he encounters on his way to that last painful line, the line stands as a dramatic moment beyond language: *their eyes met*. The moment is sited at the centre of his long version as if at the fulcrum of Christian history. And how, he asks his reader, would your eyes meet those of Christ your King, right now, this moment? He is doing the work of that church imagery in Rome,

101

effectively presenting his reader with an icon of the piercing, all-knowing eyes of Christ and requiring him to meditate upon that steady gaze.

Now we see what he thought in, poetically at least – he thought in 'image'. Language was a servant of the images fixed in the memory of a divine original and of its history worked through the Bible; he is not looking for a linguistic explanation of Peter's panic and despair here, he is searching for ways of improving the image conjured up by the words. He is painting and over-painting the wet oil of a church depiction, reaching for a more affective presentation of the eyes, in this particular verse, which all the lines lead up to; just as he no doubt saw, while the college paintings were being made in one of the chapels in which he assisted, the artist – Circignani, perhaps – touch and retouch to capture that special look in the eyes of his central figure, Southwell is pushing his descriptive medium not towards producing the story, but the moment: one that shows, as did so many of those Roman paintings, a human being in the very middle of a crisis, the worst possible crisis imaginable to an ordinary Christian, that of meeting their Lord in a state of sin.

The celebrated missioner Francis Xavier took many icons and pictures into Asia, exporting the magic of image in order to sidestep linguistic handicaps;[30] Southwell, equally aware of their potential usefulness, brought their equivalent in metaphor. His understanding of the uses of *image*, as opposed to expository language, allowed him to circumvent those complexities of phrasing up in which other university men wound themselves, in English; Campion had tried to outface the heretics in clear argument, and failed. Southwell's dislocated English may have been in part responsible for his economical style, but his tutelage under Allen and Persons will have recommended such plainness to him for didactic reasons too, I would argue, and his training in the uses of truthful image will also have informed his work. Perhaps those who accuse him of failure to achieve Sidney's or Shakespeare's 'golden' qualities have missed a point about his own poetic intentions: perhaps he never intended to.

Apart from the magic of affective imagery, there was another Jesuit pastoral practice to which Southwell's poetry may be related: the public lecture. Jesuits attached to churches were expected to lecture as well as preach, the lecture, intended to attract minds and to stimulate thought, being a more relaxed affair.[31] These were important elements of Jesuit pastoral care, and Southwell in his English ministry will have looked for ways of fulfilling this duty, despite the difficulties. But Southwell, though faced with a disaffected generation, had no pulpit from which to preach them back into church. His poetry created for him a virtual space in which to give virtual lectures, a pedagogical structure from which to reach out to hearts and minds. Just as their painting cycles were an edifying programme of interlinked themes, so Jesuit public lectures were part of a series, and so Southwell's poetry was intended to be read as a self-administered programme of personal improvement. If his congregation could not attend Bellarmine's lectures, he would import them; and if printed copies of Bellarmine could be taken from their pockets, he would disguise it as poetry.

Like the lectures (even when on Scripture), Southwell's non-religious poetry was about the life of man, not the life of the Church, tending to be elaborations on a *pericope*. Southwell writes frequently on bearing tribulation, naturally; one poem elaborates in simple language upon the subject of Jonah in a way that relates the *pericope* to those who seem reluctant to speak up for their true faith ('Christs sleeping friends', p. 19). He had a celebrated precedent: the Jesuit Bobadilla gave forty lectures on the subject of Jonah in Naples in 1552.[32] The poems are arranged in subgroups which suggest a series on a particular theme – but the fact that they arrive to us as a single group, through the efforts of various publishers, does not mean that they were originally intended by the author to be read en bloc. Such an artificial grouping suggests false inconsistencies in form and tone, especially when compared to the sonnet cycles of Sidney or Shakespeare.[33]

Lectures could also be on topics from the catechism and 'cases of conscience' too, a content reflected in Southwell's poetry. These texts were used to demonstrate God's action in history, the redemption, and humanity's fallen state and need for grace, something Southwell was easily able to sharpen into specific commentaries within the troubled English arena.

His devotional series and longer works are better equated to the sermon, designed rather to move to higher religious sensibilities than to instruct: *Marie Magdalens Funeral Teares* was taken by several of Southwell's editors to be a saint's-day sermon delivered in one of the prisons that had become the recusant Church in England. Its history of proven popularity will have made the genre of the public lecture attractive to Southwell as texts for poetic treatment, and, as I say, all the above themes are echoed in his pious poetry, making it likely that he saw in poetry a part-replacement for the lecture in his ministry of the Word in England. The commons were forbidden access to the fruits of Bellarmine's influential lectures on post-Reformation Christianity, his new *Controversies* (1586) being banned along with other Catholic works; Southwell's poetry reproduces Bellarmine where the ordinary English can best access its arguments.

Southwell, in his manuscript production, was entering into a more private sphere of discourse, in response to the interests of both himself and the circle of young seminarians and noblemen's sons in which he moved in London. Garnet himself may have seen the pragmatic, door-opening possibilities of such poetic productions amongst a rising gentry hungry for novelties – and to counter Sidney's or Spenser's Protestant-inflected poetic influence was very much in the spirit of the mission. Garnet, often up-country,[34] was in a good position to disseminate such works as Southwell saw fit to give him, but not in a position to scrutinise every line of writing that left Southwell's hand; he may not have been fully aware of the exact nature of Southwell's poetry. Although his trust in his companion's judgement was considerable, it seems to have been disturbed by at least one of Southwell's later productions.

Garnet and Southwell were seldom together. Garnet seemed especially reluctant to stay in London for longer than absolutely necessary, begging Acquaviva to send a replacement after Southwell's arrest because 'I cannot live continually in London except at very great peril'.[35] In fact, Garnet admitted to being a 'hands-off' supervisor to the extent that Southwell suffered from lack of direction. Southwell's friends 'had often seen him in tears because his superior had never in his life given him a command or even counseled him'.[36] Southwell's tears were not for lack of a clear job: his task in London was to meet, house and manage incoming and outgoing Jesuits and seminarians, to produce texts for the edification of English Christians, and to keep as many influential London Catholics as possible onside, within the parameters of the Society, which were not as strait as some. Garnet seemed to read the tears as exhaustion – he was to send Southwell up-country more than once as if to give him a break from what must have been relentless and testing work.

After the sudden posthumous release of Southwell's poetry, Garnet alerted his superior general to the possibility that Southwell might seem 'fractious or obstinate', if only to deny it. 'I allowed him always to act as he himself thought best', Garnet wrote to his general in 1595, as if distancing himself from Southwell's concept of the mission, as it appeared formally in public for the first time, firstly in the manuscript 'letter' appealing directly to Elizabeth (*An Humble Supplication*) and then as his printed poetry.[37] Both of these were distinctly Bellarminean in flavour; Bellarmine's new theories of the relationships between papal and secular power, especially (touched upon to some extent in *An Humble Supplication*), were coming under scrutiny in Rome; Acquaviva, had he had prior access to those works showing the direction in which Southwell was heading, might have wondered at Garnet's leniency.

The response of Garnet and the Continental Jesuits to the dissemination of *An Humble Supplication* in 1592 certainly suggests that control and supervision was not absolute.[38] It seems likely that Southwell's manuscript production was, although never free from self-imposed restraint, freer from outside scrutiny than was usual, despite claims made by earlier critics; freer both in the means of its production or dissemination and in the fugitive nature of meaning in metaphoric form. His poetry was, therefore, stamped with the authority of his priesthood and his personal understanding of the various agendas of the English mission, as well as that of his superior. Persons had intended that the energetic, exacting Weston should be the superior; circumstances ensured that it was, in fact Henry Garnet, Bellarmine's 'little sheep'.

THE CATHOLIC CULTURAL NETWORK: SONGS AMONG SWORDS

From their arrival, the two missioners were quickly made aware of the place of the arts in English Catholic persistence, if not resistance. Weston, met with in London, set about introducing Southwell and Garnet to important and supportive Catholics. They were part of such a group on 22 July 1586, listening to Byrd's settings for the Latin liturgy, probably as guests of an old favourite of Leicester's, Richard Bold, at Hurleyford in Buckinghamshire (a conveniently cut-off ex-priory estate on the Thames, between Marlow and Medmenham).[39] This country-house circuit was to be the centre of the Jesuit support network in England, not the usual city society amongst which Jesuits preferred to move, but a virtual city on a hill, an English Jerusalem of the mind, which had already become influential in furthering Campion's post-Tridentine cultural projects.[40] Everything that was to happen in the cause of the Society was to happen within a nexus of such cultured minds, and in the conservative country houses of the shires that were only now undergoing the artistic renaissance that had been galvanising the Continent for a century or more; Rome's churches were filled with new music and glittering imagery, but that brilliance had come late to England.

The primary focus of the mission was to place priests in as many such English households as possible, turning them into virtual churches for the help and consolation of the wider community over which the household had influence. Along with the exiled Catholic communities on the Continent, this was the quiet network that held the Catholic church intact in England. Most of our older Catholic families have tales of young portrait artists, masters of revels, or schoolmasters arriving from the Continent around this time to visit the interconnected households of a particular area, ministering to their spiritual needs under guise of their assumed professions. Many of these households came to contain paintings of the sort Southwell knew in the public spaces in Rome, if less obviously Catholic in content: a priest could also be a painter, just as Southwell was also a poet. This was part of that hidden agency Southwell was importing: cultural activities were both a disguise for and a means of expressing their religion, an admixture of cultural, spiritual or aesthetic economics that now might seem suspect, a blurring of agendas and boundaries, but which would have seemed an elegant, succinct reflection of the interconnectedness of God and his universe to Renaissance minds, its hidden potency a reflection of divine immanence.

In this project they were remarkably successful, their network surviving even the dreadful Armada backlash of 1588. Garnet was able to tell his general in Rome a few years later that 'very many persons who barely saw a seminary priest once a year, now have one all the time and most eagerly welcome others no matter where they come from.'[41]

Weston was alive to the interest in the arts developing amongst the English aristocracy, and there was perhaps a growing appreciation of the importance of the leniency shown by Elizabeth to those Catholics, like Byrd, who would share their Continental innovations with her court without publicising their religious beliefs, or encouraging contumely amongst her subjects. Southwell's 'holy family' sequence of devotional poems or hymns, for instance, was entirely apposite to this project and seems written for a different community than his lighter lyrics, using 'our' and 'we' in connection with their Mariological mysteries, where the others tend to use the confessional 'I', or the accusative 'you' or 'they', and address faults and lacks.

It seems likely that Southwell brought English translations of Eucharistic hymns to dignify just such occasions, and probably aroused much sympathy and approval, his youthful willingness to devote his talents to the cause a sign of hope for the Catholics gathered there.[42] Some of the work on Mary Magdalen that Southwell had begun in Rome may also have been intended to make an appearance here, for, as he wrote to Acquaviva on 25 July, they were to sing Mass 'with all solemnity, accompanied by special instrumental and vocal music, on the feast of St. Mary Magdalene', 22 July. This was put off to the next day; as Southwell was called away, he was obliged to miss it.[43]

To underline the multi-stranded experience of Catholicism in England in these first months of the new mission, it is worth pointing out that all this cultural activity was going on in the middle of the Babington emergency, a time of considerable upheaval and danger amongst Catholic families.

Elizabeth's counsellors had allowed (perhaps encouraged) a group of Catholic idealists to condemn themselves in letters to the imprisoned Mary Stuart,[44] before swooping to arrest them in the first weeks of Southwell's arrival. He had come to build a virtual church at a time of virtual war. His first brush with pursuivants was as they hounded Catholic suspects in a London turned upside-down by the furore. He may have arrived with his pockets stuffed with poetry, but he had 'met with Catholics first amid swords', as he wrote to his general on 25 July.[45]

Father Weston had greeted them in the same inn in which he had met Babington earlier that day.[46] Babington was under covert observation by Walsingham – Southwell and Garnet's safety was hanging on a thread. The casual way in which the not inexperienced Weston combined the two meetings suggests that he had little idea of the lethal imbroglio being developed by other minds. Southwell seems to have become aware of the plot and its cruel ramifications at some level, however. In his first letter to Acquaviva (25 July 1586), he mentions 'a matter in hand, which if it prove successful, bodes extremity of suffering to us; if unsuccessful, all will be right'.[47]

Dinner over, Weston had escorted them west out of London to the recusant refuge where they met William Byrd.[48] Walsingham had failed to find the two newcomers for the moment, but, only thirteen days after their arrival, Weston was captured, on 4 August 1586.[49] He was in a London prison by 14 August, where he was woken by the bells at midnight pealing for the capture of Babington. After four days in the Tower, Babington confessed everything, and the Catholic queen was doomed.[50] The redoubtable Weston continued his missionary activities from various prisons for many years, despite failing health, refusing offers of being bailed to Europe.[51] Southwell's superior in England was now Garnet, with his sanguine hopes for the peaceful continuation of the mission.[52]

Weston's capture left Garnet and Southwell adrift. Garnet was now superior. He had once been apprenticed in the London print shop of Richard Tottel, invaluable early training for the printing of mission texts. Along with Weston in Rome, Garnet had studied under Bellarmine, Suárez, and the mathematician Christopher Clavius, who regarded him highly enough to consider him for a chair.[53] Garnet was interested in the sciences, but also in music, music and numbers being considered aspects of the same cosmic phenomenon, and, to many minds including the Jesuit, real manifestations of God's ineffable logic in the expression of his will.[54]

Apart from Garnet's passion for music and 'numbers' both poetical and mathematical, his political attitude itself, or lack of it, must have had some effect upon Southwell's poetic production. Garnet favoured devotional practices that could reach as wisely as possible. In pursuit of this, he was given special faculties to instruct English Catholics in the esotericisms of the Dominican Confraternity of the Rosary, encouraging them to engage in the revived programme of divine number-magic that it was believed had rescued the Church during the Albigensian crisis long ago.

In the preface of Garnet's first published English work on the power of the rosary he presses Catholics to pray for the intercession of the Virgin, obtaining from her 'a new rainbow, which being a sign of God, cannot signify falsely' (as perhaps a less heavenly Virgin's rainbow might?).[55] Mary as Mediatrix was a particularly Bellarminian preoccupation, and his concept of her free acceptance of God's will being a reversal of Eve's refusal of it is reflected directly in Southwell's 'The Virgins salutation' (M&B, p. 5).

Garnet, like many of his contemporaries, believed in the transferability of the real presence of divine power from things; the rosary or corona of Our Lady was the perfect expression of that belief.[56] Anne Dillon has described the complex interface between belief and practice represented by these beads, and shows how important this element of transferral of import through object was to the Catholics in England, in desperate need of aids to daily prayer but far from priests or chapels.[57]

This transferral of belief to object is reflected in Southwell's implication of his sacred purpose into his writing; or of the sacred content of church imagery into poetic metaphor; it may well have had expression too in his more complex geometrically constructed holy poetry such as 'Christs bloody sweat', discussed in chapter 7, not 'pattern poetry' as such, but runnels of meaning as reflections of divine–human interaction flowing up and down as well as side to side, like acrostics. This was the age that had rediscovered the Alexandrians; and the Jesuits, allowing the 'New Christians' – converted Spanish Jews – to enter the Society, will not have been ignorant of the cabala.[58] Such 'magic' piety could well have been written in response to this new scientific interest in the effects of divine power on the individual.

It seems from these preoccupations that, in response to Persons's apparent change of heart about the possibility of enforced renewal of Catholicism in England, the new English mission was to give emphasis less to the reimposition of Roman rule than to the revival of pious feeling, and the transmission of an ability to self-empower that would, it was to be hoped, make the renewal of Catholicism inevitable. Garnet was importing a portable chapel and chantry in his theory of the rosary; aimed at ordinary working English folk, those 'simpler sorte' believed by the missionaries to be most at risk from Protestant propaganda.[59] Garnet's *Rosary* was designed for the lay population, and, in its new Jesuit form, ideal for the use even of a person on the move, an important consideration when prayer was so often interrupted by the attentions of the pursuivants. It was an all-inclusive, popular form of religious observance that typifies to perfection the Jesuit approach to religious observation; that it should be doable, in preference to exact. These folk shall not, Garnet stresses, be excluded from their rights of conscience because of their status, their work, their gender, their infirmity:

> Neither the husband man in the fields, nor the travailer in his jorney, nor the labourer with his toiling, nor the simple by his unskilfulnes, nor the woman by her sex, nor the married by their estate, nor the sicke by their infirmitie, nor the poore for want of abilitie, nor the blind for want of sight, yea the Religious them selves of both sexes, att all times, and in all places, when they might want either bookes, or other ordinary helpes of spirite. (*Societie*, p. 35)

The casuistical approach to sin became clear in Garnet's manual, as he struggled to accommodate his ministry to the straitened circumstances of English Catholicism: if no chapel, a recusant house with an altar-stone would do; persons could be enrolled in the graceful and beneficial confraternity of the rosary even in their absence; interruption of the rosary incurred no sin: prayer could usually be resumed later; the dead could be enrolled posthumously by the living to ease their time in Purgatory, and the prerequisite state of grace in which the rosary was to be said could be assured, if no priest was available, by the knowledge of 'perfect sorrow and repentance, and stedfast purpose of amendment'.[60] Here the gentle reworking of the action of grace by men like

Suárez can be seen in application in response to the pressures of religious oppression; to ensure the access even of the illiterate, Garnet seems to have set up local 'cells of recusants' to deliver the information, just as the Jesuit schools devolved teaching on to older pupils in order to reach more souls; as Dillon says, it replaced the church fabric as an aid to prayer, with its visual cues: 'every devout Catholicke, dailye when he saieth his beades, doth as it were in a booke, read and reverentlye laieth before his eies, Christ our Saviour incarnat in his Mother, sanctifying John Baptist his holy Precursor, lying in a manger'.[61]

Garnet provided the virtual fabric and the liturgies, and Southwell offered the supporting 'visual' aids in his poetry, the rich fabric of words, paintings and emblem-books that he had known in his Roman life. As in the argument over whether or not his poetry was a reproduction of elements of the Exercises, I am suggesting not that he was reproducing aspects of the rosary directly, but that he was using affective imagery to put the mind of the reader in a sufficiently sensitive mood to make his or her prayers more effective, opening the eye of the heart, so to speak.

SOUTHWELL'S CONTACTS: PUBLIC VOICES, HIDDEN SELVES

Alongside the reputation for religious pragmatism that the Jesuits were beginning to attract, their changeable self-identifications were beginning to arouse doubt and suspicion in conservative and hostile minds. Just as Southwell adopted the physical disguise of a black-doubleted gentleman to carry the mission work to men of his own social standing, complementing Garnet's work with the commons, so he adopted a literary disguise. How many even of the Byrd set knew that the young lyricist was also a Jesuit priest? Resorting with Cottons in London, and probably going under the name of Cotton, he organised accommodation, funds and contacts.[62] In pursuit of this, he had disguised himself as what he would have been had he remained in England, an educated and literary gentleman of fashion, albeit one lacking a certain worldliness; physical disguise could not alter discoursal inadequacies.[63] Southwell had grown up a scholar, not a sporting country gentleman. Unlike his later co-missioner John Gerard, raised on estates in Catholic Lancashire, Southwell and many of the other Southern English Catholic youths who were sent abroad were growing up lacking the knowledge of country matters of their Protestant neighbours, still in full possession of their estates. Earthy talk and sporting jargon were becoming signifiers of being 'one of us', and not knowing 'a hawk from a handsaw', as Hamlet put it (II.2.381), was a dangerous signifier of strangeness. Southwell had to ask Gerard for schooling in the unfamiliar vocabulary of hawks, horses and hounds – the only way, he said, to turn the talk in the inn away from masculine pursuits even less familiar to the young priests.[64] It was in this risky, unreliable arena of identity and dissimulation that Southwell had to abide for as long as he could in England, disguising himself as a gentleman-poet to disguise his authorship of secular, moral, lyric English poetry. These practical methods of sidestepping the impositions and shifts of the English establishment, graceful as was their intent, were what began to earn the Jesuits the reputation of religious opportunism amongst their opponents.[65]

The protective camouflage adopted by Southwell enabled him to go into dangerous territory in pursuit of souls. 'I have sometimes been to call on Protestant Sheriffs to look after secret Catholics in their households', Southwell wrote, 'and they, seeing my fine clothes and my bevy of aristocratic youths, and suspecting nothing so little as the reality, have received me with imposing ceremony and truly sumptuous banquets'. One trusts he supped with a long spoon, but can only sympathise with his pleasure at these convivial country-house suppers, in the midst of a sparkling coterie, which he piously glosses in his report as 'trick[ing] the Wicked One with his own snares and enticements'.[66]

Southwell was now a cipher, an 'o' that could contain and obscure almost any meaning. Although information about the Jesuits' activities was being amassed by Burghley from the moment Southwell arrived in summer 1586, the most vital piece, the actual appearance of Southwell and the firm identification between the physical man and the Jesuit, was not known until 25 May 1591, five years after his arrival in England.

For five years, therefore, Southwell's identity was largely an abstract, purely ideological one, mouldable according to predilections or fears: that of an attractive familiar or an invisible oppositional force; this was part of the power of the hidden that the ghostly father used to the full. Knowing which way the wind was really blowing but hiding that knowledge, being 'mad north-north-west' but sane southerly-wise, is as good a metaphor as any for Southwell's position, and that of many other scions of English Catholic families (Hamlet, II.2.380). Any writer of human drama who had witnessed one of the State's hostile readings of such 'semantics of identity', such as the execution of Father Gunter at Shoreditch, would be struck by the gross heroics and apparent futility of such a fight. It seems likely that this struggle for a self-definitive language, a system of signs that acknowledges and expresses the self-knowing rather than the subjected self, grew out of the struggles in which all literary Englishmen were embroiled in the last decades of the century, one which seems to have been most neatly embodied in the person and the *Exercises*-informed training of Southwell, a resisting Sebastian to Shakespeare's reconciling Viola; two distinct individuals in one form, inseparable yet entirely different – an inspired English gentleman-poet and an angel-aided Roman Catholic Jesuit priest.

But this duality was largely, whilst he was alive and unrecognised as a Jesuit, a potential dichotomy only. Being for the moment indistinguishable from the myriad other black-doubleted second and third sons dining their way around their relatives' country houses, he had an opportunity to renew and widen his acquaintance amongst the aristocratic youth of Elizabethan England. Devlin pays much attention to Southwell's countrywide travels, including the young Southampton in this coterie. He also notes spy reports from men such as Robert Poley and Richard Baines which speak of 'a new writer [in London] who was stealing the affections of promising patrons and reawakening sympathy with the old religion'.[67] All Southwell's biographers have accepted the likelihood that his activities and connections gave him entry to some of the highest households in the land; he disseminated his poetry as an English gentleman-poet, and it would be very difficult to believe that his innovative English style and the delicacy and strength of his moral convictions, not to mention his noble connections, did not make an impact, to some extent, upon other ambitious writers.[68]

It is possible that 'Mr. Cotton' allowed it to be known among some that he was a Catholic priest – part of his job was to give spiritual ministry to English Catholics in fear of their souls for lack of it, and it is hard to see how he could have hidden that aspect of himself entirely. 'I am determined', he wrote, 'never to desist from the works of my calling, though the works, when done, cannot long escape their notice.'[69] It is unlikely that he would have advertised himself a Jesuit, especially after the evident animosity of some other Englishmen in Rome.

Even given the polemic informing such accounts, by the last decade of the century, anti-Jesuit views had taken hold in England. Sitting in disguise listening to such animadversions, as he no doubt did at least once, Southwell's self-esteem may have suffered – as an English Catholic seminary priest prepared to come to the assistance of his Catholic countrymen he would have been lionized in many circles (Garnet described to Acquaviva the eager welcome such ministers, passed on from the Continent through his and Southwell's safe houses, were now receiving) – but if he was discovered to be a *Jesuit* he could expect less welcome in some English Catholic households, a prickly position for one who was risking his all for their sake.[70] Only during the rare weeks away with his brother-missioners could he have allowed himself a moment's relaxation from the dissembling, disguised life he was now locked into, and take the only opportunity to celebrate his Jesuitism amongst his Society brothers. The Jesuits' internalised bond of loyalty must at times have been becoming painfully stretched.

Southwell's letters to his father general Claudio Acquaviva suggest much of this existence; the rest is built up from various reports and accounts. He was given a taste of pursuivancy almost on arrival, as his temporary home (that of William, third Baron Vaux of Harrowden, in Hackney, perhaps) was raided in the wake of the Babington plot in summer 1586, and he had to lie

Robert Southwell

for days in his clothes 'in a very strait, uncomfortable place', but Southwell by and large seems to have maintained a fairly ordinary, if dissembling, existence.[71] As Brown has shown, early biographical accounts of a life spent in secrecy and isolation are only partially accurate, according to Garnet's letters from July 1586 to May 1595.[72] His letters show that he was actively engaged in missionary work, based in London but travelling into the country at times during this five-year period; they allow us a view of Elizabethan England seen from a much wider angle than the chink in a priest-hole, especially in the reports to Rome. Where one might have expected Garnet alone to take the risk of writing, as superior, in fact Acquaviva asked both men to report on local conditions without either at first knowing; the letters provide a valuable view of 1580s England from outside the pale.[73]

Southwell was clearly aware of the sensitivity and difficulty of the position of ordinary English Catholics but, as a Jesuit, he was coming not just to console them but to bring fire to those who held responsibility for them, the English Catholic aristocracy. He aimed to make changes in individual lives that would add up, in the end, to a change in the nation's way of living.

He wrote poems such as 'Joseph' for those he recognised as virtually helpless, but for those closer to government he wrote differently, seeking out those men and women he thought would be of use in his mission, an odd parallel to a secular poet seeking an influential patron. Perhaps freed by his secular disguise to follow the other poets in courting upcoming young courtiers such as Wriothesley, none the less, Southwell's 'official' patron, Philip Howard, Earl of Arundel, was chosen for his position as the new leader of the English Catholic faithful; as one of the highest nobles in the land, who had recently confirmed his Catholic faith, he was a great prize. Southwell never actually met him – he was currently in close confinement, presenting an imposing image of suffering nobility to the country and to Europe.

Philip's grandfather Henry Howard, Earl of Surry, wrote and translated Petrarchan sonnets, and a translation of Virgil's *Aeneid* in blank verse, a poetic novelty in England at the time. Some of his verse, like Wyatt's, can be read as protest poetry.[74] Southwell's connections with the old Catholic families of Vaux and Howard gave him quick access to the poetic tradition of the '"courtly makers" as represented in the works of Baron Vaux';[75] it would also have put him into that group of courtly Catholic compromisers that Heywood had been sidelined for favouring. Such masked commentaries on State affairs were circulated in manuscript form amongst an elite group who recognised the references and could read the subtext, a discourse that Southwell was to make the most of. The very position of the country house relative to Court echoed the Virgilian state of rustication and pastoral concerns as protest against central misrule: Southwell used both the geographically remote and culturally important place of such houses in his ministry.

Hidden ways and secret veins: into England

When Southwell arrived in England, then, Philip was living out the same drama of the poet-courtier in chains as his grandfather Henry, and some of Southwell's writing can be seen as a means of reinforcing that connection, working through in poetic or dramatic form the spiritual doubts that Southwell forbad the Earl himself to succumb to: David in chains; the rusticated courtier examining his conscience in affective soliloquy from behind bars; the fear and anguish of helplessness and imprisonment, yet the acceptance of it as a deservedly harsh working out of God's will, as in 'The Prodigall child', who accepts his chains in the 'dungeon of despaire' as proof of 'Gods deserved [justified] ire' (lines 58, 24). This affective exposition of suffering Catholicism can be seen to relate to Southwell's role as comforter and guide to the English congregation as well his role as chief propagandist to sympathisers in Europe, carried out via Richard Verstegan, his Continental contact.[76]

Southwell's visits to the household of Anne Dacres, Lady Arundel, wife of the lately imprisoned Philip Howard, Earl of Arundel, are taken by his biographers to show that he acted as family chaplain. It was in part under Philip's aegis that Southwell's works were at first printed, under the noses of the State authorities, any emergent notion of ideological censorship seemingly giving way to feudal precedence even in the 1580s. Whatever the reason for its continued existence, some sort of printing facility certainly existed, and Weston, Southwell, and the other Jesuits had access to it. There is mention of a secret press operating from one of the Arundel houses in the 1588 'Marprelate' pamphlet *An Epistle to the Terrible Priests of the Convocation House*.[77] 'Why set you not that printing press and letters out of Charterhouse, and destroye them as you did Walde-graves? Why did you not apprehend the parties? Why?'.[78] Fondness for popery is the suspected reason, but it may have been an official's fear of giving offence to a great lord by ordering his house to be invaded by common catchpolls.[79]

The Howards, both the imprisoned Earl and his wife, freer now to follow her own conscience in some ways, were demonstrably powerful patrons, therefore, and certainly worth cultivating in literary as well as theological works. Southwell's early understanding of the place of the influential and wealthy benefactress in the formation of his own Society may well have alerted him to the importance of making good connections with Anne.[80] Southwell wrote devotional tracts for the Earl, designed ostensibly to keep Philip from wavering from the Roman Catholic faith he had recently reaffirmed, but directed beyond this idealised reader to a much wider constituency.[81]

It seems clear that the dissemination of printed work was by no means as controlled or as ideologically consensual a process as some commentators have preferred to suggest; after all, many of the churchmen on opposite sides of the Reformation had shared the same benches in university.[82] Connections with men of influence could almost neutralise religious difference. Southwell and Garnet were alive to the danger of anti-Catholic propaganda, and desperate to disseminate their own side of the debate, but it was becoming increasingly difficult; the shield of such a patron was invaluable. But even given the patchy nature of early modern censorship in England, it might seem odd in retrospect that an ecclesiastical licence was obtained for Southwell's *Saint Peters Complaint*, especially as this licence was granted even though possession of the work had been used as evidence of recusancy in 1594.[83] Southwell's *Marie Magdalens Funeral Teares* was actually printed by John Wolfe for Gabriel Cawood 'under the hand of the Archbishop of Canterbury', appearing as such in the *Stationers' Register* on 8 November 1591.[84] In 1592 (the year of Southwell's capture), *Marie Magdalen* appears again, by the same; and in 1594 (Southwell now imprisoned and under interrogation as a known 'traitor') we see *Marie Magdalen* again, printed this time by Abel Jeffes for Gabriel Cawood. Southwell's Jesuitism, at least, was no longer part of what the texts concealed, and they still sold, just as the manuscripts spread widely and quickly.[85] All of these were licensed while Southwell was still alive, and actively connected with what the State considered to be dangerous subversion.

Southwell's sensitivity to possibilities of forwarding his interests were those of both an early modern younger son of the nobility and of a Jesuit; his use of manuscript poetry is part of that sensitivity and purpose. His dedications to his noble patron(s) and the care with which he met their aristocratic family needs with works sympathetic to their interests (such as consolations for unexpected deaths, and polite exhortations) all point towards the patron system in which he wished to place his printed work. Southwell was widely influential 'amongst Catholic families of great distinction' and his poems found their way into many commonplace books.[86] His short lyrics were distributed, not surprisingly, in anonymised manuscript form, but he had priestly tracts printed on the private Arundel press, or on a press set up by Father Weston in Essex and inherited by Garnet, under the name Whalley or Walley.[87] Illicit printers could receive the death penalty:[88] Garnet's and Southwell's promise to enter into the royal ports of self-sacrifice were not theoretical, therefore, and it was as a result of such public activities that both men eventually did so.

What was hidden in Southwell's poetry was not his Jesuitism, in the end, but something far more valuable to his wider English readership, and his efforts to describe it and stimulate its effects lie at the beginnings of our modern English poetic heritage. He was repeating a truth discovered in Rome, one linking the mystery of the Mass with human realities: that great secrets could lie hidden in simple things. The redemptive action of Christ Incarnate is rain hidden in a little cloud, or, more pragmatically, the action of Christ in history is the day's work of a Jesuit missioner. In the Roman church paintings Jesuit heroism was hidden from the public, enfolded in depictions of early Christian saints; a painted angel could represent the real angels that certain Jesuits had seen attending their masses, or encompass messages about Christian militarism, and even Spanish imperialism, and apocryphal revelation, as did the cult of the Seven Archangels.[89]

Southwell, fuelled by the meaning-charged beauties he had seen in Rome and trained in post-Trentine affectivity and dramatic realism, internalised and given voice by the Ignatian *Exercises*, comprehended those inner-space baroque beauties with a fullness that no lay English poet could match. Into the cerulean spaces between the biblical figures and their divine machinery he was able to paint a new angel, a partly self-engendered creative spirit that brought a simply expressed but passionate moral intensity into English poetry. The importance of the *Exercises* in this context is not just that they were a way into the empyrean through the power of visual memory, offering insights into psychological states, but that, in the vital discourse they created between director and exercisant, they necessitated the translation of vision and feeling into uttered language. This was Latin, in Southwell's case; he may not have been so emotionally fluent in English, but he none the less had a powerful tool in his English mission of words. He had that new vocabulary of emotional feeling, verbally or in writing expressed on a daily basis throughout his novitiate, in which to express the inner man. As if carrying some of that blue Roman sky into the English gloom, he also had his glittering visual imagery, icons carried in his head from Rome, with their refining captions and glosses, their complex, multilayered meanings ready to be poured out direct into the reader's affections, that 'boundlesse sea [...] in a little cloude', as Southwell put it ('Of the Blessed Sacrament of the Aulter', p. 26, l. 60).

Martz's argument that Southwell graced his poetry as well as supporting his spiritual strength with the technique is convincing, even if it cannot be shown that Southwell replicated the *Exercises* in his poetry. Why would he wish to? To his fellow Jesuits, the effect of the *Exercises* on the heart was beyond the artifice of rhetoric; to his fellow poets, it may have been a revelation of half-hidden methods and possibilities, a new language for deep feeling, as well as a way of legitimising, even sacralising, the newly popular creative principle of poetic frenzy, once a purely pagan concept. Southwell's own struggles to find a language in which to express the 'strange effects' he imported with his poetry offered, I would argue, suggestive possibilities to other English poets looking for a language sensitive to the individual psychology. Southwell's English mission stretched from realising the wounds of Christ for himself to empowering a new sort of creativity in others. The most obvious inheritor of this new language for invisible effects was not Donne but Herbert. In the series of metaphors he gives for 'Prayer', for instance, he seems to be directly addressing the question implicit in Southwell's poetry, even searching for ways of describing that new, inhabitable space. Those 'Angels giftes' of Southwell's become 'Angels age, | Gods breath in man returning to his birth | The soul in paraphrase'. Herbert's first school was Southwell's compact, athletic vision of what plain English could achieve through metaphor to express the vast inexpressibles of humanity's communication with the divine. It was surely Southwell's attempts to find a language for those 'strange effects' that prompted the cosmic plangency of Herbert's 'Reversed thunder, Christ-side-piercing spear'; 'Church-bels beyond the stares heard [...] something understood'.[90]

NOTES

1 Robert Southwell, 'Man to the wound in Christs side', in James H. McDonald and Nancy Pollard Brown (eds), *The Poems of Robert Southwell, S.J.* (Oxford: Clarendon Press, 1967), p. 72; hereafter M&B; further references to Southwell's poetry are from this edition, given as page/line numbers in the text.

2 See Scott Pilarz, S.J., *Robert Southwell and the Mission of Literature 1561–1595: Writing Reconciliation* (Aldershot: Ashgate, 2004), p. 21; hereafter cited in the text.

3 Christopher Devlin, *The Life of Robert Southwell Poet and Martyr* (London: Longmans, Green, 1956), p. 99; Philip Caraman, S.J., *A Study in Friendship: Saint Robert Southwell and Henry Garnet* (Saint Louis, MO: The Institute of Jesuit Sources, 1995), pp. 9–10; F. W. Brownlow, *Robert Southwell*, Twayne's English Authors Series, 516 (New York: Simon & Schuster Macmillan, 1996), n. 13, p. 137; all hereafter cited in the text. Devlin believes the recipient to be Southwell's friend John Deckers; Brownlow prefers Acquaviva, in my view the more likely option.

4 Agazzari was writing to Acquaviva on the death of the benefactor of the cycle, George Gilbert, in 1583; Gauvin Alexander Bailey, *Between Renaissance and Baroque: Jesuit Art in Rome, 1565–1610* (Toronto: University of Toronto Press, 2003), p. 160; hereafter cited in the text.

5 Ibid., pp. 163, 165.

6 See Garnet's report to Acquaviva in Caraman, pp. 14–15; hereafter, dates are by the English calendar unless otherwise noted.

7 Quoted in Caraman, p. 15. A drama about the anomaly of the dates as proof of England's departure from cosmic orderliness, *Brevis Dialogismus*, was produced at the Jesuit seminary at St. Omer in 1599; see Victor Houliston, '*Brevis Dialogismus*: an Anonymous Becket Play from the Jesuit Seminary at St Omer', *English Literary Renaissance*, 23 (1993), 382–427. Also see Dana F. Sutton's Introduction to a later Jesuit play, *Minutum*, on www.philological.bham.ac.uk/minutum/intro.html.

8 Caraman, p. 15.

9 *Calendar of State Papers, Domestic Series, of the Reign of Elizabeth, 1581–1590*, ed. Mary Anne Everett Green (London: Longmans, 1865), vol. 18, no. 21; hereafter *CSP*; and CXCI no. 35; Southwell's letter to his father General on 25 July 1586 mentions this too. John Hungerford Pollen (ed.), *Unpublished Documents Relating to the English Martyrs*, Publications of the Catholic Record Society Series, 5 (London: Catholic Record Society, 1908), p. 308; hereafter CRS; quoted in Pierre Janelle, *Robert Southwell the Writer: A Study in Religious Inspiration* (London: Sheed and Ward, 1935), p. 38; hereafter cited in the text; Caraman, p. 9.

10 This via a missive from Mary Stuart's Paris agent Thomas Morgan to Gilbert Gifford which had been handed by Gifford to Phelippes for deciphering. Letter dated 3 July 1586; Devlin, pp. 98, 109; M&B, p. xxix.

11 M&B, p. xix.

12 Devlin, p. 52.

13 Despite their letters going via the diplomatic privilege of the Spanish Embassy, Caraman notes that it was ten years before Garnet dared mention the press's existence in a letter to Rome, and then only after the press was finally seized; Caraman, pp 28, 35; see also Devlin, pp. 151–2, Brownlow, p. 11.

14 Brownlow, p. 11.

15 Michael E. Williams, *The Venerable English College Rome: A History 1579–1979* (London: Associated Catholic Publications (on behalf of the College), 1979), pp. 10–11.

16 Texts of this sort were produced from the presses in the Low Countries throughout this period, precisely the sort of thing that the missioners themselves were forbidden to produce. Persons, as Nancy Pollard Brown notes, also produced works of Christian piety from these same presses. Nancy Pollard Brown, 'Robert Southwell: the Mission of the Written Word', in Thomas M. McCoog, S.J. (ed.), *The Reckoned Expense: Edmund Campion and the Early English Jesuits* (Woodbridge: Boydell, 1996), pp. 193–214 (p. 196); hereafter 'Mission'.

17 John Bossy, 'The Heart of Robert Persons', in McCoog (ed.), *The Reckoned Expense*, pp. 141–58 (pp. 154–5).

18 Francisco de Borja Medina, S.J., 'Intrigues of a Scottish Jesuit at the Spanish Court: Unpublished Letters of William Crichton to Claudio Acquaviva (Madrid 1590–1592)', in McCoog (ed.), *The Reckoned Expense*, pp. 215–98 (pp. 218–19).

19 The part-absorption of local art forms and customs was recognised by the Jesuits as useful means of attraction; it is within the remit of a Jesuit mission as generally understood at the time to absorb the local culture, up to a point, and Southwell would have done so in England, as his brothers did elsewhere. There are, as Peter Davidson points out, 'the brocade-clad, arquebusquier angels of Cuzqueño painting', products of 'a culture based upon a fusion between the international Baroque traditions of metropolitan Spain and indigenous American traditions', in Peter Davidson, Professor D. A. Brading (University of Cambridge), et al., 'Festivals of the New World: the Viceroyalties of Mexico and Peru', in J. R. Mulryne, Helen Watanabe-O'Kelly, and Margaret Shewring (eds), *Europa Triumphans, Court and Civic Festivals in Early-modern Europe* (Aldershot: MHRA in association with Ashgate, 2004), II, pp. 345–9. Valignano instructed the missioners in China to learn Chinese and gain respect at Court by translating the Confucian classics into Latin, dressing as Buddhist monks, even finding Confucian concepts that matched their ideas of God. The Royal Academy's Exhibition, 'China: The Three Emperors 1662–1795' (2005–6), included an exquisite painting of two young men almost indistinguishable in style from Chinese works (although it includes perspective), by a celebrated court artist, Lang Shining (the Jesuit Giuseppe Castiglione 1688–1766). For a discussion of this flexible approach to 'other' cultures, see John W. O'Malley, S.J., Gauvin Alexander Bailey, et al. (eds), *The Jesuits: Cultures, Sciences, and the Arts 1540–1773* (Toronto: University of Toronto Press, 1999), especially Part Four, 'Encounters with the Other: Between Assimilation and Domination', pp. 333–438, and Andrew C. Ross, 'Alessandro Valignano: The Jesuits and Culture in the East', pp. 336–51 (p. 343).

20 See Caraman, p. 118.

21 *Saint Peters Complaint, With other Poemes* (Wolfe 1595a and Wolfe 1595b, both catalogued STC 22957); M&B, pp. lix, lviii.

22 Quoted in Caraman, p. 118. Southwell's Jesuit ministry was intended to encompass a broad range of approaches. John O'Malley describes their development of John Colet's idea of the 'sacred lecture' for the laity; its features bring it closer to Southwell's poetic activity than does the Jesuit habit of poetry on its own – poetry was used in situ in the Jesuit college to enhance some occasion, while a lecture, like the dramatic productions to which it is also affiliated, addressed a public audience from a less formal position in the church or beyond. The Jesuits defined these lectures as being 'directed to devout living' rather than formal exercises in theology or doctrine – 'an adaptation of this material to the questions and need of ordinary folk', as O'Malley puts it, which must be 'clearly distinguished from lectures on books of the Bible intended for a university audience', such as those given by Luther (p. 105); O'Malley, pp. 105–7.

23 M&B, p. lxxvii.

24 Ibid., p. xix. Southwell's Latin poetry can be seen in Peter Davidson and Anne Sweeney (ed. and intro.) *The Collected Poems of S. Robert Southwell, S.J.* (Manchester: Carcanet, forthcoming).

25 Brown discusses this aspect of Southwell's English at some length, describing Southwell's surviving English holograph pages as 'a rare record of a poet's training in his language'; see M&B, pp. xix–xxii. Brownlow notes that Brown was probably unaware of a Latin original of *Marie Magdalens Funeral Teares* and wrongly assumed that Southwell was having to translate ideas back into Latin to make his English 'work', when what he was doing was translating an existing piece from Latin into English (M&B, p. xxi; Brownlow, p. 36). See Davidson and Sweeney, 'Introduction to the Text'.

26 Alexander B. Grosart (ed.), *The Complete Poems of Robert Southwell, S.J.* (London: Robson, Fuller Worthies' Library, 1872), p. lxxxv; hereafter cited in the text; M&B, p. 103.

27 In general, I would argue, the two missioners thought in 'Roman'; a combination of Italian as the city's vernacular and Latin as the language of their career and office. Garnet's letter to Rome describing his arrival on mission with Southwell in 1586 mentioned feeling exposed by his foreign-sounding English; Caraman, p. 16, and M&B, p. xx.

28 Transcription from the holograph manuscript of 'Peeter Playnte', Stonyhurst College MS. Anglia. v. 4, fol. 50, in Croft, *Autograph Poetry*, p. 12. Also see Grosart's version (slightly different), pp. 217–18; McDonald and Brown's frontispiece carries a facsimile, and see their discussions in Appendix I, p. 173, and p. lxxxvi. See also the text alongside its Italian source in Mario Praz, 'Robert Southwell's "Saint Peters Complaint" and Its Italian Source', *Modern Language Review*, 3 (July 1924), 273–90. It is also reproduced in Davidson and Sweeney.

29 I am grateful to Peter Davidson for his work on the manuscripts in preparation for his edition of Southwell.

30 Bailey, '"Le style jésuite n'existe pas": Jesuit Corporate Culture and the Visual Arts', in *The Jesuits*, pp. 38–89 (p. 38).

31 O'Malley, p. 106.

32 O'Malley, pp. 106–7.

33 Brown, p. xciii; I agree with Brown's argument for the existence of a 'matrix' of lyrics from which all printed editions are taken, which was then collected by 'an associate' after Southwell's arrest and bundled up as one group, Brown, p. lxxi; Brownlow points out that the existence of supplementary lyrics in other manuscript collections suggests that Southwell did not release all at once, p. 76. The Jesuit rhetorical or strategic practice of adapting the message to the time, place, and circumstance also argues for dissemination of parts of his poetic canon to various people, for various reasons. No informed discussion on this point is possible, without new information on ownership of his manuscripts; see M&B, p. xxxv.

34 See Brownlow, p. 9.

35 Garnet to Acquaviva, 8 October 1592, in Caraman, pp. 88–9.

36 Caraman, p. 117; Caraman puts the tears down to Southwell's lack of self-confidence, and consequent assumption that his superior did not trust his virtue enough to give him set tasks, although Southwell seems to have been fully aware of his job in London, and to have fulfilled it well.

37 Garnet to Acquaviva, 1 May 1595, quoted in Caraman, p. 117.

38 See chapter 7, p. 254 below; also see Pilarz, p. 238.

39 Brownlow, p. 35. Byrd's 'Psalms, Sonets, and Songs of Sadness and Piety, [...] did more than anything to preserve the medieval lyric in English poetry; and it was probably with his help that Southwell first became acquainted with contemporary English verse in its current manuscript form', Devlin, pp. 114–15. See also Caraman, pp. 20–1.

40 See Brownlow, pp. 10–11.

41 Garnet to Acquaviva, 16 April 1596, Stonyhurst, Anglia, II, 16; in Caraman, p. 37.

42 Caraman proposes that Garnet sang Byrd's Three Masses at Hurleyford, p. 23.

43 Letter to Acquaviva, 25 July 1586, CRS, 5, p. 309, quoted in Caraman, p. 25; for Brownlow's rejection of Devlin's belief that Southwell was at Marshalsea Prison preaching a sermon on Magdalen to an audience including the daughters of Sir John Arundell on 22 July, see p. 35.

44 Wormald, p. 189.

45 Southwell to Acquaviva, 25 July 1586, CRS, 5, p. 307, in Caraman, pp. 18–19.

46 Caraman, p. 20.

47 See John Hungerford Pollen, S.J., 'Father Robert Southwell and the Babington Plot', *The Month*, 119 (1911), 302–4, quoted in Brownlow, p. 141, n. 15; see also Devlin, p. 248.

48 Caraman, p. 20; Devlin, pp. 114–15.

49 Brownlow, pp. 35, 11.

50 Caraman, p. 18.

51 Ibid., pp. 44–6.

52 See his letter to Acquaviva, July 1588, quoted by Devlin, p. 161; see also Caraman, pp. 51, 65, 83.

53 Caraman, pp. 6–7.

54 Devlin, pp. 90–1.

55 Roy Strong accepts the general scholarly consensus that Elizabeth's 'rainbow portrait'

was commissioned by Robert Cecil in about 1600; it is quite possible that this was in riposte to Catholic imagery such as that disseminated by Garnet. Strong describes battles for Elizabeth's imagery between Protestants and Catholics in France in 1583 and 1587, and discusses Elizabeth's own attempts to control her emblematic appearance; in *Gloriana: The Portraits of Queen Elizabeth I* (London: Pimlico, 2003), pp. 157, 34.

56 Henry Garnet, *The Societie of the Rosary, wherein is conteined the beginning, increase & profit of the same. Also the orders and manifold graces annexed unto it, with divers other things thereunto appertaining* (n.p.d. [London, 1593–94]), preface; hereafter *Societie*; in Caraman, pp. 67–8.

57 Dillon, pp. 457, 463–4.

58 O'Malley, pp. 188–92.

59 Dillon, pp. 463–4.

60 *Societie*, p. 57; Dillon, pp. 466–9.

61 *Societie*, p. 39.

62 Southwell resorted to the Fleet Street house of a 'Mr. George Cotton of Farringdon (Robert's old friend, or a cousin of the same name)', according to Devlin, p. 215; see also p. 220; see Janelle, p. 64.

63 See Janelle, p. 38.

64 John Gerard, *The Autobiography of an Elizabethan*, trans. and ed. Philip Caraman, S.J. (London: Longmans, Green, 1951), quoted in Caraman, pp. 60–1; also see Devlin, p. 208, Janelle, p. 38.

65 Southwell took this effort a stage further, beginning to present Englished versions of the 'cases of conscience' and equivocation that he had been studying in Rome both in poetry and prose. This seems to have taken the more cautious Garnet aback. Certainly Brown notes that he was 'so chary about the dissemination of a work on equivocation by Southwell that he could not find a copy in 1598 and was forced to write a defence himself, a treatise that was circulated in manuscript', 'Mission', pp. 196–7. Michael Questier opens his account of the Society by quoting Robert Tynley's warning about the Jesuits' 'capacity to transform "themselves into as many shapes as they meet with objects", "now a Courtiour, then a Cittizen; here a countrie Gentleman; there a countrie Swaine: sometimes a Servingman; a swaggerer, Pot-companion; another while [even] a Priest"'. This was to carry out that central Jesuit programme of conforming the thing to the circumstance, in order to help souls; or, if you sat on the other side of the divide, to insinuate themselves into their company to 'beguile them unawares'; see Michael Questier, '"Like Locusts over All the World": Conversion, Indoctrination and the Society of Jesus in Late Elizabethan and Jacobean England', in McCoog (ed.), *The Reckoned Expense*, pp. 265–84 (p. 265).

66 Letter, 28 December 1588, quoted in Devlin, p. 182; also see Caraman, p. 50.

67 Devlin, pp. 180–5, p. 223.

68 Janelle, pp. 54–7; M&B, pp. xxv, xxix; Caraman, p. 27.

69 Letter to Acquaviva of 21 December 1586, quoted in Caraman, pp. 38–9.

70 Garnet to Acquaviva, 16 April 1586, Stonyhurst, Anglia II, 16, quoted in Caraman, p. 37.

71 Southwell, Letter of 21 December 1586, in CRS, V, p. 313; in Brownlow, p. 10.

72 'The outline of an administrative structure within which the priests undertook vigorous

Hidden ways and secret veins: into England

pastoral work in their allotted area is now clear', M&B, p. xxv.

73 Garnet reports on his administration in a letter to Acquaviva of 9 June 1588, two months before Southwell reported the executions of Frs Gunter and Leigh.

74 See, for instance, 'Th'Assyrians' king, in peace with foul desire | And filthy luste that stained his regal heart'; in Dennis Keene (ed.), *Henry Howard Earl of Surrey: Selected Poems* (Manchester: Carcanet, 1985), p. 60. In his version of Psalm 55, Surrey is taken by his editor to be referring to Robert's grandfather Sir Richard Southwell, 'his accuser and former friend' when he translates the lines 22-3: 'It was a friendly foe, by shadow of goodwill, | Mine old fere and dear friende, guide, that trappèd me'. These lines must have resonated painfully with the imprisoned Earl. They seem to be echoed again in Peter's outcry against his false guide in Southwell's long 'Saint Peters Complaint': 'O John my guide into this earthly hell', p. 79, l. 229.

75 Martz, p. 187.

76 Verstegan disseminated news of the English Catholics to the rest of Europe, from Antwerp. See Brownlow, pp. 14-15; also see Anthony G. Petti (ed.), *The Letters and Dispatches of Richard Verstegan, c. 1550-1640*, Publications of the Catholic Record Society Series, 52 (London: Catholic Record Society, 1959).

77 This was the first of the Martin Marprelate tracts, M&B, p. xxvi. The reported house was the Charterhouse, and the printers were employees of 'J.C. the Earle of Arundels man', raising suspicions of anti-Puritanism; 'J.C.' was John Charlewood - who had the monopoly for playbills, Devlin, pp. 142-3. He had called himself the Earl's printer before Philip's fall from grace in 1585, and his books had sometimes been issued 'From Howard House', the Charterhouse, but it would have been rash indeed to continue such work in situ after the Earl's imprisonment.

78 *An Epistle (Oh read over D. John Bridges, for it is a worthy worke: Or an epitome of the fyrste Booke ... The Epitome is not yet published ... In the meane time, let them be content with this learned Epistle.)* (repr. London, 1843), p. 31, in M&B, pp. xxvi-xxvii. See also J. H. Pollen in CRS, 21, pp. 350-1, for an account of Howard House (the Charterhouse).

79 The press had probably been removed to a safer place by this time in any case, so the Marprelate writer was not working on up-to-date information, M&B, pp. xxvi-xxvii. Devlin suggests that the Jesuits met at the Acton house of the Arundels. Janelle assumes that the Countess of Arundel's house in the Strand was the meeting place after the government had seized the Charterhouse, Devlin, p. 152; Janelle, p. 42. Although the presses themselves can be identified through peculiarities of their type or typesetters, their physical locations are not so easily identified; Brown says that it was set up in Southwell's house in London. Garnet's two presses are numbered 8 and 10 in ARCR, 'Mission', p. 196.

80 Surrey's brothers William and Thomas Howard lived free of charge in the Charterhouse (Howard House) for a while, and Devlin wonders if the 'W.H.' of some poetic dedications was William Howard. Philip's mother was known to be patronising a poet in the years around 1586-92 – Southwell's years of freedom; Devlin identifies the poet as Southwell, pp. 145-6. The patronage system could operate as a mask for all sorts of interactions.

81 Brownlow, p. 28.

82 As Richard Dutton has pointed out, the forces exerted upon the production of late sixteenth-century writers rarely constituted straight censorship, or ideological suppres-

sion, as we understand it; Richard Dutton, 'Licensing and Censorship', in David Scott Kastan (ed.), *A Companion to Shakespeare* (Oxford: Blackwell, 1999), pp. 377–91.

83 Alison Shell, *Catholicism, Controversy and the English Literary Imagination 1558–1660* (Cambridge: Cambridge University Press, 1999), pp. 63, 103; hereafter cited in the text. She cites Herbert Thurston's two important 1895 essays on the significance of Southwell, 'Catholic Writers and Elizabethan Readers', nos II, 'Father Southwell the Euphuist', and III, 'Father Southwell the Popular Poet', *The Month*, 83 (January–April 1895), 231–45, 383–99.

84 *A Transcript of the Registers of the Company of Stationers of London: 1554–1640*, ed. Edward Arber, 5 vols (London: privately printed, 1875–94), II, 598.

85 The title page of the third edition of *Saint Peters Complaint* included a discreet IHS in the border, as if hinting at Southwell's Jesuitism in jigsaw-puzzle form; my thanks to Peter Davidson for this information. Anthony Bacon had a manuscript copy of 'Decease Release', Devlin, p. 147; Weston, even in prison, had a manuscript copy of *An Humble Supplication* soon after its completion, and Topcliffe passed one on to Francis Bacon, Caraman, pp. 64–5, M&B, p. xxv; a recusant owned a copy of Southwell's *Saint Peters Complaint* by 1594, Shell p. 63. Southwell dedicated a collection of poems to a 'loving Cosen', too, although we cannot know which of the printed collections constitutes this set, Brown, p. xxxv, and the 'Waldegrave' MS (Stonyhurst MS A.v.27, now at the Jesuit Archives, Mount Street), containing Southwell's letter to his father, the letters and poems to Philip Howard on the death of his sister Lady Mary Sackville (printed as *Triumphs over Death*), with a group of fifty-two of Southwell's short lyrics with introductory stanzas, was in the hands of (or at least within reach of) one 'iereneme walDegrave' around 1608 or 1609; she has scrawled on a blank page that she is 'a good garle BVt that nonBoDi cer for her'. Peter Beal suggests an earliest date of 1592; see Peter Beal, *Index of English Literary Manuscripts*, 2 vols (London: Mansel, 1980–93), I (1450–1623) (1980). 'Waldegrave' is the basis for Davidson and Sweeney.

86 See M&B, pp. xxxvii–xxxviii, xxix.

87 A man of this name had worked for Tottel the London printer to whom Garnet had been apprenticed ten years before; the real Whalley had now moved out of London to set up a press of his own, so a man buying printing materials under that name would arouse little suspicion.

88 Caraman, p. 35.

89 See Bailey, p. 106, p. 68.

90 George Herbert, 'Prayer', in Helen Gardner (ed.), *The Metaphysical Poets*, 2nd rev. edn (Harmonsdworth: Penguin, 1985), p. 124.

Chapter 4

The flight of angels: England's altered confidence

> Where can affiance rest to rest secure?
> In vertues fairest seate faith is not sure.[1]

'JOSEPH'S AMAZEMENT'

Entering England in 1586, Southwell had met with communities feeling the loss of old, familiar agencies, the active interventions once supplied by prayer now less able to offer comfort in the daily battle against doubt and anxiety. He may have arrived to take the angel's part but he was also trained in suiting his imagery to the immediate situation, and angelic agency and how he offers it up to his English readers is a case in point; Gabriel could come as himself to a Virgin freely submissive to the will of God, but Raphael had to bring help in disguise. Angels were on the front line of the post-Reformation debate. Protestantism diminished the role of angels in the revelation of God's will; Tridentine Rome, on the other hand, had a new understanding of the unseen universe, one thronged with beings of particular purpose and aspect, and one in which manifestations of grace could be as light and multitudinous as they. New Jesuit theories now characterised as congruism meant that grace was (like the angels in the many aspects in which they chose to appear to man) conformable to the peculiar circumstances and will of the recipient. Bellarmine argued a modified version of Molina's and Suárez's congruism and Southwell will have come to England full of its lively potential.[2] His lyrics seem to make the same assumptions about the conformable space opened by congruism between grace and the human will, actively working to prepare the reader to receive grace, either openly, like Gabriel hailing the Virgin, or disguised, like Raphael accompanying Tobias. He seeks to open minds to spiritually healthful questions without necessarily referring to Catholic doctrine. Wherever 'New heaven new warre' (p. 13), with its Thomistic angelic hierarchies, lay in manuscript until its appearance in print in 1602, it had clearly been intended by Southwell for a reader with a very Catholic understanding of the hidden workings of the universe. But even then, his message is modified to suit circumstance: the martial imagery and the humorous reference to Gabriel as a groom suggest that it was intended for a masculine reader who was not religiously severe, a Wriothesley, Strange or Essex, not an Arundel.

Calvin's account of angelic agency tended to reduce them to biblical manifestations, representations of Christ's intervention in history before the Incarnation had given him human form, rather than active, daily companions. The idea of a personally attentive guardian angel was dismissed as irrational and superstitious.[3] Angels as distinct agencies were as inimical to Calvin's view of things as the idea that one could call down God's mercy and grace by prayer and by independent intercession. Christianity had evolved, and the superstitious days were gone; the services of the angels were no longer required. Catholicism, by this view, was a pre-Incarnation belief that had failed to develop alongside man's understanding of things. In the metaphysical universe of the Reformed Church the skies no longer thronged with bright beings ready to come to human aid in response to invocation. The land of Angles that Pope Gregory I had identified with the angels had now decided to live without their graceful guardianship and inspiration, and without the hope of attracting their aid by invocation and prayer.[4]

Southwell is probably referring indirectly to this in noting a loss of angelic agency in 'The virgin Mary to Christ on the Crosse' (p. 71), a poem which may also be read as mourning for the loss of Christ's Presence in England's Mass:

> You Angells all that present were,
>   To shew his birth with harmony,
> Why are you not now ready here,
>   To make a mourning symphony?   20
>
> The cause I know, you waile alone,
>   And shed your tears in secresie,
> Least I should moved be to mone,
>   By force of heavy company.

This poem also represents a defiantly Bellarminian vision of the Virgin as an active participant in Christian history; Bellarmine prefers her not fainting but embracing her grief, open-eyed and courageous, an exemplar for bereaved Catholics of what St Bernard called the 'martyrdom of the heart', harder to bear even than bodily martyrdom.[5] If this is also an account of the mood of English Catholics such as Byrd, as Southwell found them, they are an unhappy company indeed; the music of such men was indeed full of complaint and sadness: perfectly natural in the circumstances, Southwell suggests.

The removal of those supports threatened a wider collapse in the spiritual state of English Christianity, accustomed as it had been to that daily help. Southwell addresses this angel-orphaned state and the fear of its effects directly in the lyric 'Josephs Amazement' and in his English prose-poem *Marie Magdalens Funeral Teares* (1591). 'Joseph' was not released in print until 1602, although it has no overt doctrinal features; it is accompanied by other first time appearances: 'The burning babe', 'New heaven, new warre', 'New Prince, new pompe', poems that, as has been discussed, contain substrata of peculiarly Tridentine Catholic meanings. Wolf had not issued them, and Cawood later either acquired a manuscript containing these more suggestive lyrics or he had decided against releasing them from the start. Something in Joseph's struggles to find the right response to the pregnancy of his betrothed without angelic guidance may have alarmed him.[6]

Mary Magdalen's loss echoes the loss of the Real Presence and the threat this poses to English piety. Seeking the body of her dead Love, she has found the tomb empty; Southwell's recreation of her distress includes her fear that 'love of her master ... would soon languish in her cold brest, if it neither had his wordes to kindle it, nor his presence to cherishe it, nor so much as his dead ashes to rake it up'.[7] This is a reasonable fear, in the context of the English mission. Calvin had dismissed Mary's tears as self-indulgent, superstitious, mere feelings of the flesh,[8] but Southwell had come to help a community that was orphaned from its spiritual family; he needed to help them to rediscover that spiritual fire and agency within themselves, now that they were almost without the external guidance of priests or holy objects. His use of Magdalen and Joseph is part of that process, at once rejecting the apparent rationalisations of Calvinism, and designed to dramatise the English Catholic's state of loss.

'Josephs Amazement' (p. 21 (1602)) is unusual amongst his lyrics in containing no prayer or consolatory element at the end. It is, on the surface, a masculine complaint of a failed love; beneath that is a debate about the relative duties to State and Self which offers no answers. Similarly, 'What joy to live?' (p. 53 (Cb)), his revision of Petrarch's *Rime* 134 (or an English translation of it) offers only a series of complaints, again masculine in mood, and to one who knows riches and fame, who wages 'no warre' yet cannot enjoy peace; it contains no overt spiritual guidance, only that implied by the last line's bare, anti-erotic warning: 'Where pleasures upshot is to die accurst' (lines 1, 30). 'Mans civill warre' (p. 49 (Ma)) has the merest slip of a homily at the end, and 'The prodigall childs soule wracke' (p. 43 (Ma)) expresses regret for past sins, but it is far more about the speaker's desperate need for direction. 'Marie Magdalens complaint at Christs death' (p. 45 (Ca)) is almost the partner to 'Joseph' in trying to live with next to no hope. These poems seem to dramatise the spiritual state of one bereft of priestly guidance, leaving the remedy to the readers themselves, whether to seek the priest, or at least to work harder for redemption; it is as if one went through all the sorrowing confessions of unworthiness prior to Holy Communion without ever reaching the respite and redemption of the Communion itself. Perhaps these poems acted in part as preparation of a 'congregation' for the visit of the priest.

'Saint Peters Complaint' is different: the Roman original is altered by Southwell into a stylised description of the after-effects of one catastrophic moment of infidelity on a great and influential man, almost certainly, in context, an English churchman; it describes not the loss but the active denial of Christ.[9] It is the shorter lyrics that address themselves to the issue of the conflicted, confused English individual, the ordinary folk left struggling to find a way through increasingly impossible circumstances, devoid of the apprehensible spiritual comforts and sacred locations of the old faith.

The *Exercises* had taught Southwell that Catholics could be guided through the shoals of spiritual confusion by their Guardian Angel, and in one sense he is performing that task for English Christians who are no longer helped to have access to one. But, echoing those new teachings on congruent grace, Southwell also insists that each must first be determined to head in the right direction; the *Exercises* encouraged exercisants to untangle spiritual quandaries and discern good or bad motivations in their own actions. Angels hardly appear in his English poetry, I would suggest, because he is, Jesuit-like, accommodating himself to the situation: reflecting the near angel-less position chosen by those who govern the English, and the spiritual quandary in which it has left the ordinary English subject.

Southwell was not seeking to return England to some older era of credulity; the Catholic youth born so near ruined Walsingham was brought up to worship without the shrine, to internalise his devotions, and his Jesuit schooling had reinforced this. Jesuits had to carry such sites in their hearts on their long journeys, internalising the imagery and the effects of real shrines. Self-reliance on the difficult spiritual journey of the soul toward God informed their whole way of proceeding, just as it informs Southwell's poetry.[10] Southwell understood free will, human thought and action, to be a divine gift. He was trained to understand Christian piety to be a matter of doing, as well as believing, of conscious actions, aided, it was to be hoped, by heavenly helpers, but at root the duty of the individual, and his poetry was a programme of works designed to lead even an averagely educated reader to a new conclusion and the all-important change of life that would allow access to grace.

This feature of his poetry is defined by 'Josephs Amazement'. The edifying imagery of the churches in Rome and the lecture programmes that reinforced their message cannot be reproduced in England's churches now, so Southwell has imported a telling moment from the Lives of Christ and the Virgin in the shape of this poem. But there is a striking omission: he has whitewashed over the angel that, in the Gospel account, appears to reassure and direct Joseph in

The flight of angels: England's altered confidence

a dream. Southwell leaves his readers, of whatever denomination, to meditate upon the implications of that absence.[11]

Southwell's lyrics contain other instances of the absent angel. Robert Bellarmine had written treatises on the Prodigal Son that included a guardian angel to guide him home,[12] but no such protection exists in Southwell's English version, 'The prodigall childs soule wracke' (p. 43). The 'child' (Southwell has universalised the gender specificity of the moral) can only cling to the wreck and see 'Heaven' so 'overcast with stormie clouds' that he or she is denied heavenly help (metaphorised as 'the Planets guiding light' (lines 15–16)), as the English were denied the guidance of their Catholic priests. In the spirit of the Jesuit method of using pagan allegory to sharpen a Christian message, Southwell's description is an emblem-picture of the storm-tossed boat, with its Christianised, college-style caption. John Busby, who entered a small collection of lyrics, characterised as 'Certaine excellent Poems and spirituall Hymnes', on the *Stationers' Register* in October 1595, acknowledges this classical aspect in naming his collection after the Lydian area associated with lyric song and with Homer.[13]

The narrative conflates journeys such as those of Jason and Odysseus with the trip to the Underworld of Orpheus, a story of souls lacking divine guidance and struggling against the anger of lesser gods and the distractions of the flesh. Southwell's speaker mentions the 'furies', those pagan workers of divine revenge (l. 17) who were moved none the less to weep for pity when Orpheus, like the speaker in this poem, 'Stept far within deaths fatall doores', in Orpheus's case to sing for his lost love (l. 31); 'With Sirens songs they fed my eares', Southwell's Odyssean wanderer cries; next he falls asleep in the lap of error, as Odysseus did in Circe's and Calypso's (lines 49–50). Medieval scholarship accepted such pagan narratives as 'Tipes to the truth' of Christian redemption ('Of the Blessed Sacrament of the Aulter' (p. 26), lines 3–4). Southwell has acknowledged this usage, tying the tales into the New Testament parable of the Prodigal Son, reminding his reader of the reach of history behind these narratives, and of his Church, tied into that history through Rome itself. Once again, as if to emphasise the loss of priestly help, he ends on a curiously flat note: it is as if the lack of divine guidance is his main point, rather than the fact of the Redemption-to-be. The ship of the English soul is adrift, the helmsman thrown overboard; indeed, it is sinking, and the lifeboats have been taken away. In this poem at least, the Christian virtues of mercy and grace do supply the smallest of lifebelts; but there is no external source of rescue at all in Southwell's 'Joseph'.

The Joseph of Matthew's Gospel is visited in his doubt over the pregnancy of his betrothed by an angel, appearing in a dream (Matthew 1.20), whereupon Joseph is comforted and does as he is told. Southwell's poem takes the Matthew version, the only Gospel narrative to mention Joseph's husbandly distress, and ventriloquises Joseph, moving from a brief six-stanza exposition into a soliloquy of internal turmoil and doubt. He expands Matthew's small moment of doubt and misery between the discovery of Mary's pregnancy and the angelic dream into a prolonged meditation upon love and faith. Southwell's Joseph is a 'stranger yet to Gods intent' (l. 3); that explanatory line recalls the prologues and epilogues of Jesuit college drama.[14] A Jesuit college production could take the form of a debate as well as a play, and Southwell will have had no difficulty in envisaging a soliloquy as part of one or the other, or of transcribing either into his poetry in the same pedagogical spirit. 'Gods intent', as all the students knew, would be revealed to Joseph only after a suitably dramatic soliloquy of doubt and self-interrogation, raising issues about civic duty, personal responsibility, fidelity, and fellowship, whilst ultimately praising the unquestioning nature of faith through love. The college audience knew that the narrative of Christian history would be re-engaged and all would be well.

But in Southwell's English version, no angel appears to explain; none can in a Calvinised Albion. The empirical, rational world merely progresses in the usual way, the swelling abdomen of his betrothed suggesting her infidelity, as 'Christ by growth disclosed his desent, | Into the pure receipt of Maries brest' (lines 1–2). The confused fiancé sees a pregnancy of unknown origin, and no heaven-informed guidance is available; he would have to travel to a Catholic place for the angelic epilogue.

Perhaps this is one of the lyric jokes Southwell reserved for his more educated reader: in a land whose churchmen believed the angels to be remote biblical phenomena of uncertain purpose, there can surely be no angelic Guardian to guide and comfort Joseph; he has, if he chooses Calvin's way, no ability to go in the company of his angel beyond this rationally apprehended surface appearance, this shameful swelling, and is forced into a debate over the relative trustworthiness of 'sense' – the senses – over belief.

The poetic genre of complaint itself becomes a rational form for what the unhappy lover feels – his poetic soliloquy is a rehearsal of his breaking heart, his anxieties over the broken promises, his fears over the broken laws represented by his fiancée's mysterious pregnancy. The matter of the locus of faith itself is contained in this simple imagery: Joseph is the undirected soul; he is also the Christian who had believed in the Real Presence and now finds that it was a false belief, as his churchmen now seem to be telling him. If God does not dwell in person in the host of Mary's humanity, then Mary must be what Joseph in this poem fears she is. English Joseph, shown the apparent viciousness of the one in which he had placed all confidence, doubts, and no angel comes to advise or comfort him, in an England which has rejected that heavenly assistance.

In showing us Joseph's pitiable confusion, Southwell is not offering a St-Peter-like self-directed meditation picking in detail over the anatomy of sin;

this and the other 'quandary' poems are personifications and dramatisations of various sorts of common anxiety or failure where the protagonists are almost blameless; their confusion is allowed to seem natural given their peculiar circumstances (none more peculiar than Joseph's, of course); they lack only external spiritual direction, and are left to find their own way.

Having allowed the reader to share with Joseph the emotionally charged space between his sad discovery and his deciding what to do about it, Southwell, most unusually, leaves something of a blank for the reader to fill in. Any Christian will know that the Incarnation has happened, although it has not yet been harvested and Joseph does not yet therefore have access to that Eucharistic redemption; they can be comforted by their knowledge of Christian history. A Calvinist reader, however, is confronted by a quandary: this angel-less Joseph, guided by his own apprehension alone, might hand the apparently adulterous woman over to be stoned. That would be the rational, the *lawful*, course, after all. Obedience and conformity are interrrogated here, in relation to belief.

'The Visitation' (p. 5), one of Southwell's Virgin Sequence, makes this separation between reason and faith more explicit. As the pregnant Virgin travels to meet her 'cosen', she has no earthly pomp on her arduous journey; but 'doubtles heavenly Quires attendant were', Southwell adds. Angelic agency is thus clearly separated from the incarnate Christ. He must himself resort to the irrational to make himself known, for, although illuminating Mary from within with his intrinsic divinity, he is as mute as any human embryo. The two women make their salutations, while 'the children' are described as greeting each other with 'secret signes', something over and above the normal movements *in utero* of the Bible account, the laws of the physical universe giving way before God's power (lines 9, 17). In 'Joseph' and 'The Visitation' Southwell seems to attack Calvin's apparent literalism and rationality, showing belief struggling to survive without skies full of cloud-borne guidance, in a cold grey place of doubt and anxiety.

CAESAR'S OR GOD'S? LAW VERSUS LOVE

In 'Joseph', Southwell is also asking his reader to consider their relationship with the Law, and the right of the Law to intervene in certain areas of human experience, revisiting the battles of Becket and More to maintain ecclesiastical over secular jurisdiction. In the Gospel narrative, Joseph's response was based not on obedience to the law, which would have called for an (apparently) adulterous woman's execution, but on his faith in his betrothed, and on the vows he had made to her. Despite her apparent participation in 'crimes for which the law condemnes to die' (l. 54), Southwell's Joseph is firm on one thing at least: his 'word shall never worke her woe' (l. 55), because he loves her. The first ordinary mortal response to the coming of Christ is therefore shown to have been profoundly irrational, and even unlawful; Joseph, in taking it upon himself to follow the way of his conscience, allows the Incarnation its full meaning in preventing the execution of Mary. The Law would have killed Christ, just as, in Catholic eyes, it had removed his presence from the Mass in England. England's law is paralleled with the pre-Christian, Christ-killing law of Rome and Israel. The subject of an individual's 'soul rights',[15] so important to Southwell's agenda, is here sited at the very inception of the Christian era, in the heart of the first ordinary man to experience the difficult choices it brought.

For an ordinary Englishman used to the management of his household, their spiritual observances included, the alterations and intrusions into his private sphere of the last two decades of the sixteenth century were offensive if not catastrophic. John Whitgift had become Archbishop of Canterbury in late 1583, and, with Elizabeth's permission, took to himself new powers in the Court of High Commission for Causes Ecclesiastical over which he presided, which operated to seek out and punish any nonconformity to the Church of England, spelling disaster for those quietly struggling to retain their preferred forms of worship, Puritan or Catholic.[16] The English Church was not only now monarch-, not pope-led, but was becoming more and more intrusive in legal ways into the erstwhile private spheres of spiritual minds. Early in her reign, Elizabeth is said not to have wanted to make windows into men's souls;[17] by the end of it these hopes were becoming increasingly unrealistic in the face of the activities of the various groups. It was supposed that Whitgift had gained the support of Elizabeth for these intrusions, despite her tendency towards toleration, by promising her the resulting fines as fees for the Crown; this was widely seen as an abuse of Whitgift's pastoral station and resented even by moderates. It provoked reactions from the exiled Catholics and from Puritans like Leicester and Burghley, who mounted anti-Whitgift campaigns in 1583–84, including the proposed legislation against Catholics which inspired the Heywood–Vaux petition for toleration; further repressions of Catholics occurred in 1587.[18]

Southwell's 'Joseph' is clearly designed to spotlight these issues, reflecting a changed understanding of the problems faced by English Catholics in the 1580s, and the intrusion of the law into their private minds. His use of manuscript poetry itself addresses this, a sufficiently private form of communication to counterbalance the effects of a State which showed an increasing determination to dominate its subjects' private responses. This authorship was for Southwell indivisible from his ministry and priesthood: he was metaphorising the direct line between reader, priest and God. Merely by accepting a manuscript containing such moral poetry and engaging with it, the reader has willingly taken the first steps towards taking responsibility for his or her own spiritual welfare, and, by post-Tridentine Catholic theology, opened up to grace, and, most important of all in the English situation, done so without the direct

The flight of angels: England's altered confidence

assistance of a priest, and away from the scrutiny of the State. Possession of Catholic tracts might be used as evidence in a recusancy trial, but Southwell might have been forgiven for thinking that possession of a poetic manuscript could not; until one of his was used in a recusancy trial in 1594, that is.[19]

The subject of 'Joseph' reinforces Southwell's message about the need for autonomy: Joseph might well have been distressed by his love's apparent infidelity, and he knew that the law had severe penalties for such breaches; but Southwell is pointing out that nobody but Joseph himself, as her betrothed, had the *moral* right to decide how to respond to the honest urging of his own heart. Southwell is here dividing responsibility up into two separate areas, personal-spiritual, and public-civic. Joseph, being (literally) engaged by love and duty to his beloved, can and should act in accordance with that love; Southwell suggests that this is a place where the law simply has no business to be. He is shining a light through the window the State has forced into the English soul, to highlight the intrusion.

Southwell was requesting not choice, of course, but the right to continue unchanged. That is the theological position that underlies his love poetry: true love does not – *cannot* – alter where it alteration finds. Recusancy only seemed like choice to those who had already exercised a choice to remove from the old faith – 'heretic' comes from the Greek *haireisthai*, 'to choose', after all.

In 'Joseph' Southwell vocalises the anguish of all pious souls who had tried both to obey the laws of England and to stay true to an ancient faith, all those who felt they had been cut off from the historical root of spiritual refreshment and its 'quickning heate', the heat that can, in the poem's context, mirror transubstantiation, calling the physical embryonic Christ into the physical self, something denied, as Southwell saw it, in Protestantism. This carefully expressed spiritual sympathy, framed as a first-person cry of anguish, must have had a profound effect on any devout English reader frustrated and confounded in their religious observances in the 'cold and barren shade' of a secular State:

> Like stocked tree whose branches all doe fade,
>   Whose leaves doe fall, and perisht fruite decay;
> Like hearbe that growes in cold and barren shade,
>   Where darknes drives all quickning heate away: 70
> So die must I, cut from my roote of joy,
> And throwne in darkest shades of deepe annoy.

How accurately has Southwell, as well-trained as he was to go 'where thought can see', in the *Exercises*, seen inside the state of mind of someone who is, as a result of the removal of the sacramental nourishment of their faith, spiritually starving. How astutely too has he, trained to make a discourse of his own psychological state, patterned a discourse for theirs, guiding them through the arguments and confusions of altered sacraments to a kernel of truth. 'Where hart pursues, what gaines the foote to flie?' he asks (l. 78). This would have been commonplace enough if it were not for the way that the image of the hotly pursuing heart challenges the State's intrusion into the heart's space, both metaphorically, and, in the executions of the faithful, literally, reminding readers of the all-too-common sight of the still-beating heart of an executed believer brandished aloft by the hangman. Southwell is painting a pre-existing virtual reality to colour the actual. The burning issue of Catholic loyalty too often worked out on the scaffold is here turned passionately aside: brandish my heart as you will, says the martyr-to-be – only God and I know what is in it. The hotly loving heart can therefore triumph even if cut out of the body. The heart of the exile is for ever cut off from him; but the hart that runs willingly onto the huntsman's arrow is no longer a victim.

But who in England can now, he asks, be allowed to get close enough to the emotional source of such spiritual heat 'to warme their harts, | Or feele [that] fire' ('The burning Babe', p. 15)? And without the fire, Southwell insists, there can be no absolution: 'The metall in this furnace wrought, | Are mens defiled soules' (lines 21–4), but the English are kept by their rational State religion too far away from such sacramental heat to participate in divine justice, in Southwell's view.

The duty (and right) of a person to be in control of their own spiritual state is a founding principle of the Ignatian *Exercises*, and a constant underlying theme in Southwell's poetry. He reworks scriptural themes into personal reader-located issues, as in 'Sinnes heavie loade' (p. 17):

> O Lord my sinne doth over-charge thy brest,
>   The poyse thereof doth force thy knees to bow;
> Yea flat thou fallest with my faults opprest,
>   And bloody sweat runs trickling from thy brow:
> But had they not to earth thus pressed thee,   5
> Much more they would in hell have pestred mee.

The individual's sin is a burden on Christ rather than the sinner, engaging the sympathies of the reader for another rather than his fears for himself. 'Alas, if God himselfe sinke under sinne, | What will become of man that dies therein?' he asks; Southwell places the reader and his God in direct contact through this shared burden of sin (lines 17–18). He goes on to portray the pathos of the scene of Christ's Passiontide prostration, pre-figured in his first fall to earth at the Incarnation:

> First, flat thou fel'st, when earth did thee receave,
>   In closet pure of Maries virgin brest;   20
> And now thou fall'st of earth to take thy leave,
>   Thou kissest it as cause of thy unrest:
> O loving Lord that so doost love thy foe,
> As thus to kisse the ground where he doth goe.

> Thou minded in thy heaven our earth to weare, 25
> Doo'st prostrate now thy heaven our earth to blisse;
> As God, to earth thou often wert severe,
> As man, thou seal'st a peace with bleeding kisse:
> For as of soules thou common Father art,
> So is she Mother of mans other part. 30

'O prostrate Christ, erect my crooked minde, | Lord let thy fall my flight from earth obtaine' he begs (lines 37–8), describing that typically Southwellian crossing of action between God and Man, the symbiosis of human will and divine grace that upholds so many of his holy poems. Fall again to lie beside me in earth, if I am to remain trapped here in this life, or raise me up to be with you, he says in his concluding prayer (lines 40–2).

Any devout Englishman or woman worried half to death about the state of their eternal soul since forbidden Mass and intercessionary prayers for their dead must have read this with a passionate recognition. Southwell here acknowledges the impossibility of maintaining traditional religious trappings; he is internalising the effects of the old sacred images of Christ in his suffering which, though effaced, still persisted in the common imagination. They are here being remodelled by Southwell into images of a Christ whose pain is the direct and immediate responsibility of whoever reads the poem; he is not recreating familiar old images to pander to nostalgia. Southwell, cutting through lukewarm attachments like a knife, rejects any merely synthetic make-believe for this insistent esemplastic immediacy.

Circumstance as he found it was again being responded to with subtlety and astuteness. 'Christ falling' is part of the 'Stations of the Cross', the sequence of moments from Christ's Passion depicted on the walls of a Catholic church, the regular progress around which was a sobering reminder to the lettered and unlettered alike. Even before the Reformation, when still up on church walls, such images had probably lost much of their poignancy, dulled by their familiarity and air of stiff antiquity. How long had it been since anyone had looked at the angels on the church roofs, now shot down like so many birds? In some respects the iconoclasts had done the Catholic Church some good in shattering complacent acceptance by congregations of these old decorations. As Southwell was taught in Douai, Paris and Rome, imagery, realised in the mind and vitalised by personal memory, has a more immediate effect than representations seen week after week for a lifetime. Southwell is here reminding his readership that if the wooden image of Christ's sacrifice has been lost from the church, there are living re-enactments of Calvary to be seen at Tyburn regularly enough.

In 'Sinnes heavie loade' Southwell is realising the Stations in the reader's mind, turning the reader once again into a participator, indeed perpetrator, not just an audience, just as, despite keeping his picture close by to remind

Robert Southwell

himself of his father's loved face, it is the (apparently) real appearance of Hamlet's dead father that has a truly galvanising effect upon Hamlet: memorial requires only observance; real presence demands action. The virtual pre-realities are again being redirected. Southwell's imagery, as ever, works on different levels, the cross-action of grace active throughout, the reader's upward-directed mind set against the falling to earth of Christ. The falling is itself a subtle prefiguring of the Crucifixion, and an even subtler reminder of the moment of transubstantiation in the Mass: Southwell knows his reader has in his or her head a powerful memory, if no more, of the blood-streaked face of the struggling figure on the way to Calvary, and manages the symbolism of the blood and the earth-bound body with consummate skill. Southwell's Lord has, before his incarnation, raised the Globe more easily than Atlas, on 'one finger' (l. 7), without a drop of sweat, but is here borne to the ground by the weight of man's sins, which are more than the weight of the entire world. The downward movement of grace of the Incarnation is set against the upward-looking idea of God willing the Incarnation and Crucifixion to happen; 'Thou minded in thy heaven our earth to weare, | Doo'st prostrate now thy heaven our earth to blisse' (lines 25–6). He adds the paradoxical image of God falling under the weight of our sins, which in turn is used to suggest what might happen to the human body as a result of that heavy load. Seemingly endless permutations and implications around the relationship between Christ, earth, body, blood, downward- and upward-ness are offered to the reader, who could sit studying these intricacies as one in meditation might sit with a mandala, achieving ever more refined spiritual insights in the absence of shrine or priest.

The concept that holds all together, though, is the fact that Christ has *chosen* this act of touching earth and relinquishing divinity for a moment: this is the magic formula, if I may put it that way, that gives power to the final prayer-stanza and its almost lover-like need to be close to the body that made that choice (or to its presence in the host). The final prayer returns agency to the reader: 'Lord on earth come fall yet once againe', he asks; 'And eyther yeeld with me in earth to lie, | Or else with thee to take me to the skie' (lines 40–2). This is why 'Sinnes heavie loade' did not appear until 1602: it is an utter repudiation of Calvin; if the words are good and the heart sure of its needs, Christ himself can be addressed and moved – bodily, actually moved – even in the midst of his great moments, thus giving that sense of personal power both over the access of grace and over one's spiritual state once offered by the Catholic Mass, and the attendant angels and now, in England, lost.

Southwell's poetry, then, not only identified the loss of personal spiritual negotiation implicit in Calvinism, but offered something approaching a holy accessing of spiritual power in itself, a space in which to engage with the heavenly powers.

Southwell's brief was not to empower English folk *per se*, of course. But even in the poems that seem as yet unmodulated by his English experience, he glosses the English generously. They are not to blame for the fault of their betters. They are only to be blamed for allowing themselves to be lulled to sleep, for having their agency quietly removed without protest, for failing as witnesses to the faith through lukewarm passions.

WAKING CHRIST'S SLEEPING FRIENDS: MAGDALEN AND THE PASSIONATE IMAGINATION

> And therefore sith the finest wits are now giuen to write passionat discourses, I would wish them to make choise of such passions, as it neither should be shame to utter, nor sinne to feele.[20]

Southwell needed more than a personification of doubt to highlight the English troubles; he needed to model a cure, exemplify a constant love that could not, for all its losses and failings, be subdued. They had lost so much, but he was bringing a new, more heartfelt piety, one demanding powerful responses. The English preferred to grieve in private over the loss of their old habits and places, judging by their own poetic expressions of complaint, which complained mostly at the loss of church beauties, the loss of the welfare brought by the monasteries, and the general sense of loss of piety and community cohesion.[21] Now the straight line of transmission from Bethlehem to England represented by Walsingham had been broken, where could faith rest assured in England? This was not just a matter of religious loss: there are also complaints of a breakdown in social order. Once, an English subject had one duty, to God, and to monarch under God; now nothing was clear. A complaint poem contains no solution, no way out; it memorialises loss. The regular religious upheavals meant that a ten-year-old of the 1530s had seen the carved Christ-cross of his village church, the central visual locus of his faith, smashed in scorn before his eyes then reverently recreated, perhaps three times before he reached fifty; after this, what could remain to him of its intrinsic or symbolic value? Each time the regime changed, he was required to transfer his old belief-system, unimpaired and unquestioning, to the new one. Where did that leave the integrity of one's personal beliefs, which, owing to State compromises in the early years of Elizabeth's reign, had in any case begun to seem negotiable?[22]

This near-*accidie* was the dominant mood of English Catholics when Southwell arrived in England, so very different from the ebullient resistance of those youthful cohorts of his South Downs years, and a world away from the exilic fervour just across the Channel. In 'St Peters afflicted minde' (p. 31), a sort of metaphysical medical report on the English condition, he describes it as a 'maladie': 'languor of the minde' (lines 9–10), associating it with loss of the

Robert Southwell

means of direct contact with heaven ('The care of heavenly kinne | Is dead to my reliefe', lines 13–14).

Despite a sharp 'letter' dated 1589, ostensibly to his father, reproving him, with priestly authority, for his graceless life, it must have quickly become obvious to Southwell that stringent reproof, however authoritative, would create animosity amongst potential supporters, especially if it seemed to be directed at influential figures, even such as Leicester or Burghley.[23] Perhaps it was in part this that gave Southwell the idea of disguising his preaching text as poetry. However he chose to do so, his community of helpable souls required some reminding of their Christian duty. Sleep, in the context of 'Christs sleeping friends' (p. 19), can be seen as another reference to the reduction of interior capability, the dulling of the individual's sense of agency, mimicking the deadly eternal sleep of the soul. Again, as if in contrast to that inertia, Christ is shown actively engaged in his own mission, a painful reflection of the missioner in his frightened, unrested state:

> When Christ with care and pangs of death opprest
> From frighted flesh a bloody sweat did raine,
> And full of feare without repose or rest
> In agony did pray and watch in paine
> Three sundry times he his disciples findes 5
> With heavy eies, but farre more heavy mindes,

He dissembles his own fears, asking them to wake up with only 'milde rebuke' (l. 7), despite knowing that his 'foes' are watching 'to worke their cruell spight'; but his 'drousie friendes' sleep on (lines 7–10). The reader, itching to shout 'wake up!' like a frustrated bystander, is thereby drawn into the drama. Southwell allows Christ his resignation, naturally, but himself goes on to sharpen the message:

> As *Jonas* sayled once from *Joppaes* shoare
> A boystrous tempest in the aire did broile,
> The waves did rage, the thundring heavens did roare, 15
> The stormes, the rockes, the lightnings threatened spoile,
> The shippe was billows gaine, and chaunces pray,
> Yet carelesse *Jonas* mute and sleeping lay:
>
> So now though *Judas* like a blustring gust,
> Doe stirre the furious sea of Jewish ire, 20
> Though storming troopes in quarrels most unjust
> Against the bark of all our blisse conspire,
> Yet these disciples sleeping lie secure,
> As though their wonted calme did still endure.

Southwell uses the Old Testament type of Christ's death and resurrection, Jonas, to prefigure Christ's predicament on finding his few supporters asleep.

The flight of angels: England's altered confidence

Jonas twice sleeps when he should be wakeful in the Lord's business. The trope of the endangered vessel will be instantly accessible to the English reader as a symbol of the barque of Peter, the Roman Catholic Church. In the following stanza (lines 19–24) the connection to the here-and-now of an Elizabethan reader becomes explicit in the background imagery of 'troopes in quarrels most unjust' (l. 21). As in the martyr paintings with their identifiably suggestive background details, the sleepers are now no longer Bible characters but have become identified with the reader and his fellow-Englishmen, especially perhaps the English priesthood hoping to lie low and ride out the storm by compliance with State demands. Southwell attacks their evident belief in an evergreen English church under which they may safely sleep out Judas's vengeful betrayals by inserting a metaphorical vine-weevil into the roots of their complacency. The 'leafe, ... fruit and flower' (l. 32), those illustrious Catholic forefathers upon whose memory the pride of the English church rests, the Alfreds, Edmunds and Beckets, perhaps even their modern-day equivalents such as Arundel, are brought to nothing while their weak descendants sleep on:

> So *Jonas* once his weary limmes to rest,   25
> Did shrowd himselfe in pleasant ivy shade
> But lo, while him a heavy sleep opprest,
> His shadowy bowre, to withered stalke did fade,
> A cankered worme had gnawen the root away,
> And brought the glorious branches to decay.   30
>
> O gratious plant, O tree of heavenly spring,
> The paragon for leafe, for fruit and flower,
> How sweete a shadow did thy braunches bring
> To shrowd these soules that chose thee for their bower,
> But now while they with *Jonas* fall asleepe,   35
> To spoile their plant an envious worme doth creepe.

Having de- then re-constructed the virtual realities, in the manner of the *Exercises*, Southwell turns to exhortation, rather than the more usual prayer:

> Awake ye slumbring wightes lift up your eies,
> Marke *Judas* how to teare your root he strives,
> Alas the glorie of your arbor dies,   40
> Arise and guarde the comfort of your lives.
> No *Jonas* ivy, no *Zacheus* tree,
> Were to the world so great a losse as he.

This, in the English context, is a clarion call, echoing the English College painting cycles and exhortations to defend the memory of the English saints and the lineage of the English church, but to what extent Southwell does not say, the six-liners typical of his more church-orientated poetry leaving the reader to supply the active context.

In this most unsententious effacement of authorial presence, Southwell shows how well he had understood his problem in finding a 'voice' in which to address the English. Magdalen, female and therefore removed from public power, the frail one who had languished, rather than worked, for Christ, might seem the perfect metaphor for these weakened, grieving English Catholics. His Magdalen is more than a representation of repentance and sorrow, however. She is castigated by the returned Christ for preferring to carry on grieving for a lost body when she has before her his newer, more heavenly reality, a reality her impassioned grieving renders her unable to recognise; the old Church is gone, Southwell seems to say, but a new Catholicism is within your grasp (*Funeral Teares*, sig. G. 5).

Whatever the means by which he had constructed his sense of self in the Novitiate and in the exile community abroad, once on English soil a missioner like Southwell had to reassess his engagement with that exiled community, losing his argumentative role, his anger, even dissembling his identity as a Catholic, a priest, and a Jesuit (depending on his company) for as long as possible to preserve his ministry intact. Where most discussions now focus on the Catholic identities expressed through overt loyalism or angry exile, in Southwell and the other missioners we have an entirely different set of circumstances governing their sense of who they were, and where they fitted into the English Jerusalem. They had somehow to maintain and internalise the exilic determination to alter circumstances, whilst presenting the irenic profile of the home Catholic, in order to fulfil their promises of ministry for as long as possible. This uncomfortable mix is represented in Southwell's poetry, perhaps nowhere more than in the personation of Magdalen – passionate but, as a woman, not puissant or threatening to (male) authority. And she is from Bethany, standing separate from Jerusalem, the community of Christians that Southwell had come to address. His *The Epistle of Comfort* spoke to a community in prison, in durance for the Catholic faith, a community who, he suggests are already living in imitation of Christ by their sacrifices. Letters to Rome often spoke joyfully of a crowd of Catholic supporters, a community that met and journeyed with him or supported him with the use of their houses. Southwell's letters were constructing an ideal English Catholic Jerusalem for the sake of the exiles and Roman Jesuits with whom he corresponded, but how far did that golden community extend into reality? Why might his ideal English Christian, his Magdalen, have preferred to live in Bethany?

A comment of Garnet's from their first days in England suggests how divided that Jerusalem was in reality: so great would be the stir if English Catholics learned of their membership of the Society, Garnet wrote to Acquaviva on arrival in 1586, 'that we are forced to conceal that we are of it, "lest the whole of Jerusalem be disturbed"'.[24] 'The' English Catholic community is identified with the community of the holy City, and in the same sentence shown to be less coherent an identity than that benign image might suggest. Jesuitism seems almost outside Jerusalem at this moment, like Jesus waiting to enter it, or Magdalen waiting amongst an inner circle of friends in Bethany. Their Jesuit identity is potentially disruptive. Admittedly, this is partly a matter of local suspicions of men who had sworn fealty to the Pope and who operated outside local church hierarchies, 'a situation which, as the Appellant controversy was to demonstrate   could lead to fatal ambiguity and conflict', as Alison Shell pointed out.[25]

The Jesuit missioners had an ambiguous role where they intersected with English society, one that must affect while never threatening. Their unidentifiability was a vital part of the arsenal which they worked to preserve. Lack of identity itself can become part of an internalised sense of hidden potency. Southwell's name may have been known, but the purposes of the Jesuits were imponderable, something that pleased Southwell: 'News of our coming has already spread abroad', he wrote in July 1586; 'and from the lips of the Queen's Council *my name* has become known to certain persons. The report alarms our enemies, who fear heaven knows what at our hands'.[26] An unknown quantity, he was able, from his Bethanian refuge, to stir Jerusalem all the more.

He is, from his femaled, non-threatening position at a respectful distance, addressing several Jerusalems, the deceptive surface blandness of some of his lyrics obscuring layers of engagement with the various discourses, the deeper layers reserved for the understanding of his Jesuit community.[27] The strains on Southwell's sense of being part of any wider Catholic community in England were doubled by his membership of the Society: when he wrote to Claudio Acquaviva in Rome of his fears of disclosure, it was not necessarily Protestant spies he was talking about. It is hard to conceive of a lonelier mission than the one that set someone at odds not only with their countrymen and their family but even with the English Catholics who harboured them. Bethany was no comfortable hideaway: allowing oneself to be walled up in an underground sewer by a semi-known English Catholic as the pursuivants thundered on the outer door must have taken a great deal of nerve in the days after Campion's betrayal; one can only guess at the doubts that flitted through the fugitive's mind as the last chinks of light were blotted out.[28]

Southwell responded to this with admirable magnanimity. He trusted in English decency, his writing beginning to show an understanding of the importance of developing a methodology that gave control over the conscience back to the English individual. As he had insisted in his letter to Acquaviva, these were an instinctively pious people: 'I beg you to give some thought to the loyal faith of the [English] Catholics, of that very same faith that has been long admired in this people naturally inclined to religious sensibility';[29] he identifies the breakdown in the church community itself – 'our domestic calamity' – as the cause of the problems of English spirituality. His poetry is part of an

Robert Southwell

attempt to build Jerusalems in each individual heart, if they cannot be built in the wider community. Quite apart from any iconoclasm amongst the intellectuals spearheading the Protestant Reformation, interest in a private religious practice, an interiorisation of spirituality, was perhaps generally inevitable, even in those least interested in change. Personal beliefs, as Duffy has suggested throughout in *The Stripping of the Altars*, might have been unchanged in fact, but necessarily transferred from public to private sphere, and subject to the unruly psychological pressures of that sphere. Southwell's trained alertness to the difference between public and private space will have informed his understanding of this necessity to 'hide' belief inside the self, in order to resist the pressures of public scrutiny and political change.

Perhaps Southwell, in 'Fortunes Falsehoode' (p. 65, lines 37–40) intends to expose the unfortunate tendency of Tudor monarchs to impose change:

> No wind so chaungeable, no sea so wavering,
> As giddie fortune in reeling varieties:
> Now mad, now mercifull, now fearce, now favoring:
> In all things mutable, but mutabilities.   40

This is a commonplace, seen from Boethius to mid-Tudor poetry. Handed for appraisal round a gathering of English Catholics by a young Catholic priest-poet risking his life in remaining stalwart in the Old Faith, though, it becomes a manifesto too. Burghley's various oaths and tests of allegiance were designed to expose the most reserved spiritual depths, creating extreme tension between personal, subjective integrity and public subjected obedience. Southwell, disguising his message in this old-fashioned sermon on the vagaries of Fortuna, directs his reader to eschew change, unlike those coat-turners and trimmers who put their trust in her and end in ruin. In the English context of the time his message is to keep the Old Faith, whatever that 'slie' woman, that 'tygre', that 'weeping Crocodile' wants (lines 2, 33, 34). Complaint poetry was becoming increasingly linked with 'anti-aristocratic' works, alongside ballad and other older-fashioned forms, as the courtly style achieved dominance.[30] Southwell, in offering nothing but the complaint in this poem, is attempting to reflect the feelings of the ordinary English, whilst at the same time identifying, indeed emphasising, the dislocation between the hopeful subject and any central, dependable truth, the essential slipperiness of subjectivity and its attendant imagery. Truth was to be found only in the individual breast, in such a place of change and dissembling; each Christian must become a lover, not just a follower, of Christ.

A GOLDEN DISTRACTION: METAPHORISING THE REAL

Sith my life from life is parted', begins Mary Magdalen, in her 'complaint at Christs death' (p. 45), 'Death come take thy portion'. She rails at the 'Spitefull speare, that breakst this prison' (l. 37), crying at the breaking of the bond between Christ's body and soul at the moment of his death on the Cross. Southwell is here dramatising part of the meditation of the morning of the Fifth Day of the Ignatian *Exercises*. 'This prison' is ostensibly the prison of the soul, the ribcage (in conventional devotional imagery), where Christ's divinity had been imprisoned until the 'spitefull speare' unlinked his soul from his body; where, also, Magdalen's heart had been held captive. As the breaking of Christ's side had given access to his heart, symbol of redemption, and blood and water, its material signs, Magdalen's misery encompasses both pre-Resurrection and post-Real-Presence Christianity.

In *Funeral Teares* Magdalen is seeing for the first time the empty tomb, also so far without any divine understanding other than that of her own instinctive love. Just as the Joseph poem occupies the space between the human and the angelic apprehension, so Magdalen is here existing in the spiritual vacuum between discovering the loss of her love and the angelic intervention that precedes the arrival of the risen Christ, a space that is explored at length in *Funeral Teares*, in which many of Southwell's short lyrics find their echoes, and, perhaps, their origins. *Funeral Teares* can be seen as a tutorial in learning to live in a place without the Real Presence, in which Southwell ventriloquises Christ himself as the teacher. Meeting the distraught Magdalen in the Garden he tells her she must learn to love him just as fully, despite being deprived of his physical presence:

> It is now necessary to weane thee from the comfort of my externall presence, that thou maist learne to lodge mee in the secretes of thy heart, and teach thy thoughts to supply the offices of outward senses. For in this visible shape I am not here long to be seene [...] but what thy eie then seeth not, thy heart shall feele, and my silent parly wil find audience in thy inward eare. (sig. I 6v)

As in 'Josephs Amazement', the all-too-human Magdalen, sent by her Lord to tell his absent 'bretheren' the good news, vacillates between love and duty, going 'as fast backeward in thought as forward in pace', sulking, turning round, or straying in a 'golden distraction', imagining 'that her Lord is present' (sig. I 7). As in 'Josephs Amazement', where any Christian reader could respond to a tearful meditation upon an aspect of Christ's life, Southwell's English Catholic readers supplied that extra context of Magdalen's tears from their own experience: they knew that she was also crying for the loss of Christ's body from the Roman Catholic Mass, and for the loss of the possibilities of wider celebration of liturgical feasts that had been part of the expression of Christian love and joy for so long. As in the impossibility of a murdered God or the pointlessness of a tomb without a body, the de-legalising of the Roman Catholic Mass meant that the loving, loyal English Catholic heart was, by the time of Southwell's mission, officially a paradox. The removal of Real Presence from the compulsory communion meant that it was impossible for a Catholic to receive spiritual comfort (legitimately) in England in the 1580s, where 'truth once was, and is not', from the Catholic point of view (l. 19). Catholics survived spiritually, both at Court and in the shires, but it was largely by mental reservation and subterfuge, wounding for them as individuals, and perpetually dangerous for their dependents. They might attend the Church of England services to save themselves from fines, but all that remained in that de-realised mass was a pretence of the real, in Roman Catholic eyes.[31] But 'Paynted meate no hunger feedes'; the mass-offerings were, by Roman Catholic standards, mere imitations and cruel reminders of the true sacrament, and therefore unable to offer salvation for the soul, mere 'Shaddowes [...] Shewing want, that helpe they cannot: | Signes, not salves of miserie' ('Complaint', lines 20–2).

'But alas, what meaneth this change, & how happeneth this strange alteration?' (*Teares*, p. 9). Southwell's poems of love and bereavement attempt to bring his readers round to new understandings of this altered state. As in 'Josephs Amazement', it is through unconquerable love that Mary transcends the rational conclusion that all is over, and she does so even before the angels bring her good news. But first she prefers merely to weep: 'I will make much of my sorrow, and sith I have no joy but in teares, I may lawfully shedde them', Mary cries, echoing English Catholic nostalgia in hovering on the cusp of accepting the apparent loss and preferring, almost, to live in a state of 'consuming languor, taking comfort in nothing but in being comfortlesse' (*Teares*, p. 14). This was the very state of sad complacency that the Jesuits came to alter. The angels seem sometimes to exchange places with the mission priests themselves as they stand ready to bring comfort that Mary's heart, weakened by doubt and fear, is barely able to hear:

> small is the light that a starre can yeeld when the Sun is downe, and a sorry exchange to goe gather crummes after the losse of a hevenly repast [...] If they come to disburden me of my heavinesse, their coming wil be burdensome unto mee, and they wil load me more while they labour my reliefe. They cannot perswade me, that my Maister is not lost, for my owne eyes will disprove them. (p. 15)

Southwell says that the light given by stars is dim in comparison with that given by the sun. In 'Complaint' Magdalen appears to repeat this, as 'Seely starres must needes leave shining, | When the sunne is shaddowed' (lines 7–8), but it is difficult to make it come out as the same thing. Whether he meant it to read falsely or not, it is a proposition which expresses the danger of recusant despair: that without the immediate succour of the Catholic sacraments and their ministers, the light of faith must fade, a proposition to which Southwell has replied in 'Scorne not the least' (p. 69), in a clear attempt to override such fading. 'Where wards are weake, and foes encountring strong', he starts, 'The feebler part puts up enforced wrong, | And silent sees, that speech could not

The flight of angels: England's altered confidence

amend' (lines 1, 3–4); but he persists in seeing a spark of something that ought to give them all hope, a reflection in the heart of a greater light that cannot be fully extinguished: 'Yet higher powers must thinke, though they repine,' he says, 'When sunne is set: the little starres will shine' (lines 5–6). Dim as it is, that glimmer of faith persists.

The 'higher powers' had, in breaking with Rome, opened up an arena of debate that was to have serious consequences in the next century: the 'magic' of directly transmitted divinity had gone from another part of the English establishment, too, in Roman Catholic eyes. Much of Southwell's poetic explores the paradox inherent in a monarchy that demanded that religious observation be kept according to its own views but that had, from his point of view, stripped away its own divinity by cutting its connection with the Pope, God's only vicegerent on earth. By the laws of the Catholic Church, only 'the hand of God' could depose an anointed king, as Shakespeare's Richard II puts it – 'no hand of blood and bone | Can grip the handle of our sceptre, | Unless he do profane, steal, or usurp'.[32] The 'Shaddowes' of God's rule that kingship once embodied are no longer reminders of the heavenly realities, they are, like the un-Real Mass, 'but vanitie' in such a kingdom – 'Signes', false seemings, that merely pretend real kingship ('Marie Magdalens complaint', lines 19, 20–2). To a Catholic, Mass without the real presence was a mockery of the truth; to a Puritan the continuing appearance of bishops' finery and other remnants of the Old Faith, and the tendency towards secularisation of the State, showed up the botched reformation that Elizabeth's church seemed to them to represent.

Reason might suggest that loyalty to the denomination of the Crown was the only option that promised a comfortable life, but the English Catholic subject had found that 'peace with sense is warre with God' ('Mans civill warre', p. 49, l. 27), resulting in confusion and, worse, desolation. Perhaps the highest Catholics could escape such desolation in exile or by throwing themselves into the hospitable life, like Sir Thomas Tresham, who deflected attention away from his private support for Mary Stuart's claim to the English throne with his public loyalism, ruinously lavish entertaining, and garden follies. Perhaps consolation for the recusancy fines and lack of advancement such men began to suffer after 1581 was to be found in such a life.

The Jesuits' concept of consolation was not of this sort, however. Nadal described it as 'an inner joy, as serenity in judgement, a relish, a light, a reassuring step forward, a clarification of insight' – everything, in other words, that was no longer available to the confused and guideless ordinary English Joseph.[33] Jesuit ministry focused on working towards this serene consolation; one must prepare and dispose oneself to allow entry to the graceful, healing love of God that the Jesuits believed to be freely available.[34] Magdalen, who was a bearer of salves before she was a weeper, seems to have been an important visual reminder of such disposition at this period; she was often depicted with her ointment-jar. In the Roman Novitiate she occupied a curiously dominant position,[35] and her appearance in refectory, dormitory, and infirmary seems to identify her with the bringer of salves for corporeal injuries rather than the penitent; she was a symbol of human appetite and bodily requirements, inescapably corporeal, but none the less capable of an almost instinctive godliness; this exemplified the Jesuits' idea of worship as passionate engagement, with ministry as an attracting and consoling of souls, as well as with their own special situation 'out in the world', where they must constantly be faced with sensuality and excess (and the company of women). Her appearance in such a private space supports this view, I would argue; in public she was more often seen as a grief-stricken penitent at the foot of the cross or at the Tomb.[36] Here are those Jesuit layers of meaning again, the private Magdalen having a different role to the public one, an emblem for a concept of penitence, which, despite Counter-Reformation preoccupations with the sacrament of Penance, was 'refashioned' by the Jesuits into something more attractive, more sanguine, predicated as much on consolation as on regret. Southwell stresses in *Marie Magdalen* that the 'funeral tears' Mary weeps are not tears of repentance but signs of 'the great vehemency of her love to Christ'.[37]

But it was as the Weeper that Magdalen was most readily taken up by other poets, expressing deep anxieties about personal sin and inadequacy: the altered English Church did not seem fully able to reassure its members that they were, or even might be, saved. In Donne's 'Show me dear Christ', the church itself becomes an unsaved Magdalen, still in a state of prostitution.[38] What had begun as the metaphorising of anxiety using Magdalen as a model had, by 1650, become an anxious understanding of the human need to feel that one has some control over one's fate. A Catholic, in loving God, was accessing grace; a Protestant at that time seemed not to be in a position to affect his or her position relative to God, hence, perhaps, the appropriation of a repentant Magdalen's despair. Puritanism had at first rejected the 'application of the senses' in devotional activity, but it allowed contrition.[39]

The whole function of the *Exercises* was based on the reading of powerful emotions, the more extreme, the better; in this sense it was a useful tool for Protestant and Catholic alike. In this intimate, private world of retreat and passionate response, Magdalen is bound to be the exemplar, as a personification of emotionalism, rather than mere repentance. Southwell's St Peter expressed the more public concerns of broken oaths and failures in high office, but his Magdalen, although he seems to show her in the same grieving role as in the public spaces in Rome, is his metaphor for the acceptability to God of the frail but passionate soul. Lukewarm Christianity was something the Jesuits deplored;[40] Magdalen was never lukewarm.

As female, too, she was connected in Renaissance minds in general with the private, not public sphere, and was therefore the perfect means of expression of the conflicted ordinary, *private* self in the paradoxical English situation; a self recognisable to suppressed Catholics, but also to Puritans, equally under attack. This contemporised, self-contained, impassioned, English Magdalen is perhaps thereby Southwell's most fecund (and most appropriated) innovation.[41]

Where reason suggested compromise, or even atheism, then, in response to the assaults of the State, Southwell had to find a way of counterbalancing such reasoning which did not itself go beyond the reasonable bounds of doctrine and morals. He had reproved the wavering congregation of Catholicism in sermon and poem, but he also had to attract them back to what seemed the *un*reasonable option. Rather than blasting the waverers with the horrors of Hell, which appear very rarely in his poetry, he did so through exemplary characterisations able to express a 'right' sort of unreason, ones that were most likely to be taken up and internalised by his readership. In other words, the effects of the teachings in the *Exercises* on honest penitence and consolation upon the exercisant's individual psyche had to be reproduced in his congregation without direct access to a spiritual director: they had to find their own internal sparks of divinity, like the little sunless stars.

Southwell needed to create a new, engaging character that was sufficiently stimulating to draw attention away from the cynical, secularising erotic poetry that was becoming fashionable, a character that could appeal to both male and female. Although the secularisation of passion was to Southwell a dangerous societal sickness that required an antidote, he had no argument with passion itself – it was central to his devotional methodology. It was the fact that Venus was Shakespeare's or Nashe's muse that made Southwell's own 'mourning muse resolve in teares'.[42] A corrupted copy of Sidney's *Astrophil and Stella* appeared in 1591, bursting with passion for an earthly love; Southwell's response, his Catholic muse, the human expression of the drama of emotional response to the *Exercises* was, of course, his Magdalen.[43]

In *The Poetry of Meditation*, Louis Martz, seeking to explain the emergence of what we call metaphysical poetry, identified a new influence on English letters, moving it from the traditional poetic language of sententiae towards newer, more dynamically personalised forms of expression. Southwell's Magdalen is central to this new, self-dramatising poetics of unreason.[44] As Southwell uses her she seems to characterise the rise of the useful, even positive, power of the emotionally affective in poetry and drama. The accessing and expressing of deeply sympathetic feeling encouraged by the *Exercises* was expressed most clearly through the model of Magdalen with her flawed, passionate personality; this psychologically multi-faceted expression of self was readily taken up by other authors after Southwell's model first appeared. A trend towards religious verse was beginning in England before Southwell wrote his Magdalen,[45] and he did not invent the characterisation – his own was based on Continental models – but, in Englishing and poeticising it, and through its appearance without any very obvious doctrinal signifiers in his earliest published poetry, the model became accessible at a moment that was clearly ready for it, and in a form that was usable, one that had wider effects on English poetry, and even drama.

Magdalen is more than an exemplar of female contrition, she is the first appearance in English poetry of a 'real' self-exposing psychology, depicted in disordered mid-thought, mid-crisis, the sort that later appeared as those realistic 'personations' in Shakespeare, the apparently *sui generis* appearance of which intrigues those of his critics unwilling simply to put it down to Shakespearean genius.[46]

Magdalen's adoption by other English poets speaks for itself; there was a flush of imitations following Southwell's innovative model.[47] *Marie Magdalens Funeral Teares* (1591) was sufficiently popular to be in ten editions by 1636, and after it came some ostentatious and probably opportunistic sobbing – Nicholas Breton's *Marie Magdalen's Love* (1595), and Thomas Nashe's *Christ's Tears over Jerusalem*, for instance, the latter openly derided by Gabriel Harvey as stolen from Southwell. Only now that Nashe has 'a little mused upon the *Funeral Tears of Mary Magdalen*, [...] is [he] egged on to try the suppleness of his Pathetical vein'; over-egged, Nashe implies, but he expressly links the model of Magdalen with the new pathetic mood in poetry here.[48]

Magdalen's capacious inner space became the locus for much serious poetic self-identification, an emotionally charged, female space to fill with personal anxieties. Henry Constable, writing sometime at or after his conversion to Catholicism in 1590 (the most active years of Southwell's private poetic production),[49] uses the character of Magdalen as 'the blessed offender' who herself 'had tried | How far a sinner differs from a saint' in one of his several sonnets to her. She keeps him warm company in his weeping while he interrogates his sinful self after the manner of the *Exercises*; her ardour, literally, lights him up. His soul becomes, by her example, 'no foolish virgin' with an 'empty lamp', but 'like a Magdalen' with her jar of precious unguents. His breast, then, like her 'ointment box', is blessed with 'oil of grace', so that 'the zeal which then shall burn in me' shall 'make my heart like to a lamp appear', and 'in my spouse's palace give me place'.[50] In the end, it is Magdalen's consolatory passion here, not her contrition, that supplies Constable with this effulgent alternative to the lightless emptiness of the virgin heart.

HAMARTOLOS: REDIRECTING LOVE

Once it is understood that Magdalen was more than just the exemplary Weeper, that she exemplified the more cheerful Jesuit idea of consolation, Southwell's reasons for bringing her to England become clear. The moral strength of

The flight of angels: England's altered confidence

English Catholicism was, under the drip-drip of hostile legislation, beginning to erode; English minds were turning away from religious conviction altogether; where passion was found, it was, as Southwell's complaint about the erotic muse suggests, all too often directed earthward. 'Passions I allow, and loves I approve,' Southwell writes, 'onely I would wishe that men would alter their object and better their intent' (prefatory letter, *Funeral Teares* (1591)); 'for in lieu of solemne and devout matter, to which in duety they owe their abilities, they now busy themselves in expressing such passions, as onely serve for testimonies to how unworthy affections they have wedded their wils' (prefatory letter, *Saint Peters Complaint* (1595)).[51] He lays out his own poetic strategy (with biblical precedents): it is 'to weave a new webbe in [the profane poets'] owne loome', laying 'a few course threds together, to invite some skilfuller wits to goe forward in the same, or to begin some finer peece, wherein it may be seene, how well verse and vertue sute together' (p. lvii).[52]

Magdalen is as closely associated with this strategy as Peter: in the prefatory poem to *Saint Peters Complaint* Southwell explains his use of biblical characterisations, apologising for a use of saints which exposed their frailties. 'Muse not to see some mud in cleerest brooke', he says: 'They once were brittle mould, that now are Saintes.' It is clear from his apology that he is quite deliberately muddying their saintly reputations in order to make them the more relevant to the reader in a fallen nation: 'Their weakenesse is no warrant to offend: | Learne by their faultes, what in thine owne to mend' (p. 75). He explicitly sets out in his *Magdalen* and his lyric poetry to 'wooe some skilfuller pennes from unworthy labours', seeking rather to redirect their loves than depress their passions.[53]

That 'Love' rather than remorse is Southwell's sermon text can be seen from the fact that the word recurs throughout his lyric poetry, apart, that is, from his Holy Family sequence. The sequence was clearly written for communal celebration and worship not improvement of others, written as it is throughout in terms of 'us/we/our'. The Virgin cannot be used to demonstrate triumph over the will; her will is not as other humans', but conjoined to God's; as the Immaculate Conception, she cannot offer herself to Southwell as a role model for the frail, errant English souls he was trying to reach.

Love of the Christ-Child, too, presented problems: although Southwell preaches it charmingly in 'A childe my Choyce', the first of the main collection of poems, the adoration of the infant can only find the chastest expression without threatening to overwhelm its subject. In one of the earliest Spiritual Exercises in Southwell's devotional diary, the Preparation for Communion, St Catharine is imagined espousing herself to God with a foreknowledge of the heavenly bliss of the union that she would complete in heaven: 'would she not, in the sweetness of the thought be bedewed with tears, would she not yearn for the heavenly embrace of the beautiful Child Jesus, His honied words, His chaste glances, His most holy union with her soul?'.⁵⁴ Here, in this metaphorical representation of the mystery of the Eucharist, we see a blending of the imagery of love poetry with its sweet talk and telling glances and the adoration of a chaste child similar to that of 'A childe my Choyce', where Southwell's desire to express passionate love seems at odds with his subject-matter.

Southwell found in Magdalen an adult characterisation to carry this ardent love to an adult Christ. When Magdalen speaks, his poetic expression seems to achieve a sureness and self-confidence that is lacking in 'A childe'. It is Magdalen as the archetypal lover that Southwell finds invaluable.

Although reduced to a bystander in Matthew, in John Magdalen is actively engaged in the events, and Bethany becomes a place of respite for Jesus in the last, crowded weeks of his ministry. Days before his arrest, Mary and Martha call him back to Bethany to help their dying brother. An apparently exhausted Jesus prevaricates; Lazarus dies. When at last Jesus comes, Mary remains obdurately in the house, despite his asking for her; later she rushes out only to confront him with her belief that Lazarus would have lived if Jesus had come when first called, whereupon he weeps.⁵⁵ Lazarus is raised from the dead by a Jesus literally groaning with the effort, and all are given supper. Martha serves, while Mary pours a pound of costly spikenard ointment over her Lord's feet, filling the house with the odour of it; she then wipes his feet with her hair.⁵⁶ This is a remarkably intense, sensual passage quite unlike the terse Matthew version. We rarely see the adult Jesus caught up in any similar familial upset. Martha is shown as the dutiful housewife; Mary is a turbulent sensualist, by comparison.

She came to Southwell's poetry with a 'past' that ought to have created problems for the priest: she was traditionally linked to other accounts in the Bible of an unnamed woman who had been a prostitute. Henry Constable makes the link explicit in one of his sonnets to her, which manages through her to complect erotic imagery with remorse for a 'few nights' solace in delicious bed | Where heat of lust did kindle flames of hell'; he then displays her 'nak'd on naked rock' in her thirty years of desert penance – the medieval tradition which gave rise to her tearful reputation.⁵⁷

Magdalen was beginning to be a metaphor for a more immediately felt sort of Christianity, appearing in more and more histrionic postures of adoration and love in the religious paintings and poetry of the fifteenth and sixteenth centuries, tearing her hair or wringing her hands in extremes of grief beside her dead or dying Lord, in contrast to the Mother of Christ, standing white and immobile. Magdalen's wilful attachment to the human aspect of Christ, to his corporeal body, drives her to these extremes of distress on seeing it so damaged, almost in resistance to the will of God, as if she loves where she does not yet understand, as in Taddeo Gaddi's *Crucifixion* of the mid fourteenth century, where Christ's Mother swoons on the arm of the Evangelist, while Mary Magdalen flings up her hands in active distress, her body twisted outward as if to make the ready availability of her emotions explicit. In Rogier van der Weyden's *Descent from the Cross* (c.1435), too, there is the same difference in response between the wilting Virgin and Mary Magdalen, writhing in distress and unable to remove her eyes from those now blood-streaked feet.[58] Trent (and, especially, Bellarmine) declared the swooning Virgin a deviation from the Gospel narrative, preferring a restrained but conscious grief, which is why it is possible for Southwell to imagine her active lament in his 'Virgin to Christ on the Cross'.[59]

Southwell is, via Mary Magdalen, able to use the complexities of adult passion to the full, exploring her physical attachment to Christ at length in his own version of the Crucifixion/Deposition, 'Marie Magdalens complaint at Christs death'. He here repeats, with greater success, the exercise of 'A childe my Choyce' where he uses 'love' in as many different ways as possible (p. 45). Using her status as an adult lover of an adult Christ, he is at last able to give full rein to his passionate nature. 'With my love, my life was nestled | In the sonne of happinesse' he writes (lines 25–6). Perhaps this puns on the Petrarchan sense of 'sun' as the Ideal Love, replacing it with Christ in the Ignatian way; it may also tip the meaning of the poem towards a more active, Bellarminian Catholicism, hinting that the speaker is Mary Mother of God, not Magdalen.[60] Love, though, is given the centrality that the new cosmology gave the sun, occupying, with its object Christ/God, the very centre of all things. 'Life' becomes external to the central 'love' felt by the protagonist, as if less important than the love itself; life is 'wrested' away from that nurturing love 'To a world of heavinesse' which reduces life to less than life (lines 27–8). It is Magdalen's emotional capacity for ardent love that has given her this deep insight into the heavenly order of things. If the impractical abstraction of her love for Christ had once been the useful model to medieval contemplatives, now it was the freely expressed passion of it. She is, as Christopher Devlin says, 'the type of the indestructible Eros, purified by contrition and thereafter made capable, through affective union with Christ's human nature, of the divine love of the Creator'.[61] Her femininity is therefore a rhetorical rather than a methodological logic.

Southwell had set out to show poets how their poetry could be better directed using several biblical characters, but it is only with Magdalen the *hamartolos* that Southwell is able to try his pathetical poetic vein in the adult genre of the love-lyric. *Hamartolos* suggests 'one who misses the mark' – 'sinner' is too prescriptive, although encompassed in the Gospel sense. Magdalen has not sinned by loving, she has loved well, but aimed too low in loving the creature Christ to distraction. Erotic love *can* be acceptable to God – even a badly made arrow, merely by being aimed, or wishing to be aimed, in the right direction, can allow the ingress of grace, in that new cross-action of up-moving will and down-pouring heavenly intention of Suárezian theology. Throughout *Funeral Teares* Southwell repeats the Magdalenic theme of 'the divine acceptance of love however misguided', something that must have fallen kindly on the ears of those whose hope and faith had been in the wilderness for so long; Southwell had made it possible for an English poet to write with erotic passion without polluting Parnassus.

The canny controversialist had also, through Magdalenic eroticism, achieved a palpable hit upon his opponents, having at once shown Sidney's Protestant Muse to be at fault, and found a morally acceptable use for the erotic poetry that so easily grabbed the attentions of youthful patrons. Southwell had 'allowed' a new expression of goodness that was sensually attractive. Some poets preferred the frankly carnal, like Nashe with his 'Choyse of Valentines', dedicated to Lord Strange; and Shakespeare with *Venus and Adonis*, dedicated to Henry Wriothesley, both young noblemen whose patronage Southwell would have considered invaluable to his mission.[62] These were probably written around the years 1592–93, after Southwell's Magdalen had appeared. Both promised graver works to follow, as if anxious not to seem to ignore the admonitions of Southwell (and others) about decency. Other poets took up the moralised model quickly, perhaps stimulated to do so by Southwell. Thomas Lodge's *Prosopopeia: The Teares of the Holy, Blessed, and Sanctified Marie, the Mother of God* (1596), for instance, refers to Southwell's challenge to aim higher. Lodge has cleaned up his poetic act accordingly, he says; as in Southwell, the betterment of love's object is expressed through female grieving.[63] Another of Henry Constable's sonnets, 'To St Mary Magdalene', comes very close to Southwell's characterisation, Constable praising her as his pattern for understanding the pleasure of 'heavenly love', which others have failed to prove (presumably he means by argument and coercion); their account of God's love has proved too unengaging. Magdalen succeeds because of her warm sensuality: 'for like a woman spowse my sowle shalbe' – that is, obedient and receptive to God's invasive love. She also succeeds because of her past experience of life: his soul/spouse was once moved by her 'sinful passions' to 'lust', but 'since betrothed to goddes sonne above' must now be 'enamoured with his deitye' alone.

Magdalen the ex-prostitute seems to be used here by Constable as a biblical model of his own journey to faith, from Protestant to Catholic. Where Peter embodied the horror of apostasy, she was the restorative for the many English who had, for whatever reason, at some time responded to fear or ambition by reneging on their old faith. She was the proof that God would forgive if remorse were felt deep in the heart.

Constable is luxuriating in the implications of Catholic belief in the Real Presence, the substance of divinity on earth. Conflating communion with God with physical consummation, as the Spanish mystics had, and Bernard and the writer of the Bible's Song of Songs before them, he takes the sexualised imagery every bit as far as Southwell does in his Magdalenic poems. The soul, once released from the body's 'garment', shall enter naked into the pleasures of the bridal night, to enjoy 'sweete conjunction' 'clasped in the armes of God' (*Verse*, p. 536; *16CVerse*, p. 467). An ancient biblical paean to powerfully felt religious response has found its English poetic metaphor, almost against reason. It needed careful handling not to become a mere stage-prop, though. Southwell's training had given him insights into human emotions and motivations that gave his characterisation a particular potency that was not always understood by his imitators. Thomas Lodge clearly found the model of the grieving female useful to express his new poetic morality in his *Prosopopeia*, but, as Brownlow notes, 'Lodge has not understood Southwell's disciplined focus on the psychology of Mary Magdalen at a particular moment'.[64] She is not just there in Southwell to catch a reader's attention by weeping prettily: she is there to enact the psychodrama of repentance; in giving a shape to deep-seated anxieties she helps to articulate the conflicts that the new forms of worship were beginning to expose.

A NEW VOICE: THE FEMALED SOUL

As with any traveller, Southwell's equipment, rhetorical or otherwise, had to fulfil many roles to justify inclusion in his 'pack'. Magdalen had transferable value as an important biblical female; she was, next to the Virgin, the closest to the centre of the Christian hierarchy. There were female as well as male patrons to attract in a kingdom rapidly losing its most important Catholic gentlemen to prison or the Continent. Breton's work of the 1590s is dedicated to Sidney's sister, the Countess of Pembroke. Hers was part of a courtly circle with a somewhat ambiguous relationship with the Crown, surrounded by the swirl of ambitious poets at whom Southwell had aimed his remarks about misguided amour.[65] Breton's version of Magdalen, *Marie Magdalens Love* (published with *A Solemne Passion* in the *Stationers' Register*, 24 July 1595), is very close to Southwell's in tone.[66] Breton was clearly alert to poetic strategies employed by Southwell; he conflates his patroness the Countess of Pembroke with the repentant Magdalen in his *Passions of the Spirit* and elsewhere, and his divine poems *The Ravisht Soule* and *The Blessed Weeper* (1601, also dedicated to the Countess) are full of Southwellian sensibilities. Breton clearly recognised Southwell's seductive, frail Magdalen as a way into both his female and his male readers' hearts.[67]

Magdalen in part represents the self awakened by the *Exercises*, and one would expect to see other Jesuits writing in similar vein to Southwell. Jasper Heywood seems to have got there first, in English at least, but without Southwell's use of biblical *dramatis personae*. Heywood's post-Exercises poetic self turns psychological aspects such as conscience and thought into characters in a personal Morality play of which he himself is the author, no longer just the audience, and in which the reader, through sympathy and recognition, must *actively* participate.[68] Heywood's exposed interiority is no mere complaint: the soul is tangled in a mess of faults; the observing mind struggles with a confusion of different and conflicting drives, conscience, whispering, secret thoughts. This is an exploration of the chaotic inner life of a living psychology, Southwell's Magdalen or St Peter agonising: a Hamlet soliloquising, not a Polonius instructing.

Where Wyatt and Sidney had introduced into English the eloquently disappointed lover, Southwell, trained as he was in the recounting of real emotion, had introduced the language of the honest but incoherent heart. In his prose, his turbulent Magdalen, helplessly exposing her doubt and frailty, can give full rein to her self; in poetry, such rhetorical abandon was less easy to imitate, although the stumbling self-contradictions of *Funeral Teares* are hinted at none the less. Joseph and Peter present similar models for similar reasons: their language sometimes leaves the bonds of reason behind, something that seems at odds with the orderliness of poetic 'number'. In Joseph the confusion is described, a matter of narration; in Peter and Magdalen it is expressed as a Shakespearean character on a stage might soliloquise it, through the simulated break-up of thought and language. In the shorter 'Saint Peters Complaynte' (p. 29) there are no explanations; the protagonist racks himself from the opening line with agonised, unanswerable questions, the ugly and discordant sounds contributing to the sense of an overwrought self-disgust: 'Were all the Jewesh tyrannyes too fewe | To glutt thy hungry lookes with his disgrace', he snarls, as if through gritted teeth, then accuses himself of spitting poison in his maker's face (lines 49–52). 'Could servile feare ... | So thrall my love', he demands, 'that I should thus eschewe | A vowed death and mysse so faire an ayme? | Dye: dye: disloyall wretch' (lines 25–8). The lines are a concatenation of bitter hisses crowded out by a rush of hard attacking 'd's; they almost beg to be shouted as a rising crescendo. In the full-length 'Saint Peters Complaint' (p. 76), the protagonist rehearses his sins fairly tidily, as a rule, although in merciless detail, but these conventional passages are interspersed with others in which the protagonist seems almost to lose his grip in his grief and shame, as if a real person suddenly overwhelmed with feeling: 'Blush craven sott', he blurts – 'lurke in eternall night: | Crouche in the darkest caves from loathed light. | Ah wretch'. Because his thoughts (and therefore the poetic structure) are disordered, it is not always clear who is being castigated, but, as in a real narrative, the emotional intensity of his feelings brings himself always back to the centre of the tale (lines 119–21). Southwell has used the structure of his source poems, the narrative of Peter's fall or Magdalen's grief, but added this simulation of disordered thought, making the personation real. 'Yet love, was loath to part; feare, loath to die: | Stay, daunger, life, did counterplead their causes' his Peter goes on; the vocabulary is beginning to become detached from linear meaning. But 'Peter' is about self-hatred, and failure. It is love that causes Joseph and Magdalen to fall apart rhetorically, Magdalen especially embodying a fresh rhetorical register. The great self-expository soliloquies of dramatists beginning with Shakespeare were written after the emergence of Southwell's characterisations of Magdalen, and his innovation deserves acknowledgement.[69]

This is less about Magdalen than about passionate engagement; one of the shorter lyrics conflates the characterisations of Magdalen and Peter as if their identity is less important than the urgency of Christian witness. 'Mary Magdalens blush' (p. 32) begins 'The signes of shame that staine my blushing face | Rise from the feeling of my raving fits', sounding like a presentation of a histrionically repentant desert Magdalen, but it becomes more confused: 'Remorse doth teach my guiltie thoughts to know, | How cheape I sould, that Christ so dearely bought' it goes on – but it was Peter who 'sold' Christ metaphorically, or even Judas, not Magdalen, whose only sin was a lustful 'past' (lines 1–2, 9–10). 'All ghostly dynts that grace at me did dart, | Like stubborne rocke I forced to recoyle' sounds even more like Peter the rock (lines 14–15). But the general drift of the poem is of a semi-coherent colloquy of shame, where the words themselves fall to cross-purposes as if in illustration both of the speaker's chaotic state and the crossing of human will with Divine purpose. 'O sence, O soule, O had, O hoped blisse, | You wooe, you weane, you draw, you drive me back' (lines 25–6). This is a soul reaching that point required by the *Exercises* of near-despairing acknowledgement of its total subjection to the forces of the cosmos, prior to gaining a new understanding of the self in its relationship with that cosmos. Southwell's Magdalen, beautiful, dishevelled and eloquent, has made a lover's demands upon Christ, and written her self on to the cosmos through sheer potency of love, confused as it is, offering both a non-dogmatic model for the loss of confidence of the English Catholics and its literary expression through the perfectly acceptable poetic ideal of love.[70] The gentlemanly disappointments expressed in Sidney's sonnets, closest of all contemporary works to those of Southwell in this respect, fall far short of this cosmic drama.

Martz made a vital early step in the recovery of the significance of such 'religious' procedures, recognising a function of the *Spiritual Exercises* that transcended the strictly doctrinal. In noting the importance to literature of that element of the *Exercises* that involves the losing of the self in ecstatic union with God, Martz has unsettled the canonical tendency to see a sudden unexplained emergence of creative genius in the late sixteenth century.[71] In Jasper Heywood Martz sees the very first 'impact of the Counter Reformation on English poetry' – and this appeared before those elements, such as Hamlet's confused inner voice, that early modern criticism identifies as innovative, and central to the new realism in characterisation seen in Shakespeare.[72] Puttenham, in his *Arte of English Poesie*, praises 'counterfait countenance', or *prosopopoeia*, the describing of the face or speech of one absent or dead, as Homer or Chaucer do 'most naturally and pleasantly'; he has no contemporary examples to offer his reader, however, leading one to suppose that such 'personation' had fallen out of usage (*Arte*, pp. 238–9). Kermode has identified a new intensity in the 'personation' of dramatic personae in Shakespeare's *Venus* and *Lucrece* – too late for inclusion into Puttenham's critique; but Southwell was already personating Magdalen and Peter, although, again, too late for Puttenham's notice.[73] It is clear that some kind of new technique in characterisation both in plays and poetry was appearing in England in the early 1590s from somewhere, and, as Heywood did not attempt such English ventriloquisations, it seems most likely that Southwell's peculiar version of imaginative realism had, whatever the other writers thought of his politics or religion, some influence on the way they approached characterisation in their own works, reflected in their readiness to take up Magdalen, the metaphor for such affective characterisation. The realistic, personalised colloquy with God, the inner self or the audience began here, with the first literary expression of Jesuit concepts of 'consolation' in English, and later through the characters of Peter and Magdalen, this self-reflexive, meditative voice took on a new, more humanistic dramatic intensity.[74] Peter's dilemma could express the technical problems of oaths and processes, but it was through Magdalen that the problems of the self or soul were expressed.

He had an English precedent for pious but worldly female complaint: Katherine Parr's 1545 meditations, which reappeared in the *Register* in 1587, the year after his arrival. That virtuous princess, though unusually strong in her own Protestantism in Henry VIII's conservative Court, became famously and tearfully repentant when her husband began to brandish the familiar arrest warrant. Not only did her model of female remorse provide a warning to overzealous Protestants, but to women in general and perhaps the present monarch in particular, to know their place. As with Southwell's Magdalenic piece, the Archbishop's licence had been obtained. Conservative, even nostalgic, forms of female obedience and conformity in a woman-monarched age were presumably considered a good thing in one London palace at least.

But this, as with other such complaints, is voiced by the poet.[75] Southwell has clearly created an English precedent in his Magdalenic exemplar, freeing the poet to explore a wounded psychology more freely than personal witness would allow, even, with Magdalen at least, to the limits of eroticism. This eroticism, an impassioning of self, not an appeal to sexual appetites, although distrusted by some critics, is, none the less, Southwell's chief gift. It was his peculiar acuity in conflating this socially acceptable model of female complaint with the sensual immediacy of the sinner and the authority of the biblical Magdalen that so excited other poets, dramatising and sacralising the genre and opening up new possibilities of identification.

Southwell's version of female remorse was different from its predecessors, or, more accurately, there was a difference in the nature of the 'husband' to whom the lesser was to owe obedience. Southwell, in comparing flawed, conflicted humanity to Magdalen, rather than an ideal princess or wife, was offering a new model of the sinful self that almost luxuriated in the depth and quality of its failings where they touched most closely Christ's own humanity. The most attractive of sinners, Magdalen was the perfect model for the secular Renaissance world: the soul fitted into the cosmic hierarchy as woman fitted into the (early modern) earthly one. God was the Ideal; Christ, husband or monarch was the self-controlled, balanced, ascetic manly perfection of humanity; Magdalen, humanity or subject the flawed, sensually distracted but love-centred 'female' partner that is capable of receiving and nurturing grace within itself. The Magdalenic model of self offered by Southwell was, being both 'female' and helplessly love-besotted, the most flawed and unassuming model of all and therefore the one with which ordinary men and women could most strongly identify. Where the idea of a female ruler might seem monstrous, an upheaval of nature to the medieval or early modern mind, this humbler model was easy to accept, conforming to natural order, or, better, acting as a bridge between humanity and God.

It was also the one model of 'female' conformity that could be seen as escaping the normal earthly constraints of household or State rule, outside secular authority, but inside God's cosmic plan. St John's Magdalen had her own house at Bethany – Christ had given her special permission to administer to his body, special rights to follow him instead of working like other women. The Bible places her ahead of other men and women in her special relationship with Christ; she was the first to recognise his potential martyrdom, last to see him alive, first to see and understand him risen. To the Virgin's empyrean Woman of the Apocalypse, Mary was the Woman of the Here-and-Now, a metaphor for femininity cut off from the norms of masculine control, making independent decisions about the locus of her faith, just like the exiled recusant's wife left in charge of the house and land. Southwell offered a female exemplar authorised by Christ to be what human society deplored.

THE ENGLISH BETHANY

But however useful Tridentine Catholicism found models of repentance and consolation such as Magdalen, Continental artistic or mystic fascinations with agony and ecstasy were not that easy to import for the English, in whom extremes of passionate intensity focused upon biblical persons seem often to have aroused suspicions of idolatry. The more febrile element of the third week of the *Exercises*, the intense fascination with the detail of Christ's injuries so readily expressed through the persona of Magdalen, was in part a sort of shared recreation through extremity of the Continental Catholic church, and was not, it must have become clear to Southwell, the proper artistic response to English habits of thought or English habits of writing (or, it must be added, a developing English Puritanism). The focus was shifting in England from external image to self. It is surely significant that Southwell's two most baroque pieces, his long 'St Peter' and his *Magdalen*, appear to be among his earliest in England, and seem to have been followed by a considerably simplified production. In the alteration of the biblical narrative, then, Southwell was, like Heywood, prepared to make changes as he saw fit. From the earliest of his English non-tractual writings he was making free in the Jesuit way with Bible narratives, licensing himself to augment them with the other rhetorical and imaginative tools at his disposal: the Word was not to be considered beyond the reach of his (allowed) imagination, if his ends were good.

He recognised the iconoclastic bent in English attitudes by modifying his output: Magdalen as a model of the disordered self works for the Puritan as for the Catholic. He seems to have further allowed himself (under his superior Garnet, and yet separated from the output of Garnet's secret press) to adapt even that licence to suit a gentlemanly English lay audience. *Funeral Teares* was probably written up for the daughter of a West Country nobleman: Dorothy Arundell, the 'Mistress D. A.' of Southwell's dedicatory epistle.[76] Here is a young woman who might see in her own situation a reflection of the independent woman of the Bethany house. Dorothy later became a Benedictine nun.

But Southwell never restricted his discourse to his immediate dedicatee: embedded in this exemplary passion are those other messages. Read in the context of the removal of Christ from the Mass, a passage as such as the following does more than offer a tearful example:

> Through too much preciseness in keeping the lawe, I have lost the lawmaker, and by being too scrupulous in observing his ceremonies, I am proued irreligious in loosing himselfe [...] The Sabboth could not have bin prophaned in standing by his corse, by which the prophanest thinges are sanctified, & whose couch doth not defile the cleane, but clenseth the most defiled. (sig. D 3)

Surely the English Jerusalem stands corrected here.

But here too, in the peculiar circumstances of the English mission and its need to reconnect the inner eye of the English to the historical English church as well as its Tridentine version, the Magdalen model grows and changes. Bethany, in Southwell's English version, comes to have the feel of a nostalgic lost kingdom of ancient piety and kindness, a sort of super-Albion where Christ once walked and supped with his people in peace. Any English Christian's sense of regret for the destruction of decorative beauties, songs and patterns of traditional English worship finds a new expression in the Magdalenic model, her grief at the loss of the physical and the beautiful, her despair at the cruelty of the Law and the baffling silence of her contemporaries. Southwell was, in foregrounding her, placing the English hearts who identified with her at the Lord's supper-table in the Bethany-Albion he had created.

No wonder that of all the new characterisations that Southwell offers it is that of Mary Magdalen that appears to have been taken up most readily by English writers at the time. Magdalen also embodies and licenses, through the approval of Christ, the human need for sacred ceremonial and display; her presence in the Novitiate refectory had taught Southwell that she had a proper, indeed a primary, place at Christ's Eucharistic supper-table. When in the Gospel narrative she had filled the house with beauty and sweetness at the supper in Bethany, and had been scolded by the officious disciple for misuse of resources and time, Christ said 'let her alone' – she was, he said, both prophesying and ennobling his burial in the only way she knew how (John 12.7). For Catholics she defined the missing heart of the host; to the poetic reader, she was the type not only of the loving sinner but of the new visionary poet who moved outside of practical, 'good' things and yet came closer to God. In his personations of her, as the Lord's lover, Southwell had found a special accommodation with passionate sensuality that transcended denominational boundaries. One wonders where such a poetic vision might have led, if only the exigencies of the age had let Southwell and his golden distractions alone for a few years more.

Just as the angel-less 'Joseph' interrogated weaknesses in Calvin's reformed relationship with God, then, so Magdalen imported and Englished by Southwell not only furnished Catholic spirituality with a new model for loving God, and a personation for the stripped and abused body of Christ's spouse the Church, but also served to expose the lacks in Protestantism, being taken up across the denominations as a biblical character closest to the self-interrogative, anxious spiritual state later exhibited by Reformed Christians such as Bunyan. Where Southwell's characterisation of Magdalen was part of an exploration of an engaging, realistically error-prone soul-scape designed to instruct and inspire, it also formed a new construct for exploring psychological/spiritual aspects of self. If it did no more than prompt poets to employ a more insightful and complex sort of personation, it at least gave a completely new function to English poetry, I would argue.

Where could Milton's Satan have come from, if not out of the kind of eloquent biblical sinners figured by Southwell, with their mercilessly exposed psychologies?

NOTES

1. Robert Southwell, 'Josephs Amazement', in James H. McDonald and Nancy Pollard Brown (eds), *The Poems of Robert Southwell, S.J.* (Oxford: Clarendon Press, 1967), p. 21, lines 47–8; hereafter M&B; further references to Southwell's poetry are from this edition, given as page/line numbers in the text.
2. See www.newadvent.org/cathen/04251b for a brief discussion of congruism.
3. John Calvin, *Institutes of the Christian Religion*, trans. Henry Beveridge, 3 vols (Edinburgh: Calvin Translation Society, 1845–46; repr. Grand Rapids: Eerdmans, 1983); the bulk of his discussion on angels is in 1.14.4–12.
4. The effects of such a loss upon the psyches of those once accustomed to the comfort of their constant presence is only now being acknowledged by mainstream commentators of the period. The work of Eamon Duffy and others on the extent of resistance to the removal of such spiritual assistance (and its persistence in the quiet places) suggests that even an English Protestant determined to do away with most of the heavenly hierarchies may have suffered a little from their loss; a Catholic undoubtedly suffered more; see Eamon Duffy, *The Stripping of the Altars: Traditional Religion in England c.1400–c.1580* (New Haven: Yale University Press, 1992).
5. See Bellarmine, 'De Septem Verbis Domini', cap. 9, 11, quoted in Fr John A. Hardon, S.J., 'Mary: Mediatrix in the Theology of Bellarmine', on www.therealpresence.org/archives/Mariology/Mariology_021.
6. See M&B, lxv.
7. *Marie Magdalens Funeral Teares*, p. 2v; text of 1591 edition from Early English Books Online (2003–4), www.eebo.chadwyck.com/search/doc. 10; hereafter cited in the text.
8. See a selection of Jean Calvin's *Commentaries*, ed. and trans. Joseph Haroutunian (Grand Rapids MI: Christian Classics Ethereal Library, 1958), on www.ccel.org/ccel/calvin/calcom.html (p. 117).
9. See Nancy Pollard Brown, 'Robert Southwell: the Mission of the Written Word', in Thomas M. McCoog, S.J. (ed.), *The Reckoned Expense: Edmund Campion and the Early English Jesuits* (Woodbridge: Boydell, 1996), pp. 193–214 (p. 197); hereafter 'Mission'; and F. W. Brownlow, *Robert Southwell*, Twayne's English Authors Series, 516 (New York: Simon & Schuster Macmillan, 1996), p. 73; hereafter cited in the text.
10. See John W. O'Malley, *The First Jesuits* (Cambridge, MA: Harvard University Press, 1993), pp. 373, 352–4; hereafter cited in the text. O'Malley shows that the Jesuits' primary operative principle was that 'the Creator deals directly with the creature, and the creature deals directly with the Creator'. Gauvin Alexander Bailey has noted how fully the Jesuit insistence on individual responsibility was reflected in the imagery of their buildings, in practical terms in the programmatic element and the need to view the programme in an active, engaged way to gain maximum benefit, and in a theoretical way, partly through the increasing depiction of angelic agency of various kinds; Gauvin Alexander Bailey, *Between Renaissance and Baroque: Jesuit Art in Rome, 1565–1610* (Toronto: University of Toronto Press, 2003); hereafter cited in the text.
11. Thanks are due to Professor Alison Findlay for bringing this significant absence to my attention.
12. Bailey, pp. 11, 243.

The flight of angels: England's altered confidence

13 III, p. 50; M&B calls the *Moeoniae* 'a second attempt by a London publisher to cull from manuscript sources a group of Southwell's lyrics that would appeal to readers of religious verse without expressing obviously Roman Catholic doctrine', p. lxix.

14 See Alison Shell, *Catholicism, Controversy and the English Literary Imagination 1558–1660* (Cambridge: Cambridge University Press, 1999), p. 191, and nn. 59, 60; hereafter cited in the text.

15 From *An Humble Supplication to Her Maiestie*, ed. R. C. Bald (Cambridge: Cambridge University Press, 1953), p. 57.

16 *Francis Bacon*, ed. Brian Vickers (Oxford: Oxford University Press, 1996), pp. 494–501; hereafter cited in the text.

17 Traditionally associated with Elizabeth, possibly from a letter drafted by Francis Bacon; see J. B. Black, *The Reign of Elizabeth, 1558–1603*, Oxford History of England Series (Oxford: Clarendon Press, 1936), VIII, p. 19.

18 Vickers, pp. 499, 495.

19 It is referred to in the examination of a recusant, the musician John Bolt, in 1594; Grosart, p. xc; see Richard Wilson, 'A Bloody Question', unpublished lecture (Sorbonne, France, 1998). For the examination of John Bolt, see *Calendar of State Papers, Domestic Series, of the Reign of Elizabeth, 1591–1594*, ed. Mary Anne Everett Green (London: HMSO, 1867), p. 467; hereafter *CSP*; Bolt claimed to have got it in Broad Oaks, Essex, from William Wiseman, a Catholic supporter; M&B, p. lxxxviii.

20 Robert Southwell, Dedicatory Letter from *Marie Magdalens Funeral Teares* (1591), printed by John Wolfe for Gabriel Cawood, London, full text version found in www.eebo.chadwyck.home, doc. 5; numbered 29950 in A. F. Pollard and G. R. Redgrave (eds), *A Short-title Catalogue of Books Printed in England, Scotland, and Ireland, and of English Books Printed Abroad, 1475–1640* (London: Bibliographical Society, 1926); hereafter *STC*; a second edition unrecorded in *STC* survives in the Folger Shakespeare Library; see M&B, p. xxiv.

21 Eamon Duffy cites several, such as this by William Blundell, of Little Crosby, Lancashire, who wrote in the early 1590s of the time when 'wee hadd one faith, | And strode aright one ancient path'; now it seems that 'each man may | See newe Religions coynd each day'. T. E. Gibson (ed.), *Crosby Records* (Manchester: Chetham Society, 1887), pp. 28–31; Emrys Jones (ed.), *The New Oxford Book of Sixteenth Century Verse* (Oxford: Oxford University Press, 1991), pp. 550–1; hereafter cited in the text as *16CVerse*; quoted in Eamon Duffy, 'Bare Ruined Choirs: Remembering Catholicism in Shakespeare's England', in Richard Dutton, Alison Findlay, and Richard Wilson (eds), *Lancastrian Shakespeare: Theatre and Religion* (Manchester: Manchester University Press, 2003), pp. 40–57, (pp. 48–50); hereafter 'Bare Ruined Choirs'. See also Shell, p. 175.

22 Even an Anglican rector, Michael Sherbrook, as Duffy observes, was able to complain in his *Fall of Religious Houses* (1591) that 'the estate of the realm hath come to more Misery since King Henry 8 his time, than ever it did in all the time before.' He lists the breakdown as social, or moral, rather than religious: 'more thieves, whores, extortioners, usurers and contentious persons striving the one against another in suits of law, and to be short, far more Beggars than ever was before'; quoted in Duffy, 'Bare Ruined Choirs', p. 52.

23 Published as *An Epistle of a Religious Priest unto his Father*; see Nancy Pollard Brown (ed.), *Two Letters and Short Rules of a Good Life* (Charlottesville: University Press of

24 Philip Caraman, S.J., *A Study in Friendship: Saint Robert Southwell and Henry Garnet* (Saint Louis, MO: The Institute of Jesuit Sources, 1995), p. 19; hereafter cited in the text.

25 Alison Shell, 'We are Made a Spectacle: Campion's Dramas', in McCoog (ed.), *The Reckoned Expense*, pp. 103–18 (p. 108).

26 Caraman, p. 19; Southwell's emphasis.

27 See also Shell, *Catholicism*, pp. 108–9.

28 See Father John Gerard's account of such an occasion in *The Autobiography of an Elizabethan*, ed. and trans. Philip Caraman, S.J. (London: Longmans, Green, 1951), p. 413.

29 Southwell to Acquaviva, 31 August 1588; CRS, 5, pp. 321–5; in M&B, p. xxviii.

30 See Gary Waller, *English Poetry of the Sixteenth Century* (Harlow: Longman, 1986), p. 268; hereafter cited in the text.

31 See Alexandra Walsham, *Church Papists: Catholicism, Conformity and Confessional Polemic in Early Modern England* (Woodbridge: Boydell, 1993), for a discussion of this.

32 *Richard II*, in Stanley Wells and Gary Taylor (eds), *The Oxford Shakespeare Complete Works* (Oxford: Clarendon Press, 1988), III.3.76, 79; further quotations are from this edition, given as act, scene and line numbers in the text.

33 Quoted in O'Malley, p. 83.

34 O'Malley, pp. 83–4.

35 Gauvin Bailey suggests that she was there for her connection with the supper table, but remains mystified over her prominence; she even appears over the doorway to the dormitories. Bailey, who identifies her with female penitence, 'the equivalent of Peter for men', thinks it 'curious that she was chosen instead of Peter'; she also appears twice in the infirmary; Bailey, p. 60.

36 But see Piero Della Francesca's monumentally calm *La Maddelena* in the Cattedrale del Duomo, Arezzo.

37 Sig. A 3; see Brownlow, p. 37.

38 Helen Gardner (ed.), *John Donne: The Divine Poems* (Oxford: Clarendon Press, 1952), Holy Sonnet 2, p. 15.

39 See Richard Baxter, *Saints Everlasting Rest* (1650); Martz agues that Baxter 'deliberately sets out to recover for the Puritans some of these devotional practices', recommending St Bernard, even citing the Jesuit Nieremberg ('Read this you Libertines, and learn better the way of Devotion from a Papist'), in order that 'the Puritan, too, through strenuous effort, might achieve that union of the powers of the soul which his dependence on Special Grace, his inward researches, and his mistrust of the senses had, for a time, disrupted', pp. 168–74.

40 O'Malley, pp. 41–2, 315.

41 Alison Shell discusses the public/private in relation to a curious imitation of Southwell's Magdalenic subject, 'Saint Marie Magdalens Conversion', that appeared from a secret press in 1603, signed 'I. C.'; it lists Shakespeare's epic works, including 'The Rape of

Lucrece', and *Troilus and Cressida*, and pleads with the reader to take those battles inside the heart, rather attend to such struggles between self-appetite and goodness only as a passive audience, p. 83. See C. M. Ingleby, et al., *The Shakespeare Allusion-Book*, 2 vols (London: Oxford University Press, 1932), I, p. 125. See also Geoffrey Hill's 'Lachrimae; or Seven tears figured in Seven passionate Pavans', in *Tenebrae* (London: André Deutsch, 1978), pp. 15–21.

42 Shakespeare's first poems, *Venus and Adonis* (1593) and *The Rape of Lucrece* (1594), may even have affected Southwell's poetic output in turn. As Grosart and Richard Wilson have noted, Southwell's long 'Saint Peters Complaint' appears to comment on the erotic poetic of Shakespeare's *Venus and Adonis*, and uses the same poetic form. It has been tentatively dated in manuscript to around 1591 by Brown, p. xxxii, and was certainly in wider circulation by 15 March 1594, judging by John Bolt's testimony; M&B, p. lxxxviii.

43 'The Author to the Reader', prefatory poem to *Saint Peters Complaint* (1595) (STC 22957), M&B, p. 75, l. 13.

44 Alison Shell discusses the rise of Mary Magdalen at this period, and her place in the characterisation of English penitence and reform (pp. 76, 79, 196).

45 See Shell, p. 64.

46 See Frank Kermode, *Shakespeare's Language* (Harmondsworth: Penguin, 2000) for a detailed discussion of this Shakespearean 'personation'; hereafter cited in the text.

47 See Alison Shell, also see Brownlow, p. 43.

48 See Brownlow, p. 44. *Marie Magdalens Funeral Teares* is altered from both the Gospel version of John 20.1–18 and the homily based upon it, identified by Helen White as a translation of a popular homily of Origen's published earlier in sixteenth century England, in Latin, *Omelia Origensis, de beata Maria Magdalena* (London, 1504?); see Helen White, *Tudor Books of Saints and Martyrs* (Madison: University of Wisconsin Press, 1963). Southwell has brought new Continental fashions for tears and remorse to his Gospel subject, influenced perhaps by poems popular in Rome such as Valvasone's *Le Lagrime della Maddalena*; see Janelle, p. 189; Brownlow, p. 37.

49 Ian Ousby (ed.), *Cambridge Guide to Literature in English* (Cambridge: Cambridge University Press, 1993), pp. 203–4.

50 Henry Constable, 'To St Mary Magdalen', *16CVerse*, p. 467.

51 *Funeral Teares*, sig. A 3v; 'The Author to his loving Cosen', prefatory letter to *Saint Peters Complaint* (1595) (STC 22957), M&B, p. lvii.

52 Spenser was writing his 'Four Hymnes' at this time; Patrick Cheney, in chapter 5 of *Spenser's Famous Flight*, sees it as testament to a new moral poetic; Patrick Cheney, *Spenser's Famous Flight: A Renaissance Idea of a Literary Career* (Toronto: University of Toronto Press, 1993).

53 Dedicatory letter from *Marie Magdalens Funeral Teares* (1591), sig. A 6.

54 Robert Southwell, *Spiritual Exercises and Devotions* ed. J. M. de Buck and trans. P. E. Hallett (London: Sheed and Ward, 1931), 10, p. 9; hereafter *SE&D*.

55 John 11.20, 32, 35; King James Version.

56 John 11.3.

57 *16CVerse*, p. 466.

58 Taddeo Gaddi, *Crucifixion*, c.1360–1366, San Croce, Florence; Rogier van der Weyden,

Descent from the Cross, c.1435, Museo del Prado, Madrid; in Christiane Stukenbrock and Barbara Töpper (eds), *1000 Masterpieces of European Painting from 1300 to 1850* (Cologne: Könemann, 2000), pp. 361, 950.

59 See Bailey, p. 239.

60 This had been corrected to 'somme' in Wolfe's second 1595 edition (Wolfe, 1595b) and is 'somme' in other manuscript versions.

61 Christopher Devlin, *The Life of Robert Southwell Poet and Martyr* (London: Longmans, Green, 1956), p. 79.

62 H. R. Woudhuysen (ed.), *The Penguin Book of Renaissance Verse, 1509–1659* (Harmondsworth: Penguin, 1992), p. 253; hereafter cited in the text as *Verse*; Oxford Shakespeare, p. 224.

63 See Brownlow, pp. 43–4.

64 Ibid., pp. 43–4.

65 See Jean Robertson's introduction to her edition of Nicholas Breton, *Poems: Not Hitherto Printed* (Liverpool: Liverpool University Press, 1967), pp. xxvii, xxix; hereafter cited in the text.

66 See Robertson, p. xxix.

67 See also Alison Shell, pp. 79–80. It may not have been the only aspect of Southwell's Jesuit poetics that Breton borrowed. On 10 October 1597 Breton's *The Figure of Four* is entered on the *Stationers' Register*, in which he arranges ideas in fours, echoing the grouping in *Marie Magdalens Love*, where he requires the reader to mark and keep in memory four chief 'notes': 'First the person named, who it was, and of what condition: Secondlie, the time, Thirdlie the place, and fourthly what was there seene and done' (Robertson, pp. lxii–lxv, xxxvii). This seems to be a close relative to the Ignatian *Exercises*, the 'mental representation of the place'. Robertson seems to skim over the possible theological origins of such patterning, merely noting other instances of groupings of four, such as 'Southwell's *A Fourefold meditation of the foure last things* and Dekker's *Foure Birds of Noahs Arke*' (Robertson, n.2, p. lxv). The fact that the four items in *Marie Magdalens Love* so closely resemble Ignatian teaching suggests a link between *Love* and *Funeral Teares* that surely requires further study.

68 See Martz, p. 182. Joseph Scallon notes the 'shift in the relationship between artefact and audience from passive admiration of classic perfection to active participation in the emotion of the event' of the new Baroque style, and links it to 'Ignatian ascetical practice', especially the 'composition of place' of the Exercises; Joseph D. Scallon, *The Poetry of Robert Southwell, S.J.* (Salzburg: Institut für Englische Sprache und Literatur, 1975), pp. 74–5; also see Brownlow, p. 79.

69 Manuscript versions of Southwell's poetry, including 'St Peter', were in circulation between 1586 and 1592. Southwell's *Magdalen* appeared on the *Stationers' Register* in November 1591 (II, 598); 'Tytus Andronicus' is entered on 6 February 1594 (II, 646) – Frank Kermode uses Shakespeare's *Titus* as the 'before' model to show how far Shakespeare's personation had developed by the time of *Coriolanus*, which did not appear till 1601/2. See Anne Sweeney, 'Robert Southwell's English Lyrics: Authorial Integrity on the Mission to Elizabethan England (1580–1595)', unpublished doctoral thesis (Lancaster University, 2004), pp. 333–8.

70 After Southwell's Magdalen had appeared, a series of variations on the theme of the madness of love are entered on the *Register*, often dignified by connection with Magdalen

The flight of angels: England's altered confidence

('Marye Magdalens love uppon the xxth Chapter of John', 14 July 1595; 'a solempne passion of the soules love', 20 September 1595; 'Maries Meditations' 30 December 1595); *Stationers' Register*, III, 45, 47, 56.

71 Martz, pp. 81–2.

72 See Kermode, p. 183.

73 Kermode, pp. 16–17, 56, 6. He notes on p. 6 that the word 'personation', which implies more than the mere gestural playing of parts, was first used as a term by John Florio (1598) and John Marston (1602), according to the *Oxford English Dictionary*.

74 Martz also describes the work of William Alabaster as being based on spiritual meditations and deems it 'Donne-like', despite its anticipating Donne by 'at least a decade', p. xxii. As Shell shows, Alabaster left a hopeful career to turn Roman Catholic in 1597–98 (under the direction of John Gerard, Southwell's Jesuit colleague, Martz notes, p. xviii). Gerard directed Alabaster in the Exercises but Alabaster never entered orders, and eventually returned to the Church of England, but 'his [...] conversion to Romanism led him to express his problems in religious poetry that clearly illustrates the impact of Counter-Reformation methods of devotion upon the spirituality of Elizabethan England'; Shell, pp. 88–104; also see Dana F. Sutton (ed.), *Unpublished Works by William Alabaster (1568–1640)*, Salzburg Studies in English Literature Series: Elizabethan and Renaissance Studies, 126 (Salzburg: University of Salzburg, 1997), pp. 99–169; also see G. M. Story and Helen Gardner (eds.), *The Sonnets of William Alabaster* (Oxford: Oxford University Press, 1959).

75 Shell, p. 82.

76 Brownlow, pp. 36–7. Pilarz, p. 180.

Chapter 5

Snow in Arcadia: rewriting the English lyric landscape

> A vale there is enwrapt with dreadfull shades,
> Which thicke of mourning pines shrouds from the sunne,
> Where hanging clifts yeld short and dumpish glades,
> And snowie floud with broken streames doth runne[1]

DISORDERED ORDER

English courtly poetry had entered the 1580s in somewhat wintry condition. Spenser's *Shepheardes Calender* began with January's 'frostie ground' and 'frosen trees', reflecting, in pastoral fashion, the 'carefull case' of the rustic lyricist-protagonist, the 'barrein ground, whome winters wrath hath wasted' being 'made a myrrhour, to behold [his] plight'. Tottel's *Miscellany*, the pattern-book for courtly poets, also began with a winter poem by the noble Howard in which the poet describes himself frozen with sorrow despite the springing season.[2] All for love unreturned, or hope blighted.

Southwell would say that this was an accurate reflection of England's fallen state. 'Like winter rose, and sommer ise', as Southwell says in 'Loves servile lot', the English State was, in his view, 'untimely' – out of step, unnatural and uncanny, not only in its apparent fall from religious engagement but in its replacing of Christ and his Mother by Elizabeth at the centre of its landscape (p. 61, l. 53). Her more pious subjects may have thought bitterly that Elizabeth wanted to make of England less a new Jerusalem than an Elizium full of May-time frolics, as she disported in the parklands of her new knights, the fancy-dress chivalric chorus to her ageing Cynthia. The courtier-poet Dyer had once carolled her from the branches of an oak tree at Leicester's magnificent Woodstock entertainment of 1575;[3] such courtly pastoral landscapes echoed, at worst, to the melancholy sounds of lack of royal attention.

Southwell was writing against that project, attempting to find in the English

Snow in Arcadia: rewriting the English lyric landscape

poetic landscape reflections of the lack of moral truth and cosmic order he believed it now embodied. He poured cold water on the perpetual May of courtly love: 'May never was the Month of love, | For May is full of flowers', he insists; it is the English April with its showers that best suits the sort of love that always ends in tears ('Loves servile lot', p. 60, lines 53–4, 37–40).

He was creating a topographical resistance-poetic of sorts, attempting to re-draw the imaginary landscape of the English national poetic agenda as he had tried to redraw the internal landscape of the English subject, to widen and deepen its sense of agency whilst at the same time emphasising its smallness in the face of cosmic absolutes. Gnomic lists of natural example proving various moral points, as in 'Scorne not the least' (p. 69), do not set him above any of his Tudor contemporaries in terms of originality, although in their social context they gesture towards certain truths about the experience of being Catholic in late sixteenth-century England.

Part of Southwell's attempt to establish a natural moral truth, though, involved the depiction of a 'real' natural scene quite unlike any existing in English poetry of the time, informed by his Jesuit theories of truthful observation and depiction. In his schooldays in Flanders he must have become acquainted with naturalism in art. Just as Southwell's English nativity poetry is set in snowy, muddy farmyards, so Peter Bruegel's *Census of Bethlehem*, for instance, is depicted in a Flanders village in bitter winter. This was an exciting and influential innovation in its day, reflected in Jesuit ideas of God found in the real world.[4] Once in Rome Southwell will have been exposed to even more sophisticated theories of realism. Mannerist fantasy was giving way to baroque pseudo-reality, relying for its effect on a clearer observation of nature, even when it was super-nature. Robert Bellarmine encouraged artistic attention to real landscapes, and Acquaviva oversaw painting cycles in S. Vitale, the little Novitiate martyrium set in the gardens on the Quirinal Hill, that were almost entirely landscape. The idea of 'composition of place' and the truths implicit in the world of nature had overtaken the depictions of martyrdom, now almost hidden by foliage; this was a 'dramatic change' in the way Jesuits looked at the world.[5] Southwell saw only the beginnings of this project, but the martyr paintings in the Novitiate generally reflected this fascination with landscape, and novices were schooled in its implications.

In 'A vale of teares' (p. 41) Southwell presents a remarkable vision: a landscape clearly taken from life, the result of actual observation of nature, but one that, in its 'disordred order', presents the truest reflection, as he sees it, of England's fallen state and the failure of vision of its ruling classes (l. 27). The 'impossibility of courtly desire' is 'a thematic dimension' of this lyric, as Gary Kuchar argues, in his Lacanian deconstruction of it; Southwell is once again using the methodology of establishment poetics to make a new point, one that, in its use of landscape, anticipates Lacan's principle of reordering 'past contingent events by conferring on them the sense of necessities to come', as Kuchar observes.[6]

This place, very far, it would seem, from the summer lawns of Leicester's or Sidney's estates, is a wild, precipitous mountain chasm 'Which thicke[ts] of mourning pines shrouds from the sunne'. In its shadowed depths icy meltwater, 'Which tumbleth from the tops where snow is thow'd', dashes itself down the rocks in 'broken streames'. The narrator is not describing a background picture for aesthetic effect; he is inside the picture, shaken to his foundations and dwarfed by the scenery's vast compass. The picture presented by Southwell overwhelms the senses. Staggered at the sight and deafened by the roar of the cataract, the narrator stands aghast, his gaze running up 'from rockes to cloudie skie', down from the 'hanging clifts' 'to dales with stonie ruines strow'd', their sides stripped bare of soil by the 'frothie frie' of 'the crushed waters', 'Where waters wrastle with encountring stones, | That breake their streames, and turne them into foame'.[7]

This is, as ever in Southwell, about sense-led immediacy of response; the narrator's presence at the scene is made to seem the more real by Southwell's description of sound effects. There are no human sounds, only the varying notes made by the churning waters, the 'blustring of the stubburne winde' as it hisses, howls or roars in 'trees, in caves, in straits', and the thunder as 'The hollow clouds [...] discharge their pregnant wombe' (lines 1–16).

This is landscape from another century, sublime and superhuman in scale; the few travellers that encounter this place are word-painted as tiny, fleeting things, passing 'with trembling foot and panting heart', overwhelmed by its sheer scale and inhospitability. 'With terror cast in cold and shivering frights, | They judge the place to terror framde by art'. But 'natures worke it is', the poet adds: he has seen it, it is real; perhaps the pass that he had taken on his way through the Alps to and from Rome. To a youth from Norfolk and the Low Countries his first encounter with the mountains must have been a terrific experience, one that spoke volumes to him, perhaps, of his own pilgrimage for spiritual certainty, and certainly one that stuck fast in his memory.[8] In any case, it furnishes him with a natural expression of cosmic power that his eye, his memory, his skill, and his pen have passed on to the reader in the channelling process between the real and the felt later to be more closely identified with Romanticism (lines 21–4). Certainly it is Southwell's version of the passes of the mountains, full of that awesome divine immanence, that a distant relative of his, Shelley, preferred when he wrote his 1816 evocation of that 'dark, deep Ravine', the 'many-colored, many voiced vale' with its 'giant brood of pines', 'where woods and winds contend, and a vast river | Over its rocks ceaselessly bursts and raves' with 'loud, lone sound no other sound can tame' – 'Dizzy Ravine!'.[9]

It is the terrible, inescapable realness of the place that makes it important to

Southwell, not any allegorical possibilities; there are no Britomarts or Corydons here: they could not survive the cold reality. He invests the landscape with the (Romantic) idea of the pathetic fallacy instead; it is, as itself, the work of a mighty spirit, 'With such disordred order strangely coucht':

> That who it viewes must needs remaine agast,
> Much at the worke, more at the makers might,   30
> And muse how Nature such a plot could cast,
> Where nothing seemed wrong, yet nothing right:

It is 'A place for mated minds', a place where distressed feelings can find their echo in the natural scene, a Shelley or a Coleridge place, not that of an Elizabethan courtier: Southwell had found a landscape where such a man was reduced to his basic humanity before a far mightier power than that of any earthly crown (lines 26–32). What precedent had he found for it in English poetry?

Southwell's own courtly poetic heritage, in the shape of his and Arundel's connections with the works of Henry Howard, Earl of Surrey, offered him an imaginary landscape space in which to explore his concerns and conflicts. Surrey's blank verse translation of parts of Virgil's *Aeneid* presented classical scenery in dignified English, but his 'The soote season', published in Tottel's *Miscellany* in 1557, recalls a Chaucerian version of pastoralism, a recognisably English scenery of budding twigs, and swallows hawking for flies; a spring-renewed landscape. Although evoked by the poet only to foreground his sorrow, the natural scenery is useful here not as a generic backdrop but in its real-seeming detail – it is in observing the real landscape that the poet finds the truths about his inner state.[10]

Southwell, perhaps in obedience to Jesuit training which encouraged the seeing of a place in as realistic a way as possible, and certainly in response to their precept of God-in-everything, seems to have found that model of poeticised landscape worth exploring in this poem. Only rarely otherwise does his use of nature rise above the merely gnomic; it is when Southwell puts an 'I' in it that his landscape begins to escape sententiousness.

The general poetic landscape that Southwell encountered in 1586 was developing rapidly. Alongside the new interest in England as an abstract notion, as an 'Albion' suddenly worth positioning historically, was springing up a recognition of the part that poetry had to play in such repositioning, and in various versions of landscape-poetic in support of or in resistance to that project. If a new land was to be created in the public imagination, the place of the poet, the creator of imaginary landscapes, became more important than ever.

There were some celebrated names associated with these imagined realms. Southwell, in the houses of Vaux or Arundel, almost certainly had access to manuscript copies of parts of Sidney's Arcadian vision. While Ralegh was extending Albion's borders out into the New World, his poems were being written and circulated at court between 1582 and 1592.¹¹ Spenser's *Shepheardes Calender* was printed in 1579, Bruno's *Eroici Furori* in 1585.¹² Southwell was at liberty in England when Spenser's *The Faerie Queene*, i–iii, appeared in print in 1590, with its allegory-loaded landscapes and characterisations. Southwell's character-led prose sermon *Marie Magdalens Funeral Teares* appeared in print a year later, alongside Sidney's *Astrophil and Stella* and another of Spenser's, *Complaints Daphnaida*.

The cultural landscape was being shaped by music and new approaches to language too. Concomitant issues of madrigals by Monteverdi and Watson and Byrd's *Psalms, Sonnets and Songs* from 1587 to 1590 suggest a revived interest in the sung lyric. As if to make plain the connection between the arts and the internal landscape, Byrd set to music Sir Edward Dyer's 'My Mind to Me a Kingdom is' ('In Praise of a Contented Mind', published in 1588), a claim to a simple inner space where he can reign as sole king, untroubled by the vanity of a world that sounds much like Elizabeth's Court. Dyer's is a moral but Godless inner landscape which Southwell in turn took up and altered into 'Content and rich' (p. 67), which, although not a reproduction of Dyer's tetrameter sestets, is clearly intended to recall them in the patterning and content of ideas, and especially in the line 'My minde to me an empire is' (l. 27); needless to say, Southwell is suggesting that an inner landscape without the hope of heaven in it is a poor one:

> I have no hopes but one,   21
>   Which is of heavenly raigne:
> Effects attainde, or not desired,
>   All lower hopes refraine.

Puttenham's *The Arte of English Poesie* (1589) shows a new awareness of the qualities and uses of English vernacular works; Sidney's revised *Arcadia*, and Fraunce's *Arcadian Rhetoric* (1590, 1588), among other similar works, on the other hand, are evidence of an interest in alternative language-registers to the rapidly centralising English one.¹³ Southwell had to decide what sort of English poetic landscape he wished to place his ideal English subject in: he had a Magdalen, now he needed an Albion-Bethany. To create the new England, he first had to deconstruct the other.

Although I agree with Kuchar's general point that Southwell was in general co-opting Petrarchan ideals in 'Vale', it was a pressganging carried out against a very different background than that of the Petrarchan love lyric; indeed, the fact that Southwell rejects the backgrounding of nature is central to his point, I would argue. It was as a result of his deconstruction of their poetics that he found the need to rebuild an imaginary landscape that was entirely new and free of other poets' registers. He found the need to distance himself stylistically as well as morally from the rest, which were, as discussed earlier, politically charged. He had no need to fit himself into the accepted form of pastoral landscape, with its uncomfortable juxtapositions of social anxieties imported from the Court and simple, honest shepherd-songsters. He did not need to adopt the semblance of rustic simplicity to give him moral authority, he was a pastor already, if from a very other place; he needed only to comment on that landscape as he found it.

As Waller argues, Sidney's Neoplatonic version of poetic creativity, suggesting as it does an ability to create worlds as God created this world, allows him to make a 'rational universe created by a rational Creator'.[14] This imaginary place of 'I', though true to the maker's own wishes, reflects few of the world's realities. As Monika Smialkowska notes, pastoral in Sidney's classical vein escapes current law and claims the higher status of classical, pagan precedent.[15] Southwell cannot enter such a Christ-exclusive landscape, and none of his English pastorals approaches the classical or the Sidneian form. He adopts the habit of disseminating poetically expressed ideas in manuscript form, however, arguably a way of controlling his ideological landscape, at least.[16] It can readily be seen how the Jesuit principle of adapting one's methods to achieve one's targets of reaching as many as possible as appropriately as possible suited the process of manuscript dissemination in Elizabethan England, with its 'special status, its personal appeal, relative privacy, freedom from government control, its cheapness, and its ability to make works quickly available to a select audience'.[17] Southwell was encouraged to adapt his communication to his audience as a pastoral strategy, and manuscript poetry can be seen as such an adaptation. One of the readerships he courted was in effect that of men like Dyer and Wriothesley, and even Essex, who was becoming an important possibility for the throne in some English Catholic minds, owing to his apparent sympathy and support for loyal Catholics.[18] Such readers would have understood, even admired, Southwell's grave interrogation of Petrarchan poetics.

Southwell viewed the details of any imaginative landscape actively, forensically. His training was designed to encourage discernment of motivations and results: if he invented, what were the fruits of his inventions, good or bad? These questions over self-generated authorship and its relationship with God are wrestled with by the novice in his devotional diaries; the question goes to the heart of his creativity. The Neoplatonic poetic claim of God-like creative autonomy troubled a youth so responsive to beauty and so interested in its literary recreation. In his diaries he refers over and over again to the problem of telling whether in his ardour he is adoring God, or whether he has transferred his love 'from the Creator to the creature'; or whether he has used the 'inspirations' sent by God for or against God (*SE&D*, 13, 16.4, pp. 16, 23). How does the poet's creative urge relate to that of the Demiurge? God plants the seed and sends the nourishment but it is the nature of the plant that decides what it makes of that goodness – as a producer of works and effects, is Southwell, he asks himself, a tree that gives good fruits or poisonous ones?

Once in England he was free, to some extent, of such anxieties, or at least able to externalise them on to more obvious targets. The identification of the new English realm with a poisoned garden crops up more than once in his lyrics, by way of reclassifying the garden of love, a favourite amorous conceit, into a deceit; Venus's luxuriant and well-watered deer park, in which she gives Adonis the right to roam in Shakespeare's *Venus and Adonis*, and many other pretty, amorous plots come under Southwell's reproving gaze once he is in England. Denigrating the fruits of their trees, he no longer has to inspect his own production quite so closely; and, freed from that eggshell-delicate college environment, his condemnation of others seems to have been free, enthusiastic, and, perhaps, cathartic. In his communications with Rome he regularly overstepped the mission rule that he was to be discreet in his letters and not attack others. In a letter of 12 August 1587 about the burning of a Protestant for heresy in Norwich, he derides the relics removed from the site as 'faeces'; '"crap" would be an apt modern synonym', as Brownlow says drily.[19] In another letter of early 1588 Southwell attacks a cleric, describing William Whitaker, Regius Professor of Divinity at Cambridge, as 'a well-known maker of lies and a "miles gloriosus"'. Less surprising perhaps is his letter reporting the death of Leicester of 7 September 1588, in which the Queen's favourite is described as 'an abstract of wickedness, a glutton for crimes, who left no sin uncommitted, and who has made a spectacular entrance into hell'.[20]

Here he was on safer ground. Yet in his implicit criticism of courtiers, court poets, and the Court that encouraged their excesses, or in his use of the suggestive metaphor of royal David suffering for his sins, Southwell is deploying a poetic that goes against the grain of the mission instruction to avoid controversy. In 1588, two years into the mission, there comes an interesting suggestion in a report to Rome by Southwell's mission superior Garnet that Southwell might have been doing too much of his own thing. Garnet writes that Southwell believed himself abandoned by his superior because of his wilfulness,[21] presupposing some misbehaviour on the part of the young Jesuit at the root of this apparently guilty conscience. Garnet is, very gently, telling tales here. Whatever its nature, does this implied wilfulness, on top of the more generalised willingness to 'other' his enemies in his letters, prose and poetry, mark the point at which he became, in terms of his authorship at least, self-sufficient? Has his own view of himself in relation to the landscape altered?

IN AN ENGLISH GARDEN

Southwell's environment had changed utterly from the collegiate, companionable gardens and corridors shared with his brother Jesuits and scholars in Rome. There, his place in the wider scheme was reflected back to him in pictures of Jesuit community activity; in England he was alone in a hostile place very like that described in 'A vale of teares'. Some of Southwell's altered landscapes are conceived in a far less sympathetic register even than the nature-created 'Vale', and connected more directly with the consciously shaped landscape of the garden, currently of great interest among Elizabeth's top courtiers and ministers. There are similar identifications in Shakespeare's *Richard II* (III.4.41–8) and *Hamlet* (I.2.135–7) of the garden with the realm.

In one of his garden poems, 'Loves Garden Grief' (p. 64), possibly a riposte to one of Breton's and certainly a comment on the new craze for gardening and specimen-collecting, Southwell attacks the wrongly directed idea using metaphors that would have been unmistakeably pointed to contemporary ears. John Gerard of Cheshire was achieving a reputation as a plantsman; he supervised Burghley's gardens in his houses in the Strand and at Theobalds, and had his own garden in fashionable Holborn.[22] The vogue for making new garden estates also touched the group of noblemen that supported the Catholic priests in their mission work, notably Sir Thomas Tresham, whose plans for garden and building programmes based on sacred formats, numbers, symbology, and imagery will have been much talked about in such circles: Lyveden was intended to symbolise the passion of Christ.[23] Garnet the mathematician must have been delighted by Tresham's vision. He and Southwell recognised this sort of garden design both from the thematically planned Novitiate garden, which was in the early stages of execution when the pair left Rome, and from the devotional idea of a 'sequenced pilgrimage of the soul' through a carefully planned landscape.[24] Tresham and his Throckmorton wife were spending a fortune on their garden at Lyveden, work which was all but halted by his imprisonment for hosting Edmund Campion in 1581, but which was clearly near enough to his heart for him to keep up the work from his cell, as a letter written from Ely prison to his gardener John Slynne on 9 October 1597 shows. There was a bowling alley (to be 'kept very short with oft mowing', naturally), and gravelled pathways laid 'all over a full foot deep of stone'. The carefully planned spiral ascents of the mounds and the terracing were 'very convenient both to walk in open air, as well in summer in shadow', whilst the Christian symbolism of the retired garden lodge was to 'delight and edify the beholder', as the proud owner observed. If Southwell did not see such gardens on one of his country house calls, he will certainly have heard about them, in the form of admiring descriptions of their novel delights. English Catholic upset at Burghley's repressions and the treatment of the loyal courtier Tresham will have been commingled with this garden project in his mind.

Perhaps fresh from a visit, or keen to raise in his reader's mind the comparative images of these two celebrated new English gardens, one so close to the Christian symbolism of his novitiate, the other, in Southwell's view, the fruits of a vicious and vainglorious heresy, Southwell re-employs his devotional diary metaphor of poisonous production, this time in the accusative. 'Your beds are sowne with seedes of all iniquitie, | And poys'ning weeds', he accuses. This garden is evil in concept, vain of ornament, its fruit 'misdeedes'. The new specimen trees boasted of by fashionable garden-owners like Burghley are nothing more than 'dismall plantes of pyning corrosives' without health or grace or any medicinal worth at all (unlike the sweet cherries and pears about which Sir Thomas was anxiously instructing his gardener from prison). Their bark (perhaps in mocking contrast to the medicinal 'Jesuit bark' of the quinine tree, news of which had begun to arrive from the Americas[25]) is 'bale' – poison; their very core, the 'pith', is 'untruth'. There is a hint of displacement, too, given the anxieties in Southwell's private diaries, when he changes the sweet voices of the birds in the trees into the 'screeching note' of the 'guiltie conscience' (lines 13–24). Perhaps Burghley had a rookery amongst his town garden trees, where his neighbour, Southwell's patron Arundel, had nightingales?

Amusing as it may once have been to exiles or college friends, such satire will have left a sour taste in the mouths of those like Southwell's family who had profited from the breakup of the old abbey estates, the 'poys'ning weeds' of whose new gardens perhaps recalled the medicinal plots of the old monasteries (lines 13–14). Thomas Tresham's grandfather, a wealthy supporter of Mary Tudor, had been made Grand Prior of England in the Order of Knights Hospitallers of St John of Jerusalem in 1557, and his grandson Thomas may well have seen his own building project as a recreation of the mystic architecture of the Holy City and the history of the Hospitallers, a restorative, recreated English Jerusalem, after Elizabeth in 1559 had dismembered the Priory in Clerkenwell, seizing its rich lands and assets, as if in imitation of her father.[26]

In this new, godless English garden the 'force and operation' of the herbs work 'To banish grace' (lines 17–18), not to nurture it as before. Where there had been holy song, now there is only disharmony and ruin (l. 24). 'Loves garden grief' is an example of how carefully Southwell had to balance his poetic effects to make his points without alienating the wrong people: what may have seemed the simple 'good'/'bad' dichotomy of college days, was, once he was on English ground, far more complex, as his family complications showed. Some of his poems seem less than sensitive to this problem, as in his rewrite of Dyer's 'Phancie' (p. 36), where he castigates the easy target of a courtier – clearly associated with Dyer – 'As one that lives in shewe, | And inwardly dooth die' (lines 25–6); or where he employs their English gardens in medieval-seeming moralisations on the withering of the true faith – 'Alas the glorie of your arbor dies', he warns in 'Christs sleeping friends' (p. 19, l. 39); you think your England green and pleasant but you are mistaken: 'So *Jonas* once his weary limmes to rest, | Did shrowd himselfe in pleasant ivy shade', but the tree was killed by a 'worm' at the root while he slept, which had denatured the landscape, bringing 'the glorious branches to decay' (lines 25–30). Only a sleeper could not have noticed the spiritual decay of this Eden. This can have been of little spiritual use or comfort to those families (like his own or Sir Thomas's) caught on the horns of the Elizabethan Catholics' dilemma.

When he enters into the landscape of regret, however, appearing to refer to the old medieval poetic tradition of a courtly Orpheus gone wild at the loss of his Euridyce, he is making a far more obvious critique of the mindsets of the courtly poets and the object of their adoration. Their new use of pagan imagery, as in Dyer's complaint, was being further redirected by Southwell towards that of another great man run wild – Nebuchadnezzar, pagan Orpheus's biblical twin. In Daniel 4 the potentate is driven to the wilderness by God, to 'eat grass as oxen […] till his hairs were grown like eagles' feathers, and his nails like birds' claws' (4. 33). Where Orpheus was a courtly song-maker and poet, and lost his mind through loss of love (or, in Dyer's case, favour), Nebuchadnezzar is the monarch; his crime, to set his will and law above God's; rustication is divine punishment, not romantic predicament. He eventually acknowledges that God, not any earthly ruler, owns the earth and makes the law; a reminder of God's humbling of a mortal crown would not have been missed by any Elizabethan reader of Southwell's poetry, courtly or common.

In looking for the motivations and circumstances of the personalities in any poetic/biblical situation, Southwell begins to show the poetic 'I' interacting with the space – in 'A Phansie turned to a sinners complaint' (p. 36), for instance, his imagined landscape is becoming a more psychologised space. There is a dissolution of boundaries between the spiritual and the physical: his thoughts are 'like ruines olde, | Which shew how faire the building was, | While grace did it upholde' (lines 37–40). His garden realm, too, which was one of pre-lapsarian innocence, has become rank:

> I sow'd the soyle of peace,
> My blisse was in the spring;   50
> And day by day the fruite I eate,
> That Vertues tree did bring.
>
> To Nettles now my corne,
> My field is turn'd to flint;
> Where I a heavie harvest reape,   55
> Of cares that never stint.

Despite this sense of a space inhabited by something approaching a real psychological persona, he refers constantly back to the imagery of biblical or pagan precedents, merely reminding his reader of how they represent the breakdown of order – harmony gone to discord, time no more orderly than an owl's sporadic cries:

Robert Southwell

> My teares shall be my wine,
> My bed a craggy Rock;
> My harmonie the Serpents hisse,   135
> The screeching Owle my clock.

When Southwell writes in this accusative vein, Christianising Orpheus or decrying the ruin of England's Paradise, he seems to have little new to say, Gascoigne, for instance, having presented the same scene in 'the Green Knight's Farewell to Fancy' (1575), although his use even of these well-worn rhetorical forms must be acknowledged to be purposeful, targeted as they are on a wide and conservative readership (or, in the case of his 'Dyer' pieces, courtly readers); they are best seen in the light of public sermons on recognisable themes. His encouragements, though, are in the Jesuit mode of attracting minds through graceful works and sympathetic conversation.

This attractiveness was a bone of contention: indulgence of the senses was the primrose path to perdition to Protestants: Catholicism was negatively associated with sensual beauty and decorative excess, partly through the efforts of Southwell's great teacher Bellarmine, who argued that an informed appreciation of the multifarious beauties of creation was a valid means of approaching closer to their Creator. His *Controversies* were exercising English Protestants in 1588. Elizabeth was reportedly determined to have them rebutted,[27] and the representation by Spenser of a garden of earthly delights in 'Muiopotmos' (1591) can perhaps be read as part of that anti-Bellarminian effort. He implicates by suggestion the blossoming of Tridentine Catholic baroque: the prodigies of art in all their 'riotous excesse' are not English but 'fetcht from farre away' (lines 168, 201–3). His butterfly, Clarion, spiritually independent and unwilling to accept guidance, and therefore unable to tell the flowers from the 'weeds of glorious feature' (l. 213), is distracted and drawn by this dizzying sensual excess towards death in a spiderweb of destructive envy. Pagan precedents and godly motivations are employed, including the myth of Psyche, the soul-butterfly, to dignify what might otherwise seem a slight tale.

Southwell presents the beauty-laden 'Seeke flowers of heaven' as if in riposte (p. 52; see Introduction, pp. 9–10), in which the soul, implicated as a caterpillar capable of eating only the crudest weeds while trapped in the fleshly body, is admonished to let its imagination take wing and seek heavenly flowers – no caterpillar or butterfly ever being specifically mentioned. 'Soar up my soule', he says, 'Cast off this loathsome loade', this 'strait abode' (lines 1–4). The released soul will feed no longer on 'worldly withered weede' but on flowers whose 'sugred vaines' are filled with 'nectared drops' and 'Life giving juice of living love' (lines 5, 13–16). The poet's classical imagery cannot be mistaken here, nor his Christianising purpose: where Spenser's Clarion is only a descendant, this butterfly's model is the Greek maiden Psyche, who, through Cupid's love and intercession, is given immortality and restored to him in heaven, a classical type of Christ's redemption of the human soul.[28]

Southwell is here repeating the technique employed in 'The prodigall childs soule wracke' (p. 43), poeticising pagan tales that prefigure Christian redemption, but with Christian inflections to disguise their pagan origins, leading his more educated English reader, via that Renaissance fascination with classical imagery, towards Christian truths. He preaches the Counter-Reformation idea that the action of Christ can be seen throughout history; but is he also suggesting that England, or her poets, have returned to the pre-Christian era?

Spenser's 'Muiopotmos or The Fate of the Butterfly' appeared in 1591, dedicated to Lady Elizabeth Carey and presented as a meditation on the world's vanity.[29] Scholarly suggestions as to the identity of Spenser's vaunting flutterer include Sidney, Ralegh, Essex – even Spenser himself. Southwell, astute enough to avoid the trap of employing the very effects that he is decrying, praises such created works, but insists that all remain caterpillars of the spiritual commonwealth unless they can re-engage their creativity in support of the living Church. The flowers in this garden are designed both as products of, and to appeal to, the richest imagination. They are given powerfully physical existences, the lost beauties of the Church: stained glass, painted images, illuminated manuscripts, 'staind in beauties die', 'inameld with delight, | And limbde with glorious gleames' (lines 9–12); they 'spring from fertile soile' and offer 'most glittering gold' not 'glebe' or mundane harvest (lines 17–20). Southwell's imagery is unusually brilliant and painterly here; the visual beauty of his description is the main point, as if in direct reply to Spenser's suggestion that such beauties lead the butterfly-soul into danger. Southwell rejects these iconoclastic accusations of worldliness and vanity; the relationship between art and the sacred is beautifully and emphatically celebrated here.

Once again, it is in his attempts to reproduce the powerful effects of the visual without a pagan plethora of classical props, or risky doctrinal signifiers, in the pursuit of a simple moral point, that Southwell achieves his best effects in English.

For if beauty in pursuit of holiness is to be considered suspect, what is the beauty of Spenser's garden for? Is cultivating noble patronage a sufficient justification for such lush descriptions? Southwell's gardening is more meticulous. There is a suggestion of the *hortus conclusus*, full of the Mariological imagery that was beginning to flower in Rome. In a painting in the Collegio Romano church of SS. Annunziata, God sends the Holy Spirit to the Madonna and Gabriel, and symbols of the Virgin, including the Garden, the Tower of David and the Well of Living Water, occupy the background.[30] The mystical attributes of the Virgin were of great importance to the Jesuits; Henry Garnet and Southwell made a detour on their journey to England to the shrine of the Blessed Virgin of Loreto, in the hills near Ancona, where Ignatius and Xavier had prayed before their first entry into Rome. Xavier had experienced a miraculous access of zeal there which helped him on his mission to India; no doubt Garnet was hoping for such a blessing.[31] He was, incidentally, taking a less-travelled route up Italy; their effort to hide their presence from even other English Catholics in Boulogne suggests that the missioners saw a need for unusual discretion. They certainly caught Burghley by surprise, in spite of all his contacts in Rome, as discussed earlier, so perhaps the Virgin of Loreto smiled on them.

Although the college decorations in 1580s Rome did not emphasise these Mariological features to the extent of seventeenth-century decorative programmes (or those in Germany, where Canisius's 1558 Litany of Loreto was popular), the *hortus conclusus* and Loreto will not have been far from Southwell's mind whenever he described a garden. The Litany identified Mary with 'the Seat of Wisdom, the Tower of David, the Tower of Ivory, the House of Gold, the Ark of the Covenant, the gate of Heaven, the Mystical Rose, and the Morning star, among other titles', the majority of these appearing in the Song of Songs and other Old Testament passages.[32] But Southwell's Marian poetry has less than one might expect of such emblems: she is just '*Elias* little cloude' in 'The Virgine Maries conception' (p. 3, l. 3). In 'Her Nativity', however, she is the 'Orient starre', 'little cloud', 'royall throne', the 'quarry to cut out our corner stone', fruitful soil, Jesse's Rod (p. 3, lines 1, 9, 13, 15, 16, 17). It is in 'Her Spousals' that we come closest to the *hortus conclusus* imagery: she is the Garden of Paradise, lent to Joseph; she is described as a tripartite persona too, Virgin, wife, and widow (p. 4, lines 7, 17).[33] Symbols pertaining to her position as Queen of Heaven are not mentioned at all in 'The Virgins salutation' (p. 5): rather, the idea is presented as if describing a painting of her as Queen of Heaven. She is described as a flower in 'Christs returne out of Egypt', but mostly in order to provide Southwell with a series of flower symbols to make into a word-bouquet, punning on an old identification of Nazareth with a flower: 'Flowre to a flowre he fitly doth retire. | For flower he is and in a flower he bred, | And from a thorne now to a flowre he fled.' She is also a 'virgin branch' in order for Christ to be described as a bud which flowers and fruits and, which, when ripe, 'must with thornes hang on a tree' in a garden of *our* making (p. 10, lines 10–12, 16–18). Southwell's garden imagery is precisely that: a discussion of how we, as much as God, create our own landscapes.

Such emblems became a conveniently concise and obscured way of introducing Catholic meditative imagery into England in the seventeenth century, and the Jesuits, used to going into places of poor literacy, were skilled in the use of such pictorial aids. Southwell's poetry, as I have said, can be seen in the light of this pastoral usage, but his failure to include specific flowers in his garden, such as the rose and lily emblems symbolic of Mary, suggests that, although picturing the garden as a device, he is not attempting any direct reference to the Marian emblems; also, like the secular *impresa* of Elizabeth's

Snow in Arcadia: rewriting the English lyric landscape

Accession Day tilts, Southwell's can carry a sting, in context.

The garden, to Southwell, was a microcosm of our troubled relationship with God's cosmos; the attributes of the Virgin were less his pastoral concern once in England than the wrongness of Elizabeth's alleys and arbours. He had carried with him from Rome memories of a garden that may have seemed to him the model for all good gardens, and one that both circumstance and devotional habit connected in his mind with pious femininity. His 'Poema de Assumptione B.V.M.' speaks of a place

> worthy of report from the first beginning of the Universe, planted with trees amongst which the mild air breathes with gentle whispering and soft murmuring and, flowing through the grass, rippling water sends forth sweet-sounding melodies, and flowing back on itself in even curves divides into various meandering paths [...] Who could tell of all the wonders of the place? Whatsoever of beauty is spread over the immense globe and is seen, scattered and solitary throughout region after region: all this is enclosed in one garden.[34]

The Novitiate gardens (shown behind the new Novitiate buildings in a near-contemporary engraving) were being renovated as Southwell's time in Rome was ending.[35] They represented the natural world ordered to God's work. Terraces with different horticultural emphases and filled with emblematic references expressed the diversity of global cultures.

The Novitiate's blessed plot contained beehives, drinking-fountains, orchards, herbers and potagers full of what is good for the body; flower beds to please the senses; fountains to reflect the source of the divine inspiration; statuary to represent ideals. The bees themselves perhaps symbolised the communal work of the Society, while the clipped topiary hinted at the violence done to private inclination to shape the natural man to the proper Jesuit ideal. Most Ignatian of all, along the entire side of the terraced and multifarious site, a single communicating pergola-ed walkway, emblem and microcosm of the global Jesuit network, linked each terrace from bottom to top. And at the top, commanding the view across the world-garden, stood the Novitiate building, on the wall of which the IHS of the Society sent out rays of divine light, with a wall sundial beneath it as if to remind the wanderer in the garden that the light was to illuminate the work of God, not the beauties of the garden. Novices strolled the gravelled alleys of the geometric terrace by the Novitiate, engaged in devout conversations or solitary prayer. This was a place enfolded within the iconography of the Virgin as the *hortus conclusus*, full of subtle reminders of her mysterious symbols: roses, lilies, trees, tower and gate, stairway and fountain. Her symbolic presence engendered an air of loving companionship as well as piety. In Southwell's 'Poema de Assumptione B.V.M.' he makes a suggestive connection between Paradise and the Catholic Virgin, of earth, but uniquely unstained with earthly sin.

> Quicquid in immenso pulchri diffunditur orbe,
> Et sparsum solumque alias aliasque per oras
> Cernitur, hoc uno totum concluditur horto.
> Haec sedes antiqua fuit, quam Lucifer Adae
> Invidit[36]

(Whatsoever of beauty was spread over the immense globe and is seen, scattered and unique throughout region after region: all this is enclosed in one garden. This was the one-time abode, which Lucifer begrudged to Adam)

The Novitiate Garden was a representation of biblical Paradise, translated into Latin and Italian. If Garnet talked with Weston his English friend there, it was in Latin, and if Southwell learned about the garden and its trees and flowers, he did not learn in English. 'Loves Garden Grief' (p. 64), written in English, is the antithesis of that Roman Paradise. Unlike the hilltop gardens of the Quirinale, the summer breeze in England's garden is enervating, and its birdsong dreadful to the ears. The English palace is a prison 'that allureth | To sweet mishap' (lines 5–6); Southwell's Latin palace, the Novitiate, was the house of a better sort of Love than the one derided in his poem.

Most of all, the Novitiate garden was a Paradise associated with pious women, and here Southwell's comparison becomes pointed. Southwell's Novitiate in all its splendour and refinement was a place funded by the jewels and treasure of at least two wealthy and pious benefactresses.[37] It is likely that Southwell was remembering this devoted and celebrated womanhood – not to mention making unflattering parallels with Elizabeth – when he accuses 'Vaine loves' English garden of being built on the wages of sin: 'your jewels jests, and worthless trash your treasure' (lines 1–2). His first experience of well-directed wealth in his novice years was connected with pious women, while his English experience of wealth included that of his grandfather, product of the Dissolution, in Catholic eyes the work of a sinning female, Anne Boleyn; and that of Elizabeth her daughter's Court, founded on heresy, piracy, sycophancy, and vanity, in Southwell's view. His mission orders prevented him from saying so directly, and perhaps in any case he felt tongue-tied in trying to express such sentiments in English; if so, he need only turn to the imagery of the garden itself, and he had his English homily, designed as an abstraction founded in the real.

MAPPING THE NEW ALBION

Mary's are heavenly attributes, and one has to die to the world to reach them. This is an idealised, unattainable soul-scape, not an altered nation-scape: the ordinary English reader needed something more useful, a map to help find the way around the England they inhabited. 'vale of teares' and the wintry nativity poems are in this sense far more useful, overlaying a simply conceived Christianity on to a recognisably local environment, one that, in its wintriness, echoed the bitterness of Catholic experience at the time.

It is when Southwell takes on the Court poets most directly that we see him begin to sketch out a viable alternative landscape to that of the original: one can see the beginnings of an inhabitable interior space being formed, even though the 'I' he invents is merely a riposte to that of the other, standing only in opposition. In 'Content and rich', for instance, he constructs his alternative space carefully from the centre out. 'I dwell in graces courte', he begins; virtue and faith, not ambitious courtiers, are his companions. He takes his pleasure walking in 'lowlie vales' (p. 67, lines 1, 5); this estate is not in defiant competition with Burghley's, but neither is it, on the other hand, in heaven: it is 'poor' (l. 8), but very much here. Now we are seeing a space all too familiar to an English gentleman, especially a Catholic one, down on his luck, unable to attend Court and constricted into ever tighter corners of his countryside by State controls, or even, like Arundel, literally confined to prison. Where a Ralegh is pushing out the bounds of English national expansion, creating a new empire, Southwell may claim at least the ownership of his mind; where a Dyer might say 'my mind to me a kingdom is', this courtier can say, in direct riposte, 'My minde to me an *empire* is' (l. 27; my emphasis); the Catholic Church is claiming universality; this mind is inhabiting its own internalised realm, self-constructed and 'other' than that of the national project, which Southwell implies has cost a Ralegh or a Dyer the free ownership of his own mind, and lost him the only empire worth having.[38]

This Southwellian alternative mind-map defines a gentleman's right to inhabit, maintain, and direct the estate of his own conscience.[39] Even a Protestant Englishman could identify with this issue, if in the negative. The alterations wrought by Protestantism in humanity's ability to access grace meant that, in witnessing for the Faith and suffering rejection for it, a man might become a martyr, but he would not know if he were capable of accessing grace until he reached the heavenly city at the end, like Bunyan's Christian. Bunyan's *Pilgrim's Progress* is an interior landscape bereft of security of tenure or even hope of it, if it has not already been divinely determined.

Other poets had been redrawing Albion too. Sidney, in his *Certaine Sonets*, perhaps reflects a spiritual loss when he describes a place where once he walked with mind at rest which has now become a metaphor for rejection and isolation from joy:

> In wonted walkes, since wonted fancies change,
>   Some cause there is, which of strange cause doth rise;
> For in each thing wherto mine eyes doth range,
>   Part of my paine me seemes engraved lyes.

> The Rockes which were of constant mind the marke 5
>   In clyming steepe, now hard refusall show;
> The shading woods seeme now my Sunne to darke,
>   And stately hills disdaine to looke so low.
>
> The restfull Caves now restlesse visions give,
>   In Dales I see each way a hard assent: 10
> Like late mowne meades, late cut from joy I live.
>   Alas sweete Brookes do in my teares augment:
>   Rockes, woods, hilles, caves, dales, meads, brookes, answer me;
>   Infected mindes infect each thing they see.[40]

The new subject, stripped of its old imagery or simulacra, can no longer 'see' the world fully: it has no point of pre-reference to replace that lost. If Sidney, a hero of English Protestantism, can be taken, with Bunyan, as an example of Protestant imaginative subjectivity, this poem suggests that something was wrong at the very heart of the individual Protestant's world view. The Catholics were suffering too: the imaginative faculty and 'focused visuality', the very loci of love of traditional Catholicism, had been doctrinally excised from the English psychological/spiritual landscape, whatever its denomination, leaving the individual in a spiritually arid, lonely place.

Southwell, especially in his poetry, was offering his readership both Catholic and Protestant – his *English* readership – a new set of simulacra, mapping a new way around this frightening place. His 'vale of teares' goes much further than Sidney's complaint to become effectively an illustration of the unmapped wilderness in which they all wandered, a place where the wellsprings of true spirituality, the 'christall springs', creep 'out of secret vaine', only to disappear immediately down 'some envious hole that hides their grace', swallowed up by the godless landscape like the fugitive priests themselves.

Is Southwell giving a poetic riposte, if not reproof, to Sidney's own version of the redrawn scene? It is hard not to find parallels in the phrasing and core concept of 'Vale' with Sidney's heartsick place. 'A vale there is', Southwell begins, and mentions rocks free to the view from earth to high heaven, and streams and dales – a wide landscape but, to a troubled view, threatening, infected, as in Sidney's poem, by a wrongness at the core. In Southwell's version, though, the wrongness is in complete accord with the spiritual state of the English viewer, removed from the true observance of God. In this early appearance of the pathetic fallacy, the grief of the good English Catholic is wrung from Southwell's landscape:

> A place for mated minds, an onely bower,
> Where every thing doth sooth a dumpish mood.
> Earth lies forlorne, the cloudie skie doth lower,
> The wind here weepes, here sighes, here cries aloude. 35

Snow in Arcadia: rewriting the English lyric landscape

'The strugling floud betweene the marble grones, | Then roring beates upon the craggie sides' like a man trapped in some unyielding place (lines 37–8); as if writing a more suitable landscape for a heavy soul, or as if giving the heavy soul an explanation for its state of misery, Southwell seems to be attempting to wrap the Sidneian mourner in Southwell's own vision of an English landscape of betrayed and shattered self-hood. Cling to that sorrow, Southwell is saying – it is the only honest response to your condition. It is, far from a sign that you have gone wrong, a sign that your understanding is alert and fully functioning:

> All pangs and heavie passions here may find
> A thousand motives suitly to their griefes,
> To feed the sorrowes of their troubled minde,   55
> And chase away dame pleasures vaine reliefes.
>
> To plaining thoughts this vaile a rest may bee,
> To which from wordly joyes they may retire.
> Where sorrow springs from water, stone and tree,
> Where everie thing with mourners doth conspire.   60

The *Exercises* had taught him this sensitivity to the appropriate response. And a remedy of sorts is offered: number the sorrows and sins, turn the grief into music, then at least in sorrow the soul can continue to imitate God's creative urge:

> Set here my soule maine streames of teares afloate,   61
> Here all thy sinfull foiles alone recount,
> Of solemne tunes make thou the dolefulst note,
> That to thy ditties dolor may amount.

Southwell's imaginary soul-scape is not the terrifying spectacle one would expect of a man looking hard at the prospect of martyrdom. He ends it in flames: but not the oppressive medieval landscape of hell or the hope of martyrdom, but an entirely individual and Renaissance idea, a limbeck of the heart heated by the severity of former sins and regrets, vapouring up tears to the eyes (lines 69–72) to be turned into sad melodies. 'Let teares to tunes, and paines to plaints be prest' (l. 73): the English affective art manifesto, and certainly one that described the artistic activities of William Byrd and the other Catholic creatives of Elizabeth's Court. These were the butterflies released upwards into holy music and poetry in England, the project Southwell had come in part to foster.

In comparison with this, Sidney's landscape seems a tamer place altogether, a place of well-managed brooks and woods, where caves are for taking one's ease in and meads are mown by rustics, a place of regular resort, an owned place, an estate, if one clouded by disappointments. As if to address this more familiar sort of scenery, or more to the point, to enfold it into his own newly formulated soul-scape, Southwell writes about it in full pathetic vein. As I have mentioned above, 'Loves Garden Grief' describes this more recognisable, domestic scene, but one deliberately made wrong, emphatically not the community place addressed as 'ours' in his Virgin sequence; this is '*your*' landscape:

> Your garden griefe, hedg'd in with thornes of envie,
>   And stakes of strife:
> Your Allyes errour graveled with Jelosie,
>   And cares of life.   10
> Your bankes are seates enwrapt with shades of sadnes,
> Your Arbours breed rough fittes of raging madnes.

With Satan as the gardener (l. 29), small wonder that the work has produced the opposite of Paradise, visionless, joyless, untrue at the very root; yet so many of Southwell's readers themselves were luxuriating in the newly planted acres of England's new demi-paradise.

The image-landscape chosen by Southwell was therefore political as well as spiritual in nature, a direct assault upon the actual landscapes being built by the mushroom growth of 'new men' at Elizabeth's Court. Surely few ordinary Englishmen of any sort approved of the way in which certain men around Elizabeth were enriching themselves at the country's expense.

He also witnessed a more particular resentment: why should a gentleman not decide for himself how to direct his prayers, whether under monarch or pope?[41] Southwell appears to have understood this less as an issue of correct doctrine than one of freedom of conscience: given the right conditions, the right choice would be made. He shared Puritan alarm at the general slide towards atheism.[42] The God-indwelt English landscape yearned for by Puritanism was not dissimilar to the one he was creating in his writing. In offering his soul 'map' Southwell was identifying his readership and their needs very precisely: English, and proud of it (and therefore 'ashamde of their decay': 'Vale', l. 47); shorn of their rights ('hedg'd in with thornes of envie': 'Loves Garden', l. 7), and sick of it.

Wyatt's and now Sidney's English map was a smaller-scale one of courtly complaint at injustice or lack of advancement, expressed within the existing courtly structure: the generic landscape is there to be mastered – 'hard refusall' meets Sidney's attempts to climb the rocks, and the 'Sunne' is darkened only because it does not favour Sidney (Sonnet 18, lines 6, 7): hardly a soul-scape. Lodge's sonnet from *A Margarite of America* (1596) is another 'backdrop' depiction of nature:

> O shady vales, O fair enrichëd meads,
> O sacred woods, sweet fields, and rising mountains,
> O painted flowers, green herbs, where Flora treads
> Refreshed by wanton winds and watery fountains [43]

It is, like Sidney's, a landscape of symbol and background colour, like the accoutrements of a Queen's Day Tilt, no more than something to strike attitudes in front of. Bees, lilies, myrtles, bowers, and fountains: these – Flora's, not Mary's – are the generality of nature-poetry tropes from the 1590s, blazon-simulacra of the real.

Southwell's approach is sharper and more focused, at worst a response that disguises its political implications under its drab medievalism, at best an entirely new vision of a landscape that focuses, even determines feeling.

Responding to discussions of the landscape at all in the 1580s and 1590s was a form of political opposition. To speak about the land of England was *not* to speak about its monarch. As Richard Helgerson says, the 'extraordinary burst of cartographic and chorographic descriptions of England [...] necessarily displaced the royal body as the chief sign of national identity'. A landscape without the Queen in it was a landscape which problematised the rights of monarchy.[44] Sidney had done it in his pastorals, other less poetical men were doing it in their estate record-keeping. Even Burghley with his new garden was inventing a landscape outside Elizium, and Tresham's temple-building suggests an intention to reinstate, in as many private ways as possible, that ancient tradition of sacred architecture that the Iconoclasts had tried to erase.

But Southwell was not merely inserting himself and his own agenda into this new landscaping; what the young Jesuit-poet added to this cartographic commentary was an extra layer of sermonlike authority. Landscape to a missionary Jesuit trained to find God in the real could never be a mere collection of blazons to be assembled in response to a personal agenda. Where the others were using self-created landscapes to comment on the political, or at least their place in it (as Dyer in his tree), Southwell was in turn commenting on the self-created landscapes, the paucity of spiritual creativity that in his view rendered them invalid. Obedient to his training, he was insisting that a landscape, whether internal or not, is informed by God, and must have God acknowledged in it.

I have already discussed the poetic formulations regarding English nationhood and monarchy addressed by Southwell at the level of the poetic; my point here is the special level of real authority invested in his poetry, and what it implied for English poets. Whether or not it was his prime intention, Southwell was criticising the integrity and scope of Englishmen's vision, and most specifically as it was reflected through other English poets' creativity, their artistic landscape, so to speak. Through his critiques of their approaches, he was addressing not just their subject matter but their subjecthood as authors: the nature of their audience and addressee, where they placed the 'I' in their imaginary landscape.

Robert Southwell

'ASTONISH'T DREAD': LAZARUS IN PARNASSUS[45]

The Parnassian picture was, for Southwell not merely incomplete; he was trained on Bellarmine's view that a generic backdrop was an artistic lie, and nothing worthwhile could be said before it. It was Southwell's more truthful rhetorical vision that persisted and eventually dominated English poetry. It is somewhat ironic that by George Herbert's time it was Southwell's, not Sidney's, landscape that had become part of a distinctly Protestant poetic position. In 'Jordan (1)' Herbert criticises poetry that is recognisably that of Sidney and the courtly set:

> Is it no verse, except enchanted groves
> And sudden arbours shadow coarse-spunne lines?
> Must purling streams refresh a lovers loves?
> Must all be vail'd, while he that reads, divines,
>   Catching the sense at two removes?
>
> Shepherds are honest people; let them sing:
> Riddle who list, for me, and pull for Prime:
> I envie no mans nightingale or spring;
> Nor let them punish me with losse of rime,
>   Who plainly say, *My God, My King*.[46]

Southwell was writing into a tightening formula for poetic discourse, led at that particular moment by Puttenham and by the emerging importance of Sidney's works. In his *Arte of English Poesie* Puttenham hierarchalises poetic production according to classical precedent, ending with the lowly Eclogue or Bucolic – the native expression of the natural man, before the arrival of farming and nation, politics and princes.[47] Southwell does not, in English, employ pagan pastoralism. He has, with the one exception, no nymphs, and no overt classical allusion, as if he does not intend his discourse to be carried on outside the arena of the political or princely.

Southwell does have shepherds, but not Parnassian or May-time ones. Bruegel-like, he uses a more realistic pastoral imagery to site his Christ-Child in the discomforts of here-and-now, his descriptions a metaphor for English rejection of the Catholic sacraments no doubt sharpened by his own travels, carried out in winter to deter pursuivancy. The north European Christian landscape experienced by Southwell was a cold one. Bucolic language appears in 'Losse in Delaies', too, and 'vale of teares' has those remarkably realistic descriptions of a far-from-classical pastoral scene. General discomforts like 'chilling cold' and 'freesing Winter night' appear in 'New heaven new Warre', and 'New Prince, new pompe' (p. 13, l. 7; p. 16, l. 2), to emphasise the pitiable image of the Christ-child born into the cold heart. Only in 'The burning Babe' (p. 15) is the English poetic 'I' fully exposed, 'shivering in the snow' out on a winter's night, experiencing to the full the twilight of England's Albion.

Southwell's choice of bucolic poetry is interesting given that Puttenham cannot admit it to be the first among the poetic forms: what business has a priest to be dabbling in it? Puttenham does, however, claim that the pastoral style was later developed as a ruse to cover comment on greater matters which it would not otherwise have been safe to make (*Arte*, p. 38), a claim interestingly pursued by scholarship in the light of Sidney's pastorals. Southwell's 'Deere cosen' apology for turning to light poetic matter seems to hint at ulterior motives; in his prefatory letter to *Marie Magdalens Funeral Teares* he clearly understands the use of light poetry as a 'mask' without which moral truths 'would not find so free a passage' (sig. A 7v). Here are parallels again with William Byrd, who released four volumes of holy songs and more mirthful ones, including simple country airs and lyrics, during the years of Southwell's English mission; they too appear to disguise darker matter.[48]

There is a glimpse of Parnassus, however, as Milton was later to do in combining the grandeur of the classical with the authority of biblical traditions, in the unique appearance in Southwell's English poetry of direct classical referents, in Peter's description of Mary Magdalen and her sister Martha:

> O sister Nymphes the sweet renowmed paire,   589
> That blisse *Bethania* bounds with your aboade:
> Shall I infect that sanctified aire,
> Or staine those steps where *Jesus* breathd and trode?[49]

'No: let your praiers perfume that sweetned place', he adds. With this stately passage, Southwell seems to bypass the florid nymphomanias of the Elizabethan pastoralists in perhaps the earliest example of the dignified, restrained classical-biblical combinations more typical of a later age. Even Milton sometimes falls short of the effortless Christian neoclassicism of these simple lines.

But Southwell was not joining Parnassus with Bethany only to constitute a new congregation, but also to recall the old church, as Milton later did, reflecting the continuity of God's action in human history. There was another dweller in Albion's Bethania that connected it to the blessed dead of Christian tradition: 'could I revived *Lazarus* behold, | The third of that sweet Trinitie of Saints', his protagonist muses, 'Would not astonish't dread my sences holde? | Ah yes, my heart even with his naming faints' (lines 595–8). Southwell's neoclassicism is used to give access to an ancient faith: Lazarus is both a reminder of the old Catholic saints of Albion, and a man of the Gospels come from beyond death to remind the English Peter of all that he has let go.

COLD COMFORTS: A BRETON AND A SOUTHWELL CHRISTMAS

A comparison between Southwell and Nicholas Breton, also interested in plain English poetry, shows the layers of meaning hidden in Southwell's apparent simplicity. In Breton's version of our vale of tears, a 'wretched wight', betrayed by a cruel mistress, converts his anguish into music which consists of 'beating on my breste, | And sobbing sighes, which yeelde a heauy sounde, | My harte with panges of paine is ouerpreste' and 'for delights, in dumps I passe my dayes'.[50] His complaint is of a false mistress, his response sorrowful song and tears, the poetic environment merely a vehicle by which to convey those external details; the Petrarchan foregrounding of the body and the effects of emotion on it are there: he goes little further than the physical body itself, the 'breste', the 'harte', as the site of all the action. When he does turn to the inner landscape of the mind he places it in the dream-world, and the scenery through which the dreamer passes is merely a backdrop to the allegorical figures, as it is in Spenser, peopled with characters out of morality plays, heroic, monstrous or pitiable. Breton uses poetic landscape the way the theatre might – a prop against which to present his text, or as emblem, not as a method of eliciting a response which gives him insights into his own psychological state. Despite any external similarities in form and subject matter, Southwell's poetry is doing something different and new: as Kuchar says, Southwell's interrogation of Petrarchan desire 'reflects a significant moment in the history of *anthropopathia*': he puts God into the human interior landscape.[51]

The closest precedent to Southwell's non-generic landscape is in the poetry of Thomas Sackville, Earl of Dorset, to which Southwell almost certainly had access.[52] The nature described in his poetry is specific, well-observed and delicately realised, but used only to reflect his raindrop misery. Southwell's 'vale' offers us a more complex and psychologised landscape than this, although still one absolutely integral to the narrator's self; in this it is quite unlike the landscape of either Sackville or Breton; it is created *by* the narrator's interior experience, not merely *for* it to be played out upon. The viewpoint is matched by the internal state of the viewer – as the anxious traveller's eye ranges from the barren to the green and back to the horrid waste, seeking a way through, so his hopes spring and wither. 'Here gaping cliffe, there mossie plaine is seene, | Here hope doth spring, and there againe doth quaile' (lines 42–3). The landscape in turn reflects the disordered view of the traveller: 'huge massie stones' hang overhead, kept up 'by tickle stay' and ready to fall at any moment; and there are those 'withered trees ashamde of their decay' (lines 44–6). Perhaps the massy stones are men of standing, ever at risk of a moment's mistake and a fall, or even England, hanging on the thinning thread of an un-heired Elizabeth; perhaps the withered trees that are 'forcde gray coats to weare' amongst

Snow in Arcadia: rewriting the English lyric landscape

the overweening evergreens are the Catholic families ruined and humiliated by the State (l. 47), but they are also real elements of recognisable mountain landscapes, stunted birches, perhaps, leafless amongst the mountain pines; there is not an allegorical grotesque in sight. Southwell is telling us that the state of real nature itself has been disrupted and made monstrous by the changed circumstances in heretic England, just as Shakespeare suggests by his descriptions of storms and prodigies in *Hamlet, Julius Caesar, Lear* or *Midsummer Night's Dream*.

Southwell's poem is also a musical and poetic mission-statement, describing the 'dolefull' landscape of the assailed soul, with its 'fearfull quier' of thunderstorms, water and winds, the 'musicke' of the destructive forces of nature, 'where none but heavy notes have any grace' and any springs of solace, creeping out of 'secret vaine', are immediately swept into the envious ground; laments and 'solemne tunes', 'the dolefulst note', are the only musical response that could resonate with such a state (lines 17–20, 49–50, 63). Southwell, in emphasising the realness of the place, has told his readers that the state of nature itself is troubled; in conflating the place and the persona's mood, he also makes it into an interior landscape, equally, if subjectively, real. In fact, drear as it seems, the place is suitable because it is in a state of harmony with a 'troubled minde' (l. 55):

> To plaining thoughts this vaile a rest may bee, 57
> To which from wordly joyes they may retire.
> Where sorrow springs from water, stone and tree,
> Where everie thing with mourners doth conspire.

Instead of the body being the only thing moved by feeling, in Southwell, the landscape and the body are integrated as a psychological or spiritual and physical entity, a whole. The melancholy of the place in turn feeds into the response of the musician-pilgrim, who recounts to himself his sins and lacks, in an elegy sharpened in its 'dolor' by its sensitivity to the sadness all around (l. 64). We are again being referred to a medieval-style, or classical-pagan, Orpheus-in-the-wilderness poem, but seen from an entirely different angle – from inside a 'real' psychology, situated in a 'real' landscape. As in his disguised 'Psyche', Southwell never refers explicitly to his classical-pagan model, but the Orphean musical frame of the poem becomes more obvious towards its close. In the original myth, Orpheus could move the beasts, indeed the very stones themselves, with his music; Southwell, in his penultimate stanza, describes a sort of madrigal of self-accusation and sorrow as the sorrowing persona and the sorry landscape make a harmony of melancholy sounds:

> When *Eccho* doth repeat thy plainfull cries, 65
> Thinke that the verie stones thy sinnes bewray,
> And now accuse thee with their sad replies,
> As heaven and earth shall in the latter day

Robert Southwell

Southwell has taken classical motifs, those of Echo, cursed by a cruel goddess and rejected by a vain youth, and left able to reflect only what the world says to her, and Orpheus, which he has not only Englished, but conjoined with Christian teleology. It could as well be the biblical Nebuchadnezzar, or, more likely, David in the wilderness: the political ups and downs of David's life, as well as his multiple roles as beautiful shepherd, royal favourite, fighter for the crown, prince, song-maker, and, ultimately, ruler, make him a suggestive model for courtly poets under Elizabeth. The very invisibility of the persona and the lack of a recognisable narrative, though, put all the emphasis upon the interior spiritual or psychological state – the narrative is not the point. The landscape, or the apparent realness of it, is part of the point, but it fades into the background at the end along with the sad music, as remorse becomes the main theme:

> Let teares to tunes, and paines to plaints be prest,   73
> And let this be the burdon of thy song,
> Come deepe remorse, possesse my sinfull brest:
> Delights adue, I harbourd you too long.

Apart from an appearance here and there of suggestive words or phrases such as 'pilgrim wights', 'christall', 'grace', 'sinfull' and 'the latter day', and the remorse for a life wasted on 'dame pleasures vaine reliefes' typical of the Orphean or Davidic genre, there is no religiosity, not even in the shape of a prayer at the close, as in so many of Southwell's other poems. There is only the sad acceptance of the fallen state, the failure of Petrarchan ideals, the wasted time. 'In Southwell's vision, Nature, guided seemingly at random by God's creative hand, steps in and touches a deeper vein of soothing resignation'; Southwell is describing the artistic production of the Byrd set, Catholics creating music in a 'wrong' landscape, 'waiting', as Devlin puts it, 'until the Sun of God's supernatural consolation should break the clouds again'.[53] If this is the best Arcadia has to offer the lyricist, it is a cold, unlovely place, in truth.

Cold comfort as it seems, it is closer to the articulation of the self than that of Breton, a confession of inner feelings and how they change the *Umwelt*, not a semi-detached description of a scene. Breton, who seems not to have shared Southwell's sharper understanding of psychology, ends his own allegorical trip sounding even more like a Morality player, with this cheering communal prayer (*Poems*, 18, p. 50):

> And then awake I gan to call to minde,   385
>   this vision strange, that thus appearde to me:
> Theffect of which, who so could justly finde,
>   I doo not doubt some matter rare should see:
> And thus I end, when worldly woes are past,
>   God send us all the joyes of heavne at last.   390

Snow in Arcadia: rewriting the English lyric landscape

Southwell's landscape is not a dreamed place. He uses something like this dream-sequence only once, in 'The burning Babe', but, rather than the persona recalling a dream once 'reality' has been regained, Southwell's narrator calls 'reality' to mind after living through a vision. That vision was not one had while asleep or in some allegorical hinterland, but in the all-too-recognisable cold of an English winter, sketched in with a self-confident lightness of touch never achieved by Breton. 'As I in hoarie Winters night | Stoode shivering in the snow, | Surpris'd I was ...' he begins, introducing the simplest of apparitions: a baby, in a blaze of light.

The Babe metaphorises his condition in a few stanzas, without recourse to allegory, in a passage full of highly sophisticated meditations on complex relationships between man and divine law. A Renaissance mind of any education would have been deeply involved in unpicking such a passage. But Southwell once again is not content with such externalising of feeling, finishing with a shot that must carry deep into the heart of his reader, recalling him to a more childlike relationship with his Maker. Then, the narrator concludes, 'With this he vanisht out of sight, | And swiftly shrunk away, | And straight I called unto minde, | That it was Christmasse day' (lines 31–2).

Breton's use of the idea of Christmas itself illustrates the difference between his and Southwell's poetic scope. In 'Christmas Carol', Breton shows a 'gentleman, being on Christmas Eve in a very solitary place, among very solemn company', singing a complaint of his hard hap lost in the 'desert woods and plains' where he dreams wistfully of the high life at the distant Court. In 'The burning Babe' the narrator also shivers for obscure reasons in the night (surely only an exile or a shepherd would be out there at that time?) and also has a vision of splendour: not the obvious one of the belly-filling seasonal grandeur of royal tables but the frightening sight of the Child sobbing in the bonfire of vanity.

In 'Another Christmas Song' Breton's narrator swears, at the end of the feast-days, that he came not near 'old Christmas games, or dancing with fine dames, | Or shows, or pretty plays' but wandered 'In woods from tree to tree, | For want of better room', praying God send a better one next year.[54] Southwell's frozen-hearted wanderer, instead of warming his heart at a lighted window, sees a fire in the sky, and dreams of a landscape of heavenly justice and mercy, and, after experiencing the mystery of the Passion in this metaphoric furnace, calls to mind only at the end of the poem that 'it was Christmas day', that light touch that ties us back into the Breton Christmas but now with added spiritual ballast: a very Southwellian trick. He has taken Sidney's Arcadia and shown it to be in the grip of bitter winter; he has concentrated all the moral power of Breton's vale-of-tears-type moralisation into a blinding, Damascene moment, all superfluity or words burned away to the central universally Christian image of the sacrificed and resacrificed Christ, and all in thirty-two lines in the simplest of ballad or common metre.

The landscape of this Albion cannot possibly be pictured in May greenery by an honest poet, Southwell seems to be saying. Despite the brief and fading flare of Christmas daylight described in 'The burning Babe', the Sun does not shine here; 'here' is out in the spiritual cold, with more snow on the way.

NOTES

1 Robert Southwell, 'A vale of teares', in James H. McDonald and Nancy Pollard Brown (eds), *The Poems of Robert Southwell, S.J.* (Oxford: Clarendon Press, 1967), p. 41; hereafter M&B; further references to Southwell's poetry are from this edition, given as page/line numbers in the text.

2 Hugh Maclean and Anne Lake Prescott (eds), *Edmund Spenser's Poetry*, 3rd edn (New York: Norton, 1968), 'Januarye', 'Argument', p. 506, and lines 19–20, p. 507; and Paul Alpers, 'Spenser's Domain of Lyric', in *Edmund Spenser's Poetry*, p. 788; hereafter cited in the text.

3 Gary Waller, *English Poetry of the Sixteenth Century* (Harlow: Longman, 1986), pp. 61–3; hereafter cited in the text; biographical information on Dyer is from Ian Ousby (ed.), *A Cambridge Guide to Literature in English* (Cambridge: Cambridge University Press, 1993), pp. 285–6.

4 Musées Royaux des Beaux-Arts, Brussels; see Christiane Stukenbrock and Barbara Töpper (eds), *1000 Masterpieces of European Painting from 1300 to 1850* (Cologne: Könemann, 2000), p. 148.

5 Gauvin Alexander Bailey, *Between Renaissance and Baroque: Jesuit Art in Rome, 1565–1610* (Toronto: University of Toronto Press, 2003), p. 49; and '"Le style jésuite n'existe pas": Jesuit Corporate Culture and the Visual Arts', in John W. O'Malley, S.J., Gauvin Alexander Bailey, et al., *The Jesuits: Cultures, Sciences, and the Arts 1540–1773* (Toronto: University of Toronto Press, 1999), pp. 38–89 (pp. 69–70; both hereafter cited in the text.

6 Gary Kuchar, 'Southwell's "A Vale of Tears": A Psychoanalysis of Form', *Mosaic*, 34.1 (2001), 107–120 (pp. 117–18); hereafter cited in the text.

7 This is reminiscent of Southwell's Latin 'Poema de Assumptione B.V.M.', with its description of Lethe in Tartarus (in Stonyhurst MS A.v.4 at Stonyhurst College, Clitheroe, Lancashire); Southwell's description in 'A vale' contains more, and more realistic, detail, as if taken from a real encounter.

8 See Pierre Janelle, *Robert Southwell the Writer: A Study in Religious Inspiration* (London: Sheed and Ward, 1935), p. 35.

9 Percy Bysshe Shelley, 'Mont Blanc', in Margaret Ferguson et al. (eds), *The Norton Anthology of Poetry* (London: Norton, 1996), pp. 796–9; hereafter *Norton*.

10 From Emrys Jones (ed.), *The New Oxford Book of Sixteenth Century Verse* (Oxford: Oxford University Press, 1992), pp. 102–13; hereafter *16CVerse*.

11 See Waller, pp. 282–3.

12 Edmund Spenser, *The Shepheardes Calender* (London, 1579); *The Faerie Queene* (London, 1590); see Giordano Bruno, *The Heroic Frenzies*, trans. Paul Eugene Memmo, University of North Carolina Studies in Romance Languages and Literatures Series, 50 (Chapel

Snow in Arcadia: rewriting the English lyric landscape

Hill: University of North Carolina Press, 1964); also Edmund H. Fellowes (ed.), William Byrd, *Collected Works*, vol. 12, *Psalms, Sonnets and Songs* (1588) (London: Stainer & Bell, 1965).

13 See Waller, pp. 282–5.

14 Ibid., pp. 42–3.

15 Monika Smialkowska, 'Skipping Sports and Solemn Rites: Popular and High Culture in the Early Stuart Court Masque' (unpublished doctoral thesis, University of Gloucester, 2001), p. 171.

16 For a discussion of dissemination and authorial strategies for resisting control, see, for instance, Arthur F. Marotti, *Manuscript, Print and the English Renaissance Lyric* (Ithaca: Cornell University Press, 1995); H. R. Woudhuysen, *Sir Philip Sidney and the Circulation of Manuscripts, 1558–1640* (Oxford: Clarendon Press, 1996); Annabel M. Patterson, *Censorship and Interpretation: The Conditions of Writing and Reading in Early Modern England* (Madison: University of Wisconsin Press, 1984).

17 Woudhuysen, p. 15.

18 See Patrick H. Martin, and John Finnis, 'Thomas Thorpe, "W.S.," and the Catholic Intelligencers', in *English Literary Renaissance*, 33 (2003), 3–43; Alison Shell discusses connections between Wright, the ex-Jesuit priest favoured by Robert Persons despite his overt loyalism, and Essex in 1595, pp. 127–33. For an account of connections between Catholic madrigals and Essex's switchback fortunes, see Lilian M. Ruff and Arnold Wilson, 'The Madrigal, the Lute Song and Elizabethan Politics', *Past & Present*, 44 (1969), 3–51.

19 F. W. Brownlow, *Robert Southwell*, Twayne's English Authors Series, 516 (New York: Simon & Schuster Macmillan, 1996), p. 130; hereafter cited in the text.

20 Brownlow, p. 130.

21 M&B, p. xxv.

22 Breton, 'A Strange Description of a Rare Garden Plot', published in *The Phoenix Nest* (1593); H. Thurston S.J. made the comparison in *The Month*, 1895, p. 2; also see Brownlow, p. 101; John Gerard, *Catalogus arborum* (London: *exofficina Arnoldii Hatfield, impensis Ioannis Norton*, 1599); his *Herball* (1597), a catalogue of 1033 plants and trees, was not published until after Southwell's death, but one of the works on which it was founded, Dodoens's *Cruydeboeck*, had been highly popular (in Lyte's translation) since 1578. See also http://apm.brookes.ac.uk/publishing/contexts/elizabet/mechanis.htm; www.rembert-dodoens.biography.ms/.

23 See www.nationaltrust.org.uk/places/lyvedennewbield/history_papers.html; also see Sir Gyles Isham, *Sir Thomas Tresham and his Buildings*, Northamptonshire Antiquarian Society, Reports and Papers Series (Northamptonshire Antiquarian Society, 1966), vol. 65 (1964, 1965), Part 2.

24 This medieval idea was designed to echo the pilgrim-routes in the Holy Land, and found Counter-Reformation expression in the pedagogical image progressions of the Roman churches; see Bailey, p. 9.

25 First mention of quinine appears to have been by Spanish authors in the 1560s and 1570s. See Fernando Ortiz-Crespo, *History of Chinchona*, uncompleted English translation, on www.cuencanet.com/ortiz/chinchona.htm.

26 See www.newadvent.org/cathen/15037b.htm; www.orderofmalta.org.uk/priory.htm.

27 See Pilarz's discussion of Bellarmine in relation to Southwell, pp. 160–71.

28 Thomas Bulfinch, *Bulfinch's Mythology* (New York: Avenel, 1978), pp. 81–91. 'Psyche' having been associated with 'butterfly' as well as 'soul' in Greek, she is often painted with butterfly wings, and appears in the work of many poets, including Milton and Keats.

29 Hugh Maclean and Anne Lake Prescott (eds), *Edmund Spenser's Poetry*, pp. 546–59.

30 See Bailey, p. 117.

31 Philip Caraman, S.J., *A Study in Friendship: Saint Robert Southwell and Henry Garnet* (Saint Louis, MO: The Institute of Jesuit Sources, 1995), pp. 2–3; hereafter cited in the text.

32 Jeffery Chipps Smith, 'The Art of Salvation in Bavaria', in O'Malley, Bailey, et al., *The Jesuits: Cultures*, pp. 568–99 (p. 582); see also Karl Josef Höltgen, 'Henry Hawkins: A Jesuit Writer and Emblematist in Stuart England', in the same volume, pp. 601–26, for a discussion of how emblematica were taken up by English writers after Southwell's time.

33 Mary is also the enclosed garden of Paradise described in Southwell's Latin 'Poema de Assumptione B.V.M.', in Stonyhurst MS A.v.4.

34 'Poema de Assumptione B.V.M.', Stonyhurst MS A.v.4, lines 9–27; from Peter Davidson and Anne Sweeney (ed. and intro.), *The Collected Poems of S. Robert Southwell, S.J.* (Manchester: Carcanet, forthcoming).

35 See Bailey, fig. 14; pp. 167–8.

36 'Poema de Assumptione B.V.M.', Stonyhurst MS A.v.4, lines 25–9. Translation from Davidson and Sweeney.

37 Bailey, p. 41.

38 'In praise of a contented mind', attributed to Sir Edward Dyer, in *16C Verse*, p. 322.

39 The map was in need of redrawing. Being predestined either heaven- or hell-wards effectively made conscience obsolete, and self-examination an anxious search for 'signs' of sainthood, as later evinced by Bunyan: 'But how if you want Faith indeed? But how can you tell you have Faith?'; 'Behold, then, his Goodness, but your self to be no partaker of it.' From John Bunyan, *Grace Abounding to the Chief of Sinners*, ed. John Brown (Cambridge: Cambridge University Press, 1907), pp. 19–20, 56; quoted in Louis L. Martz, *The Poetry of Meditation* (New Haven: Yale University Press, 1954), pp. 160–1.

40 'Certaine Sonets', 18, in Richard Dutton (ed.), *Sir Philip Sidney: Selected Writings* (Manchester: Carcanet, 1987), pp. 165–6.

41 An entry in a collection of records and accounts of Catholic martyrs from 306 to 1910 describes the outrage of Catholic gentlemen and their families, 'trailed' from prison to hear Protestant sermons by force, who seemed more upset at the attempt by other gentlemen to dictate their consciences than at the physical abuses they suffered in the process, a Mr. Stillington protesting that 'they were men and that it was meet they were suffered to be their own guides; it was strange and very grievous unto them, to be forced against their wills and consciences'. Robert Smith, *Chronicles of Blackburnshire, &c.*, I (Nelson: the author, 1909), p. 132.

42 In letters to Acquaviva in summer 1587 and January 1588 Southwell reports a Puritan named Wigginson who, preaching in church against bishops, was rescued by apprentices from arrest by catchpolls, who got a 'handsome beating'; but perhaps it was the defiant setting up of Wigginson in another pulpit that Southwell really admired; the

minister of the church insisting 'that there were twenty thousand men in London who were ready to risk their lives in the same cause. Thus far has Puritanism made progress' Southwell finishes, a note of admiration colouring his warning; in Devlin, p. 150.

43 Norman Ault (ed.), *Elizabethan Lyrics* (New York: Capricorn, 1960), p. 229; hereafter cited in the text.
44 Richard Helgerson, 'Shakespeare and Contemporary Dramatists of History', in Richard Dutton and Jean E. Howard (eds), *A Companion to Shakespeare's Works, Volume II: The Histories* (Oxford: Blackwell, 2003), II, pp. 26–47, p. 42.
45 'Saint Peters Complaint', M&B, p. 76, lines 595–8.
46 Helen Gardner, *The Metaphysical Poets*, 2nd rev. edn (Harmondsworth: Penguin, 1985), p. 125.
47 George Puttenham, *The Arte of English Poesie*, ed. Gladys Doidge Willcock and Alice Walker (London: R. Field, 1589; repr. London: Cambridge University Press, 1970), p. 38.
48 Joseph Kerman, *The Masses and Motets of William Byrd* (London: Faber, 1981).
49 'Saint Peters Complaint', pp. 76, lines 589–92.
50 Nicholas Breton, *Poems: Not Hitherto Printed*, ed. Jean Robertson (Liverpool: Liverpool University Press, 1967, first published 1952), p. 24, lines 31–3, 37.
51 Kuchar, p. 119.
52 Sackville was connected with Southwell's noble coterie: he was father of the Robert Sackville who married Arundel's sister Margaret and for whom, on her death, Southwell's *Triumphs over Death* was written.
53 Devlin, p. 187.
54 From Breton's *A Flourish upon Fancy*, 1577, in Alexander B. Grosart, *A Bower of Delights; being interwoven Verse and Prose from the works of Nicholas Breton* (London: Elliot Stock, 1893), pp. 41–5.

Chapter 6

Southwell's war of words

>Hoise up saile, while gale doth last;
>Tide and wind stay no mans pleasure[1]

DIES IRAE

Two years into the English mission, as the two Jesuits struggled to contain the multiple hopes and agendas of the English with whom they came into contact whilst never losing sight of the orders of their superiors, something changed which left them strung uncomfortably between two polarities. After the attempt on England of the Armada in 1588, the courtly Heywoodian compromise became an impossibility. On 5 November, as if to underline the alteration, Persons was put in charge not only of Englishmen supporting the Spanish forces in the Low Countries but of the Jesuits working in England too: he was now their superior; his concerns, now largely associated with the English succession, were theirs. Yet Garnet and Southwell were still bound by Acquaviva's orders to keep apart from any such concerns.[2]

In a ministry so intimately connected with the written word, one wonders how these uneasy relationships were worked through in all those network letters and missionary texts. Southwell tried to write to both horns of the dilemma: on the one hand he did his pastoral duty with aids to devotion and uplifting poetry; on the other he did his duty by Persons and the exile community, with their need for eyewitness reports of Catholic suffering at the hands of the English heretics to augment and update the martyr imagery being disseminated to rouse support for the Catholic cause.

But his own inclinations might be guessed from the nature of the private correspondence that survives: no letters of his to Persons of the mission period survive, while we have several to his father general Acquaviva, confiding and confident of support in return. It is also worth noting here that the first person the distraught Garnet informed of his companion's arrest in 1592 was his superior general, Acquaviva, not his mission superior, Persons, as Philip Caraman gently points out, 'for Southwell had formed closer ties with [Acquaviva] than with Persons'.[3]

His two last known written works while free sum this doubled duty up; both were based on the same information: one was his plea to the Queen for mere justice for her loyal Catholic subjects, the other was one of those grim reports to Richard Verstegan in Antwerp, detailing the increased torturing of Catholic prisoners to raise awareness abroad of the desperate need of the English Catholics.[4] He had used almost the same words to engage the heart of Britannia as to raise anger against her in the hearts of her enemies abroad.

In the private as in the public sphere, Southwell seemed to be struggling against the current. He had arrived in England with poetic shrines to replace those another Southwell had ruined. He had offered this new, redemptive vision to his family, and it had been rejected.

In the dark of the winter of 1587–88, Southwell wrote an uncharacteristically bitter letter to his father general in Rome. 'We seem to have fallen upon times full of grandeur in their promise and very mean in their performance', he complained.[5] What grand promises had been reneged upon, and by whom? And of what 'performance' had he been disappointed?

Southwell's relationship with his family, who had dropped contact with him after the Campion crisis, appears to have worsened once he was on their doorstep. His spiritual hopes for them, his promise to the Society of his own inheritance, such as it might be, all appear from writings of his of this period to have been dashed. Alongside that angry letter to Rome, there exists a somewhat more personal one, ostensibly to his father, which exposes Southwell's private disappointments: 'In my own country I have lived like a foreigner, finding among strangers that which in my nearest blood I presumed not to seek', he writes bitterly.[6] Southwell's father's estate was sold in 1588, and he was in prison for debt by 1589; Southwell's general sense of frustration may have been sharpened by the collapse of these private hopes. Just as his winter letter to Rome shows an uncharacteristic acidity, Southwell's letter to his father is unique amongst his writings in the bitterness and depth of its anger.[7]

Southwell seems to have been painfully aware that his status and affiliations may have alienated his father, and other Englishmen like him.[8] After all, Southwell's letter to his father is, in asking him to restore himself in the faith, requiring him to become a hostage to a now vengeful English State. Part of his war of words was in this fraught personal arena, therefore; his letter and the several poems that seem to echo its sentiments suggest that he is struggling to reconcile within himself such awful demands on the people around him; perhaps he saw the collapse of the family fortune of his lapsed Catholic father as a microcosmic reflection of the ruination of the nation. As the angry letter to Robert Cecil quoted in the Introduction (p. 14) reveals, he had in all conscience to recall his people to their spiritual duty, but at the same time Burghley was illegalising that duty, the prisons were filling with Catholics, families were being ruined: what were they to do for the best? What was he to advise them to do? His anger over his family's rejection of his Christian zeal can be seen to stand for all hopes dashed in that dreadful time, even, in a way, for the hope of a Catholic survival in England: at this dark moment the thought that he could ever have made a difference must indeed have seemed to be 'a blind, and now abolished faith'.[9]

Southwell's familial experience was only a backdrop to that greater one preserved by history, those two great religio-political dramas that so fundamentally affected the Catholic English in the years 1587 and 1588: the execution by the English of the Catholic Scottish Queen Mary Stuart, and the attempts by Spain to invade England in order to restore, in Catholic eyes, the true Christian rule of law. Both of these were the focus of much propagandising from both (or, rather, all) sides, but the instructions given to the missioners on their departure from Rome were explicit: they were 'not to meddle in the affairs of state; in their reports to Rome, they were to avoid political news and gossip; in company they were to shun all talk about the Queen and were not to countenance it in others'.[10] Their letters abroad make no mention of the Scottish Queen's execution, in obedience to their instructions. Southwell clearly considered his 'disguised' poetry exempt from such strictures, however, because he wrote himself poetically into the centre of both issues, unarguably so in the case of the Queen, and even, I would argue, in the case of the proposed invasion.

To what extent and at what level was a mission-priest able to engage in such actions? To a greater extent than has been assumed, I believe, if Southwell's poetry is looked at as part of a historical discourse rather than a purely artistic exercise. Looked at from the perspective of creative genius, 'Josephs Amazement' (p. 21), for instance, offends some of Southwell's commentators. Louis Martz calls it 'incredibly bad'; Frank Brownlow thinks it 'very peculiar', and the placing of it next to the two Eucharistic hymns strikes him as arbitrary.[11]

But looked at as an expression of Southwell's ministry, 'Joseph's Amazement' is in part a metaphysical discussion in the simplest English of the non-reasonableness of pure faith. It personalises the complexities of the Incarnation, the first 'transubstantiation'. Both the Eucharistic hymns that follow argue for an act of unreasoned faith in accepting the miracle of transubstantiation of Christ's body into bread: all three are therefore about the core difference between a Catholic and a Calvinist, and, although very different in tone, all are, in this respect, on the same subject – one that was highly controversial at the time of writing. Southwell was risking his life writing about it. It is 'peculiar' perhaps, but not 'bad', and certainly not misplaced in the context of Southwell's English mission.[12]

Southwell himself admitted that he was engaged in a war of words. On 12 January 1587 he had also written to Acquaviva in dismay about the success that Protestant literature, widely disseminated and in plain English, was having in souring attitudes to the Catholic cause.[13] There was a rhetorical, as well as a military, war on, and Southwell's poetry was written as part of the action.

In 1587, four years after pulling back from joining with Guise forces in an assault on England, and after Robert Persons had obtained a renewal of the papal excommunication of Elizabeth, Philip of Spain obtained the Pope's permission to launch a crusade against England.[14] If it had been intended to rescue England's only hope of a British Catholic monarch, the imprisoned Mary Queen of Scots, it was too late: she had been executed in February. Perhaps unsure that she would not ally against him with her French relatives if installed on the throne of England, Philip had prevaricated; he believed himself a rightful contender for the English throne in any case.[15] But matters dragged on without immediate action; during the winter of 1587–88, when Southwell sent his bitter letter, the Spanish forces were still sitting across the Channel waiting for the arrival of their orders, and their supporting fleet, and, indeed, the Pope's money.

Southwell and the Jesuits almost certainly knew about the proposed invasion; it was, for both sides, the endgame for the moment. For some of those English Catholics still resolute in their resistance to the altered faith, and suffering dreadful deprivations for their recusancy, it constituted rescue; others would have preferred rescue by an English, rather than a Spanish Catholic prince. Their would-be liberators cross the Channel naturally tried to prepare that incipient recusant Resistance for their coming. Unfortunately Burghley had obtained a copy of Allen's *Declaration* instructing English Catholics how to respond on the landing of Spanish forces; he now used it to drive the last of the recusant English families to the wall, including Southwell's imprisoned patron, the Earl of Arundel, accused by Burghley of praying for the success of the Spanish Armada. Burghley's notorious 'Bloody Question', allowing no vagueness about whether one supported the Pope or the Queen, put a final end to the possibility of keeping Catholic faith in secret while being a loyal English subject in public.[16]

Southwell's anger in his letter to Acquaviva may have been at the Continental power politics that had spoiled the armed rescue;[17] he may equally have been referring to failures of his own countrymen. Certainly there had been no sign of change from his father, who (with his family) continued to shun his company, Southwell saying angrily in his letter that he has perceived 'that many were more willing to hear of me than from me'.

There is a shared mood of bitterness in private letter, public letter and certain poems. The imagery in his 'A Phansie turned to a sinners complaint' (p. 36), for instance, of the courtly gentleman whose fortunes have collapsed, whose 'hope is fallen, whose faith is cras'de, | Whose trust is found untrue' (lines 2–3), and whose 'field is turn'd to flint' (l. 54), is echoed by the imagery in his letter to his father where he accuses him of having 'long sown in a field of flint which could bring you nothing forth but a crop of cares and afflictions of spirit' – a crop that is identified as 'Nettles' and 'a heavie harvest [...] | Of cares that never stint' in 'Phansie' (lines 53–6). The fallen courtier in 'Phansie' has ample time now to grieve over his wasted life, but there is a hint of wasted fortunes as well: 'Too late I finde, (I finde too well) | Too well, stoode my estate' (lines 71–2); the estate was fair when it was still upheld by grace (lines 39–40). The ireful Southwell, in a very rare direct reference to damnation, reminds both his father in the letter and the fallen courtier in the poem of their 'prospect into hell' (l. 142), the 'fear lest the whole become fuel for hell-fire'.[18]

His mood at this time will also have been darkened by the tragedy of the Scottish Queen, her long imprisonment drawing to its end on the back of the Babington Plot as Southwell had arrived in England. This was a complicated case: here was a lawful monarch, a faithful Catholic, and a now unsupported woman, who had, against all laws of kinship and courtesy, been arrested and held in confinement in increasing sickness, abandoned even by her son James. She had become the figurehead of hot-headed escape attempts and plots against the English throne, yet even to quiet English Catholics her arrest and captivity was a source of unease; she was becoming a reproof to the English Crown, a symbol of religious oppression, a living martyr.[19] Southwell's first letter to his general in Rome speaks unequivocally in terms of swords, alarms and plots.[20]

Does Southwell's poetry reflect this crisis? In his *An Humble Supplication* he later accused the Queen's advisers of warping inexperienced minds into extreme positions,[21] and perhaps one of the Virgin sequence, 'Flight into Egypt' (p. 9) was written for those, such as Babington, swept up in this catastrophe. Southwell uses the Gospel imagery of the Innocents killed by Herod as an opportunity to show a realm under the sway of a bloody-handed tyrant who, 'to be sure of murdering one', the principal target of their hatred, 'doth pardon none' (lines 11–12). It was Elizabeth herself who asked for 'special punishments' to be applied to the Babington plotters; Burghley seems to have reassured her that the ordinary manner of execution could, by ensuring the briefest of hangings before disembowelment, be made sufficiently cruel. This was done to the first seven victims, until the crowd became enraged and the Queen was forced to back down; the next seven were mutilated unconscious or dead.[22] The well-documented portraiture of Elizabeth does not include any showing her in the guise of Herod; Southwell has here word-painted his own. This darker picture was very much the image of England and the Queen that the Continental

Catholic powers wished to promulgate: Southwell was conflating his role as news reporter with that of poet.

Southwell stresses that 'Sunne being fled the starres do leese their light | And shining beames, in bloody streames they drench' – although his little stars are extinguished because of the cause, they are not directly part of it: Christ – the Sun – is absent. They have merely fallen foul of the State's cruelty, 'Their lives and lightes' quenched 'with bloody showers' by '*Herods* mortall spight'. They are faceless victims 'untimely cropt', not willing sacrifices, Babingtons, not Campions, although they still merit their martyr's 'garlands' (lines 7–8, 10, 9, 14). As such they are not a central part of the action and have no voice but weeping, the instruments of their death playing out the martyr theme:

> O blessed babes, first flowers of christian spring,
> Who though untimely cropt faire garlands frame,
> With open throats and silent mouths you sing   15
> His praise whom age permits you not to name,
> Your tunes are teares, your instruments are swords,
> Your ditty death, and blood in liew of wordes.

Blood will, Southwell says, speak their cause where they cannot; and, as we have seen, the carnage of their deaths spoke loudly to the crowd, and more than recusants will have been outraged by the spreading stains of cruelty.

In this piece we see an accounting system building up in the writer's mind around the cultural, political or religious value of such deaths in the war of words, informed by the martyr cycles of Rome. There is little sense of a personal involvement in such sacrifices however, strengthening my feeling that such work was written in Rome or very early in Southwell's English mission. It is the ideological uses to which such sacrificial deaths can be put that occupy the writer here. It reminds us again that an important part of Southwell's mission was to send accounts of English Catholic suffering abroad, to move Continental Catholics to take action: action, as we have seen, that was not forthcoming.

TWO QUEENS AND AN ORPHANED STATE

Southwell's flair for affective English rhetoric was being put to service in this general cause but in his poetry he underlines the pathos and inhumanity of such acts, not their savagery. The nature of Mary's last days supported a tragic view of her as the hapless victim of a repressive State.[23] Mary's plea to be allowed her rights of conscience as a Catholic was sympathised with by many in England, and not only Catholics;[24] Mary was becoming the locus for criticisms of the State that went wider than her immediate projects, criticisms that might be accessed most easily through her appeal to general English sensibilities. Southwell's 'I dye without desert' (p. 48), one of the well-balanced, smooth sestets that I have come to associate with his college or early mission output, seems to be an attempt to appeal to the chivalric sympathies of his reader:

> If orphane Childe enwrapt in swathing bands
> Doth move to mercy when forlorne it lyes,
> If none without remorse of love withstands
> The pitious noyse of infantes selye cryes,
> Then hope, my helplesse hart, some tender eares 5
> Will rue thy orphane state and feeble teares.

The trope is that of a heart orphaned from its beloved, the language register highly affective: babies, orphans, 'Relinquisht Lamb in solitarye wood'; the repetition of the word 'orphan' immediately removes it from association with the Christ-Child, despite the suggestive capitalisation of 'Child' (l. 1), 'Lamb' (l. 7), and 'Innocent' (l. 29). This persona is to be associated in the readers' minds with the infant Christ, Christ the sacrificial Lamb, and the slaughtered Innocents, the Bible's first Christian martyrs, though these are never actually mentioned, and do not match the orphaned state of the persona. Southwell, by multi-layering his imagery and its associations, *impresa*-like, packs a great weight of interpretation into a compact space. All the multiplicity of supporting texts and images of a sermon are here collapsed into a few suggestive phrases.

The repetition of the imagery of helpless baby animals may seem to remove it also from the case of the now middle-aged Scottish Queen. Nowhere does the poet say that the subject itself is an infant, however – merely comparable in his or her helplessness and pitiable innocence to an unsupported child in a hostile place 'Whose happ would force the hardest hart to bleede', 'A case that might even make the stones to crye' (lines 7–12, 30): very much Mary's unenviable state in her stone tower in 1586. The chivalry of her youthful would-be rescuers was misguided however. Southwell's line 18, 'Men pitty may, but helpe me god alone', may be a gentle reminder that such things are best left to God to sort out. This poem appeared only in manuscript collections of Southwell's poetry, harmless as it seems.

Babington and the rest were tried and condemned to that more than usually painful death in mid-September, Chidiock Tichborne having the presence of mind to leave a poetic memorial – poetry was deeply connected in these men's minds with their Catholic mission, if only the passive poetry of complaint.[25] His sestets are very reminiscent of Southwell's, in simple English, with a series of contrarieties in fashionable Petrarchan mode to underline the paradox his life has become: 'My prime of youth is but a frost of cares', he says, 'My feast of joy is but a dish of pain'. Some of Southwell's 'David' imagery is echoed here: the cornfield turned to tares, his idea of good being a 'vain hope of gain'.

But if Southwell views their greenness with pity, he does not share their poetic outlook. It is Southwell's revision of Petrarch, 'What joy to live?' (p. 53), that comes closest to Tichborne's unhappy paradoxes, and then only to reject their premise, including the idea implicit in them that such deadly chivalry shown to either of the mortal queens in England was misguided. 'I wage no warre yet peace I none enjoy, | I hope, I feare, I frye, in freesing cold' (lines 1–2); Southwell's persona is almost reversing Tichborne's elegy for murdered youth, exposing its Petrarchan contrarieties for their lack of what Southwell was trained to consider a proper indifference to the body. Southwell may have known Petrarchan work in Rome, but the only references to its genre are in his rewrites of love-poetry, here of Petrarch's *Rime 134*.[26] Southwell follows Petrarch's or Watson's first four lines, then begins to weave into the standard pattern of complaints about non-returned love a new thread, of love returned, but on a higher level, beyond bodily existence. He leaves the Petrarchan pattern altogether at line 7, heading into a new zone of a clear individuality untied by love for any earthly thing: 'That others love I loath, and that I have: | All worldly fraights to me are deadly wracke' (lines 8–9). But Southwell is adding more than this pious and elevated hope: where Tichborne repeats 'and now I live, and now my life is done' as if dazed at the speed of his downfall, the Southwell persona despises the bodily life and looks for its ending, in pious enough mood, but Southwell has rejected the recusant's elegiac Petrarchan tone and replaced it with bitter, pointed anger and quite specific description which owes nothing to Petrarch. He is not writing sadly in the abstract about the woes of this life – he is writing about 'heere', now. Southwell is writing about the London into which he was flung on arrival:

> Heere love is lent for loane of filthy gaine,
>   Most frends befriend themselves with frendships shew,
> Here plentie perill, want doth breede disdaine,   15
>   Cares common are, joyes faultie, short and few.
> Here honour envide, meanenesse is dispis'de,
>   Sinne deemed solace, vertue little pris'de.

Southwell and his co-missioners were extremely vulnerable to false friends, and 'Friendships shew' was certainly instrumental in bringing down Babington and his companions.[27] Southwell's is an unusually dour poem; there is no prayer or comfort at the end: 'O who would live', Southwell asks, in this charnel-house of faiths and hopes? 'Where best in shew, in finall proofe is worst, | Where pleasures upshot is to die accurst' (lines 29–30). Tichborne's imagery remains to the end an unresolved paradox, and a regret at the sudden cutting-off of his youth – fruit fallen while the 'leaves are green'; 'My glass is full, and now my glass is run, | And now I live, and now my life is done'.

Mary's recorded determination to die a good Catholic was to earn her the martyr's garland, not to mention some general sympathy, something that Southwell's poem plays upon.[28] 'My dying plaints I daylie do renewe, | And fill with heavy noyse a desert place', the persona of 'I Die' mourns (lines 15–16); perhaps England under this regicidal regime might seem a spiritual desert to her supporters. The sex and status of the persona are not defined, but the case is desperate, tragically so:

> Rayne downe, yee heavens, your teares this case requires,
> Mans eyes unhable are enough to shedd, 20
> If sorow could have place in heavenly quires
> A juster ground the world hath seldome bredd.
> For right is wrong'd, and vertue wag'd with blood,
> The badd are blissd, god murdred in the good.

Again we see Southwell's reflective landscape – the rain is a sympathetic natural response to some vast wrong: even the 'heavenly quires' might almost forgo praising God to reflect this earthly sorrow, so mightily bad is the case: this is not an elegy for an ordinary personage. It is a matter of blood and murder too, an execution or assassination. Most of all, this is the arena of false justice, right *wronged*, not just a pitiable mischance; natural and heavenly justice are here conflated, to emphasise, perhaps, what was Elizabeth's weakest point in her treatment of Catholics in general and Mary in particular – its illegality. Star Chamber cited the Act of Association of 1585 (which allowed the law to be exercised upon any beneficiary of a treasonous act as well as its perpetrators) to justify trying Mary for her life. Mary, without proper defence or support, was in an orphan-like state indeed; it can hardly have seemed that justice resided in those courts.

The next stanza defines the status of the persona more clearly: 'A gracious plant for fruite, for leafe, and flower, | [...] A noble peer for prowesse, witt, and powre'; this is a prince (lines 25–30), and a well-connected one: Mary herself was connected to Tudor and French royalty, as well as the kings of Scotland. In Catholic law she was the rightful owner of the English throne;[29] she, unlike Elizabeth, had borne fruit. 'Thus vertue still pursued is with spight' suggests a royal person vindictively imprisoned and waiting to die, as does the title itself (l. 33). It also recalls a motto associated with both Mary and the Arundels: the Oxburgh Hanging, worked by Mary for Philip's father the Duke of Norfolk, a powerful sympathiser and potential husband, shows a vine being cut back, with the motto *virescit vulnere virtus* (wounding makes virtue stronger).[30] It may be about Philip, Earl of Arundel, also imprisoned, and condemned to death a few years after; but the very childlikeness of the register suggests a claim on the reader's chivalry or protectiveness – Mary seems the likeliest subject.

Mary was found guilty (in absentia) on 25 October 1586, but not until 4 December did Elizabeth, apparently desperate not to be seen to commit regicide herself, allow a public proclamation of Mary's condemnation.[31] This long hiatus must have been a dreadful time for the Scottish Queen and her sympathisers; hope of her rescue by force of arms may well have burned hot through the autumn and winter of the year, without necessarily implying a wish to see England itself fall. Perhaps Southwell's poem was written after the Babington fiasco but while there was still some hope of saving her. But the only possible hope came, in cuirasses, from France or Spain: was Southwell writing to engender pity in the English in order to soften the blow of a potential invasion?

Spain had promised much. From the point of view of Philip of Spain, England was a pariah state, a nest of barbarian heretics who fomented rebellion in his realms (the Netherlands and elsewhere), and – with their heretical sovereign's blessing – pirated the lawful proceeds of his empire on the seas. To these outrages against a legitimate state was now added the crime of regicide: Mary was executed on 8 February 1587, in secret, with an axe, and that inexpertly; she wore martyr's red.[32]

This cutting-off of a royal cousin under her protection made Elizabeth something of a hostage to fortune herself. Southwell has his Magdalen as a moral or spiritual model to counterbalance what he sees as the wrongly directed carnal love of the English court. He also has a model of Catholic queenship to present in his only identifiable non-biblical poetic subject, and his only datable poem, written after the death of Mary in 1587. There can be no doubt as to the subject this time, but the form is very different to that of 'I dye without desert'. The ballad style seems an odd choice on the face of it.[33] Frank Brownlow justly praises the 'strength and limpidity of its language', but, given the stately sestets of Southwell's holy work, it seems strange to choose a popular song form in which to celebrate the martyrdom of a queen, the cutting off of princely divine right by another prince.[34] It was a form of verse calculated to please ordinary English readers, though, and perhaps it was aimed at the commons. This lyric was not intended, it seems, as a secret between gentlemen, but as semi-public pamphleteering, an expression of honest outrage. This was not just poetic commentary on a sad death, but a central part of Southwell's war of words. Forbidden even to mention politics and affairs of state in his prose and correspondence, with this poem Southwell took the metaphoric war right to Elizabeth herself. She, too, had written a poem about her troublesome cousin, which Southwell may well have read; that Southwell's attack was on the spiritual rather than the national predilections of the English subject can be illustrated quite neatly in a comparison of these two poems. The English Queen's 'ditty', included in George Puttenham's *Arte of English Poesie*,[35] was part of the material revised whilst in press in 1589 – two years after Mary's execution. It stresses the foreignness and the unreasonableness of her enemies, famously naming Mary 'daughter of debate' (l. 11). No 'forreine bannisht wight' shall overturn Elizabeth's national peace, built on reason, steadiness of purpose and foresight (not religious conviction, it may be noted). Like many other disturbed polities before and since, Elizabeth's is here built upon that dangerous metaphysical entity, non-foreignness (despite England's historical relationship with incomers); 'Our realme' is identified against a polarised otherness: 'it brookes no strangers force, let them elswhere resort' (lines 13, 14).

Where Elizabeth sees that 'subject faith doth ebbe', she seeks not to renew faith itself, but to redirect it back to her as the central defender of 'reason' and 'wisdome' (lines 3–4). The agenda or method for the re-subjectification of the English subject under the crown is set out clearly. Elizabeth's (or her ghostwriter's) use of the phrase 'tois untried' (l. 5) and 'graffed [grafted] guiles' (l. 8) insists that Catholic sympathy is not the return to an old faith that Southwell (and, more so, Persons) would have us believe, but innovation, a new departure, something foreign artificially fixed onto a strong central *English* stem, to its detriment. Always the pressure was on the new Protestant nation's rulers to resist accusations of faithlessness and breaking with tradition; always their accusers tried to stress that very issue. Hence the telling addition of 'subject' to 'faith' (l. 3) in this poem, an attempt to link subjecthood to God via the English Crown, not via individual conscience, again, something that Southwell worked in every way to resist in preaching the rights to an individual conscience.

The Crown, in the shape of Elizabeth, also tries to deny the heights to ambitious climbers, threatening them with 'ruth' (bitter regret) and ruin (l. 7). Southwell in 'Scorne not the least' (p. 69) counsels his readers to turn their backs on the heights and work quietly in the background, focusing on the humbler English subject and showing it to be naturally subjected away from Elizabeth's lofty centre. In fact, he seems largely to have rhetoricised against active revolt – in 'Decease release' (p. 47) he makes a tiny reference (perhaps) to Marian plotters, the 'frendes' who procured her 'foyle': it certainly seems to have been Mary's adherents who did her most harm (l. 18).

The Crown's centralising project is assisted by its intelligencers and strategists, 'worthy wights' such as Burghley and Walsingham: her sword is rusty because of her counsellors' success in preventing conflict; they defend England against 'forrein'-ness, which here openly links anything not English with illegitimacy (l. 13).

Elizabeth's counsellors had in fact been busy making acts that increasingly othered English Catholics, loyal or otherwise, pulled by personal visions of what was best for their State and pushed by religio-political activities abroad. The confused and heated atmosphere made it easy to gain the ageing Elizabeth's approval for new laws that seemed designed to strengthen security around her.[36] The specificity and severity of the Acts and penalties increased towards and during first Campion's, and then Southwell's mission, beginning with 'An Act to retain the Queen's Majesty's subjects in their due obedience' (1581) (p. 431); and 'An Act for provision to be made for the surety of the Queen's most royal person' (1585) (p. 78), for instance. The culmination was 'An Act against Jesuits, seminary priests and such other like disobedient persons' (1585) (p. 433). This Act made the practice of the Catholic religion treason, and forbade youngsters a Catholic education abroad (in other words, a Catholic education of any sort); Southwell and other Englishmen, in aiding the passage of young men to Catholic schools on the Continent, were rejecting this law and the right of the monarch to decide such things. These young Englishmen, merely by following their own or their families' wishes in education, were now, apparently, traitorous, Tyburn-fodder. An English nation had been invented that did not include them in it by law, something that, politics and high purposes apart, must have caused some bitter distress and anxiety amongst many perfectly ordinary English families, not to mention deep anger. Richard Bancroft, a supporter of Whitgift's, in his *Sermon Preached at Paules Crosse* (February 1589), developed this further into an anti-foreign theme, naming all but Church of England sympathisers 'false prophets', maintainers of propositions that were 'strange' and 'rebellious', plotters of 'the overthrow of all government'; any reforming urge had an 'intolerable and popelike maner', a piece of chauvinism that earned rebukes from many foreign churches.[37]

The new virtual nation of Protestant, anti-Catholic England became explicit in 'An Act against popish recusants' (1593), which links 'sundry wicked and seditious persons' with 'Catholics', 'spies and intelligencers', 'foreign enemies', and 'rebellious and traitorous subjects' who 'shift from place to place' 'under a false pretext of religious conscience'.[38] The travels of Southwell the Englishman in his pastoral work of consoling English Catholics was, by this law, 'traitorous' of itself; indeed his very conscience, and the consciences of any who had helped him in his care for their souls, were now deemed 'false'. Windows into souls and bars around England's borders were now very much in place. To the Jesuit with his global outlook, this inward stare was England turning her back on God's wide universe; Elizabeth's poem summed up for Southwell the wrongness at the heart of her reign.

EMBLEMS AND IDOLATROUS IMAGES

If the Catholic Queen could not be saved, Southwell could turn his attentions to the Protestant one. As a female in the public gaze, Elizabeth was open to assaults on her position and character. After Mary's execution, she was portrayed as Jezebel by the Catholic exile Adam Blackwood.[39] Southwell's many counterblasts against fickle and destructive Fortuna can be seen as part of his opposition to her centralising movement, the royal poetic which attempts to control minds by public pronouncement and display of constructed stability, centred upon Elizabeth herself and her motto *semper eadem* – 'ever the same'. Indeed he seems to deride the Queen's claim explicitly in 'Fortunes

Falsehoode' (p. 65); 'shee never altereth' he ends at line 15, recalling her boast to his reader's mind, only to follow up on the next line with 'But from one violence, to more oppression' (lines 15–16).

One method of deconstructing without actually attacking the body politic is to pull the rug from under it by suggesting a lack of *bona fides*. Elizabeth's claim of *semper eadem* was her weakest point, after the shifts of the English Reformation and her own apparent movement amongst the various doctrinal and ritual options debated in the English Church in her time; Donne's cry about the confused identity of Christ's spouse the Church, 'Show me dear Christ, thy spouse, so bright and clear', is a caustic reflection upon a century of alterations.[40] Elizabeth could not, from the Catholic point of view, be said to have kept the faith of her fathers (Henry VIII himself, after all, was named 'Defender of Faith' by the Pope), whatever the need for reformation. So one of the principal branches of the counter-argument from the Catholic English across the Channel was that she or her churchmen had betrayed the British Christian heritage. Robert Persons addressed this time and again.[41]

Southwell, by hinting at the faithlessness of the Crown, disguised as a false-fair or haggish, over-powerful female Fortune in the medieval mould, makes the troubling suggestion that the English hierarchy is a falsely directed one, not because the female head is *female*, but because it is the wrong sort of female, not in the mould of Our Lady the constant and meek, but in the mould of the changeful, luxurious and irrational Fortuna. His training in Rome had taught him the distinction between images and idols; there was the image of the Madonna 'supposedly painted by St Luke in the church of S. Maria Maggiore ..., credited with allowing the victory over the Turks at Lepanto'; Borgia had faithful copies made which found its way 'to the four corners of the globe': it was an *archeiropoieton*, an image above the human-made, even copies of which possessed miraculous qualities. Bellarmine had translated the legitimacy of the cult of the saints into the legitimacy of the image, insisting that 'sacred images had the advantage over pagan ones in that they depicted the Truth and not falsehood'.[42] Southwell's Fortuna is the pagan version of that gift-giving, miraculous Virgin; truths, when applied to that pagan image, are untruths in reality, he insists.

He places what would otherwise seem a commonplace moral into a specific site: the Court and all the business surrounding it, as in 'Fortunes Falsehoode' where he builds a picture of something approaching a court masque, but one where masks are gradually lifted to expose the vicious scowls beneath. He is making his point specific and unmistakable: truth is not with Elizabeth or her English Court, because they are not with the true Church: images of Elizabeth are idols; praise of Elizabeth is idolatry, as Bellarmine had preached.

Southwell shows a canny manipulative power over his reader's imagination. By the piling-on of a certain sort of imagery, an increasingly insistent courtly language-register, Southwell pricks the reader's imagination towards something more particular than is apparent at the start. No courtier in the latter days of Elizabeth's reign could fail to be aroused by phrases such as 'fawning flatterie', 'mens ruines', 'oppression', or the notion of 'idle menages' being 'wagde with wearinesse in frutless drudgeries'. 'To humble suppliaunts tyrant most obstinate' is pointed too: many once-wealthy Catholics were reduced to petitioning the Queen for their daily livelihood; the petition direct to the Crown was a viable legal option, in principle, but only where the laws of equity held good. Richard Shelley, a relative of Southwell's, had petitioned the Queen for toleration of her Catholic subjects; he died in prison around the time of Southwell's arrival.[43]

The 'weeping crocodile' places this Fortuna more firmly yet – Fortuna did not care whom she hurt, but the Queen had been known to shed crocodile tears, notoriously in the case of her cousin Mary. No Catholic would miss the reference to men's fortunes being ruined by the change of doctrine that made them virtually outlaws in their own land: 'shee never altereth, | But from one violence, to more oppression' also serves to emphasise this point (lines 15–16). This is all very Bretonish and traditional in feel, yet once again Southwell's awareness of possible tensions in the reader's mind allows a more complex reading, allowing it more potential than appears on the surface, to paraphrase Grosart.[44]

Although the phrase 'untaught to mitigate | rigour with clemencie' is the only moment in which Southwell admonishes wrong government directly, the rest of 'Fortunes Falsehoode' seems to be an argument against total power being left in the unruly and unpredictable hands of secular monarchy, appealing directly to those most able to consider and produce alternatives, the men that surrounded and attempted to influence her, to whom her *semper eadem* must at times have had a hollow ring.

Puttenham, in an apology for her treatment of Mary, proudly emphasises the openness and honesty of Elizabeth's dealings in his comments about her 'not hiding' her power while Mary's is exercised in 'secret'. The new English subject is to be formed and subjectified by public responsibility and centralised control; Mary, with her foreign connections and secret plans, subverted and threatened that national agenda. The arena of the closet arts, with their decorative motifs, innocent-sounding lyrics or poetic metaphors, and unlicensable shades of private interpretation, was perhaps one of the secret ways Puttenham had in mind; recent scholarship has begun to expose links between even the most innocent-seeming pastimes and the political arena. Southwell had his manuscript lyrics, after all, and Mary Stuart had her embroidery. There is the delicate link between Mary, her Southwellian epitaph, and the Arundels with whom her own fate was entangled, the Oxburgh Hanging. This is a link which shows the importance of the arts to the communication of thought between even the most repressed of a repressed community. The vine, set in an orchard, carries leaves on both sides, but fruit only on the right side. An almost bare branch among the weaker left-hand branches is being cut back by a heavenly arm, descending from clouds with a billhook, hence the motto: 'Virescit Vulnere Virtus' – 'virtue is made stronger by wounding'. As the Gardner in *Richard II* says, it was common practice to 'wound ... our fruit trees, | Lest, being over-proud in sap and blood, | With too much riches it confound itself', and to borrow the imagery for the pruning of over-ambitious or wasteful aristocrats, the 'Superfluous branches | We lop away, that bearing boughs may live'. His requirements that his First Man go 'like an executioner' to 'Cut off the heads of too fast-growing sprays | That look too lofty in our commonwealth' seems to paraphrase Elizabeth's 'ditty'.[45]

Mary's point in employing this commonplace imagery is ostensibly to comfort the man whose power is being pruned by Elizabeth, and whose church too is being attacked: the best fruit is obtained only from the hardest-pruned plants. But the lopped branch in its barrenness also represents the end of the Tudor line in the person of the childless Queen.[46] Southwell, who was clearly keen to involve himself in Howard family matters, seems to have drawn on the same theme for the poem he wrote in memory of Mary herself, perhaps to comfort in turn the next generation to suffer. Perhaps he had been shown the Marian Hanging by the Countess, when he arrived in the Arundel household after Mary's execution. By echoing its images and themes he ties himself to both to the Marian and the Howard tragedy, by metaphoric or emblematic repetition.

Mary's needlework has recently come under scholastic scrutiny; the emblems and devices she incorporated into them seem to have been as significant as any of the courtly *impresa* of the time, certainly in the eyes of her captors. As Michael Bath has shown, some of her embroidered motifs were used as evidence in court in 1584, when Elizabeth's ministers were trying to persuade Elizabeth to put Mary under a more strict surveillance, and Mary certainly sent Anne Dacres a piece of embroidery with motifs representing love and endurance during a time of great neglect by her husband Philip, Earl of Arundel; that the motifs were accompanied by some indicating her own position after the death of her putative rescuer, the then Duke of Norfolk, shows that she was in the habit of communicating in this way.[47]

Southwell's poem repeats the emblems to explain her death as a martyr without actually saying so in incriminating words. All the main motifs of her embroidery appear in the first stanza of Southwell's poem, line 4 repeating the motto: 'The lopped tree doth best and soonest growe'. Other images are less commonplace: in the work, a miller stands by his grinding mill; in the poem, 'The pounded spice both tast and sent doth please' (l. 1); Southwell has increased the value of the grist, as he is now discussing a prince, not merely a principle. He says that 'The perisht kernell springeth with encrease' (l. 3), while along the bottom border of Mary's work runs a row of acorns, hazelnuts and such, buried (a squirrel is busy in the left-hand corner) and waiting to spring up. Amongst the orchard trees creatures damaging to plants and in their turn subject to human predation are shown, such as deer, rabbits, snails, and even worms; a butterfly has escaped its earthbound stage and rises heavenwards, and next to it, on the hill, by the descending arm of God, stands a church, high-steepled and triumphant: all these symbols of resurrection and increase through suffering are achieved through *this* God and *this* church, the imagery seems to say. Southwell's poem makes this explicit: 'Death was the meane my kyrnell to renewe | By loppinge shott I upp to heavenly rest' (lines 7–8). Around the border, the repeating cycle of the seasons is shown in the nuts below, the fruits ranged along the top. This is Mary's garden landscape, its fruits hers, not barren Elizabeth's. The side borders are stitched with flowers, those nearest the top being the symbols of the martyr and the lover, the lily and the rose. Her own coat of arms is shown, crowned, and in each corner is a thistle or a rose: England united with Scotland, which only could be achieved through her branch of the vine.[48]

The motif of England as a vineyard that would grow rank and unfruitful for want of priestly gardeners appears in many places in Jesuit writing and imagery of the period. The new English Jesuit College at Valladolid, which Persons had helped to set up with the financial aid of Philip II, celebrated its founding in 1592 with a display of verses, emblems, and mottoes. Another solemnity is recorded there in 1600 for the installation of the Vulnerata; accompanying the images of England's martyrs at the High Altar was a statue of the Virgin, deliberately damaged during Essex's raid on Cadiz in 1596, an eloquent witness to England's fall from Christian decency and grace.[49]

Southwell, in the Jesuit way, looks for speaking pictures; no doubt all too aware of codes and plans on all sides of the debate, and clearly alive to the subtleties of such imagery, he is unable to refute the State's accusation of secrecy. 'Decease release', having begun with the theme, goes on to relocate the primary subjecthood of the maligned Mary in her individual conscience, in direct resistance to the Crown's apparent agenda of central control and public demonstration of loyalty. By remaining true to her Catholic conscience, she has neutralised the new Crown's claims. Now, from prisoner her death has promoted her to 'prince'; the 'Crosse' of her execution has translated her to a heavenly martyr's 'Crowne'; 'ruth' turns to 'right', the 'trapp' laid for her by others has served only to advance her nobility:

> By death from prisoner to a prince enhaunc'd,
> From Crosse to Crowne, from thrall to throne againe,
> My ruth my right, my trapp my stile advaunc'd,   35
> From woe to weale, from hell to heavenly raigne.

Mary's own last attempts to make a martyr of herself had been supported, in a way, by the State's rigorous attempts to prevent any scrap of body or blood escaping the death chamber in Fotheringhay as if they were spiritual dynamite, although her possessions were distributed as she wished. Southwell, attending Anne Dacres's household at this difficult and depressing time, may well have been there when some arrived. Perhaps he wrote 'Decease release' for Anne, as the female figurehead of English Roman Catholicism after Mary's death, Mary's 'cheynes', as Southwell wrote, being now 'unloo'sd to lett the captive goe' (l. 28). Here, as in his elegy for the murdered Innocents, 'Flight into Egypt', Southwell is conflating his role as news reporter with that of poet.

Elizabeth, in unconscious imitation of Southwell's fickle Fortuna, turned on the ministers who had allowed her to sign the death warrant, but in London there were public demonstrations of relief. On the Catholic Continent, though, Mary was generally considered a true martyr; even sainthood was under discussion. The future Pope Urban VIII wrote an elegy about her 'darkened sorrows turned to glorious joy'. Mendoza, Spanish ambassador in Paris, carried Mary's ring to Philip of Spain. He, who had had it in his power to make a creditable attempt at military intervention to save her and had not done so, decided that the time was ripe, and now moved accordingly.

To Southwell the times were bleak; the fury of his bitterness is obvious in his letter to Acquaviva. The plight of English Catholics seemed readily fixable at first. News of an invasion to rescue Mary had no doubt encouraged him to believe that all was about to be put right at a stroke – even after her death, the Pope's spiritual footsoldiers needed only to last until the Papal swords arrived, restoring normality and a lawful Christian monarch to a long-suffering realm. The confusion in the hearts of English Catholics would be over; Burghley's great estate would be sown with salt, and the sun would shine again. But the army did not come, despite war-talk everywhere: Catholics were under the harrow, executions were going on and on, and nothing was being done.

The war of words was becoming more and more explicit, however. If Southwell could not discuss politics *per se* in his correspondence, he could discuss its literary discourses. Part of his winter letter to Acquaviva in Rome included a sharp account of certain books that had just appeared. One, arguing at length whether war or peace was more to the advantage of the kingdom, and coming down on the side of war, is identified by Devlin as Ralegh's *Discourse of War*, based on Machiavelli's notion of calming local strife by foreign wars.[50] A second work against Allen's position on the surrender of Deventer (purporting to come from English Catholics) Southwell called a 'vapid production, quite alien to a Christian sense of justice', deriding it as 'the work of some atheist or agnostic courtier who is playing at theology and mistaking military precedents for moral principles'.[51] Southwell clearly knew the difference between military and moral precepts, but he was writing at a time in which the two were becoming increasingly blurred. Allen's tract had caused more problems for English Catholics trying to demonstrate loyalty. This was the impossible position that Southwell's mission of words was trying to address, and it is possible that its rationality began to break down under such tensions at this point, at least temporarily, a view supported by the bitter tone of his letter to Acquaviva.

If it seems unlikely that a mission priest should be involved in such debates, it should be remembered that Southwell himself acknowledged from the start that he was engaged in a mission of words, as his letter to Acquaviva about the undesirable success of Protestant propaganda suggests. Southwell's training was partly in disputation and rhetoric, to add to which he had his Order's formidable new systems of discourse, including the Suárezian model of tight point-by-point argument, which may have been what allowed him to strike such a confident note in his refutations of the English churchmen. Where many commentators have insisted on Southwell's innocence of political involvement and ill-will, Devlin censures Southwell for the 'vein of mocking irony' that he exposes in discussing the works of rival churchmen with his general in Rome; Southwell's winter letter of 1587–88 derided the attempts of English theologians to refute his teacher Bellarmine's *Quaestiones*: 'Reynolds managed after many months of labour to discover three falsehoods in the book of Tobias, but has fallen into three hundred himself in the process', mocks the young priest; 'even his most faithful disciples are beginning to look the other way'.[52]

But alongside this official debate, Southwell was addressing less doctrinal, more personal areas of difference. He had, in Magdalen, created a pattern for all demoralised Christians, that of an errant but unshakeable loyalty, requiring little other than that it kept on loving, and loved Christ first. He seems also to have found a persona through which to attack church leaders in his recreation of Peter; here was a great personage who had failed, not only to love sufficiently, but to act rightly. Worldly and responsible in his position as Christ's chief Apostle, the Gospel original had broken his sacred vows of fealty and gone, out of fear, to the other side. It is the moments after this betrayal, the extended moment of remorse and shame, a metaphor for Calvinised England that Southwell's Peter is made to explore at length. The character has had to negotiate an earthly power, ill-wishing priests, a sycophantic court, ruffianly enforcers – and at the last has succumbed to a wily woman and broken the vows he made to be true to his proper faith. As Richard Wilson has argued in his comparison of 'St Peters Complaint' with Shakespeare's *Venus and Adonis*, Southwell had, in his Peter, created a poetics which clearly identified and rejected a thinly disguised version of the English Court or State that seemed increasingly bent on annihilation of what to him were the true Christian traditions and lineages.[53] He reproduced that condensed version as if anxious to make the message more accessible: 'What trust to one that trewth it self defyde? | What good in him that did his god forsweare?' ('Saint Peters Complaynte', p. 29, lines 2–3).

Not only are his biblical ventriloquisations sharpened and aimed at contemporary figures, then, but even the biblical references at the end of some of his poems are suggestive in context. In 'Scorne not the least' (p. 69), which seemed harmless enough to appear in the very first edition of *Saint Peters Complaint, With other Poemes* (Wolfe, 1595a), what seems like a sententious list of natural examples of patience in the face of overwhelming odds ends with a reference to the Old Testament book of Esther: 'In Hamans pompe poor Mardocheus wept; | Yet God did turne his fate upon his foe' (lines 19–20). Unlocked, the reference seems far more threatening than the rest of the poem. The ruler of the empire of the Medes and Persians, Ahasuerus, particularly favoured one Haman, who became proud. Mardocheus (Mordecai), an Israelite in the king's service, who had not only supplied the king with a new wife (Esther) but warned him of a plot on his life, refused to bow to Haman, and Haman, discovering that he was a Jew, told the king that 'there is a certain people scattered abroad and dispersed among the people in all the provinces of thy kingdom; and their laws are diverse from all people; neither keep they the king's laws: therefore it is not for the king's profit to suffer them' (Esther 3.8). Haman, having worked up feelings against the Jews, asked leave to destroy them, and the king acquiesced, especially when Haman offered to bring the riches of the Jews into the king's treasuries. This is unmistakably relevant to English Catholic experience as Southwell encountered it, with Protestant arrivistes enriching themselves at the Catholics' expense through dubious accusations of disloyalty, and using their riches to subsidise the Queen's enterprises and entertainments; oddly enough, it also echoes Puritan complaints against Whitgift.[54]

The poem would seem to be another call for patience in the face of persecution, except that instead of ending with patience (Job, for instance), the story ends with revenge. Mordecai, through his service to the king (and Esther's courageous intervention at the highest level), was reinstated, while Haman, having fallen from favour through his own ambition, was hanged on the very gallows prepared for Mordecai (7.10). Not only revenge but war: the Jews were then given royal permission to 'gather themselves together, and to stand for their life, to destroy, to slay, and to cause to perish, all the power of the people and province that would assault them, both little ones and women, and to take the spoil of them for a prey' (8.11). To those who knew where to look in the Bible (accessible in plain English now) this was a sharp and relevant lesson, and not one of fatalistic acceptance. Mardocheus succeeded through being one of God's chosen people, through loyal personal service, but also through having influence inside the royal household; and the upshot was a just war.

At any moment of Southwell's mission this would have spoken of injustice and righteous anger to a recusant with access to a Bible, but in the anxious months of the Armada, the corollary of this poem was a clarion call. Although it respects the biblical monarch despite his obvious weaknesses, there is that dig at Elizabeth, the Queen of the May as Sidney had portrayed her in his first entertainment for her, in the final couplet: 'We trample grasse, and prize the flowers of May: | Yet grasse is greene when flowers doe fade away' (lines 23–4). Southwell is reminding his trampled recusant readership of the historical persistence of their faith. What could not be said in public debate, for fear of causing scandal, he was here able to say in disguise, but it was no less an attack for all that.

DEATHLY LOVES: SOUTHWELL'S POINTED POETRY

It is clear that Southwell, who had shown himself capable of sharp criticism in his rhetoric, was equally capable of disguising political comment under the matter of his light lyrics. What other lyrics of his can be unlocked in this way? The group of what I would call 'court' lyrics deals with the interactions between personal hopes and a cruelly unpredictable fate. These lyrics, in the light of Southwell's disguised critiques, bear harder scrutiny than they have, in general, previously received. Public refutation of powerful men was dangerous (and against his orders); in his closet poetry, he expresses much whilst saying little. Whether from a genuine wish to show a better alternative (according to his own lights) or from a desire to satirise and attack pomp, Southwell uses mimicry as one of his weapons.[55]

In the circumstances of recusant poetry, there seems little need to enter into the critical debate that sees parody or mimicry as a failure of artistic vision. Whatever we now think the 'proper' aim of poetry, Southwell almost certainly thought differently. College records show that he was capable of attack-rhetoric; indeed, he clearly had a well-developed sense of satire, and no hesitation whatever in applying it vigorously, to the point of earning censure from his masters. College plays included farcical *intermediums* such as the *Minutum* (1613), discussed earlier.[56] Why, then, should Southwell's lyrics not include burlesques or satires? The assumption that a priest would never so depart from propriety seems unrealistic even in the twenty-first century, and it is likely that Southwell wrote his burlesques either 'in disguise' or for a smaller, like-minded readership in any case, and therefore had no need to turn the other cheek; he certainly felt no such need in his letters, as we have seen.

This concept of a 'disguised' or private rhetoric might help to explain an odd fact: there are positions taken up in his sermon, *The Epistle of Comfort*, which are altered, even reversed here and there, in the more combative of his lighter lyrics. Another possibility is that, closely involved, in disguise both physical and mental, with his set of gentlemen's sons of varying levels of conviction or none, the boundaries between one 'life' and another sometimes became blurred.[57] Sojourns in the company of Cambridge scholars (probably including Christopher Marlowe) with their sharp views of God and government, may, after the closet dreariness of the London safe houses, have encouraged the young priest to engage that Jesuit flexibility beyond the hair's breadth a time or two, if only to attract the stragglers back to his fold.

In any case, part of Southwell's pastoral anxiety was that the old definitions of religious conviction were under assault even within denominations; the crude polarities exposed by the killing of the Scottish Queen had become increasingly complex after her death. Southwell's letter to Acquaviva about 'a matter in hand, which [...] bodes [...] suffering'[58] may have referred to Walsingham's intriguing, but it underlines his recognition of the poisonous nature of almost any outcome for English Roman Catholics. Any assault on England from the Catholic Continent would have to succeed utterly or spell the ruin of Catholicism in England – and then there were the rivalries between the Catholic powers themselves, each feeding unpredictably back into the political vortex. Could even the nimblest of gunners have worked out the right way to face his guns on such a confused field?

To hold the attention of young men such as the university wits in this increasingly excitable period, Southwell needed to do more in his poetry than sermonise, he needed to attract and amuse. He had experienced the Roman tradition of the *pasquinade*, anonymous and scurrilously anti-authoritarian comments and epigrams that would appear, by way of popular commentary on matters of state, affixed to a crumbling classical statue (still standing behind Palazzo Braschi).[59] Some of his English poetry expresses a similarly satirical, even comical humour, something barely addressed by earlier critics, perhaps because it seemed to muddy the waters. That Southwell himself was anxious about the appropriateness of humour is suggested by the air of uncertainty that creeps into his lighter poetic production, exposed even in the dedicating of his lyrics: Southwell's apologia suggests a more than usual anxiety about the light nature of the content. The prefatory letter to the collection of lyrics he put together for an unidentified relative suggests that he was known to the dedicatee as a sober or scholarly man, and felt the need to explain this departure into 'mirth', even though it appears to have been solicited by this 'cosen'.

There was much for a Pasquino to satirise. It must have seemed a vainglorious hypocrisy to have stripped the churches of their so-called 'idolatrous' imagery only to redeploy it in promotion of the Queen. Ralegh had made her the centre of a moon-goddess cult of his own, expressed partly in poetic hymnody, partly in emblematic form, but Roy Strong and others argue that a deliberate subsumation of the Catholic iconography, especially that of the Virgin, was also under way; medallions were made of Elizabeth in the style of saints' talismans, in costly materials for courtiers to swing, or base metals for poorer bosoms. Strong argues that these were entirely new, and appeared suddenly in the mid-1580s, perhaps in reaction to threats to royal safety; it was 'a Protestant use of the sacred image of the Virgin Queen exactly paralleling the wearing of holy images by Catholics'.[60] Elizabeth's (or her chief ministers') estimation of the importance of such iconography can be measured by the lengths gone to in the control and dissemination of it.

Spenser's poetic project was part of this process: consider the Marianism implicit in Mercilla's divine melding of majesty with mercy. The Virgin had interceded for humanity with God, and it is unlikely that a contemporary reader would miss this veiled allusion to the Catholic Virgin of Mercy.[61] Had Walsingham been ruined only to be set up again by courtly poets as the shrine of an earthly queen?

Southwell, obedient to his training, tried to hate the sin, not the sinner, by separating those features he regarded as transgressive from the rest and personalising them in his poetry, to counter these poetic recreations of the earthly Virgin Queen ('look here upon this picture, and on this' (*Hamlet*, III.4.55)). Where Ralegh praised the virgin Cynthia, and Spenser wrote the medievalised Faerie Queene, Southwell created a character which seemed to encompass both these conceits of moon and medieval female, but in negative: the old medieval persona of Fortuna, balding, fickle, bringer of bad luck, with her ill-chosen favourites, the ruination of good and bad alike. What later readers of Southwell have seen as imitative medievalism seems more likely, given his readiness to excoriate, to be outright satire, though necessarily shorn of overtly offensive material. The offence was not after all so much in the person of the lawful monarch, but in the contradictions and injustices, and especially the unlawfulnesses, of the Queen's reign – seen from the Catholic point of view.

It is in pursuit of this project that he makes an interesting departure from the *Epistle*; in which semi-public sermon (evidently a work of refined scholarship), he lists the works of the Devil:

> The Devill kisseth where he meaneth to kyll, he giveth us a draught of poyson in a golden cup [... quoting Eusebius, *Emissenus* ...] While with pleasures without he delighteth us, inwardlye he deceyveth us, and killeth our soule, while he flattereth our fancye. For when he moveth us to labour our wittes, and settle our affection in these inferiour things, what doth he perswade us, but with a golden hooke, [...] With *Sirens* sweete notes he woeth us into the salte sea of perdition, with *Crocodyles* teares, he endevoreth to intrappe us, and when he sheweth a mans face, and glorious lockes adorned with a crowne of golde, as the *Locustes* of the *Apocalips* did, then meaneth he even like the same to byte us with his Lions teeth, & stynge us with his *Scorpions* tayle [...] He shrowdeth his bitter poyson, under a deceiptfull sweetenesse, the pleasant savour of the cupp inviteth, but the sweete taste of the poyson choketh.[62]

In 'Fortunes Falsehoode' (p. 65) Southwell repeats these malfeasances but alters the sex of the ill-doer from male Devil to female Fortuna, using a rhythmic, prancing metre reminiscent of one of Elizabeth's favourite pastimes. He emphasises the feminine by use of artful prosody – 'falling' metre: dactylic tetrameter gives a slipping, skipping quality, its insubstantial nature emphasised by the 'weak' or 'feminine' endings to the lines. Of all his lyrics this is the one most obviously designed to be sung; and with the Elizabethan vocalisation of '-ed' endings it becomes as regular as a dance tune, an apparently inappropriate conjoining of the language of sin with the tone of a ballad or jig. The strange combination works in context of a sinful, flighty Court. 'With fawning flatterie deathes doore she openeth, | Alluring passengers to bloudie destenie'; 'Slie fortunes subtilties in baites of happinesse | Shrowde hookes, that swallowed, without recoverie | Murder the innocent'; she is 'like weeping crocodile to scornefull enemies' (lines 9–10, 2–4, 34). Some of these activities seem inappropriate to this characterisation – surely the medieval Fortuna never opened death's door to anybody? This is an attribute of Death, or mortal Sin, not giddy Fortune.

Oddest of all is the reversal of sense in one particular act – in *Epistle* the Devil, spider-like, ignores the already sucked-dry sinner to work on the man rich in piety and therefore full of heaven's treasures, ripe for spoiling (*Epistle*, pp. 11a–b). In 'Fortune's Falsehoode' Southwell rearranges the sense to allow for a Fortuna who, against the arbitrariness of her standard characterisation, favours sinners. Although at first saying that she is, as one would expect of the medieval Fortuna, 'Blinde in her favorites foolish election', and that 'Chaunce is her arbiter in geving dignitie', he then adds a little extra layer of implication, saying that 'Her choyse of visious [vicious] shewes most discretion, | Sith welth the vertuous might wrest from pietie' (lines 25–8). He is saying, in highly condensed language, that when she elevates men of vice she is actually doing God's work, because preferment would tempt men of virtue away from 'pietie'. It seems an odd adjustment of sense to introduce this comforting idea into what is so obviously a depiction of the ill-doing of the powerful; and if he had wanted so many of the attributes of the Devil, why change the characterisation at all? It may repeat Boethius's animadversions on Fortune, though, who through adversity 'frequently draws men back to their true good' despite herself, or shows the true friend from the false;[63] it was almost certainly therefore an attempt to comfort those Catholics impoverished by their faithfulness, a way of giving it the best possible gloss; it may also be designed to turn a generalised moralisation upon Fortune into an anti-portrait of the Queen.

Many features of the poem are connected with the standard medieval Fortuna, than which 'No wind [is] so chaungeable, no sea so wavering' – Boethius could well have penned the last couplet: 'Now mad, now mercifull, now fearce, now favoring: | In all things mutable, but mutabilities.' Other aspects of her are in a language-register that seems designed to remind a reader of aspects of current Court life, such as 'To humble suppliaunts tyrant most obstinate | She suters aunswereth with contrarieties' (lines 29–30). Contrarieties can mean perplexing poetic expressions, a form of word-play of which Elizabeth was reputedly fond, but Catholic supplications to the Queen were being treated with increasing harshness and no Catholic reader would have missed this criticism. One wonders what Elizabeth, who had translated Boethius's *Consolations of Philosophy*, would have thought of Southwell's pointed characterisation.[64] Medieval Fortune makes or breaks at a whim, and is not usually depicted as 'Constant in crueltie', altering only 'from one violence, to more oppression'. 'Suing for amitie where shee is odious' while 'forswearing curtesies' to her 'followers' sounds like one more actively engaged in human affairs than the usual model of 'giddy fortune' (lines 15–16, 35–6, 38). The final verse, Boethian as it is, has, when read aloud, a finely patterned, skirling quality of Englishness that lifts it out of the sententious entirely; it was clearly written to be sung:

> No wind so chaungeable, no sea so wavering,
> As giddie fortune in reeling varieties:
> Now mad, now mercifull, now fearce, now favoring:
> In all things mutable, but mutabilities.   40

This alteration from a biblical to a semi-pagan and certainly profane characterisation is perhaps what Southwell apologises for in his prefatory letter. But why did Southwell need to make this sort of change at all, and why only in his lyric poetry? Is it because the poetry constituted the discourse with his courtly contemporaries that he was not allowed to have in his more formal rhetoric – does his lyric poetry contain the political comment refused him by his superiors?

'Loves servile lot' (p. 60), similarly, seems on the face of it a Tottelian moralised homily about the fickleness of love. 'Love mistris is of many mindes, | Yet few know whome they serve' is commonplace enough, and we again see elements used in his *Epistle* piece on the Devil:

> Shee shroudeth vice in vertues vaile,
> Pretending good in ill: 10
> Shee offreth joy, affordeth griefe,
> A kisse where shee doth kill.

Perhaps he was responding to a poem in Byrd's *Psalms, Sonnets, and Songs* (1588), which shares this language-register of the deceits of 'false love'. It has been attributed to Ralegh. 'False Love' is described as 'the oracle of lies', a poisoned serpent covered all with flowers, | Mother of sighs and murderer of repose', a 'net of deep deceit, | A gilded hook that holds a poisoned bait', a 'siren song', a maze 'wherein affection finds no end', the confusion of reason and hope – homiletic enough, if odd work for a man at that time at the height of his favour at Court.[65]

If the first half of Southwell's ballad-style poem is on a similarly standard Petrarchan 'cruelty of love' theme, the second half begins to touch more on the sin of it – acceptable for a moralising poet perhaps, but again, the language-register brings the reader close to uncomfortable areas. The first edition of Southwell's poetry, Wolfe's earlier 1595 edition (Wolfe, 1595a), printed only the first half to line 48, oddly, although it was complete in the second (Wolfe, 1595b). Is it possible that Wolfe had a manuscript that omitted half a poem, then found it so soon after? Changes such as 'much good will' for 'good in ill', and 'the fire' for 'her fire', suggest an attempt to soften the effect of the poem (lines 10, 36). Perhaps a line like 'Shee hath the blush of virgine mild, | The mind of viper race' is a little too personalised for comfort, but it was the stanzas that list the deathly danger she presents to the soul that were 'lost' from Wolfe, 1595a (lines 15–16); they trod too close upon the heels of current religious debates, perhaps.

Sweet moments that bring 'immortall harmes', or eyes like 'murdring dartes' are deliberate assaults upon the spirit of Petrarchan idealism surrounding the Queen (lines 50, 51), and no courtly lover would wish to be reminded of the 'Moodes, passions, phancies jelous fits' that all too often attend upon encounters of the heart, Elizabeth herself being notoriously jealous of rivals for her courtiers' attention (l. 57).[66] But Southwell seems to cross the threshold of decency with this description of Love's brothel-like abode:

> Her house is slouth, her doore deceite,   61
> And slipperie hope her staires,
> Unbashfull boldnesse bids her guestes,
> And every vice repaires.

This is emphatically not the vocabulary even of failed Love. Just as he has tried to find the weakest points in the argument against the breakaway Church, he has looked for the weaknesses of Elizabeth's self-centred Court erotics, and, in being a good scholastic rhetorician, has been a mannerless love-poet.

His view of the changes brought about by 'love' in men around him is an unfavourable one, as one might expect, judging by his discussion of it in *The Epistle*. His use of archaic chivalric language perhaps expresses his belief that it was, in Elizabeth's court, an artificial and self-serving recreation – he is, in other words, burlesquing again; 'an enamored knight', he says:

> hath no greater felicitye, then to doe that, which maye be acceptable to his paramour, and the fadinge beautye, of a fayre Ladyes countenance, is able to worke so forceiblye in mens myndes, that neyther losse of riches, daunger of endurance [...] is able to withholde where she inviteth [...] Euery perill undertaken for her, seemeth pleas-

ante, everye reproch honorable, all drudgery delightsome, yea the very woundes that come from her, or are suffered for her, are voyde of smarte, and more rejoyced is the wounded wretch, with hope that his hurte will purchase favoure. (*Epistle*, pp. 34b–35a)

In passages such as this in *The Epistle* he deconstructs the artificiality of carnal Love – but in his poetry he complects her with death.

BATTLE LINES

One of Southwell's oddest poems is 'Losse in Delaies' (p. 58). Its implicit martiality has troubled some of his biographers; one of his earliest, Grosart, for instance, raises and rejects the possibility that it could have been written with the Armada emergency in mind; more recently, Pilarz, working on the theme of reconciliation, does not address it at all.[67] Grosart's insistence that some of Southwell's poetry was written in prison as an expression of heartfelt feeling made any political construction inadmissable. But Alison Shell (and Louis Martz before her) noted that even a brief study of Southwell's life and work suggests that he engaged in late sixteenth-century religio-political discourses; Nancy Pollard Brown, too, has little hesitation in suggesting a political statement hidden in Southwell's poetry, such as 'Scorne Not the Least':

> The Marlyne cannot ever sore on high,
> Nor greedie greyhound still pursue the chase:
> The tender Larke will find a time to flie,   15
> And fearefull Hare to runne a quiet race

The hawk and the greyhounds are taken to represent assiduous harriers of Catholic families. General critical reluctance to allow any political dimension is based on Southwell's own stated position. Janelle, for instance, quotes Southwell's own insistence that 'about Parliament I say nothing, as I desire my letters, like my soul, to have absolutely nothing to do with matters of state'.[68] But Southwell attacks types of error rather than personalities, and perhaps unattributed manuscript poetry was a different matter, written as it was in a different arena to that of public discourse. Southwell's intellectual, morally robust poetry, enriched by voguish Continental features, was bound to get about, perhaps introducing its critiques into the minds of readers almost unnoticed, like the 'secret vaine' mentioned in 'A vale of teares' (p. 41, l. 49).

On 1 July 1587 '*Deferre not Repentance for tyme will not staye &c.*' was entered by John Wolfe on the *Stationers' Register*.[69] Southwell may have written 'Losse in Delaies' at about the same time: it does not mention repentance though (p. 58).[70] 'Shun delaies, they breede remorse: | Take thy time, while time doth serve thee', Southwell's *carpe diem* begins; 'Lingred labours come to nought' (lines 1–2, 6). His tetrameter, a lively enough rhythm at the best of times, is further spurred by use of trochaic stresses throughout his six-liners, the trailing female foot in the second and fourth, which underline the theme of delayed action, being flung off in the final rhyming couplet of each stanza; these offer briskly articulated variations on the theme of do-it-now. In a time so inclined to punish the wrong step, what is he hurrying along? 'Hoise up saile, while gale doth last' he urges, it is too late to ask for time, 'when time is past'; 'Sober speede is wisedomes leasure: | After wits [hindsights] are dearely bought' (lines 7, 9). Something is happening that requires his reader to put aside all normal constraints of caution and patience – all the things, in other words, that the mission priests had been counselling their English flock to maintain (although never in regard to the state of their souls, of course). 'Workes ajournd have many stayes, | Long demurres breede new delaies' (lines 17–18). 'Works' could have meant works of grace, of course, but the obvious frustration in his lexis of 'long demurres', 'stayes', and 'delaies' chimes only too well with the words of his angry letter to Acquaviva.

He next talks of injuries: of the fresh wound that is best mended however painful such mending might be. Tempting as it was to escape the immediate pain of such ministrations, 'festred woundes' ultimately need harder medicine. He is demanding that some dreadful self-hurting remedial act be undergone. But what had been wounded? This is a commonplace reference to the soul in sin, but perhaps he also hints at the wounding of the English Church, or reflects Continental Catholicism's outrage at recent English actions on what it could reasonably consider its own soil in the Low Countries (lines 19–20). Wounds had been dealt both in England and abroad that would require much bloody surgery to remedy; Southwell was making painful demands of his readership. As in the Jonas imagery in 'Christs sleeping friends' (p. 19), he warns his countrymen not to think to ride out the times and settle things later: 'After cures are seeldome seene' (lines 21). This is unique among his poems in describing a pinch-point, a moment beyond which nothing can be the same again. His imagery points to irrevocable and inevitable damage if something is not done 'now'. 'Ill' is to be stifled 'In the rysing', because it will grow whatever we may wish, and become unstifleable (lines 29–30).

After this hard beginning, his theme turns a little in stanza six; now, to enlarge upon his point, he is metaphorising the action and effect of these innocent-seeming but dangerous little beginnings if not defeated at once: a drop of water can carve out a 'stubborne flint' not by its 'force', but by its very persistence, and 'custom' blunts the will in the same way, 'More by use then strength prevailing'. He is arguing for forceful action against the grain of the times, making his case by showing that stability can be an illusion, disguising danger: 'force' can come in different ways – terrible damage can be done as much by tiny, gentle actions as by invasive ones. Is this not to argue for some sudden, intrusive force in order to prevent the continuance of

Southwell's war of words

a destructive one? He uses a more obviously moral metaphor of the wreck of the soul-ship when he ends by warning that a grain of sand is tiny, but 'many make a drowning fraight' (lines 31–6). It moves from urging action towards a warning of deadly *spiritual* danger if such action is not undertaken. What was the source of such bloody stridency?

He had at least one biblical precedent, fulfilling that older function of the poet as excoriator of tyrants and fallen peoples: Jeremiah, the biblical prophet imprisoned for putting obedience to God before king. He had a musical milieu in which to perform such warning canticles, too: a cursory look at William Byrd's catalogue of motets and canticles shows that many have been taken from Jeremiah. In an apocalyptic age, Jeremiah's is the voice best suited. Some of Byrd's biographers have noted that the worthy biblical texts are chosen and ordered to act as an accompaniment to Catholic miseries.[71] Texts such as 'Weeping, my eye shall bring forth tears, because the Lord's flock has been taken captive', or 'Tell the king and the queen, Be humbled, sit down, for the crown of your glory has fallen from your heads' were pointed in the years around the Armada invasion. As for the invasion, in the book of Jeremiah the Lord himself becomes a warmonger; angry at the wickedness of his people, he stirs up their enemies to battle: 'come up, ye horses; and rage, ye chariots; and let the mighty men come forth [...] For this is the day of the Lord God of hosts, a day of vengeance, that he may avenge him of his adversaries: [...] for the Lord God of hosts hath a sacrifice in the north country by the river Euphrates' (46.9–10).

This was the mood amongst some English Catholics, at least, during 1586–88, and 'Losse in Delaies' echoes it. Southwell's generally gentle nature-poetic is here beginning to show a touch of tooth and claw, offering a much more explicit threat to that macrocosmic state body against which he had been trying to constitute a new microcosmic English Catholic community.

His community of meek things is disrupted in 'Losse', the patience of the timid hare and creeping worm of 'Scorne not the least' rejected. Now 'Creeping Snailes' are too slow, too weak. All at once the reader is promoted from small fry to somewhere near the top of the food-chain. Where in 'Scorne' Southwell addressed his readers as helpless prey hiding from the hawks and hounds, in 'Losse' they are empowered to kill what threatens their spiritual well-being: the serpents of State or the 'ill egges' and 'bad chikins' of a nation going to the bad (lines 26–7). Nature has become unnatural. The macrocosmic body is that of a harmful animal and can longer be tolerated.

Animal and nature imagery is now left behind; the specificity of the ending shocks. Where normally in a Southwell lyric there would be a biblical character typical of the quality he poeticises, a prayer, or a promise of action, here he is calling upon a biblical precedent for the desirability of smashing the skulls of enemy babes against a rock – the destruction of an enemy at the very source; a moral commonplace, yes, but in context something more: 'Happie man that soone doth knocke, | Bable babes against the rocke' (lines 41–2). In *Epistle of Comfort*, oddly, Southwell uses this same motif as an example of the work of the wicked: he shows Pharaoh and Herod killing infants and the Devil dashing our good babies against the rock (p. 5a).

Southwell was in hurt, frustrated and martial mood by the beginning of 1588. 'Losse' seems homely enough, but in the context of those times there are undeniable and disturbing subtexts, perhaps the most odd of which is the vocabulary itself. Ironically, it was Grosart, the editor least in sympathy with the idea of a political Southwell, who troubled to identify this oddness: Southwell, whose English, though plain, is otherwise generally elegant, uses country imagery and dialect in the lines 'Kill bad Chickins in the tread, | Fligge they hardly can be catched' (lines 27–8). 'Fligg' has been identified as a Norfolk form for 'flown'; it was also used in the North-East for flight in general, but specifically for fledged birds.[72] In a poem which is in any case a collection of simple sententiae, some of the phrases seem more than usually countrified: 'Out of season out of price' is calculated to appeal to a country community (lines 23–4). Was this chivvying song designed to help prepare the Catholic commons along the Norfolk coast for invasion?

If so, it had little effect. Nobody seemed inclined to 'Crush the Serpent in the head' or 'Breake ill egges ere they be hatched' (l. 25). If this was indeed written at the time when Southwell's mood was most frustrated at the lack of action, it was perhaps in bitter self-parody of those lines that he wrote to Acquaviva on 11 July 1588, 'Now at long last the Serpent's eggs are hatched, and a poison gushing that looks likely to be the ruin of many' ('Losse', l. 25).[73] Indeed, many friends and acquaintances went to the gallows that year.

The direct confrontation, as Garnet and Southwell feared it might, had ended in disaster for the English Catholics caught between the Scylla of the Elizabeth and Rome's enraged Charybdis. Burghley had imposed upon many prominent Catholics the ignominy of close confinement or house arrest, and now devised that *point non plus*, the 'Bloody Question', which looked likely to doom Arundel and anybody, however noble, who wanted to be true to both secular sovereign and the Catholic God. Fear – 'loves frost' as Southwell called it in the long 'Saint Peters Complaint' – had 'cand[i]ed with ysie colde' the hearts of the community he wished to serve (lines 300, 251).

Southwell's war of words had made only a small difference. For all the fervour of Catholic youths at college in Rome, and the promise of generals across the Channel, performance had been lacking. The cream of English recusancy was in prison or fled abroad. Poor Joseph was now more than confused, he was in chains; Peter remained obdurate, and Magdalen had for the moment fallen silent. The arenas for debate were closing down: Southwell was going to have to find a different rhetoric altogether.

NOTES

1 Robert Southwell, 'Losse in delaies', in James H. McDonald and Nancy Pollard Brown (eds), *The Poems of Robert Southwell, S.J.* (Oxford: Clarendon Press, 1967), p. 58, lines 7–8; hereafter M&B; further references to Southwell's poetry are from this edition, given as page/line numbers in the text.

2 Francisco de Borja Medina, S.J., 'Intrigues of a Scottish Jesuit at the Spanish Court: Unpublished Letters of William Crichton to Claudio Acquaviva (Madrid 1590–1592)', in Thomas M. McCoog, S.J. (ed.), *The Reckoned Expense: Edmund Campion and the Early English Jesuits* (Woodbridge: Boydell, 1996), pp. 215–98, pp. 218–19.

3 Philip Caraman, S.J., *A Study in Friendship: Saint Robert Southwell and Henry Garnet* (Saint Louis, MO: The Institute of Jesuit Sources, 1995), p. 77; hereafter cited in the text.

4 M&B, p. xxv.

5 Christopher Devlin, *The Life of Robert Southwell Poet and Martyr* (London: Longmans, Green, 1956), pp. 152–3; hereafter cited in the text.

6 Southwell's letter to his father is his *The Triumphs over Death*, ed. J. W. Trotman (London, Manresa Press, 1914), pp. 36–64; cited in Caraman, p. 54; also see Nancy Pollard Brown (ed.), *Two Letters and Short Rules of a Good Life* (Charlottesville: University Press of Virginia, for the Folger Shakespeare Library, 1973); Brown believes the letter to have been written in 1587 or 1586; see Scott Pilarz, S.J., *Robert Southwell and the Mission of Literature 1561–1595: Writing Reconciliation* (Aldershot: Ashgate, 2004), pp. 29–37, for a meticulous discussion of the *Epistle*; see also Brownlow, pp. 45, 47.

7 See Brownlow, who criticises Southwell for 'arrogant high-handedness' in some of his poetry too; pp. 103, 45–6.

8 Pilarz, p. 31.

9 In Brown, *Two Letters*, p. 81.

10 Caraman, pp. 2, 33, 43; from John Hungerford Pollen, S.J. (ed.), *Unpublished Documents relating to the English Martyrs*, Publications of the Catholic Record Society, 5 (London: Catholic Record Society, 1908); hereafter CRS, especially 361ff.

11 Louis L. Martz, *The Poetry of Meditation* (New Haven: Yale University Press, 1954), p. 186; F. W. Brownlow, *Robert Southwell*, Twayne's English Authors Series, 516 (New York: Simon & Schuster Macmillan, 1996), p. 98; both hereafter cited in the text.

12 An additional point that lies largely outside the sphere of this book but seems worth noting here is that Southwell's Latin poetry was even less squeamish about current affairs. Grosart, the first editor to print it, notes that 'the first of a fragment of a series of elegies seems to relate to some disaster to the Spanish arms, probably the Armada collapse of 1588; [...] and that "Elegia IX" is historically interesting as being put into the "fair lips" of the "Shade" of Mary, Queen of Scots'; in Alexander B. Grosart (ed.), *The Complete Poems of Robert Southwell S.J.* (London: Robson, Fuller Worthies' Library, 1872), note preceding Grosart's Appendix on the Latin poems, p. 190; hereafter cited in the text; Grosart found the Elegies at Stonyhurst. The Latin poems and translations can be seen in Peter Davidson and Anne Sweeney (ed. and intro.), *The Collected Poems of S. Robert Southwell, S.J.* (Manchester: Carcanet, forthcoming).

13 Southwell to Acquaviva, 12 January 1587, in Caraman, p. 35. Also see Nancy Pollard Brown, 'Robert Southwell: The Mission of the Written Word', in McCoog (ed.), *The Reckoned Expense*, pp. 193–214.

Robert Southwell

14 John Bossy, 'The Heart of Robert Persons', in McCoog (ed.), *The Reckoned Expense*, pp. 141–58 (p. 145); hereafter cited in the text.

15 Mary had gone some way, in earlier wills, towards confiding her right to the English throne to Philip on her death, provisional on her disinheriting her son James should he fail to profess Catholicism. Although her last will included no such clause, Philip understood this as permission to reach for the English crown; see Jenny Wormald, *Mary Queen of Scots: Politics, Passion and a Kingdom Lost*, rev. edn (London: Taurus Parke, 2001), pp. 186, 191.

16 Devlin, pp. 191, 167; 'If the Pope ... pronounce her Majesty to be ... no lawful Queen, and her subjects to be discharged of their allegiance and obedience unto her; and after, the pope ... do invade this realm; which part would you take, or which part ought a good subject of England to take?'; discussed in Devlin, App. B as Petyt MSS Series 538, vol. 43, fol. 304; Devlin, p. 330, Brownlow, p. 71.

17 See Devlin, pp. 152–3.

18 Folger MS V.a.421, 8, 10; cited in Brownlow, p. 45.

19 Wormald, p. 13; Alison Shell, *Catholicism, Controversy and the English Literary Imagination 1558–1660* (Cambridge: Cambridge University Press, 1999), p. 116; see also Michael Lynch (ed.), *Mary Stuart: Queen in Three Kingdoms* (Oxford: Blackwell, 1988), p. 1; previously unseen documentary material on Mary Stuart is discussed in John Guy, *My Heart Is My Own: The Life of Mary Queen of Scots* (London: Harper Collins, 2004).

20 Southwell to Acquaviva, 25 July 1586, CRS, 5, p. 307, in Caraman, pp. 18–20; see John Hungerford Pollen, S.J., 'Father Robert Southwell and the Babington Plot', *The Month*, 119 (1911), 302–4, and Devlin, pp. 114–15.

21 Pilarz, p. 238.

22 Frank Brownlow discusses this, and the strange relationship between Elizabeth and her chief torturer Topcliffe (called 'homo sordidissimus' by Garnet), pp. 13–15; against the trend of historical accounts, Brownlow finds only twenty cases of victims left to hang until dead, p. 166. On this subject he cites Lacey Baldwin Smith, *Elizabeth Tudor: Portrait of a Queen* (London: Hutchinson, 1976), pp. 65, 71–2; Philip Hughes, *The Reformation of England*, rev. 5th edn, 3 vols (New York: Macmillan, 1963), III, pp. 270–1, 327, n. 1; and John Hungerford Pollen, S.J., 'Religious Terrorism under Queen Elizabeth', *The Month*, 105.489 (March 1905), 271–87.

23 Wormald, pp. 13–14, 191.

24 Shell, p. 122.

25 Bodleian Library MS Tanner 169, fol. 79r; see 'Tichborne's Elegy', in Emrys Jones (ed.), *The Oxford Book of Sixteenth Century Verse* (Oxford: Oxford University Press, 1992), p. 393; hereafter *16CVerse*.

26 Perhaps Southwell borrowed from Watson's translation, 'Passion XL', from his 1582 *Hecatompathia*, text in eebo.chadwyck.com/home.

27 See Brownlow's discussion of this and Southwell's exposure of it in his *Humble Supplication*, p. 67.

28 She is associated with martyrs in *Jesus Praefigured*, a poem by John Abbot published in 1623; Shell, p. 143.

29 See Shell, p. 152.

30 See Margaret Swain, *Needlework of Mary Queen of Scots* (New York: Van Nostrand-Reinhold, 1973), pp. 77, 98; the work is in the Victoria and Albert Textile Collection. See Donald King and Santina Levey, *Embroidery in Britain from 1200–1750*, The Victoria and Albert Museum's Textile Collection Series, 7 vols (London: V&A Publications, 1993), III, p. 47.

31 *Calendar of State Papers and Manuscripts relating to English Affairs, Venetian, 1202–[1675]*, ed. Rawdon Brown (London: Longmans, 1864–1947), VIII, p. 226; hereafter *CSP, Venetian*; Leah S. Marcus, Janel Mueller, and Mary Beth Rose (eds), *Elizabeth I, Collected Works* (Chicago, IL: University of Chicago Press, 2000), p. 193.

32 Wormald, p. 190; Shell, p. 121.

33 Grosart, pp. 172, 174–5; Pierre Janelle, *Robert Southwell the Writer: A Study in Religious Inspiration* (London: Sheed and Ward, 1935), p. 160; Devlin, p. 147. Devlin also notes that Southwell's 'Decease' shares 'phrases and turns of speech' with *The Epistle of Comfort* (London: secretly printed, 1587); repr. in D. M. Rogers (ed.), *English Recusant Literature, 1538–1640* (London: Scolar Press, 1974), vol. 211); hereafter *Epistle*; Caraman, p. 33; M&B, p. lxxx.

34 Brownlow, p. 115.

35 George Puttenham, *The Arte of English Poesie*, ed. Gladys Doidge Willcock and Alice Walker (London: R. Field, 1589; repr. London: Cambridge University Press, 1970), Introduction, p. cii; hereafter *Arte*.

36 See G. R. Elton (ed.), *The Tudor Constitution: Documents and Commentary*, 2nd edn (Cambridge: Cambridge University Press, 1982); see also Brian Vickers (ed.), *Francis Bacon* (Oxford: Oxford University Press, 1996), pp. 494–501; both hereafter cited in text.

37 Vickers, p. 497.

38 Ibid., p. 437.

39 Wormald, p. 13.

40 Helen Gardner (ed.), *John Donne: The Divine Poems* (Oxford: Clarendon Press, 1952), Holy Sonnet 2, p. 15; see Gary Kuchar, 'Southwell's "A vale of teares": A Psychoanalysis of Form', *Mosaic*, 34.1 (2001), 107–20 (p. 119), for a discussion that connects the 'radically anthropomorphic expressions of divine love' of Donne's 'Show me' and 'Batter my Heart' with Southwell's 'vale of teares'; in 'advocating a religious application of Petrarchan modes', Southwell was offering a possibility of stability through *anthropopathia*.

41 See Persons's *Briefe Discourse why Catholics refuse to go to Church* (Doway (Douai), 1580), quoted in John Bossy, *The English Catholic Community 1570–1850* (London: Darton, Longman & Todd, 1975), p. 125.

42 Gauvin Alexander Bailey, *Between Renaissance and Baroque: Jesuit Art in Rome, 1565–1610* (Toronto: University of Toronto Press, 2003), pp. 10–11; hereafter cited in the text.

43 Brownlow, p. 66, n. 14, p. 141.

44 Grosart, p. lxxxi.

45 Stanley Wells and Gary Taylor (eds), *The Oxford Shakespeare Complete Works* (Oxford: Clarendon Press, 1988), III.4.58, 34.

46 See Michael Bath, *Speaking Pictures: English Emblem Books and Renaissance Culture* (London: Longman, 1994), for a discussion of uses of such emblems.

47 William Camden, *Annales: The True and Royal History of the Famous Empresse Elizabeth* (trans. Abraham Darcie, 1625), p. 72; Anon., *Lives of Philip Howard [...] and Anne Dacres* (1857), pp. 173–4; see the testimony of John Leslie, Bishop of Ross, describing how the embroidery came into the possession of the Duke of Norfolk, in William Murdin (ed.), *A Collection of State Papers relating to Affairs in the Reign of Elizabeth, 1571–1596, transcribed from original papers and other authentic memorials left by W. Cecill Lord Burghley, and reposited in the Library at Hatfield House* (London: William Bowyer, 1759), pp. 46–51; I am indebted to Michael Bath for this information.

48 See King and Levey, *Embroidery in Britain*, p. 47.

49 My thanks to Peter Davidson for bringing the Valladolid material to my attention, and for the paper on the subject that he kindly lent me, 'Emblems for the Vulnerata, Valladolid, September 1600'.

50 Devlin, p. 154.

51 The reply to Allen was called *The Answer of diverse Catholick English Gentlemen to a certain seditious book veiled with the name of D. Allen*, and Devlin says it was probably the work of Gilbert Gifford, pp. 154–5.

52 See Devlin, pp. 156–8.

53 Richard Wilson, 'A Bloody Question' (unpublished lecture, Sorbonne, 1998).

54 See Anthony G. Petti (ed.), *The Letters and Dispatches of Richard Verstegan*, Publications of the Catholic Record Society Series, 52 (London: Catholic Record Society, 1959).

55 The most frequent criticisms of his lyrics seem based on a view of poetry that denies the possibility of its use as an assault weapon in such discourses, and insists on its originality and purity of purpose. It is the 'parodic' poems of Southwell's lighter lyric collection that have most often fallen foul of this critical tendency. A large part of Southwell's lyric poetry, as Frank Brownlow reminds us, consists of poems based to a greater or lesser extent on the work of other poets (p. 103); Southwell himself acknowledges it, claiming for his lyrics 'neither Arte nor invention', only an ulterior motive – that of redirecting poetic vision; from 'The Author to his loving Cosen', prefatory letter to *Saint Peters Complaint* (1595); see M&B, p. lvii. For a discussion of poetic parody, see Brownlow, p. 101, and Rosamund Tuve, 'Sacred "Parody" of Love Poetry, and Herbert', *Studies in the Renaissance*, 8 (1961), 250.

56 In English College Archives MS Lib. 321, fols. 102r–121r; see Dana F. Sutton (University of California, Irvine: www.philological.bham.ac.uk/minutum) for her Latin text, English translation, and introduction.

57 This is a possibility opened up convincingly by Brownlow in his discussion of Southwell's last work, *An Humble Supplication* (pp. 64–72).

58 See John Hungerford Pollen, S.J., 'Father Robert Southwell and the Babington Plot', *The Month*, 119 (1911), 302–4, quoted in Brownlow, p. 141, n. 15; see also Devlin, p. 248.

59 See B. C. Foley, *The Story of the Jubilee Years 1300–1975* (Lancaster Cathedral Library), pp. 46–8.

60 Roy Strong, *Gloriana: The Portraits of Queen Elizabeth I* (London: Pimlico, 2003), pp. 121–2; see also Roy Strong, *The Cult of Elizabeth: Elizabethan Portraiture and Pageantry* (London: Pimlico, 1999), and Helen Hackett, *Virgin Mother, Maiden Queen: Elizabeth I and the Cult of the Virgin Mary* (Basingstoke: Macmillan, 1995).

61 Robin Headlam-Wells, *Spenser's* Faerie Queene *and the Cult of Elizabeth* (London:

62 *Epistle*, pp. 20v–21.

63 All of Book II concerns Fortune: 'With domineering hand she moves the turning wheel | [...] No cries of misery she hears, no tears she heeds, | But steely hearted laughs at groans her deeds have wrung'; in V. E. Watts, trans., *Boethius: The Consolation of Philosophy* (Harmondsworth: Penguin, 1969), pp. 76, 56.

64 Elizabeth I, 'From Boethius' *The Consolation of Philosophy*' (1593). Ralegh, for one, had fallen foul of Elizabeth's poetic ripostes, such as: 'Ah, silly pug, wert thou so sore afraid? | Mourn not, my Wat, nor be thou so dismayed. | It passeth fickle fortune's power and skill | To force my heart to think thee any ill', in *16CVerse*, pp. 184–5.

65 Bodley MS Rawl. Poet. 85; in Norman Ault (ed.), *Elizabethan Lyrics* (New York: Capricorn, 1960), pp. 126–7.

66 Ralegh was sent to the Tower when his secret marriage to Elizabeth Throckmorton was exposed by her pregnancy in 1592; in Ian Ousby (ed.), *Literature in English* (Cambridge: Cambridge University Press, 1993), p. 774.

67 Grosart, p. xlvi.

68 Martz, p. xxii; Shell, p. 67; Brown, 'Robert Southwell: The Mission of the Written Word', in McCoog (ed.), *The Reckoned Expense*, pp. 198–9; Janelle, pp. 50–1; Southwell's letter in CRS, 5, pp. 311, 314; Janelle, p. 51.

69 *A Transcript of the Registers of the Company of Stationers of London 1554–1640 AD*, ed. Edward Arber, 5 vols (London: privately printed, 1875–1894), II, 472.

70 It appeared in the first edition of his poetry to be published in 1595; see M&B, p. lvii.

71 See for instance Joseph Kerman, *The Masses and Motets of William Byrd* (London: Faber, 1981).

72 Grosart, p. 77.

73 Devlin, p. 167.

Chapter 7

The 'performing Word': Southwell's sacralised poetic

> All that he had his image should present,
> All that it should present he could afford:
> To that he could afford his will was bent,
> His will was followed with performing word.
> Let this suffice, by this conceive the rest,
> He should, he could, he would, he did the best.[1]

THE CROSS-ACTION OF GRACE

Southwell could be forgiven for thinking that appeals to other English poets to better their aims were not having much immediate effect. There was a new literary interest in the idea of England/Albion and its poets, and Sidney's translations of Christian works were in print, but so were his lovesick sonnets, and it was not a Catholic England being envisaged by the poets, not even in some cases a moral one. Southwell had vocalised aspects of his ministry through Peter, Magdalen, Joseph, and David; the voices of the executed Scottish Queen and English Fortuna had been ventriloquised to address those matters of political power that he could not touch in his tracts and sermons. Nothing had changed but for the worse. He had disguised his poetic voice, distracting from his Jesuit affiliations while in private carrying out his ministry in full, risking his life with every sacrament; if it comforted his secret congregations, it had not seemed to alter those minds that could make a difference.

None the less, Southwell had brought treasures back to England, word-painting a new sort of Catholicism, the visions of the Counter-Reformation opening in the new churches in Rome, the sacralisation of individual vision and creativity, and the elegant magnanimity of that Suárezian interaction between grace and free will.

To Southwell in 'heretic' England this new concept of grace was pure gold, modifying considerably the less forgiving Calvinist conception of predestination, the doctrine that was to trouble Fulke Greville when considering the untimely end of his friend Sir Philip Sidney. Creativity was being linked by Southwell not just with human capabilities, as Sidney seemed to propose, but with the access of the divine, a privileging – sacralising – of the imagination not known in English poetry before. Whether or not Southwell had intended to, in the need to give pious minds the wherewithal to work independently of Church and State, he had allowed a use of the human imaginative faculty that brought authorship far closer than before to godlike self-sufficiency. A right-minded authorship could be a channel for grace.

It is possible that the canon that critics such as Barbara Lewalski have treated as a separate and self-contained Protestant devotional poetic might never have developed without the injection, largely via Southwell to begin with, of poetic theories that were based, if almost imperceptibly, upon this more flexible concept of free will as it applied to creativity and sensitivity to the Muse – and without, it must be added, the Catholic devotional works that supplied Protestant needs until they could legitimately produce their own.[2] Southwell's English phrase 'soul rights' was innovative, but he did not invent meditational literature, nor did he have sole rights over the thinking of men such as Suárez, Lessius, and Bellarmine; but his transmission of such concepts into popular poetry was unique at the time in England, and helps to explain the interest aroused by his work. Although the whole arena of the autonomous self had become inextricably interwoven with themes of creativity and religious doctrine (with the writings of Sidney and Southwell both expressions of this in their different ways), only Southwell had studied such theories in depth, and had formulated pastoral strategies that included their use. And only Southwell was, through his ordination, *alter Christus*: another Christ.[3]

At the hub of his poetic was the 'Performing Deed', an act which expressed a giving up of self in response to downward-moving grace, the transubstantiation and cross-action which lay at the centre of his faith. For himself, that included a willing submission to an actual Calvary, part of that complete identification with Christ implicit both in his priesthood and in membership of the Society of Jesus. In his attempt to teach the English how to remember God, Southwell had one last resource to call upon: himself. His very presence in England was self-sacrifice, but what had seemed a pious hope for his congregation in his poetry would become something very different in respect of himself if – when – he died a martyr.

Southwell's contribution to English poetry includes more than poetics. He was, as we have seen, a man of peculiar sensitivity to the visual and the affective; he had also, of course, brought two new ideas to English poetry: firstly, a new emotional realism, an expressed interiority, the integrity of personal response; and, secondly, poetry as the metaphorising of the visual, not just the explication of ideas. His training, including the Ignatian *Exercises* and keeping a spiritual diary, had given him access to a language of individual response new to English literature; also he had, in attempting to attract hearts by reproducing in his poetry the visual splendours of the religious art of Rome and Catholic Europe, begun to create a poetic based on real observation of nature and the potential of the suggestive metaphor. There can be no doubt that the best English poetry after Southwell was no longer just a matter of exposition of the thought but an expression of the felt. Southwell was part of what made that change possible. Taught by his lyrics, a reader could now experience a personal, even intuitive, moral response to agonistic characterisations, as if to real personalities. The reader was no longer part of the audience at a sermon or lecture, but engaged in an immediate experience with whatever the poet cared to give form to, be it demonic or divine. Southwell's sinning David or mad Fortuna is given as vital an existence as his Gabriel, if not more, and painted in contemporary detail.

But Southwell brought another, even more special, attribute which helped, as it were, to drive the other two home. His ability envision images and reproduce emotional states was married to his status as an ordained priest, one who was authorised to act as a channel between God and humanity in the Mass. He could write about the mysteries of the Mass, and most importantly, that of transubstantiation, both feelingly and from a position of one authorised to deliver the sacraments; in offering his poems on these mysteries he was, in a sense, offering something of the mysteries themselves. His understanding of grace meant that the poems he offered to elevate the souls of his readership contributed directly to its reception.

In addition, Southwell was, to all who knew him to be a Catholic priest on English soil, after Campion a potential martyr; if executed, he could himself hope to enter into the Real Presence, sharing body and soul in the sacrifice. This altered the impact of his poetic output considerably.

Firstly, it made his utterances pastoral rather than merely conversational or poetically conventional: he could discuss wrong loves or sinful living from a position of authority, and write authoritatively around the rites and dogma of his Church (although doctrinally explicit material was not included in early printings). Some of his manuscript poetry communicated his priestly status to a special community, but even within this community there were natural variations of apprehension. Southwell made sure, in his poems about the Mass especially, that the intellectual scope of all his readerships was fully catered for. His lyrics sparkle with Neoplatonist grandeur and new concepts of response and sacred connection, while as simple songs they could be enjoyed even by the illiterate.

Southwell's poetic practice expresses the thinking inculcated in him by his training. The recurrence that we have seen in his poetry of imagery involving simultaneous upward and downward action, for instance, can be related directly to the mutuality between the individual and grace that the Jesuits preached, stressing always the importance of human action in its acquisition. In the hands of the reader, a poem on this theme stood as a simple Christian hope; but a further layer of meaning would be acquired after the author's death. His choice of subject matter, even the titles themselves, seem to court this acquisition, titles such as 'I die alive' (p. 52), which plays with the desirability of a 'right' death over a 'wrong' life, through the delicate intertwining of upward impulses – feelings of remorse, pleas for forgiveness, confessions of love – with a hoped-for downward movement of grace in response:

> Not where I breath, but where I love I live,
> Not where I love, but where I am I die:
> The life I wish, must future glory give,   15
>   The deathes I feele, in present dangers lie.

It is impossible not to read Southwell's own deadly experience into these lines, as many of his critics and biographers have done. For Southwell the cross was action, a living geometry not a static shape, combining metaphoric exemplar with real experience. He carried it in metaphor before him in his poetry, like a processional crucifix, to focus the minds of his congregation; but on his death it became Itself, his poetry transfixed upon it alongside its author, participating in his sacrifice. It was his experience of the cross, not sought but freely submitted to, that was to complete the meaning of his poetry for his reader.

In 'At home in Heaven' (p. 55) there is that cross-action again, the good soul winning God into human form through a loving understanding of its relationship with him. The cross-action here is an aesthetic one, soul's beauty rewarded by heavenly sights. It is expressed with utter simplicity as a natural reciprocal movement in 'Lewd Love is Losse' (p. 62), where, amongst natural examples of movements between the observer and a desired earthly object (including that of a hawk stooping to false lures, and a fly falling with burned wings), only one interaction works both ways to the good of the creature: 'All grace [runs] to God from whom all graces runne' (l. 6).

Just as in the Ignatian model, prayer was not abstract, but directed inward to improve the ever troubled self. Doing, not merely contemplating, was the point. The soul was to be joined with God, even if it meant a rough wooing. In 'At home in Heaven' (p. 55), Christ is 'Sampson' to the human soul's Delilah (though she is never named), lulled in the seducer's lap into a state where joining with our physicality became possible, and from which, as those familiar with the Bible would know, only self-sacrifice could effect a release. Samson, taken as an Old Testament type of Christ, did not die a soldier defending the Temple of God, but a martyr pulling down the Temple of the heretics upon their heads, an image which suggests an identification between the martyr-in-waiting Southwell himself, in his battle against heresy, and his Christ-Samson.

On joining the Society, the seventeen-year-old Southwell had been told: 'Thou art made a member of the Society of Jesus, a son of the Blessed Virgin, a part of the very body of Christ, and therefore with the rest thou too must be crucified.'[4] In the English College, it became habitual to say Te Deums before Durante Alberti's altarpiece, *Holy Trinity with St Edmund and St Thomas of Canterbury*, on the death of each college man.[5] Southwell, standing with his colleagues, knew the inscription of the painting: *Ignem Veni Mittere in Terram* – 'I have come to bring fire to the earth' (Luke 12.49). Alberti's innovative depiction of Christ as a realistically dead figure, freed from the formality of the Cross, forced upon the viewer the physical reality of sacrifice. The rustling busyness of the angelic actors in the picture, the diminishment of the instruments of Calvary, and the foregrounding of the two English churchmen, shown in almost photographic clarity, helped to suggest that Christ's martyrdom was accessible to the English in the here-and-now. The 'fire' of the inscription conflated the downward action of grace with the act of martyrdom, emphasising the martyrs' mystical place as part of that sacrificed body.[6] But this is not a calvary: the disposition of Christ's body itself represents the Cross, he, in his death, is *Logos*, his arms echoing the arched wings of the Spirit above, and the flying curve of the caption at his feet, and below that the arched door of the church through which the college youths were to carry the message. The rest of the picture is all supporting arcs and intersecting triangles, the great caped shoulders of the Father the apex, as he bears up his dead Son. This was a depiction of the self-giving of the Christian in support of Christ's sacrifice, the conflation of art and sacrament.

As a member of Christ's body, Southwell was realising God's will on earth, and his poetry is part of that realisation, a point never more clearly defined than in the poems on transubstantiation.[7] Even in these, though, doctrinal issues are combined with the need to engaging the reader rhetorically. This is not the observance of divine rites, but the calling-up of semi-divine understanding of the mysteries involved through poetic imagery and the integrity of the poet. The 'Son' becomes the human equivalent of God's creative urge, implicit in all Southwell's work and at the same time represented by the creative product of Southwell the priest-poet. In that sense, all of Southwell's poems are proofs of Christ with us, he merely the pen for the transcribing of the Word of God, in the Jesuit ideal of a priest as 'nothing more than "an instrument" united with God, in God's hand'.[8]

Southwell's lasting effect on English letters lies in this: that he was not a poet but a priest who – brilliantly, sensitively – included poetry in his pastoral activity. To close-read Southwell is almost to pray; a Southwell poem is almost an item of liturgy, not in any lexical sense, but in that it recalls its readership to

The 'performing Word': Southwell's sacralised poetic

God. As a priest, his creativity was the inspiration of the hierophant, the interpretive channel between the mortal and the divine, not merely an upwelling of native wit; and his role as a poet, as he saw it, was to remind English poets of the divine origins of that native wit. The use of the sacred memory is immanent in almost all of Southwell's poetry, especially the Holy Family sequence, but he refers to the idea in more direct ways, picking up on current interests in Neoplatonism, just as he borrowed from the modish Petrarchanism, on Christ's behalf. Memory is placed at the centre of the Mass in 'Of the Blessed Sacrament of the Aulter' (p. 26), defining the central rite of his Church as a soul-memory of the divine original. The Bible tells us that the spirit of Man originated in God, although his body was made of earth: his spirit's memory must therefore be of God. But although our memory has been clouded by our mortality, forgetting its Godly origins, we can obtain in these rituals a glimpse of those heavenly, or what Plato called perfect, Forms – '*trewe* wisdome', 'good', and 'blisse' (my emphasis), which is the lasting heavenly version of the fleeting bliss of earthly delights:

> Here to delight the witt trewe wisdome is,
> To wooe the will of every good the choise,
> For memory a mirrhor shewing blisse,
> Here all that can both sence and soule rejoyce: 40

'And if to all all this it do not bringe', he finishes, 'The fault is in the men, not in the thinge' (lines 41–2). Sacrament is memory of being one with God. If there is no resultant response in a human mind, then he has fallen too far from those bright origins to be reached through the shadows, and is in need of correction.

Southwell's poetry is indistinguishable from his pastoral attempt to mend what he sees as a deadly blindness to the light which is all around us, if we only have eyes to see. Southwell's prefatory address to his reader's 'deare eie' ('The Author to the Reader', p. 75) sums up this idea. It begins with an appeal to his imaginary reader, a 'thou' which, in being addressed as a pair of eyes, is understood as an entry point for Southwell's (or anybody else's) poetry. But the addressee at the end is 'you', always second person plural in Southwell's poetry. This is no longer an address to the reader's eye but an appeal to the creative imagination of a generation of poets, and to those special forces in them that can bridge the gap between the mortal and the divine: those 'heavenly sparkes of wit' that raise and illuminate our native skills. The sinful state of things literary has forced this writer's pen alone into a sober discourse of complaint, 'to plaine in prose'; he now asks for divine inspiration to enable his sterner discourse to be matched – gilded – with pious poetry. What God gave must be returned pure to its original, not wasted on 'mistie loves' (lines 14, 20, 21).[9]

Robert Southwell

The soul is addressed as separate from its host body, to emphasise the lesson in divine, rather than earthly, memory or inspiration. In 'At home in Heaven' (p. 55), for instance, the soul – feminised, as so often in mystical Christian symbolism, here as an errant wife – is offered a place back in the heavenly 'home' from which mortal life has removed it, and asked to 'Content [its] eye' with the attractions 'native' to it, not earthly beauty but heaven's grace (l. 27). The poet is doing the work of memory of Origins on the reader's behalf, as one might prompt forgetful pupils in the hope that, through emulation, they will eventually inwardly digest the lesson.[10]

It is followed in the McDonald and Brown edition by 'Looke home' (although only 'At home' appeared in the first edition (Wolfe, 1595a), and only 'Looke home' in the second (Wolfe, 1595b), as if exchanging places (p. 57). In 'Looke home', Southwell makes the link between memory and 'origins' explicit, and ties it more closely to Christianised Neoplatonism. In 'At home' he recalls the double-entendre of the imagery of the Novitiate – home to him for a while – by subtly conflating Christ with the language community of his brother missioners. It is 'our flesh' in which God enters in the Incarnation or the Mass; our 'exile', 'our Pilgrim weede', and 'tormentes' that he shares. In its plainness of thought and imagery it seems to address a less educated reader in terms which simplify and personalise the great mystery of humanity's relationship with God, applying it to a more simple domestic morality (lines 14, 17, 23–4). A straying priest might feel a renewed sense of Christ's claims upon him; another Jesuit would, in addition, recognise that controversial self-identification with the preaching Christ played out in the Novitiate paintings.

In 'Looke home' he is addressing a well-educated person, perhaps a poet, judging by the complex Neoplatonic theorising and the mutilayered meanings. Here his 'Deare eie' poem finds a more specific application. 'Mans mind a myrrour is of heavenly sights', he begins (l. 3), applying this Platonic elevation of the status of memory to the process of poetic creativity itself. Perhaps he is also recalling the creation of some of the beauties of the Gesù, seeing day by day a supernaturally realised heaven stretching across the shadowed walls and ceilings, wound out of the mysterious inner spaces of the creative mind.

Now he introduces the Ignatian principle that combines one's personal experience (his, and perhaps his reader's, as a poet) with the memory's inclination to return to its Original. 'The mind a creature is, yet can create, | To natures paterns adding higher skill' (lines 7–8): Southwell has used the Ignatian idea in the service of God, but also to elevate and justify his own (and a poetic reader's) poetic status, the better to make it a pattern for other poets.[11]

He seems to understand words themselves in the metaphysical, seeing a deeper meaning beneath their semantic flexibility, an ordering of the cosmos reflected in their interconnectedness, even in their ludic possibilities. Acrostics, algebra, music, poetic numbers, all were expression of divine order. There is an undeniably Neoplatonic interest in 'figures, correspondences, symmetries, antitheses, and paradoxes', in Southwell's Virgin sequence at least.[12] Southwell applies these intriguing puzzles only to his more religious subjects, as if seeing the game of sound and number played via his poetry as something approaching a mystery in its own right, a sort of Pythagorean transubstantiation. The poet, by the Neoplatonic model of creativity so attractive to the new breed of courtly makers such as Sidney and Ralegh, was, in his imaginative inspiration, an imitation of God the Maker.

The priest, however, was an interpreter of the Word in the mind of God.[13] Southwell's double status addressed this new conception of poetic creativity directly. As an anointed priest, he was, in Catholic terms, a living channel of transmission of Christ's body into earthly matter; nothing he wrote with sacred intent is mere writing, any more than Belshazzar's 'MENE MENE TEKEL UPHARSIN' (Daniel 5.25) is just a collection of letters. In encouraging poetic production in these circumstances, he was offering English poetry a potentiality beyond anything that had gone before.

HEARTS AND THORNS: SIDNEY'S AND SOUTHWELL'S POETIC VISION

The second fact of importance to the manuscript production of this particular priest is that he died. Even before his death, because of the peculiarities of sacred (as opposed to religious) art according to Church practices, his manuscripts acquired, I would suggest, the physical quality of relics. Religious art could be directly connected with the process of the Church, such as liturgical music (Byrd's Masses, for instance), in which case it was sacred in itself; or it could be in addition to, in support of, such processes, in which case it was not of itself sacred but none the less holy in intent, and therefore acceptable to the Church (the poetry of George Herbert, for instance).[14] Southwell negotiates these arenas with care, naturally.

Medieval models of religious or sacred art tended to reduce the position of the creator to its most functional, but in the peculiar conditions of the centralised culture of the English Court things were becoming rather different. The author and his intentions were becoming as important as the work itself; a Psalm Englished by Sidney or Spenser carried a very different dialogical effect from one by Southwell. If every party claimed Zion's high ground as their own, it became increasingly important to know who was making the claim, whether to applaud or anathematise. The identity of the individual author was thus foregrounded, and, in this arena at least, Southwell was in direct competition with Sidney or Spenser. In this light, Southwell's identity as a moral poet rather than a priest can be seen as strategically central to his enterprise: when the unarguably moral Englishness of his poetry had been appreciated, the author's identity, exposed by his eventual capture or death, might come as an epiphanic light to some of his readers. Certainly, in neutralising the polarities in this way, he (or his editors) ensured the delivery of his moral message to the widest possible audience, thus making the ambitions and concerns centred upon the Court seem almost irrelevant and isolated from the moral and spiritual concerns of the ordinary English reader.

Although a fine moral Englishness appears in the work of Spenser and Sidney, among others, Southwell's poetry was different, I would argue, in that it encompassed his priestly authority to perform the 'magic' of transubstantiation, and the potentialising significance of his martyrdom, his personal imitation of that sacrifice. Work produced in the support of this godly project was work produced to the greater glory of God, and therefore with the potential to become sacred of itself, after his death. The phrase repeated through his work, 'Performing Deed', especially in its ultimate, Eucharistic manifestation as Christ the Word, is Southwell's reminder to his reader of what his poetic ultimately means. When he says, in 'A holy Hymme', 'What power affords performe indeede' (p. 23, l. 4), he means: return the deed symbolised by the Eucharist, 'That sacrifice to Christe [we] may retorne' ('Christs bloody sweat', p. 18, l. 20).

To Catholics (and some Anglicans) his work encompassed a supernatural mystery, that of transubstantiation, worked into his poems as if to inform the texts themselves. As in the Gesù paintings, all acts of sacrifice for God are conflated into the act of Communion, with Southwell as *alter Christus*, the human expression of it. The mystical exchange of humanity for divinity is implicit in a phrase in the first of his lighter lyrics, 'A childe my Choyce' (p. 13), 'He mine, by gift: I his, by debt: thus each to other due' (l. 7). In 'New Prince, new pompe' (p. 16), Holy Communion and the Nativity are conflated in images that call to mind a secret Mass in a remote barn, where a 'wooden dish' becomes Christ's Communion 'plate', in the spirit of a Bruegel painting. It is as if Southwell is asking those collected there to 'highly prise' the homely miracle of bread into God, the 'humble pompe, | Which he from heaven dooth bring', for its intrinsic value, not for any celebratory finery that might or might not accompany it (lines 20, 27–8); this would seem to preach against art were it not set out in poetry itself, and poetry that imported such beauty.

In 'Sinnes heavie loade' (p. 17), there is another reminder of mystery disguised by metaphor: it is the union of God and man sealed with a 'bleeding kisse' (l. 28), as God/Christ, Father of our souls, mates with the earth, Mother of our body; it is she who drinks his 'dearest blood' (l. 31) and entombs Christ's body, 'And with them all thy deitie to have, | Now then in one thou jointly yeeldest all' (l. 34). This is less to describe than to conjure, almost in the form of a physical recipe, the basic elements of the central truth of a Christian tradition that it is death to practice in Southwell's England. Southwell's poetry thus

The 'performing Word': Southwell's sacralised poetic

contains both the elements and the reality of total self-sacrifice.

St Augustine says that God, 'in knowing Himself in His Son', knows 'all the ways in which His infinite perfections can be mirrored by creatures. The consubstantial Word is, therefore, the uncreated model of all creatures'.[15] Southwell's 'Looke Home' is a superbly condensed poetic expression of this. St Thomas Aquinas likens the preconception of a thing in the mind of a craftsman to the concept of God's intellect, 'which is His Wisdom conceived from eternity, namely, the Word of God, the Son of God. And so it is impossible that He does anything except through the Son.'[16] As in the Alberti altarpiece, the Son is the metaphysical and actual point of contact between God and Man; Southwell, as a Jesuit, believed he stood at that point of contact. This, to Southwell, was the locus of the rightness, the truth of his art. 'Of the Blessed Sacrament of the Aulter' (p. 26) is closely connected to Thomist thought; in it Southwell writes, of the moment of transubstantiation, that 'What thought can thincke, what will doth best approve | Is here obteyn'd where no desire ys voyde' (lines 21–2).

Sidney's *Apologie* can be read in part as an attempt to Protestantise this theory of art, removing the religious requirement and replacing it with artistic quality and skill. Southwell rejects this attempted removal. In writing poetry at all, Southwell was engaging with an international debate over creative intention, and also creative originality. Originality was a religious issue – there was only one Original, one Author/ity who had the right to be creative, who was not required to work into the established structures. Priests and poets alike made this discussion their business. Puttenham's was the standard view: only God was *Autharcos* because only God was 'in every respect selfe suffizant'.[17] The writer was to reflect that ideal self-sufficiency, not attempt to recreate it in himself; his work was a mirror polished by the best skills of his craft. Skilful authorship resided in skilful imitation of the best precedents, not the imposition of self. Even in a work celebrating the cream of English poets, such as Richard Tottel's 1557 (and much reprinted) *Miscellany*, the authority of the poet was subsumed under the need to mirror perfection in form, Tottel 'improving' the noble Wyatt's own choice of metre in places.

Poets were in a precarious position historically. It was not just that the material had to be decorous and fitting, but that the very responses to it, its affective capabilities, and the position of the author/artist, had to be carefully balanced against accusations of using the Devil's tools or trespassing on the self-confidence of God, a Christianised version of Plato's concerns over poets and their place in the ideal *politis*. There was therefore an inevitable and multifaceted anxiety about creativity that poets such as du Bellay and Sidney felt constrained to address in their defences of poetry. The affectivity of a work had always to be justified by its improving force. Southwell's repetition of 'performing deed' underlines this necessity, 'Such distance is betwene highe wordes and deedes', as he says in the short 'Saint Peters Complaynte' (p. 29, l. 11). He was ahead of the game here in some respects, his priesthood implying that his poetry was part of the authorised scholastic methodology of interpretation and symbolism developed by men such as Augustine and Aquinas. Protestant poets, having apparently rejected that lineage, were somewhat at a disadvantage, and Southwell's use of poetry can be seen as an attempt to deny them the high ground.

Sidney's *Astrophil and Stella* sonnet sequence was published in 1591, although his *Defence of Poesie* was not in print until the time of Southwell's death in 1595. Although it is perfectly possible that part of Southwell's mission was to engage a somewhat disaffected Sidney's interest, his death during Southwell's first summer in England meant that it would make more sense to build upon Sidney's poetic legacy, but attempt to adapt it towards Jesuit agendas. It would be tempting to set these two poets in opposition, but in fact much of Southwell's poetic agenda concords with and builds upon that of Sidney. The differences are almost exclusively informed by Southwell's mission agendas and status as Jesuit priest.[18]

Sidney in his *Defence of Poetry* championed the affective in literature, with provisos, trying to establish creative rights for an author based on self-initiated imaginative faculty rather than imitative skills alone.[19] Where to most early modern writers creative freedom was little different from lying, Sidney argued generally in his *Defence* that self-authored poetic licence, the expression of 'may-be' rather than 'is', was a powerful educative tool rather than a foolish distraction. This is very close to the artistic outcome of debates at the mid-century Papal Council of Trent.[20] Sidney will have encountered these artistic outcomes in Europe, especially around Campion in Prague, and saw that affective art could 'imitate both to delight and teach; and delight, to move men to take that goodness in hand, which without delight they would fly as from a stranger'. To Southwell, likewise, 'The best course to let [poets] see the errour of their workes' is, according to Southwell, 'to weave a new webbe in their owne loome', borrowing the delight of their style 'to invite some skilfuller wits to goe forward in the same, or to begin some finer peece, wherein it may be seene, how well verse and vertue sute together'.[21]

Sidney finds pagan precedent for his claim, linking it wherever possible to divine action, likening the Greeks' understanding of the Poet as Maker to God's role as Creator (lines 174–81, 235–40)); or discussing the Romans' belief in the power of song to charm spirits (lines 143–5). The Roman concept of poet as *vates* included prophecy, and Sidney reminds his reader of this supernatural function even while seeming to laugh at it (lines 129–54). Southwell, through his Roman Church, may have inherited some of the mysteries of the Sybil, but he still needed to find doctrinally satisfactory biblical precedents: 'not onely among the Heathens, whose Gods were chiefely canonized by their

Poets, and their Painim Divinitie Oracled in verse: But even in the Old and New Testament it hath bene used by men of greatest Pietie, in matters of most devotion'.[22]

Here at least there is a division: Sidney names the royal song-maker, David, with many anxious apologies for linking the holy words of the Bible with what he regrets has become regarded as a debased art (lines 167–70); he gives such godly song-makers the prime position as imitators of the excellencies of God (lines 258–67); he then passes over a 'second kind' of poet, men, like Virgil, concerned merely with natural, moral or other philosophising, without creative invention (lines 273–8). It is Sidney's third, the most creative, 'right' sort of poet (l. 282), that comes closest to godly *vates* such as David or Orpheus – able to create new imagery in the mind, better than life (lines 295–8, 286). Pure inventivity is higher, in Sidney's model, than moral rectitude. Southwell pounces on the weakness exposed. Having allowed the use of imaginative poetry by men such as David for 'matters of most devotion', he problematises its use outside that strict definition: inspiration can come from the Devil as from God; poets, even the best, can harness their talents to the bad, harming where they should have inspired to good: 'For in lieu of solemne and devout matter, to which in duety they owe their abilities, they now busy themselves in expressing such passions, as onely serve for testimonies to how unworthy affections they have wedded their wils.'[23]

Aspects of Sidney's poetry made him something of a hostage to fortune; it is possible to make unfortunate connections between Astrophil's Stella and David's Bathsheba, and many have done. But Southwell need only show how far Sidney's view begs the question about authority to raise questions about the moral direction and moral authority of such secular Neoplatonic poetry. Sidney's authority to invent is self-authorised; he asks his reader to accept that his will to authorship is right and proper, and yet, faithful to the tenets of Calvinism, he allows that the human will is 'infected' in ways that we can neither know nor remedy (l. 244). How, then, can an untrained lay person fallen from grace and subject to the prescription of election know if he or she is moved by the 'Divell' or the divine? Sidney seems to writhe and struggle in these complexities without ever finding an answer. The Petrarchan resolution of human into divine love, via the beloved's virtue and guidance, falls, in some of Sidney's sonnets, into 'a downward spiral of false elation, depressive nightmare and self-mockery', as his editor Elizabeth Porges-Watson puts it, as if failing in its own poetic self-confidence.[24] In such deep matters, surely only a lifetime's training in piety and self-denial can confer such discriminating ability and guidance, Southwell seems to say. Here the priest has the upper hand over the poet, in terms of authority, at least.

Southwell, like Sidney, acknowledges from the start that authorship is a position of power; Nature can only ape the Ideal, while a poet's imagination can figure it forth to a new perfection. God has created Man above Nature, which, according to Sidney, 'in nothing he showeth so much as in Poetry, when with the force of divine breath [the Poet] bringeth things forth far surpassing [Nature's] doings, with no small argument to that first accursed fall of Adam – since our erected wit maketh us know what perfection is, and yet our infected will keepeth us from reaching unto it' (lines 239–44). But does Sidney not stray towards saying that in this third, imaginative category of poet God has created certain sorts of humanity – those discerning, creative, sensitive ones – semi-divine, above mortal Nature, a view that not only is controversial, to say the least, but which could imply a near-Nietzschean disregard for the laws of both Nature and less divinely creative individuals in the hands of one who did not acknowledge such laws to be God-given? Southwell would surely have to reject this view, but in writing poetry he is skating towards it, and on thin ice. It is the priest who is in an ambiguous position now: as a poet he must claim only to reflect God's creation, but as a priest he is an active interpretive channel for its most heavenly mysteries. How does he mediate between the two in his poetry? Is the Pythagorean cosmos revealed in some of his poetry the priest channelling, or just the poet synthesising?

SOUTHWELL'S POETIC SACRAMENT

The question resolved itself in his death. Southwell's poetry could claim a sort of reliquary status among those who knew he was a Roman Catholic priest even before his death because he had, in remaining committed to his priesthood in the face of martyrdom, both an official and a sacred authority; and the subject matter of his poetry called that authority into the minds of his readers. That his poetic inspiration was divinely sanctioned and inspired, therefore, there could be little doubt amongst Catholics; and those that could not accept (or did not know of) his authority could at least admire his moral integrity and courage. This implied position of authorial authority of the very highest must be seen in relation to the claim that divine inspiration could be accessed by a secular poet calling upon the internal fires of his own creativity, as Giordano Bruno had argued in the work he dedicated to Sidney, his *Heroic Frenzies*, in a debate on self-sufficiency similar to Puttenham's in the *Arte of English Poesie*.[25]

What is missing in Sidney is Southwell's emphatic closure. Gary Waller, like Porges-Watson, notes the contradictions inherent in Sidney's view of creativity, torn as it is between Neoplatonism's 'erected wit' and Calvinism's 'infected will'. Sidney, in what Waller calls probably his most 'ecstatic sentence' on the autonomous creativity of the poet, none the less ends with this 'inability to embody what the poet is inspired to perform'. 'How did poets reconcile such oppositions?' Waller asks.[26] Southwell reconciled the unattainability of the

The 'performing Word': Southwell's sacralised poetic

Petrarchan Ideal with the lover's desires through his theory of a theologised Petrarchanism, what Gary Kuchar describes as a 'self-conscious thematization of religious desire' reflecting 'a significant moment in the history of *anthropopathia* (the [...] expression of God's attributes in language that is normally reserved for describing human characteristics) as it occurs in the early modern lyric'.[27] This, as I have argued in earlier chapters, was less a poetic strategy than a direct and inevitable result of his Jesuit theology, which encouraged a more-than-usually human visualisation of God. Southwell's ideal lover, as he reminds us through his repetition of 'Performing Deed', achieves physical consummation with the only beloved he thinks worth loving, a real death, through the real fire, either of a lifetime of earthly sacrifice, Purgatory or martyrdom. Southwell insists again and again that the beauty comprehended in his poetic is heavenly, and therefore supreme; the blisses it brings are not the momentary ones of earthly consummation. For him the Petrarchan Ideal is realisable only through Calvary – apparently an unreasonable position. Any authorial insistence upon the reasonable as a means of knowing God undermines, in his view, God's prime authority in unfolding his creation through history as he alone sees fit.

In 'Of the Blessed Sacrament of the Aulter' (p. 26), a poem closely connected to Thomist thought, he writes of the moment of transubstantiation that 'What thought can thincke, what will doth best approve | Is here obteyn'd where no desire ys voyde' (lines 21–2). Southwell is, in accessing this mystery, answering Sidney and the courtier-poets; such is the perfection of the act that it transcends the reach of man's wit, however 'erected': 'No witt can wishe nor will embrace so much'; it outreaches the most infected of wills: 'Selfelove here cannot crave more then it fyndes, | Ambition to noe higher worth aspire'; 'In summ here is all in a summ expressd' (lines 25–30). Southwell is offering poeticised transubstantiation as a means of erecting the wit beyond human capacity. To take it makes us semi-divine; merely to comprehend it, he seems to be saying, is to reach beyond mortality. He has borrowed, as he put it, the 'course threds' of Sidneian passionate poetry to 'weave a new webbe' of (Catholic) Christian virtue in the 'loome' of love poetry.[28]

Both 'Of the Blessed Sacrament' and 'A holy Hymme' (p. 23), the translation of Aquinas's *Lauda Sion salvatorem* which Brown doubts to be Southwell's work,[29] attempt in their different ways to metaphorise the mystery of the Mass as well as instructing in its typology and meaning. Perhaps this was one of Southwell's attempts to recapture his English as a novice in Rome; certainly the words of the old 'holy Hymme' strain to encompass transcendental mysteries even in the sort of numerological puzzle so dear to Renaissance intellectuals, the Jesuits not the least:

> Under kindes two in appearance
> Two in shew but one in substance,
> Lie thinges beyond comparison:
> Flesh is meat, blood drinke most heavenly: 40
> Yet is Christ in each kinde wholy
> Most free from al division.
>
> None that eateth him doth chew him,
> None that takes him doth divide him,
> Received he whole persevereth. 45
> Be there one or thousands housled
> One as much as all received,
> He by no eating perisheth.

This is a homely look at the most complex of mysteries; 'Housle' was an ancient Germanic-English word for 'sacrifice', later taken to mean the Christian sacrament itself – Shakespeare has Hamlet's ghostly father use it, either as deliberate anachronism or because this was the word he knew and used at home (*Hamlet*, I.5.77). If Southwell did write this poem, he was reminding his readers of an ancient tradition of communal worship now lost. Elizabeth had replaced the great Roman Catholic communal festivities of Corpus Christi and Ascension-tide with her own feasts, her Accession Day and her birthday.[30] Southwell is here perhaps reminding the English commons, in simple form, of that secularising piracy. This translation has the cheery tone of a drinking song – not at all the ascetic mood of Southwell's other holy poems. It ends with a prayer to Jesus, 'food and feeder of us' (l. 67), asking him to take us to a heavenly table that seems more inn than altar. Perhaps because this work, though of unimpeachable scholastic authority, lacked something of the intellectual flights admired by his peers, Southwell saw fit to present the more elegant version, 'Of the Blessed Sacrament', stressing the mystery of the Old Testament's 'dymm glymses to the light' that was the 'Performinge Deede', the incarnation or self-sacrifice or transubstantiation itself (lines 3, 4).

This is Southwell the *vates* in the sense of Sidney's first, not his third (though second-best) kind of poet, interpreting the mysteries of the *Logos* to the people. This version focuses far more on the mysterious presence of Christ in its various manifestations; expressed through word games and repetitions, it amounts almost to Pythagorean number magic. 'Here truth beleefe, beleefe inviteth love' (l. 20) is a typical example of the patterning of the words and syntax almost into algebraic formulations to reproduce the God-ordered mystery of the thing itself, a very Southwellian (and Garnettian) poetic preoccupation, that cosmic 'summe' or total that expresses the mathematical 'summe' or paradox of three into one. The central (and centrally Catholic) mystery is the wellspring of the most excellent and holy music, algebraic order, nourishment, art, even perfumes – in fact 'all that can both sence and soule rejoyce'

The 'performing Word': Southwell's sacralised poetic

(lines 30, 41); the sum total of everything lost to the English churchgoer, in other words.

It is as a poet of skill that Southwell can best digest and translate the mysteries to his reader; it is as a priest that he has the authority to do so.

SOUTHWELL AND SPENSER: TRUTH AND BEAUTY

Southwell's project of importing the rich experience of Rome into Protestant England is clearly seen in 'Of the Blessed Sacrament of the Aulter' (p. 26). What few of his English flock could hope to experience he supplied directly into their imaginations, as it were, through poetry, the angels acting in historic, poetic, and real time, carrying the inspirations they brought Southwell to the readers in their turn, via his memory of the beauties of church celebrations in Rome, and the suggestive magic of poetic imagery. Father Southwell's poetic Mass, complete with sweet music and the scent of incense, is assisted by real angels, who therefore help to bring the sacred bread to the table of the English reader's imagination – the poet-priest's way of offering his congregation a virtual Eucharist, to console them for the loss of the actual one:

> To ravishe eyes here heavenly bewtyes are,
> To winne the eare sweete musicks sweetest sound,
> To lure the tast the Angells heavenly fare,
> To sooth the sent divine perfumes abounde,
> To please the touch he in our hartes doth bedd,   35
> Whose touch doth cure the dephe, the dumm, the dedd.
>
> [...]
>
> A body is endew'd with ghostly rightes,   55
> A natures worke from natures law is free,
> In heavenly sunne lye hidd eternall lightes,
> Lightes cleere and neere yet them no eye can see,
> Dedd formes a never dyinge life do shroude,
> A boundlesse sea lyes in a little cloude.   60

The restorative role of Christ is quite explicit here, in the idea of 'ghostly rights', the part of our body that has been remade divine by consuming Christ in the Eucharist.

This metaphorised Mass appeared at first only in manuscript, as if to underline its sacramental significance, and the priest's role in its delivery. 'Of the Blessed Sacrament' appeared in the St Omer edition of 1616 (with lines 31–6 on the sensuality of the experience omitted).

The poet is using the words, sacralised by his status as priest, almost as the particles of the host are used, each carrying the same weight as the whole, no matter how small and diminished into apparently light matter, a magic that transcends mere numerical correctness as alchemy transcended chemistry, transforming the 'numbers' of his poetry into something more than the sum total of the parts. If the original authorial intent is true, the words themselves are equally so. 'Forme' of words might be less elevated, but in conveying the mystery of Real Presence, they themselves are part of the Word itself, disseminated like the bread broken and handed out by the priest. Southwell was handing out his manuscripts almost like wafers at Mass, to be consumed for the betterment of his readers. Just as the real priest arrived to deliver the Mass disguised in a doublet, so he does it here metaphorically, disguised as a poet.

Southwell's 'Performing Word' informs his poetry through both his metaphorising of the Mass and through the affective power of the physical beauty of his Church. 'The holiness of beauty is ordered to the beauty of holiness' as Saward says, summing up Thomist theology on the transmission of holiness via the Sacraments; the 'Triune Godhead' is 'the principle efficient cause of our sanctification' while 'the humanity of Christ' is 'the instrumental cause'. This was the Church's response to the debate: art cannot sanctify us in the same way as a sacrament, but Christian art can, as a 'sacramental', sanctify us *ex opere operantis*, 'through the intercession of the Church and the devotion of her members'.[31] This is very much Southwell's strategy: to improving the soul through meditation on an image, a *poetic* image 'of the Suffering Christ, the Ecce Homo'.[32] Aquinas gazed on a crucifix as he prayed, the visual conditioning the spiritual. Southwell has merely incorporated such visual stimuli into his affective poetry, dismissing Spenser's anxieties over the use of beauty.

The drawing back and pushing forward action of the Holy Ghost working through such affective art is metaphorised in 'Mary Magdalens blush' (p. 32) as the cross purposes of *eros* and divine love:

> All ghostly dynts that grace at me did dart,
> Like stubborne rocke I forced to recoyle:
> To other flights an ayme I made my hart,   15
> Whose wounds, then wel-come, now have wrought my foyle.
> Woe worth the bow, woe worth the archers might,
> That drave such arrowes to the marke so right.
>
> To pull them out, to leave them in, is death:
> One, to this world: one, to the world to come: 20
> Wounds I may weare, and draw a doubtfull breath:
> But then my wounds will worke a dreadfull dome.
> And for a world, whose pleasures passe away:
> I lose a world, whose joyes are past decay.

Sensuality is allowed to inform 'good' poetry, but in Southwell's Thomistic model it is a thief if it inspires to anything but. Spenser's and Sidney's secular use of semi-divine inspiration is stealing fire from God. If either had applied it to the Queen of heaven, perhaps it would have stood Southwell's test, but Spenser's courting of the earthly Virgin and the gradual entanglement of Sidney's heavenly Stella and the fleshly Penelope Rich served only to prove Southwell's point about misdirection. In his own poetry Southwell accepts the implied challenge of Sidney's inspirational authority, offering us Magdalen's Christ-directed erotic love for Astrophil's cloudier one:

> O heaven, lament: sense robbeth thee of Saints:
> Lament O soules, sense spoyleth you of grace.
> Yet sense doth scarse deserve these hard complaints,
> Love is the theife, sense but the entring place.
> Yet graunt I must, sense is not free from sinne,   35
> For theefe he is that theefe admitteth in.

The undogmatic muscularity of Southwell's poetry here fixes the cross-action of grace in the trope of a sword-fight, a knightly combat that must contain an implicit reproof for the love-distracted, idle Astrophil. The arrangement of the verse on the cross-action of grace caught between the physical love of Christ and the spiritual return to God in the fifth stanza is a vertical one: the sentences read down as well as across. Southwell is weaving in and out of the sensual versus the spiritual, the had versus the hoped-for pleasure:

> O sence,   O soule,   O had [blisse],   O hoped blisse,   25
> You wooe,   you weane, you draw,   you drive me back.
> Your crosse-encountring, like their combate is,
> That never end but with some deadly wrack.

This is an almost literal weaving of threads of his own into the other poets' loom, their carnal pleasures against his better ones. Having pictured within the stanza the crossing elements of the battle of the senses against the wish for piety almost as patterns, or even mathematical equations, he then solves the equation, or elucidates the situation, in more literary form:

> When sense doth winne, the soule doth loose the field,
> And present happes, make future hopes to yeeld.   30

Sense woos to pleasure, soul weans the speaker off it, 'had', or remembered, pleasure draws him back into sensuality; hope of bliss drives him back to Godly behaviour. Somewhere in the middle, caught in the crossfire, is the feeling, responsive, confused self that Sidney/Astrophil was writing out, and that Southwell is here seeking to express through a form of sympathetic magic.

The concept of the magic contained within the right words is more explicit in one of Southwell's Virgin sequence. This sequence, not seen in print in its entirety until 1856 and not in proper order before McDonald and Brown's edition of 1967, is, of all Southwell's poems, the group most deeply immersed in the complexities of Mariology. Martz suggested that the sequence was related to the use of the rosary.³³ This fits with Garnet's interest in the rosary, and with a theory of words as holy artefacts; connections between Neoplatonic poetry and the Pythagorean concept of the numbered universe have been argued more fully elsewhere.³⁴ None the less, the poetry is full of complex relationships between the word and a universe of measured order as expressed through the Marian mysteries. In the fifth of this sequence, 'The Virgins salutation' (p. 5), the cabalistic word-magic is made clear in a relationship between words, such as the medieval 'ave/Eva' mirror-image used by Southwell here:

> Spell *Eva* backe and *Ave* shall you finde,
> The first began, the last reverst our harmes,
> An Angels witching wordes did *Eva* blinde,
> An Angels *Ave* disinchants the charmes,
> Death first by womans weakenes entred in,   5
> In womans vertue life doth now begin.

Gabriel is set in simple opposition to the Devil here, as in Southwell's Latin 'Poema de Assumptione', where the mystery of the Virgin's assumption into heaven is debated.³⁵ In the tenth of the sequence, 'The flight into Egypt' (p. 9), a bizarre transubstantiation of words themselves is effected by the horrid image of the slit throats of the martyred Innocents like lips calling out wordlessly but eloquently to God. The words have become part of the Eucharist through the transforming 'magic' of martyrdom coupled with the material magic of poetry: 'Your ditty death, and blood in liew of wordes' (l. 18). Writing this, could his own proposed martyrdom be far from the poet's mind? Reading it, could it be far from that of his reader?

LOVE SONGS TO THE SOUL: THE PRIEST-POET

Only a priest could have written authoritatively on such a sensitive subject as the Mass, but surely only Southwell, among all other English priests of the time, could have written a love poem to the Soul. He is exploiting the duality of his position of gentleman-poet and priest, and, again, weaving a few threads in the profane poets' own loom, subverting (superverting?) their erotic agenda. Brownlow notes Southwell's ability to write love poetry in his discussion of one of Southwell's Latin elegies, 'Elegia VIII', which contains what Brownlow considers 'two of the most moving lines Southwell ever wrote': 'I said, Doubt not, we shall live in the memory of love, | As I am yours, truly yours, so you will always be mine'.³⁶ In his English lyrics he adopts a lighter tone while still privileging love. In 'At home in Heaven' (p. 55–6) Southwell is playing with the same flirtatious subtlety as that in 'Seeke flowers of heaven' (p. 52), in which he addresses the whole poem, by implication only, to the feminised soul in the

The 'performing Word': Southwell's sacralised poetic

form of Psyche. Now Southwell addresses himself to that feminine principle in the statelier vein of his polished sestets:

> Faire soule, how long shall veyles thy graces shroud?
>   How long shall this exile with-hold thy right?
> When will thy sunne disperse this mortall cloud,
>   And give thy gloryes scope to blaze their light?
> O that a Starre more fit for Angels eyes,   5
> Should pyne in earth, not shine above the skyes.

At first it seems to address a lady – 'sweet saint' and 'fair soul' were not unusual at the time – in the form of a beautiful body veiled in clothing like a sun hidden behind a cloud, the bright star of the Petrarchan Ideal Love. A Catholic reader might recognise the first part as a disguised hymn in Petrarchan mode to the Virgin, she being the archetype of the pure soul who 'seduced' God into manhood, the Empress of mercy who intercedes between God and mankind. Southwell's teacher Bellarmine had insisted that God sought her permission, like any good husband, before the Incarnation. Perhaps this is the coolly courteous Gabriel of Fra Angelico's *Annunciation* pressing God's amorous suit on the Virgin; perhaps she waits for her Assumption, or for England her Dowry's renewal of her devotions. Certainly, the cruder applications of Petrarchan imagery are overstepped: Southwell has overpainted the Petrarchan canvas – the beautiful element of this lady is not her body, which veils her true beauty as clothing might veil an earthly one in a less elevated poem; neither is the lover the poetic 'I' of Petrarchan poetry: although the poet addresses the lovely one, it is, Gabriel-like, on behalf of someone else. 'Thy ghostly beautie offred force to God', this messenger tells her, 'It cheyn'd him in the lynckes of tender love' (ll. 7–8). God's is the Petrarchan eye, the poetic 'I', while the poet, like the angelic assistants at the Mass, is merely the channel and recorder of the upward-downward movement of love. It is the beauty of the human soul that has seduced God into the human body, turning the vengeful sword he wielded in the Old Testament into a loving communion. That beauty 'made the rigor of his Justice yeeld, | And Crowned mercye Empresse of the feelde' – a reminder of Mary's intercessionary role, now lost to Protestants:

> This lull'd our heavenly *Sampson* fast asleepe,
>   And laid him in our feeble natures lapp.
> This made him under mortall load to creepe: 15
>   And in our flesh his god head to enwrap.
> This made him sojourne with us in exile:
>   And not disdayne our tytles in his style.

But here, Southwell-like, a metaphysical multiplication of meaning occurs, and the simple identification with the Virgin ends. We now discuss the generality of humanity, it is 'our flesh', not just that of the Mother of God. And having praised the lovely lady-soul for her seduction of so great a lover, he pleads with her to stay true to what is at 'home', in her natural, native demesne, heaven. Having played with an artfully dissembled skill and delicacy upon the heart-strings of the English Catholic nostalgia that composed the melancholy 'Walsingham', he now directs his sermon into the individual reader's breast. This could not, after all, be said to the Immaculate Conception:

> O soule do not thy noble thoughtes abase 25
>   To lose thy loves in any mortall wight:
> Content thy eye at home with native grace,
>   Sith God him selfe is ravisht with thy sight.
> If on thy beautie God enamored bee:
> Base is thy love of any lesse then hee. 30

But the priest neither proselytises nor condemns: he is writing, on God's behalf, God's love-song to the human Soul, borrowing the imagery and implications of Mary's impregnation; only an ordained priest, one who was authorised to administer that consummation of God and humanity in Holy Communion, could claim the authority to do so without causing offence. Southwell is here metaphorising the Performing Word, that moment of transubstantiation he praised in 'Of the Blessed Sacrament', a remarkable and daring exercise in cross-action, this time between the art of poetry and the action of grace itself.

A newer element yet appears in the final stanza: in yet another of those multiple implications so often hidden within his sermonising, Southwell the poet-priest seems to be admonishing high-placed female Court Catholics and addressing the legality of the Crown all at once; perhaps this is why it was removed from the second issue of 1595 *St Peters Complaint* (Wolfe, 1595b) and replaced with the uncontroversially Neoplatonic 'Looke home'. Its inclusion in the first set of lyrics acquired by Wolfe and issued immediately on Southwell's execution, all of which seem to deal with domestic or womanly concerns, reinforces my supposition that this set was collected for, or by, a woman.[37] In January 1592 Topcliffe had arrested Anne Bellamy, a daughter of one of the families who regularly supported and housed the priests; he was closing in hard on Southwell with this arrest – Southwell and Garnet stayed regularly at the recusant Bellamy household at Uxenden, Harrow, on their road north-west. She was taken to the Gatehouse prison for recusancy, where she was interrogated and in some way impregnated by Topcliffe or one of his officers – was it from Anne that this presumed collection was taken?[38]

The imagery is too finely honed to be dismissed, as it so often has, as poetic fancy or mere sermonising;[39] we have already seen Southwell using the Bible to make hard socio-political points, and I believe he does so here. Southwell addresses the legality of the Crown, no less, through the courtly Petrarchanism of Elizabeth's own favourite poets, borrowing the hierarchy of beauty to plead his better way:

The 'performing Word': Southwell's sacralised poetic

> Queene *Hester* was of rare and pearlesse hew,
> And *Judeth* once for beauty bare the vaunt,
> But he that could our soules endowments vew,
> Would soone to soules the Crowne of beautie graunt,   40

He foregrounds 'Queene', and, with 'Crowne', reminds his reader of famously beautiful and powerful earthly ladies, biblical Esther and Judith. It might seem a dry priestly diatribe on the theme of *vanitas vanitatum* and no more, but this is no ordinary priest, and, on further investigation (which his original reader, if pious, would not have required), we find that both ladies are united in more than their good looks: both have high places in heretical courts; both act, by conscience and loyalty to their God, to destroy, within that court, a powerful hater of their own people (Haman; Holofernes). He is therefore asking the soul or the reader to remember that however beautiful a Queen and powerful a Crown, it is the self-soul of the individual that bears the responsibility of real beauty and power, and its prime duty is not to any earthly royalty, or to evil counsellors, however powerful. 'O soule out of thy selfe seeke God alone: | Grace more than thine, but Gods, the world hath none', he finishes, relating the issue of 'soul rights' directly to the claim to legal superiority of earthly crowns (lines 41–2). That cross-action sidesteps duty to any earthly monarchy, it seems.

In 'From Fortunes reach' (p. 66) Southwell uses poetic structure itself to imitate the action between earthly and divine force that happens in transubstantiation in a cycle of light (the 'light that ever shines' – divine inspiration), a light which engenders love, which in turn gives (eternal) life. He directs this light/love/life cycle inwards onto 'one' (Christ/God) who becomes the centre of radiating lines of the force of love, and who alone, as the centre of it all, constitutes the eye's only light, the only proper site of the heart's love, the only source of life for the soul. These three forces become a sort of trinity of divine energy in the person of that 'one':

> My light to love, my love to lyfe doth guyde
> To life that lives by love, and loveth light: 20
> By love of one, to whom all loves are ty'de
> By dewest debt, and never equald right.
> Eyes light, harts love, soules truest life he is,
> Consorting in three joyes, one perfect blisse.

The recipient and engenderer of this love is never named, leaving the reader free to form his or her own locus for the energy Southwell has theologised so completely in so few lines – this highly complex weaving of ideas and images on the loom of love-poetry is only four stanzas long.

Despite Sidney's courtly assault upon scholastic precedent, Southwell seems to share many of his views on creativity, in his poetry, at least. 'Looke Home' (p. 57) might be patterned upon Sidney's last sonnets, so closely does it reiterate Sidney's attitude, with its Neoplatonic expression of inspiration as the soul's urge to return to its true Original. The last two items in Sidney's *Certain Sonnets*, first published in 1598 but circulated in manuscript earlier, perhaps as early as 1580, seem drawn from the same fountain as Southwell's, or vice versa, on the theme of *splendidis longum valedico nugis* ('I bid a long farewell to splendid trifles').[40] But Southwell could not have approved of Sidney's claim for autonomy via his skill as a poet alone: he had an active agenda and an inherent authority that Sidney could not share, and these (and his critique of Sidney's poetic theories) are subtly expressed in his repetition of the phrase 'performing word/deed'. Milton, too, seems to have distrusted Sidney's confidence in the acceptability of *poetic* integrity alone, judging by the many caveats he set about his own poetic revelation, *Paradise Lost*.

In 'Looke home', Southwell is addressing himself directly to the creative imagination, this time playing with the idea of vanity, the 'selfe beholding eye' (p. 57, l. 2). As the eye of vanity pleases itself by admiring its own beauty in the mirror, so 'retyred thoughts' please themselves by seeing in their meditation a reflection of the divine mind: 'Mans mind a myrrour is of heavenly sights | A breefe wherein all marvailes summed lye' (lines 3–4). In the human imagination are memories of the ideal forms of things, if only, as Plato said, we could remember them; our memories are intrinsically good, but 'thought may grace them more' (l. 6). 'The mind a creature is, yet can create, | To natures paterns adding higher skill', adds Southwell (lines 7–8); our imaginative abilities give us a semi-divinity, as Sidney argued, and we can through imagination transcend nature. Southwell concurs: 'wit' could certainly better nature's 'finest workes', but only 'If force of wit had equall power of will' (l. 10). If prudence and art, or the intention and the ability, agree, they add up to something more than mere nature.

Here the poem turns. We are taken from Sidney's creative agenda, which puts the individual imagination near the centre, into Southwell's, which sees human skill at its best as a reflection of true creativity. Refracting the simple image of the vain eye and the self-pleasing mirror at the start into a divine insight, he says 'Mans soule of endles beauties image is, | Drawne by the worke of endlesse skill and might' (lines 13–14); God is the Artist, even a Sidney is only a reflection of that skill, and then only coming close to it if his attention is focused on God, not on ambition or self-love:

> Mans soule of endles beauties image is,
> Drawne by the worke of endlesse skill and might:
> This skilfull might gave many sparkes of blisse,   15
> And to discerne this blisse a native light.
> To frame Gods image as his worthes requirde:
> His might, his skill, his word, and will conspirde.

Southwell's agenda was in part to improve the creative aspirations of the English, and here he makes his hope explicit. The soul is forged by the great

Artist as the image of perfect, divine beauty, capable, through its own, lesser 'native light', of discerning the 'sparkes of blisse' given off by its creator. God has used a creative foursome of elements to make it: power ('All that he had his image should present'), skill ('All that it should present he could afford'), will ('To that he could afford his will was bent'), and word ('His will was followed with performing word') (lines 19–22). Southwell then wraps up these divine attributes in the grammar of good intention: 'Let this suffice, by this conceive the rest, | He should, he could, he would, he did the best' – and so can you, he leaves it to his reader to add, conflating God's creative capabilities in producing the Incarnation with man's in reflecting the beauty of it (lines 23–4). The skill is God's, the result a creature imbued with a 'native light' of its own with which to reflect God's artistry, Sidney's ambitious individuality, certainly, but now redirected outwards and upwards towards its Original in Christianised Neoplatonic mode. This should not, in my view, be seen as the standard pious exhortation to turn away from life; nor do I think Southwell's Jesuit training and way of proceeding would have allowed him to expect such a thing of his readership; the full engagement with the senses required by the *Exercises* requires full engagement with the world. Southwell praises the richness of human memory-stores, which contain those 'heavenly sights, | A breefe wherein all marvailes summed lye. | Of fayrest formes, and sweetest shapes the store' (lines 3–5), but also the human mind's ability to add value to that Platonic memory-ideal, enhancing and extending those memories 'Most gracefull all, *yet thought may grace them more*' (l. 6; my emphasis). The wideness of God's creation is a source of inspiration and a site for godly meditation, not something to be feared. This is the writing of a man who has been outside the walls of the Citadel and has learned to find God where he can in a wider world, not the uncompromising ascetic suggested by some critical interpretations.

GOD'S NUMBERED UNIVERSE: SOUTHWELL'S DIVINE SYMMETRY

Southwell's was ultimately the authority of priest and martyr; poetry was the way he chose to express that authority, imitating as it did the numerically perfect Creation, the cross-action of divine grace as experienced by humanity. The first stanza of 'Christs bloody sweat' as it appears in McDonald and Brown's 1967 edition, based on the printed texts, is just another of Southwell's disciplined verses on elements of the Passion. An alert reader would, however, notice a perpendicular as well as the more usual horizontal structure, patterned on four 'columns' in the first four lines. This structure is made graphic in the relative privacy of the 'Waldegrave' Manuscript, however, where the poem becomes an embodiment of the numerically patterned and reciprocal beauty of God's cosmos in its paired and mated concordances, poetically observed and described within the neat and narrow frame of Southwell's poetic authority:

> Fat soile, full spring, sweet olive, grape of blisse,
> That yeelds, that streams, that pours, that dost distil,
> Untild, undrawne, unstampt, untoucht of presse,
> Deare fruit, clear brookes, faire oile, sweet wine at will:
> Thus Christ unforst prevents in shedding blood
> The whips, the thornes, the nailes, the speare, and roode.[41]

Fatt soyle,	full springe,	sweete olive,	grape of blisse
That yeldes,	that streames,	that powres,	that dost distil
Untild,	undrawne,	unstampde,	untouchd of presse
Deare fruit,	cleare brooks,	fayre oyle,	sweete wine at will
Thus Christ unforc'd preventes in shedding bloode			5
The whippes the thornes the nailes the speare and roode.[42]			

This links Southwell's poetic with more esoteric Renaissance interests in Moorish sciences and Jewish studies based on the cabala, interests which produced such prodigies as astrology, alchemy, conjuration of spirits, and especially graphic magic such as the word square:

```
R O T A S
A R E P O
T E N E T
O P E R A
S A T O R
```

As in the ROTAS–SATOR square, Southwell's poem contains vertical as well as horizontal relationships, in a direct graphical imitation of each individual drop of Christ's sweat as it rolls down his face; the result is far more subtle than any of its later imitators' shape-poetry. The conflation of the blood, sweat and tears Christ shed during his agony in Gethsemane with various liquid comestibles should not surprise, coming from a writer who believed he consumed Christ's actual body and blood, willingly offered as food, and, more importantly, who was authorised to administer such a miracle food to others. Southwell is here administering in the magic of poetic numbers the holy emanations of Christ's Passion, just as he would if giving Holy Communion. This poem becomes the written testament to that authority and that miracle in one. Read with the blocks of related meaning separated from each other by extra spacing, we have four separate poems, defining four different substances: wheat/bread, water, oil, and wine. The last element of the fourth of the downward set, 'at will', leads us out of the mere action of the moisture and into its significance (wine here linked to blood, as if caught in the very act of transubstantiation): Christ volunteered; the sacred substances are produced 'unforst' (l. 5). His freely offered emanations anticipate the enforced emanations of his crucifixion drawn out by the Five Wounds, 'The whips, the thornes, the nailes, the speare, and roode' (l. 6) (potent emblems in English Catholicism). The Latin-fluent Southwell gives 'prevents' a meaning closer to its Latin root, 'praevenire', the obliging anticipation of the wishes of others. Christ, by choosing self-sacrifice, offers freely what was supposed to be produced by force, neutralising the enemy's intentions and snatching back the initiative from the jaws of defeat. Southwell is creating a sacralised space for the blood of martyrs. 'He Pelicans, he Phenix fate doth prove' continues Southwell, opening out the number-square into the logical impossibility of paradox: 'How burneth bloud, how bleedeth burning love? | Can one in flame and streame both bathe and frie?' (lines 7–10). Christ bled but he did not burn; Southwell conflates Christ with Elias's sacred fire that burned beyond the power of natural flame, consuming everything including stones and water, then he attributes that consuming power to love: 'Such fire is love that fedd with gory bloode | Doth burne no lesse then in the dryest woode' (lines 17–18). Southwell has prefigured Christ's sacrifice, but he has also reminded his reader of the gore and fire of contemporary martyrdoms, thereby 'preventing' also his own. It ought not to be forgotten that he is, in this, contemplating open-eyed his own death, the 'performing deed' where he at last becomes part of the 'Performing Word'. No part of this poem appears in the first collection of Southwell's work (Wolfe, 1595, STC 22957, a or b). The first two stanzas, clever and Gospel-related, were printed in the *Moeonae* (STC 22955), the second-string edition of Southwell's poetry, but the last stanzas, clearly related to more modern martyrs, were not.[43]

The artful structuring and logic-games break bounds in the last stanza, escaping from the merely authorial into the divine sphere via Southwell's own intended martyrdom. It is 'no less than a prayer to be subsumed into figures, to have one's body transformed into a text of typological correspondences, and [...] a preparatory contemplation of the nature of Southwell's own martyrdom':[44]

> O sacred Fire come shewe thy force on me
> That sacrifice to Christe I may retorne,   20
> If withered wood for fuell fittest bee,
> If stones and dust, yf fleshe and blood will burne,
> I withered am and stonye to all good,
> A sacke of dust, a masse of fleshe and bloode.

This is no longer an exhortation to other minds, but a statement of personal intent. Too hot for secular poets to handle in its ambitions for the author, perhaps, but a stirring hint to other poets of what an authorship entirely committed to the integrity of its art could achieve.

LAST LINES: SOUTHWELL'S FIRST AND LAST PUBLIC SERMON

Poetry, however interesting, only goes so far. The Catholic Queen had not been saved; the avenging hosts had not come down on their enemies, nor, with Philip now infirm, were they likely to do so. Southwell's family had turned their backs on him, his family home was lost, his father ruined, and Southwell had watched, helpless, as friend after friend went to the gallows to die dreadful deaths for a cause that must have begun at times to seem a forlorn hope, that hopelessness itself being a black sin to add to any sense of failure in his mission he might have felt in his darker moments.

In 1590 Southwell wrote 'I am living in the very mouth of Hell'.[45] Efforts to capture him were at fever pitch by 1591. Something about his activities had alarmed the authorities, and not, it appears, just those of the English State; the secret Catholic presses that had so busied themselves with his *Epistle* in 1587–88 and his sermons on Magdalen in 1591 fell still over his last piece of writing, *An Humble Supplication*, probably written late in 1591.[46] Did *An Humble Supplication* demonstrate, as Brownlow has argued, a hair's breadth too far beyond the mission agenda given him in Rome?[47] Was it a step too close to Bellarmine's complex arguments on papal authority? If so, time has softened the perspective. In the Jesuit church at Farm Street in London there is a booklet which describes *An Humble Supplication* as 'a highly important document' that has been 'shamefully ignored'.[48]

Southwell, writing in furious response to a proclamation of Burghley's issued in the autumn of 1591 in an attempt to smear seminary priests, threw aside all past habits of disguise, addressing the Babington plot head on and attacking a government which, he said, had used the plot to 'net such green wits as [...] might easily be overwrought by Master Secretary's subtle and sifting wit' (*Supplication*, p. 18).[49] The unfairness of the deaths of Tichborne and friends had at last been addressed overtly – they were not fair game, unlike the priests. Yet, he wrote to the Queen, 'it hath been objected sometimes against priests that they should pretend to kill your sacred person'; not only was the mission priest addressing himself to the hottest of political issues, but addressing himself directly (ostensibly) to the monarch, bypassing all his proper channels of authority. He is not criticising Fortuna any more, but calling down Elizabeth's royal justice upon the head of Master Secretary Burghley, characterised almost as Aragnoll to Babington's Clarion. The regicide that Burghley suggests is planned by Catholic priests would be 'so contrary to their calling, so far from their thoughts, so void from all policy, that whosoever will afford reason her right, cannot with reason think them so foolish to wish, much less to work such a thing' (*Supplication*, p. 32). Burghley does not 'afford reason her right'. Southwell here sets his authority as a priest apart from Elizabeth's as a prince;

in doing so, he is also, by implication, going some way towards acknowledging that the laws of the Papal See do not obtain in England. He no longer insists upon his papal priestly authority but appeals, as an English subject, to English laws of equity, and to the monarch's own sense of justice in order to make his case for the unjust and unreasonable behaviour of Burghley's government. This surely represents something of a sea-change in Southwell's view of the matter.[50]

Perhaps this is less of a change than an altered rhetoric, though. Southwell's private views can be guessed at through his letters and other writings, but he was always the master of whatever rhetorical framework he was writing in, adapting his communication to its dialogical requirements, be it diary, lyric, letter, or sermon. Here, Southwell is rehearsing in rhetoric the process of lawful petition allowed any English subject (in theory); his use of this form is not necessarily a sign of a softening of his attitude, however: the death in Marshalsea of his relative Richard Shelley demonstrated to ordinary English subjects that such justice did not obtain in practice. Just as his holy hymns replaced missing metaphysical counterparts such as intercession by the Virgin or transubstantiation, this, through using a rhetoric appropriate to real petitions, draws attention to the lack of an ordered, merciful justice in England and interrogates Elizabeth's adoption of the Virgin's mantle of Mercy.

Had it been widely released, it would have found a home in many English hearts, and not just Catholic ones, but that does not make it any truer a depiction of Southwell's inner thoughts. It reflects Southwell's assessment that an insistence on the legal primacy of the Pope will no longer be helpful in the English debate at that particular moment.[51]

More importantly, perhaps, Southwell, in denying Burghley's accusations of murderous intent, insists upon his right to die:

> We come to shed our own, not to seek the effusion of others' blood. We carry our desires so high lifted above such savage purposes, that we rather hope to make our own martyrdoms our steps to a glorious eternity, than others' deaths our purchase of eternal dishonour.[52]

So utterly had the English State removed every possibility of decent continuation of faith and loyalty from the recusant community served by Southwell that the only high ground left to him was a martyr's death. He had envisioned the scene of that death clearly, as he was trained to do in the Exercises, and seen how easily it could be made to look like that of some regicidal wretch. He could not allow the State to throw weeds into the crop he was making of himself, ruining the harvest towards which his whole mission had been growing with smears of malevolence and illegality. *An Humble Supplication* was, in part, his sweeping-clean of his own threshing floor, with characteristic Jesuit thoroughness.

Robert Southwell

There was 'nowhere left to hide', as Garnet wrote to Acquaviva from London in February 1592.[53] Political determination, increasingly detailed spy reports, and the missioners' own efforts were combining to box the Jesuits in; Southwell was sent off for another recuperative tour of the country. Dark as things seemed, somewhere in his dangerous travels up and down the wintry country, Southwell had created his English Joseph, Magdalen, and Peter; he had restored an English Virgin, helping to repair, at least in poetry, her shrine now in ruins at Walsingham. If Byrd's holy music was sad, it was still sounding, there was a well-established network of priests ministering quietly to the Catholic families of England, and there were still young men coming through Southwell's London entry-point from the seminaries on the Continent.

Once back in the capital after his travels in youthful company, probably having written 'The burning Babe', as well as some of his more playful lyrics, Southwell clearly made the most of his time. Chomley (who also accused Marlowe of atheism) reported 'Mr Cuthwell, a Jesuit' at the houses of Dr Smythe and Mr Cotton in Fleet Street. Long ago, John Cotton had been Southwell's first companion to the Continent; 'Mr. Cotton' had been Southwell's cover name on his English travels, and he was taken under that name by the pursuivant Topcliffe.[54] The wheel was come round full circle.

He had been active for exactly six years, a remarkably long time compared with other missioners in England.[55] The time for action had come and gone. Most of the young Hamlets of his acquaintance, when faced with the sticking-point, had prevaricated or fled, or been outwitted and taken, but Southwell's ministry had survived. His sermons, *Magdalen* and *Epistle*, had been printed and disseminated; his poetry was spread in manuscript as befitted a gentleman. He had been busy with his reports to the Continent and his duties to incoming priests and existing recusant families; special works were in train: *Triumphs* and *St Peter*, *A Short Rule of Good Life*; *Humble Supplication* was finished late in 1591.[56] He had helped keep unhappy Arundel staunch, and played a major part in establishing a basis for a new English poetic that resisted the distorting pull of patronage and insisted, on the strength of its own authorial integrity, upon its right to be written and heard, building (perhaps on Sidneian foundations) a stronger moral or creative imperative. He seems to have helped create the basis for an undogmatic English holy writing. A glimpse at William Byrd's 'playlist' for the years of Southwell's mission show many songs that echo Southwell's poetic preoccupations as presented in the first editions of his poetry, Wolfe's and Cawood's of 1595, especially the complaints. Byrd's list is not predicated upon Southwell by any means, but one can see the centrality to both men of the same set of themes, approaches and moods.

One theme that is not to be found in Sidney's poetic or Byrd's selection (apart from the protest about Campion) is that celebrating martyrdom. In Sidney there is a sense of impotence: his heroic furies end in loss or suicide.

The 'performing Word': Southwell's sacralised poetic

In Byrd, the sad elegy is there, and the gentle protest of the complaint, as if the music itself stands in place of action; only Southwell's poetry is able to insist on total commitment to the cause: the poetry is part of the 'performing deed' that in his case must end, in Protestant England, in death. To Southwell it was where the two personae of poet and priest, and the twin lines of persuasion and violence separated out in his diary, came together. His Passion performance of Christ becomes the unifying element of his life in England, and his poetic production bears on it over and over again.

His dual role had suited his mission purpose of re-engagement of English hearts and minds, in the manner of Campion's mission; but it was, as for Campion, a trap. It was the necessary but dangerous performing deed of his ministry that enabled his pursuers to catch up with him at last.

Accounts of Southwell's end generally agree. Southwell's description had at last been given by another priest who had known him in Rome, one of that group of English students that had caused him such grief in 1584. Sent from Valladolid to join the secret English mission by Persons, despite Southwell's earlier warnings, John Cecil, with Fixer, Blount, and Warnford, had made use of Southwell's priest network, obtaining clothes and money in the house at Lincoln's Inn. Cecil had been arrested suspiciously soon after his arrival in England in 1591, and immediately told all to Robert Cecil (identified in transcripts only as 'John Snowden').[57] They sold the secret narrative of the priests' entry into England – the arrivals in hidden creeks, disguised as 'Soldiers, Mariners, Merchants', some coming disguised 'as gentlemen with contrary names in comely apparel, as though they had travelled in foreign countries for knowledge'. Some acted the part of 'Ruffians', not to be suspected of being 'Friars, Priests, Jesuits or Popish scholars' on their way to the universities, or into the service of 'Noble men, ladies and gentlemen', where they would insinuate themselves by 'hypocrisies' into the household, to perform priestly offices.[58] Southwell's arrest by Richard Topcliffe on 26 June 1592 followed hard upon the heels of this disclosure.

Southwell had left plague-ridden London on 26 June for Warwickshire, perhaps making for the Ferrers house at Baddesley Clinton. Rented at that time by the Vaux sisters, it provided a welcoming retreat for the Jesuits, although they had been sent to ground by pursuivants there on one of their regular meetings.[59] Southwell was persuaded to stop and give Holy Communion to the Bellamy household at Uxenden near Harrow on his way, just as Campion had been sidetracked from his road north in 1581 by his priestly responsibilities. The imprisoned Anne Bellamy knew of the visit to her family home; she also knew where the priest-holes were.[60] Topcliffe was beside himself at taking the now notorious Southwell, secreting him away from Privy Council eyes in his private torture chamber, and writing directly to the Queen for permission to torture Southwell, not to the Privy Council; perhaps this is why Garnet, who appears to have had reliable, regular intelligence from someone who knew Council business, knew nothing about it for some days.[61]

By the time of Southwell's arrest Garnet was writing that London was altogether too 'whot' for comfort, but whatever waverings Southwell had occasionally been prey to, it says much for the faith Garnet had in Southwell's constancy after capture that he carried on with the same round where Southwell had left off, writing to Verstegan, their contact on the Continent, that 'my marchant was arrested, but his elder brother hathe undertaken his busynesse'.[62] The elder brother was Garnet himself, of course, the language that of Campion's and Person's 'business' letters from the 1580s mission. Southwell was at last a full partner in the bloody enterprise.

Perhaps sensitive to the sort of international accusations of barbarity raised in Southwell's own reports, the Queen appears to have given Topcliffe permission to torture Southwell using a new method guaranteed to get results whilst leaving no incriminating marks (what might now be termed 'stress posture').[63] On Topcliffe's failure to produce results, which really says much for the young priest's spiritual strength, an official order was made on 28 July 1592 for Southwell to be received by the lieutenant of the Tower and 'kept close prisoner so that no one may be suffered access to him but such anyone as Topcliffe shall appoint as his keeper [to which has been added] Herein we require you to take this order for his close restraining, he being a most lewd and dangerous person'.[64] Southwell's absolute isolation was unusual (and quite unlike Father Weston's at Wisbech); he was clearly considered to be too dangerous to allow writing and visits. He took with him a Bible, a breviary Garnet had sent him and the works of St Bernard, apparently given by the Countess of Arundel.[65] Garnet wrote to Acquaviva on 4 September that Southwell was safe from his torturers in the Tower, forbidden visits but being treated with some humanity by the lieutenant of the Tower (Sir Richard Berkeley) at least.[66]

For eight months after his imprisonment Southwell continued to refuse to identify himself as anything other than a gentleman. Then he at last acquired paper and pens and wrote to Sir Robert Cecil, identifying himself and asking to be tried and sentenced, probably in part to forestall accusations that he was ashamed of his ministry and mission.

Southwell had been Garnet's only Jesuit assistant and close companion, certainly until John Gerard's arrival in 1588, and his loss seems to have unhinged Garnet to some extent. 'At last it has happened', he wrote to Acquaviva in two letters in the weeks after the capture, 'Our very gentle dear companion has been captured by pirates, and now in a broken and battered vessel we are sailing without a helmsman.'[67] A Hamlet could betray his false companions to escape such exigencies; a priest, in good conscience, could not. Verstegan writes that Southwell would not reply when asked whether he acted for the Pope or the King of Spain, telling them that he was afraid they would make

The 'performing Word': Southwell's sacralised poetic

inferences from whatever he said, thereby getting more from him than he knew.[68] All Southwell would say was that he was 'a priest and a religious man, true to the Queen and State, free from all treasons, only doing and attending to his functions'.[69]

His execution was by no means assured after his captivity. There was some talk of ransom, and Southwell's unusually long and close imprisonment suggests hopes among members of the Council that that he would just fade away, perhaps to return eventually to Europe, broken in health like Weston, a weapon put beyond use.[70] Acquaviva forbade this: having done his utmost to talk the lamb out of going to the altar, he was now insisting that he lie on it. The ransoming of English Jesuits, as he told Garnet shortly after Southwell's capture, could expose the Society 'to criticism and scandal'.[71] There is no suggestion that Southwell himself asked for quarter.

Southwell appears to have given nothing away under torture or in his dreary confinement, despite his fears of failing through weakness. Garnet later told Acquaviva that Southwell had remained 'dumb as a tree stump' throughout.[72] Garnet could now counter Elizabeth's *semper eadem* with his own motto for Southwell: *semper pertinax* – always constant.[73]

On 21 February 1595 a 'notorious criminal was led to Tyburn with all the public notice that could be arranged'. No doubt many wanted to see the celebrity's last jig; Garnet wrote that 'almost all the city went out to see the execution and knew nothing of what was happening to Father Robert'. What was happening was Southwell's trial, arranged at a moment's notice after his seemingly interminable imprisonment. A few days before, as Garnet reported, he had been pushed into Limbo, 'a subterranean cell of evil repute where condemned felons await the hangman's stroke',[74] to weaken him and further spoil his standing before his trial. The execution of a 'highwayman' on the day of Southwell's trial is also noted in Grosart; all commentators seem in general agreement that the haste with which his trial was brought and the fact that Southwell was quickly hanged after a rapid condemnation (after only a fifteen-minute deliberation, according to Caraman) suggest an attempt to divert popular attention and deny Southwell a platform from which to speak.[75]

There seemed no good reason to condemn Southwell other than his now illegal priestly calling: he had been accused of no other crime.[76] Southwell based his defence, such as it was, on the unacceptability of the 1585 law that had made it treasonous to be a Roman Catholic priest. By refocusing attention upon the detail of the new law designed to disempower foreign-trained priests he exposed its weakness. How could it be right that a pious, loyal Englishman could be executed for offering the Mass of ancient tradition to his fellow-Christians, fellow Englishmen who had asked him to minister to them as a priest? Who, on earth, had the authority to make such alterations to precedent? To repeat these concerns is to synopsise his English poetry, so closely were the purposes of his mission and his writing intertwined.

Garnet was concerned with the spiritual aspects of Southwell's incarceration, an exile from the comforts of the sacraments far worse than that endured by his English congregation; this would certainly be a test of the powers of the rosary Southwell had been given to substitute for the real presence of the priest and sacraments. Perhaps anxious to show its efficacy, as well as the toughness of Society fibre, Garnet's letters deal with Southwell's strength in transcending spiritual handicaps, his ability, whilst never once being able 'to celebrate Mass or to confess himself or to speak with anyone who might bring him a little consolation' to come forth at last 'with such an undaunted spirit, so calm and serene, that it seemed that he had been with a company of angelic souls'.[77]

Garnet's letters about his companion's semi-mystical ability to appear serene without recourse to the sacraments are explicit: the young victim, from the moment of his disappearance into prison, was being converted into part of the body of Christ by sharing in his Passion. This is more than a trope – Garnet, through his 'mystical fellowship' with the imprisoned Southwell, was 'one of the first Englishmen to develop at some length St. Paul's doctrine of the mystical body of Christ';[78] he was locating his brother within Christ's Wounds. This identification as the actual body of Christ made the suffering endurable: 'Stricken as we are we feel that God through his sufferings will enhance his glory, strengthen his church and confound his enemies'; 'What seems insufferable for one person, when it is shared by all the members [of the mystical body] becomes sweet indeed, not by any means because it is less severe, but by reason of the love that binds us all together'.[79]

Southwell himself made a considerable effort to manage his last act; sick and weary as he no doubt was, he is recorded addressing the crowd bravely from the platform at Tyburn; it is likely that those in the crowd were waiting in silence to hear the last set-piece of a popular or notorious sermoniser and poet, of course.[80] Via his already disseminated sermons, not to mention the manuscripts of his poetry that had found their way into various hands, his English readership had been given certain expectations of him as a courageous victim which the State seemed equally determined to have him disappoint. Their prolonged harsh treatment of their prisoner and the nature of his death were intended to work to the detriment of his cause, showing him as a traitor, something outlandish and hostile. It was the popular Englishness of his Catholicism, as expressed in his poetry and prose, that had made him dangerous; in the international arena, such writing would tend to lose its nationalistic appeal, but here in the capital such appeals could be incendiary.

Once it became clear that they must send Southwell, however briefly, into the not fully controllable public arena, the representatives of the State seemed most anxious to prevent controversial outbursts, but Southwell now held centre stage: he had his pulpit at last.

The 'performing Word': Southwell's sacralised poetic

Strapped to the hurdle, he had tried to keep his head up and away from the road's muck on the long haul to Tyburn, anxious to present the most dignified appearance possible; he must have aroused some pity in the crowd as he stood in his shift in the wintry air, trying to wipe the filth from his face with a handkerchief. Once on the scaffold he may have remembered a time of pain and fear from his novitiate, fifteen years ago, because he repeated, in Latin, the words that had been used in his diary to quiet his fears: 'if we live, we live to the Lord, or if we die, we die to the Lord. Whether we live or whether we die we are the Lord's'.[81]

Here was a new panel of the English College martyr cycle, coming to life in England: a Paul speaking to the Romans at Tyburn. As with his poetry, there is more here than meets the eye; in using Latin Southwell was addressing the educated in the audience, men like Mountjoy, there to witness his dispatch, and even the English churchmen. They would have known that in the preceding verse St Paul had told the Romans that no man is an island: 'none of us liveth to himself, and no man dieth to himself (Romans 14.7); Southwell was telling his Jesuit brothers, at least, that he was in immediate hope of entering into the body of Christ through his wounds and death, but any English churchmen listening would have understood this message, too, and knew that they could not easily alter its spiritual implications.

But after the verse quoted by Southwell, Paul asks 'why dost thou judge thy brother? Or why dost thou set at nought thy brother? For we shall all stand before the judgement seat of Christ [...] let us not therefore judge one another any more: but judge this rather, that no man put a stumblingblock or an occasion to fall in his brother's way' (verses 10–13). This implied text is intended for the English churchmen, the Jesuit priest's estranged brothers in Christ. Southwell's words seem, when investigated at their source, to reprove, certainly, but also to plead for a wider toleration of different approaches to God.

In English, for the wider crowd, he had admitted frankly and with pride to his priesthood and membership of the Society of Jesus, acknowledged his sufferings to be the way to spiritual regeneration, and prayed for the Queen, the country, and his own soul. The crowd muttered at the attempts of the Chaplain of the Tower to trip him on the stumbling-block of religious controversy, attempts quietly refused by the young Jesuit.[82] His was not to be the fate of the Babington plotters; the crowd demanded that he be fully hanged before being taken down to be butchered, Lord Mountjoy adding his voice to their insistence that Southwell be allowed to die as cleanly as was possible in the days before the 'long drop'. None the less, he had long enough to offer himself into God's hands, and Caraman tells us that on removal the young man's heart leaped in the hangman's grasp.[83]

Garnet, overwrought, wrote twice to Acquaviva the next day, trying to work through his feelings. 'Whether I should be sorry now or glad, I do not know.

My sorrow is that I have lost my most dear and loved companion; my gladness, that the man I have cherished so much has risen to the throne of God'. He described Southwell as an 'unvanquished soldier of Christ, my most faithful subject and the bravest of martyrs, once my closest companion and brother, now my patron, lord and ruler together with Christ in his empire'.[84] Southwell had effected, at least in the minds of his life's readership, the translation from maker of words to the Word Itself, from poet to patron.

Before his poetry was released to them, the public wanted a piece of the martyr himself. Even before his death the event was beginning to crystallise into the mythical, as if his body was already dissolving into relics: his more reverent biographers note every word, every item of clothing handed out to the crowd. Some managed to dip cloths in his blood after the butchering was done, or offered the hangman money for pieces of bone or hair. The body, exposed by the authorities to show how ordinarily helpless it was, inside and out, had none the less been pre-written, claimed for God as the body of a martyr. No one who had read or attended the Jesuit's sermons, taken the Host from his hands, or heard of his courage in defying Topcliffe could fail to see the gory chunks and tatters of what had been a man as anything other than glorious trophies in the martyrological rag-and-bone shop of the heart. 'I have a rosary which he threw from the scaffold and also the bone of one of his knees', Garnet wrote to Acquaviva on 1 May 1595.[85] He also had the breviary that he had sent to Southwell on his transfer to the Tower. It had come back with enigmatic additions: no writing in ink, presumably because he had none, but the word 'Jesus' and 'My God, and my all' scratched into it with a pin.[86] In the light of Garnet's mystic transubstantiation of imitator into Christ, the 'Jesus' scratched on the breviary begins to take on the aura of a signature.

NOTES

1 Robert Southwell, 'Looke home', from James H. McDonald and Nancy Pollard Brown (eds), *The Poems of Robert Southwell, S.J.* (Oxford: Clarendon Press, 1967), p. 57, lines 19–24; hereafter M&B; further references to Southwell's poems are from this edition, given as page/line numbers in the text.

2 Greville was, as Gary Waller puts it, 'uneasily aware that the ideals Sidney represented had failed'; as a Protestant, he was certain that he was subject to 'the absolute incompatibility of man's actions with God's will'; see Gary Waller, *English Poetry of the Sixteenth Century* (Harlow: Longman, 1986), p. 131. Southwell's Suárezian *scientia media* was a useful riposte to such doubts. See Barbara Kiefer Lewalski, *Protestant Poetics and the Seventeenth Century Religious Lyric* (Princeton, NJ, Princeton University Press, 1979), p. ix. 'The purpose [of the Ignatian *Exercises*] was to enable an exercisant to develop a plan for a modern life lived outside the Church in an increasingly secular society: a decision-making system, a method of self-appraisal that emphasised the importance of the (right-thinking) self in autonomous acts of discernment. It was a model that could be effective to any Christian in a secularising world, though; subsequent Protestant

The 'performing Word': Southwell's sacralised poetic

interest in medieval and even Catholic meditational texts shows how far this was the case [...] Jesuit and other devotional tracts were imported into Britain towards the end of the sixteenth century and "borrowed", even those by Jesuit authors, and even by Puritan communities. A devotional work by de Piñeda of the Inquisition appeared in the town library of Puritan Ipswich, for instance'; from Anne Sweeney, 'Robert Southwell's English Lyrics: Authorial Integrity on the Mission to Elizabethan England (1580–1595)', unpublished doctoral thesis (Lancaster University, 2004), pp. 26–7; see also Anthony Milton, 'Qualified Intolerance: the Limits and Ambiguities of Early Stuart Anti-Catholicism', in Arthur F. Marotti (ed.), *Catholicism and Anti-Catholicism in Early Modern English Texts* (Basingstoke: Macmillan, 1999), pp. 85–109 (p. 85).

3 For a work investigating the circumstances surrounding Southwell's formation as a Jesuit, see Thomas M. McCoog, S.J. (ed.), *The Mercurian Project: Forming Jesuit Culture, 1572–1580* (Rome: Institutum Historicum Societatis Iesu, 2004).

4 Robert Southwell, *Spiritual Exercises and Devotions*, ed. J. M. de Buck and trans. P. E. Hallett (London: Sheed and Ward, 1931), no. 21.2, p. 30; hereafter *SE&D*.

5 Michael E. Williams, *The Venerable English College Rome: A History 1579–1979* (London: Associated Catholic Publications (on behalf of the College), 1979), p. 9; the painting, reproduced in pl. 64, is discussed in Gauvin Alexander Bailey, *Between Renaissance and Baroque: Jesuit Art in Rome, 1565–1610* (Toronto: University of Toronto Press, 2003), pp. 158–9; hereafter cited in the text.

6 See Bailey, p. 159; see also Alexandra Hertz, 'Imitators of Christ: The Martyr-Cycles of Late Sixteenth Century Rome Seen in Context', *Storia dell'Arte*, 62 (1988), 53–70 (p. 65).

7 Garnet to Acquaviva, 16 July 1592; 26 July 1592, Westminster Archives, 4, 305; quoted in Philip Caraman, S.J., *A Study in Friendship: Saint Robert Southwell and Henry Garnet* (Saint Louis, MO: The Institute of Jesuit Sources, 1995), pp. 82–3; hereafter cited in the text.

8 John W. O'Malley, *The First Jesuits* (Cambridge, MA: Harvard University Press, 1993), p. 83; hereafter cited in the text.

9 Southwell's use of 'phere' (fere) is interesting here: it was a Chaucerian archaism, meaning a companion of the way, a mate, even a spouse. Spenser was to use it at the end of Canto III of his *Faerie Queene*, Book IV, printed in 1596, a year after Southwell's death.

10 It is very similar to the diary entry on communion commemorating his joining the Society, where he is exhorted to feel like St Catherine of Siena offering herself to 'her Spouse [...] overwhelmed with love and tenderness', or as Mary awaiting the incoming of God, accompanied by the blisses of a heavenly marriage-bed; from 'Preparation for Communion', *SE&D*, pp. 9–10.

11 One wonders, given the Jesuit connections of Shakespeare's schoolmaster, John Cottam, whether his promising Stratford pupil had been given an early glimpse of such an imaginative empowerment, and if so, what he would have made of it, once away from Stratford and relatively free of religious scruple. Shakespeare, at least in his theatricals, recognises the pragmatic uses of artistic inspiration, and often has his (male) characters gleefully embrace the less elevated uses to which a poet's imagination can be put, something Southwell preached hard against in prose and poetry. If Shakespeare had been taught the affective powers of literature, then, he did not care to put it to pious use, and even laughs at such uses. In *Two Gentlemen of Verona*, for instance, Proteus, acting as the absolute reversal of a spiritual director, teaches the Duke how to win his

love in terms of envisaging her as a goddess, using music to carry his praise to her 'For Orpheus' lute was strung with poets' sinews, | Whose golden touch could soften steel and stones'; see Stanley Wells and Gary Taylor (eds), *The Oxford Shakespeare Complete Works* (Oxford: Clarendon Press, 1988), III.2.77–8; hereafter cited in the text. John Cottam and his family were recusants; his brother Thomas entered the Jesuit novitiate in 1579, and was executed in 1582 for carrying Catholic items to the Stratford area; see Park Honan, *Shakespeare: A Life* (Oxford: Oxford University Press, 1998), pp. 63–4; see also Eric Sams, *The Real Shakespeare: Retrieving the Early Years, 1564–1594* (New Haven: Yale University Press, 1995), p. 203, n. 99. See Peter Milward, S.J., *Shakespeare's Religious Background* (London: Sidgwick and Jackson, 1973); Milward also discusses this in 'Shakespeare's Jesuit Schoolmasters', in Richard Dutton, Alison Findlay, and Richard Wilson (eds), *Lancastrian Shakespeare: Theatre and Religion* (Manchester: Manchester University Press, 2003), pp 58–70.

12 F. W. Brownlow, *Robert Southwell*, Twayne's English Authors Series, 516 (New York: Simon & Schuster Macmillan, 1996), pp. 106–10; hereafter cited in the text.

13 See Sidney's *Defence of Poesie*, in Richard Dutton (ed.), *Sir Philip Sidney: Selected Writings* (Manchester: Carcanet, 1987), further references, cited in the text as *Defence*, are from this edition; see also Giordano Bruno, *The Heroic Frenzies*, trans. Paul Eugene Memmo, University of North Carolina Studies in Romance Languages and Literatures Series, 50 (Chapel Hill; Valencia printed: University of North Carolina Press, 1964), for a discussion of late Renaissance theories of Neoplatonic creativity.

14 See John Saward, *The Beauty of Holiness and the Holiness of Beauty: Art, Sanctity and the Truth of Catholicism* (San Francisco: Ignatius Press, 1997), pp. 77–8; hereafter cited in the text. None of Southwell's English lyrics is in this category, on the face of it. Southwell was writing largely 'religious art', and clearly had a well-developed sense of what Brian Oxley calls 'the artifice of holy things, and ... the holiness of artifice'; from Brian Oxley, 'The Relation between Robert Southwell's Neo-Latin and English Poetry', *Recusant History*, 17.3 (May 1985), 201–7; hereafter cited in the text; see Brownlow, p. 109.

15 Saward, p. 89.

16 *Lectura super Ioannem*, cap. 1, lect. 2; Saward, p. 89; also see Robert J. O'Connell, *Art and the Christian Intelligence in St Augustine* (Oxford: Blackwell, 1978).

17 George Puttenham, *The Arte of English Poesie*, ed. Gladys Doidge Willcock and Alice Walker (London: R. Field, 1589; repr. London: Cambridge University Press, 1970), p. 28.

18 For a discussion of possible points of contact or overlap, see Katherine Duncan-Jones, 'Sir Philip Sidney's debt to Edmund Campion', in Thomas M. McCoog, S.J. (ed.), *The Reckoned Expense: Edmund Campion and the Early English Jesuits* (Woodbridge: Boydell, 1996), pp. 85–102.

19 I use the account laid out by Richard Dutton in his introduction to *Sidney: Selected Writings*.

20 See *Canons and Decrees of the Council of Trent*, trans. H. J. Schroeder (Rockford, IL: Tan Books, 1982).

21 Philip Sidney, *Defence*, lines 298–300; Robert Southwell, 'The Author to his loving Cosen', prefatory letter to *Saint Peters Complaint* (1595), in M&B, p. xxxv.

22 Southwell, 'To his Loving Cosen', p. lvii.

23 *Defence*, lines 152–70, p. 106; Southwell, 'To his Loving Cosen', p. lvii.

The 'performing Word': Southwell's sacralised poetic

24 *Sir Philip Sidney: Defence of Poesie, Astrophil and Stella, and Other Writings* (London: Dent, 1997), p. xliii.

25 See Francis Yates, *Giordano Bruno and the Hermetic Tradition* (London: Routledge & Kegan Paul, 1971); or Giordano Bruno, *The Heroic Frenzies*, trans. Paul Eugene Memmo, especially pp. 128–9.

26 Waller, p. 43.

27 Gary Kuchar, 'Southwell's "A Vale of Tears": a Psychoanalysis of Form', *Mosaic*, 34.1 (2001), 107–20 (p. 119).

28 'The Author to his loving Cosen', prefatory letter to *Saint Peters Complaint* (1595); M&B, p. lvii.

29 M&B, p. lxxviii.

30 See Roy Strong, *The Cult of Elizabeth: Elizabethan Portraiture and Pageantry* (London: Pimlico, 1999), p. 16.

31 Second Vatican Council, *Sacrosanctum concilium*, no. 60 (CCC 1667), quoted in Saward, pp. 84–5.

32 'Era de Cristo muy llagado', *Libro de la Vida*, chapter 9 of *Obres de Sta Teresa de Jesús*, ed. el p. Silverio de Santa Teresa, Biblioteca Mistica Carmelitana Seriès, 1 (Burgos: Tip. de 'El Monte Carmelo', 1915–24), p. 63; in English in E. Allison Peers (ed. and trans.), *The Complete Works of St Teresa of Jesus*, 3 vols (London: Sheed and Ward, 1946), I, 54; cited in Saward, p. 85.

33 See Brownlow, pp. 104–5; see Southwell's 'Poema de Assumptione B.V.M.', in Stonyhurst MS A.v.4, at Stonyhurst College, Clitheroe, Lancashire. See poem and translation in Peter Davidson and Anne Sweeney (ed. and intro), *The Collected Poems of St Robert Southwell, S.J.* (Manchester: Carcarnet, forthcoming). Martz, pp. 101–7.

34 See S. K. Heninger, Jr, *Touches of Sweet Harmony: Pythagorean Cosmology and Renaissance Poetics* (San Marino, CA: Huntington Library, 1974).

35 In the 'Waldegrave' MS (Stonyhurst MS A.v.27, now at the Jesuit Archives, Mount Street, London).

36 Brownlow, p. 109; see Alexander B. Grosart (ed.), *The Complete Poems of Robert Southwell, S.J.* (London: Robson, Fuller Worthies' Library, 1872), pp. 189–215; hereafter cited in the text. See also Brian Oxley, 'Southwell's Neo-Latin and English Poetry'. See Davidson and Sweeney.

37 'Mary Magdalens blush'; Marie Magdalens complaint at Christs death'; 'Times goe by turnes'; 'Looke home'; Fortunes Falsehoode'; 'Scorne not the least'; 'The Nativitie of Christ'; 'Christs Childhoode'; 'A childe my Choyce'; 'Content and rich'; 'Losse in delaies'; 'Loves servile lot' (with the last four stanzas of 'Seeke flowers of heaven', which is not in, substituted for lines 49–76; lines 49–76 are reinserted and the stanzas from 'flowers' omitted in Wolfe, 1595b). M&B, pp. lix. All these are relatively non-intellectual homiletic or complaint poems, focusing on love, the repentant female, the helpless child, and the weak.

38 Garnet to Acquaviva, 16 July 1592, in Christopher Devlin, *The Life of Robert Southwell Poet and Martyr* (London: Longmans, Green, 1956), p. 277; hereafter cited in the text; Caraman, pp. 74–5; M&B, pp. xxx–xxxi. Other possible candidates are the Countess of Arundel, the Vaux sisters, Dorothy Arundell – it is quite in keeping with Southwell's ministry to have kept a central 'pool' of his works to make up smaller collections suitable

to particular wants. Despite the reliance of the priests upon the ladies of recusant households evident in contemporary reports, the possibility that Southwell wrote poetry for female readers has not been discussed in any depth to date.

39 See Brownlow, p. 115.
40 Dutton, pp. 167–8, 178.
41 'Christs bloody sweat', lines 1–6, M&B, p. 18.
42 'Christs bloody sweate', lines 1–6, 'Waldegrave' MS (Stonyhurst MS A.v.27, now at the Jesuit Archives, Mount Street, London).
43 See M&B, p. 19.
44 Brownlow, p. 114.
45 From John Hungerford Pollen, S.J. (ed.), *Unpublished Documents relating to the English Martyrs*, Publications of the Catholic Record Society, 5 (London: Catholic Record Society, 1908), p. 332; hereafter CRS; quoted in Pierre Janelle, *Robert Southwell the Writer: A Study in Religious Inspiration* (London: Sheed and Ward, 1935), p. 49; hereafter cited in the text.
46 M&B, p. xxv.
47 Robert Southwell, *An Humble Supplication to Her Majesty*, ed. R. C. Bald (Cambridge: Cambridge University Press, 1953); hereafter *Humble Supplication*; see also Geoffrey Hill, 'The Absolute Reasonableness of Robert Southwell', in *The Lords of Limit* (New York: Oxford University Press, 1984); hereafter cited in the text.
48 Fiorella Sultana De Maria, *Robert Southwell: Priest, Poet and Martyr* (London: Catholic Truth Society, 2003), p. 32.
49 See Brownlow's discussion of this, p. 67. While allowing the justice of some of its claims, Brownlow calls parts of Burghley's Proclamation 'an affront to any decent standards of discourse', p. 64. Geoffrey Hill calls it 'wilful and monstrous cant', p. 24.
50 See Brownlow, p. 70.
51 R. C. Bald believed that Southwell had dropped the idea of Papal supremacy in English State matters by 1591; if Southwell was indeed influenced by Bellarmine's ideas of modified papal authority, he may well have been arguing that the secular monarch had legal rights, but only in order, it seems to me, to insist that the monarch also had legal responsibilities, and that these were being usurped and abused by counsellors such as Burghley. R. C. Bald, pp. xxi–xxii, quoted in Browlow, p. 71.
52 *An Humble Supplication*, p. 32; see Brownlow, p. 69.
53 Devlin, pp. 255–6.
54 *Calendar, S.P., Dom, 1591–1594*, vol. 241, no. 35 (?January 1592), p. 176, quoted in M&B, p. xxx; Janelle, p. 64; also referred to in Devlin, p. 215. See also 'Remembrance of words and matter against Richard Cholmeley', Brit. Mus., Harleian MSS 6848, fol. 190, for reference to Southwell's 'Epistle of Comfort' (Devlin, pp. 223, 267), which it was claimed was given to Cholmeley by Burghley: Southwell had a wide range of readership.
55 Patrick MacGrath and Joy Rowe, 'Anstruther Analysed: the Elizabethan Seminary Priests', *Recusant History*, 18.1 (May 1986), 1–13; cited in Frank Brownlow, 'Richard Topcliffe: Elizabeth's Enforcer and the representation of Power in *King Lear*', in Richard Dutton, Alison Findlay, and Richard Wilson (eds), *Lancastrian Shakespeare: Theatre and Religion* (Manchester: Manchester University Press, 2003), pp. 160–78 (n. 24, p. 176);

hereafter 'Topcliffe'.

56 Brownlow, p. 64; Pilarz, p. 229.

57 John Cecil was sent to England from the seminary at Valladolid. He claimed, among other things, that Robert Persons had instructed him to assess Lord Strange as a candidate for a Catholic succession, this being revealed 'to none but Southwell or Garnet'. *Calendar, S. P., Dom.*, 1591–1594, vol. 238, no. 160 (21 May), p. 39, and no. 179 (25 May), p. 45; M&B, p. xxx.

58 Devlin, pp. 227–8

59 Devlin, p. 277; Caraman, pp. 61–2; M&B, p. xxviii; an account of the incident is in John Gerard, S.J., *The Autobiography of an Elizabethan*, trans. and ed. Philip Caraman, S.J. (London: Longmans, Green, 1951), pp. 41–3.

60 Garnet to Acquaviva, 16 July 1592, in Devlin, p. 277; Caraman, pp. 74–5; M&B, pp. xxx–xxxi.

61 The incident is described without hyperbole by Brownlow, who has made a close study of Southwell's captor and torturer, Topcliffe, a man Elizabeth trusted enough to keep close throughout her reign; Brownlow, *Southwell*, p. 14, and 'Topcliffe', pp. 160–2. Brownlow shows a darker side of Elizabeth's Albion, arguing that Topcliffe corresponded directly with her, often bypassing the Council (p. 162), and that the true number of torturings ordered by Elizabeth is higher than that suggested by the official warrants: 'nearly double'; for a transcription of Topcliffe's letter to the Queen describing his plans for the torture of the captured Southwell, see Christobel M. Hood, *The Book of Robert Southwell* (Oxford: Blackwell, 1926), p. 48.

62 CRS, 52, p. 68; see M&B, p. xxv; see also Caraman, chapter 7, especially p. 85.

63 Brownlow, *Southwell*, pp. 14–15, and 'Topcliffe', pp. 161–3.

64 Privy Council Registers, X, fol. 504; in Caraman, p. 86.

65 Caraman, p. 87.

66 Garnet to Acquaviva, 8 October 1592 (the letter of 4 September had not arrived in Rome it seems), in Caraman, p. 88.

67 Garnet to Acquaviva, 16 July 1592; Garnet to Acquaviva, 26 July 1592, Westminster Archives, 4, 305; in Caraman, p. 78.

68 Richard Verstegan, despatch of 3 August 1592, CRS, 5, p. 212; in Janelle, p. 67.

69 Garnet, letter of 26 July 1592, in Christobel M. Hood, *The Book of Robert Southwell* (Oxford: Blackwell, 1926), p. 46; Janelle, p. 67.

70 Caraman, pp. 87, 93.

71 Acquaviva to Garnet, 10 October 1592, General Archives, S.J.: Flandro-Belgae, 1. 507; see M&B, p. xxxii; see also Janelle, p. 70.

72 Garnet to Acquaviva, 7 March 1595, MS transcript at Farm Street, London; quoted in Janelle, p. 66.

73 Garnet to Acquaviva, 16 July 1592, Garnet to Acquaviva, 26 July 1592, Westminster Archives, 4, 305; in Caraman, p. 81.

74 Garnet to Acquaviva, 22 February 1595, in Caraman, pp. 97, 95.

75 Grosart, p. lvii; Caraman, p. 106; Brownlow, p. 16.

76 All accounts of Southwell's trial come from the same few sources: *A briefe Discource of the condemnation of Mr Robert Southwell*, by an unnamed eyewitness, in Stonyhurst: Anglia XXXI, 1; 'The Relation of Thomas Leake, a Secular Priest', Stonyhurst: Anglia VI, in CRS, 5, pp. 333–6; Henry Garnet's two Italian letters, of 22 February, and 7 March 1595, Archives S.J., Rome: Anglia XXXI, 1; Henry Garnet to Claudio Acquaviva, 1 May 1595, in Caraman, n. 5, p. 99.

77 Garnet to Acquaviva, 22 February 1595, Archives S.J., Rome: Anglia, XXXI, I, fols 107–8, quoted in Caraman, p. 91.

78 Caraman, p. 83.

79 Garnet to Acquaviva, 16 July 1592, and 26 July 1592, Westminster Archives, 4, 305, quoted in Caraman, pp. 82–3.

80 Garnet's letter of 1 May 1595, in M&B, p. xxxiii; Devlin, p. 294.

81 'Whether we live or whether we die, we belong to Christ' (*SE&D*, p. 69); Caraman, p. 110; Brownlow, p. 21.

82 M&B, p. xxxiii.

83 See also Caraman, pp. 111–13. Accounts of Southwell's death include those of Diego de Yepes, *Historia Particular de la Persecucion de Inglaterra* (Madrid, 1599); *A brefe Discource*, in Foley, III, 164–75; Garnet's two Italian letters, 22 February, and 7 March 1595, Archives S.J., Rome: Anglia, XXXI, 1; 'The Relation of Thomas Leake, a Secular priest', in Stonyhurst: MS Anglia, VI, printed in John Hungerford Pollen, S.J. (ed.), CRS, 4 (London: Catholic Record Society, 1908), pp. 333–7; Garnet to Acquaviva, 1 May 1595.

84 Garnet to Acquaviva, 22 February 1595; Garnet to Acquaviva, 22 February 1595, Stonyhurst, Anglia, II, 4; quoted in Caraman, p. 115.

85 Caraman, pp. 117–18.

86 Described as 'various other signs which might have been used in the examination of conscience', in M&B, p. xxxii; see also Janelle, p. 69. This is the evidence that leads some (including Garnet) to conclude that Southwell had no free access to ink and paper and could not have written poetry in prison.

Chapter 8

Conclusion

silver, weighed, tried, and sevenfold purged from earthly dross in the fire[1]

'A SHARP SWORD, YET AS I SUPPOSE WELL SHEATHED'[2]

How can one individual exist in both flame and stream? Those aspects of Southwell's life and work visited by this book, the importation in metaphor of sacred imagery and sacraments, his pedagogic use of the reader's poetic apprehension, and those all-informing paradoxes of violent care and self-preserving self-destruction, as disparate as they seem, all fold together in the person of Southwell himself, and in the last physical act of his life. Southwell's ministry, his correspondence, his sermons, his poetry were all predicated upon his wish to be dissolved in Christ. From the private self-identifications with Christ crucified of his college diaries to the *Epistle of Comfort*'s public affirmation of the place of martyrdom in the English Catholic mission, the probability of a public, disgraceful, agonising death was part of Southwell's daily understanding of himself.[3] He and his fellows lived both with and (after their executions) within the imagery and reports of English State butchery; nor must it be forgotten that Southwell had seen men burned alive at the behest of his mother Church in Rome. That quotidian violence was as much a part of the methodology of spiritual direction as the poetry.

Such paradoxes as the use of violence to further religious ends and the active desire in an individual for the apparent self-annihilation of martyrdom are, to the twenty-first century mind, at once incomprehensible and all too familiar; the young man of education and sensitivity throwing himself upon the sword of a State he believes himself no longer to be part of is no early modern freak.

Southwell, in his last letter to his captor Robert Cecil, responds to Topcliffe's having put it about that he refused to say who he was because he was ashamed of his vocation by defiantly identifying himself as a Catholic priest in England; having done so, he tells Cecil 'I am become suitor for my own execution'.[4] He does not talk about the miseries he has suffered, reassuring Cecil that his Jesuit training has inured him to the harshest of conditions. He does not seek death, but is entirely ready for it, as the silencing of his voice has made him 'apostolically useless', as Pilarz puts it; his Order is more precious 'than a thousand other lives, so to live by relenting in the one or swerving from the other in the least duty I reckon more odious than as many deaths' (l. 82). He describes the missive as 'a sharp sword, yet as I suppose well sheathed' (l. 243).[5] It is likely that he knew he had sheathed it in his own bosom, but he seemed entirely indifferent to his death or his life, except in that the expenditure would help souls.

How can any creative act fit into such a bleak scheme? Where in Southwell's poetry can sense be made of it? There is, however, an informing theory running through his vision of violence and its place in the cosmos, and it is only by understanding that theoretical violence that Jonson's admiration of 'The burning Babe' can be properly understood.

In the peculiar, extreme circumstances of the English mission – circumstances never anticipated by the Society of Jesus, which preferred not to send missionary priests to their own country – Southwell's martyr-poet-priest-hood is almost unique. In his efforts to recreate the edifying vision of the Roman artworks, to word-paint Rome's brilliant new baroque for English minds, as in the dramatic and self-defining autonomy of his status, this uniqueness represents a wellspring of creativity, and a new direction in English lyric poetry, but it was his death that elevated his poetic strategies above the earthly, and fixed the message like a thorn in the hearts of his readers. He admits in his letter to Cecil that he trembled and wept when he was taken, in anticipation of the agonies he knew were ahead (lines 189–90, p. 275), but he takes comfort in sharing in Christ's agony in Gethsemane, the image he metaphorised so often in his poetry (l. 191, p. 275). Southwell's poems therefore served to soothe him as well as his readership, but only, for him, in that they pre-scripted his death, presenting him as an imago of Christ.

Southwell's creative autonomy was a theological proposition, not a mere claim for authorial status, as we have seen. In an age struggling for Self-creation and freedom from constraint he was the repressed of the repressed; the silenced, by fear of the Other and even by his own strict codes and training; the abused; the Self willingly subjected to destruction by the laws of the State in order to prove his point about their illegality. The self-defined and redefined self that had survived the war-disrupted novitiate and the College stirs, conformed itself to its changing circumstances, and negotiated the manifold attempts to negate it, is curled up within a snailshell of resisted assaults and hard positions. Yet still, when finally exposed by agents of the State, soft as it seemed, it could resist all attempts to alter it because it had already accepted and pre-scripted its own annihilation, using poetry itself to remove the last possibility of power over its vulnerable selfhood by the oppressive Other.

Henry Garnet, in the preface to Southwell's *Short Rule of Good Life* written after Southwell's death, describes unflinchingly the depth of that resistance:

> Yet is there a certain disposition in those which are chosen to so high a dignity ordinarily required of God, which is, first, to have killed their passions before they be killed by the persecutors [...] first to have become their own butchers before they be delivered to the hangman's shambles.[6]

Such self-butchery is reconstructive, paradoxically. Southwell had to do extreme violence to his self in order to maintain its autonomy against attempts at conversion and control from a State which had little understanding of a training that so effectively Othered oppositional forces that it taught its soldiers to 'love Christ all the way to Calvary', and to reconcile the paradoxes of their training in such an extreme fashion; 'only at the point of death does the martyr become a whole, fully realized person, when the life of inward denial and violence is finally manifested sacramentally in an outward and visible sign'.[7] The importance of Southwell's readership had become the importance of the audience in acknowledging the significance of his act. As in the Alberti altarpiece, the cross-action of grace becomes the Cross itself, in the shape of Christ's dead body: the martyr-priest is elevated to become part of the Host that he has been raising for the congregation, just as Christ descends into it – it is in the 'Performing Deede' of total self sacrifice that they become one:

> That which he gave he was, o peerelesse gifte, 7
> Both god and man he was, and both he gave,
> He in his handes him self did trewelye lifte:[8]

This is what Southwell meant to say all along, and such is the looking-glass rhetoric of resistance that it was his oppressors who had made this utterance finally possible.

'Christs bloody sweat' (p. 18) is the poetic expression of this transformation through paradox, through that imagined pain shared with Christ, 'Whom flames consume, whom streames [of blood] enforce to die', imagery which describes the death of the sixteenth century martyr as much as Christ (l. 8). Southwell here sets his mind to deal with such a death, perhaps anticipating the moment when he, or the bleeding remains of himself, may feel the lonely horror of the end. Here he is translating it, through the magic formulae of number-puzzle and metaphor, into the agony felt by Christ, the resurrecting 'Phenix fiery paines' which burn 'In fainting Pelicans still bleeding vaines'; the fire of this, more violent, love is fed, not quenched, with 'gory bloode' (lines 11–12, 17).

Robert Southwell

It is set out for his reader to wonder at, not to emulate, but also for his reader to recall, on the day of Southwell's ending, as a mystic self-dissolution into Christ: an English Jesuit foresees his death. In writing himself as Christ, though reduced to 'A sacke of dust, a masse of fleshe and bloode' in the hands of his torturers (l. 24), what cruelty could now be inflicted on him that did not simply reinforce his point and ensure his phoenix-like salvation? What physical annihilation could the State attempt that did not, in the very moment of its success, send him, as a martyr, immediately to heaven? Though denied access to the sacraments, any sins he may have committed would be wiped clean the instant his butchers subjected him to this purgatory-substituting baptism of fire. Viewing the flames as a phoenix-bonfire like the burning Babe's, rather than annihilation, he was neutralising the authority of his executioners over his body, just as he did in 'Decease release', on behalf of Mary Stuart. In prescripting his own death, he became his own butcher, and made a free offering of himself, thus 'preventing' the instruments of the Passion, like Christ.

TERRIBLE SEMBLANCES: LOVE'S VIOLENCE

Expressions of pain, in Southwell's poetry, are associated with spiritual, not physical discomfort. It is his sinners, deaf to the needs of their spirits, who make themselves prey to the physical hell of an existence in denial of God's love. Repentance brings pain, but it is a blessed, constructive pain: his Babe cries in a fire, but it is of Love fed by Justice and Mercy, and it is felt only within his 'faultlesse breast' (l. 17); and his Queen of Scots, caught in the moment of her martyrdom, feels no anguish at all, smiling at the block and the axe which have delivered her into heaven. His spiritualised view of pain allowed submission to it, and his submission meant that he, not the State, was asking the questions. The very vulnerability of his body was a political statement, a sort of sermon on the wrongness of the path England was treading, an interrogation of the perceived loss of individual autonomy. Where does the public body, the site of ideological interventions, end, and the private body, the one that is rightly the 'property' of the self, begin? Southwell's doubled physical appearance as gentleman or priest, and his disappearances into cellars and holes, as much as his ultimate bodily dismemberment, are rejections of the idea of the ruly, static, containable body demanded (and legislated for) by the Tudor State in which he lived. They offer a variety of bodies for the State to play out its verifications and judgements upon, while always keeping aspects of his self reserved, by disguise, by resistance rhetoric, by silence, by equivocation, and, when those other strategies were no longer possible, by the allowing of his body to be taken from him but always in the knowledge that he had scripted, in his poetry and prose, his preferred implications of these apparent failures, turning them into expressions of power to empower other resistances and to undermine the State's apparent supremacy.

From his point of view as a Catholic, too, he had, he hoped, ensured the same immediate rise into heaven as he had written for Mary Stuart. His was a resistance founded on paradox and interpretation and the reality of Christ's death: he had not been denied life, he had escaped into real life within the person of Christ, via the 'royall rifte' of God's wounds ('Man to the wound in Christs side', p. 72), as he had prayed to do in his college diary.

The poetics of this sort of resistance is expressed through Southwell's Magdalen and Joseph, in the rhetoric of the self-annihilated individual who finds a new autonomy behind what had been a false face. Magdalen the whore, Joseph the cuckold, both reconstituted themselves by effacing their egos and giving themselves up to love – which in turn redefines them as lovable. Southwell submits them only to a metaphorical martyrdom; as Hélène Cixous said, the recreative, recombinative action of metaphor is the only possible voice of the repressed 'I'.[9]

Love might have been the motivation for readmission into Christ's body, but violence was the method. In his private prayer Southwell did not call for peace or reconciliation on his own behalf; his was a manifesto for violence, and for ownership of violence, headed by that strangest of all the young priest's preferred texts: 'The kingdom of heaven suffereth violence, and the violent [bear it away]' (Matthew 11.12); This strange theme of aggressive assaults on the kingdom of God is repeated in Luke 16.16, where the arrival of the Baptist has changed everything utterly: 'since that time the kingdom of God is preached, and every man presseth into it' (Luke 16.16). This is as much about internal violence as social unrest: the text appears again in Southwell's spiritual devotions, preceded by the remark that, in seeking perfection, 'It is a great hindrance to refrain from using violence to oneself.'[10]

Southwell, trained up on such auto-austerity, points out that Christ was found in places of dearth and hardship, in desert, mountain, fire and thunder:

> Thincke we to fynde in doune & deyntinesse, him, that to them appeared so terrible, and fearfull. Doe we thincke, that his rigor and justice, signified by these terrible semblances, is so relented [...] Surelye we are greatlye deceyved [...] For albeit the new testament be fuller of grace, yet is it no lesse full of agonyes.[11]

God is love, yes: a hard, excoriating love. One of Ignatius's favourite writers, the fourteenth-century Ludolph of Saxony, had written that Christ's side was wounded with love's wound for our sake; if we loved him enough to enter, we would find his heart and become incandescent with love, just like iron cast into the fire. In the *Epistle*, Southwell builds on this idea of loving self-violence: though the Redemption enfeebled our enemy, the kingdom of heaven still suffers violence, and goodness alone is no longer enough for a crown in heaven – violence must be countered with violence (*Epistle*, p. 32v). How can we allow ourselves to be less hurt and frightened than Christ, if we claim to follow him? The wanderer who observes the torments of the child in 'The burning Babe', with its furnace imagery, is musing on the same theme: violence, and self-violence, as sacrament.

The violence of Christ's re-entry from human life into heaven can be matched only by similar levels of violence done to the sinful self – and in matching the brutality to be applied to the self by the enemy, theirs is neutralised.[12] Public execution, as identified by Southwell, was a battle for the self. In engaging with its processes, Southwell had finally done what he set out to do, and he did it with a most un-poetic hardness. His last letter to Arundel, after the Earl's death sentence, an uncompromising insistence on Arundel's sacrifice of himself and his family to further the cause, was 'a curious combination of congratulation and exhortation'.[13] Southwell's own interest in the 'art of martyrdom', rather than the pieties that can be assumed to lie behind it, is clearly seen in his advice to the condemned man: rather than improving the coming hour by sacrifice and prayer, as one might expect a priest to suggest, Southwell advises the Earl to leave his pious exertions and preserve his strength for the last fight, as if martyrdom was an important sporting event. Once again we get a sense in Southwell's writing that the martyrdom was in itself important, like an act of prowess in a contest. The mere fact of self-sacrifice was no longer enough, in the face of the Protestant competition displayed in Foxe's *Book of Martyrs* (although Southwell still troubles to make a case in the *Epistle* that heretics can never be martyrs (p. 184v)). The true Christian's death must be perfectly crafted and long studied-for and rehearsed, as if to match the moving perfection of an Alberti or Circignani altarpiece. It was, as *presented* by Southwell, primarily a dialogic act of audience-management – it mattered, more than ever before, what the recipients of the act thought, just as he had learned in viewing the martyr cycle paintings in Rome.

TORN AND FRETTED VELVET: THE PATTERN OF A POET

Southwell seems to have had this concept of the glamour, the desirability, the applicability, of violence from the start. Brownlow, more than any previous commentator, sees a self-annihilative bent in Southwell's diary entries, but their expostulations seem to me to be in part a response to the terrible beauty of violence with which he was surrounded in Rome, a drive in response to strip away the ugliness of failure, or smother it with a fretwork of wounds and blood as if putting on a rich robe.[14] A suicidal urge could have found rapid satisfaction in London, but Southwell kept out of the fire for longer than most.

Southwell's rhetorical sensitivity allowed him an understanding of a being created by words, and much of his English lyric poetry seems to be an attempt to recreate an ideal English Christian in such terms. In the *Epistle of Comfort*,

Conclusion

Southwell writes of the loyal follower of King Saul who, on seeing his master throw himself upon his sword, follows suit, admirably, in Southwell's view '(though wickedly)'.[15] Taking the Old Testament ruler as a type for Christ (and perhaps the martyred Campion or the imprisoned Earl of Arundel too), he tells his English readers: 'Yea our *Saule* falleth on the most rigorous sworde of his owne justice, for our sakes. And shall we for whose benefite all this is done, ungratefullye refuse to follow his example?' (*Epistle*, p. 28v). He wrote this early in his mission, ostensibly in spiritual support of the imprisoned head of the English Roman Catholics, who could be said, in refusing to recant his faith, to have fallen on his sword for the Church. Here Southwell has demonstrated why his metaphors, even the apparently simple ones of a little lyric like 'The burning Babe', cannot be considered at face value alone: he has conflated a biblical precedent for self-sacrifice, Christ the very pattern of it, and a striking contemporary example of it, all in one triune metaphor, a conflation of the immanent, the imagined and the real as potent in its way as one of those deeply agonistic and affecting altarpieces of his Roman years.

His training insisted that one's own body was the enemy where sensuality entered in; one's soul, to survive, had to kill it – literally – or commit spiritual suicide: this was the 'Civill Warre' of which he wrote ('Mans civill warre', p. 49), where the 'halves must disagree' or betray the whole self (l. 23). In the narrow, polarised *Umwelt* of Southwell's mission it was not possible to be both fully obedient to God's will and to remain alive, and Southwell increasingly had to find ways of expressing that as the intention of God, not the State. He had used tropes in his college writing which turned the ugly physical deformations of a martyrdom into a Godly act of creativity: 'If a prince should chance to tear a precious robe upon a nail, the craftsman will repair it with such care and diligence that far from spoiling the appearance of the robe, the rent will even add to its beauty and value.' This trope re-identifies damage as enhancement: Christ is the princely cloth torn by the Jews or 'heretics' and repaired and embellished through sacrifice and grace.[16]

The same theme appears later in the *Epistle*. Here, Southwell paraphrases St Chrysostom, developing the saint's practical metaphor of the craftsman-sculptor into something more courtly and secular, better suited to his audience. Southwell imagines the cloth that was Christ's body now become the body of English Catholics, torn by the Protestant authorities. His identification of them as 'you' increases the sense of an identification through suffering with Christ. He starts with the familiar metalworker imagery:

> But St. *Chrysostom* well saith that as the cunning artificer to abetter an image doth first melt and dissolve it; to cast it afterward in a more perfect mold: So God permitteth our flesh by you [Protestant authorities] to be mangled, to make it more glorious in the second casting. (*Epistle*, pp. 203–203v)

Southwell then expands into imagery that calls immediately to mind the richly worked and reworked stuff of late sixteenth century costume:

> And as a cunning imbroderer having a piece of torn or fretted velvet for his ground, so contriveth and draweth his work, that the fretted places being wrought over with curious knots or flowers, they far excel in show the other whole parts of the velvet: So God being to work upon the ground of our bodies, by you so rent and dismembered, will cover our ruptures, breaches and wounds, which you have made, with so unspeakable glory, that the whole parts which you left shall be highly beautified by them. (*Epistle*, pp. 203–203v)

George Puttenham had used a similar trope in exhorting the good poet to add value to his Court as the embroiderer 'sets stone and perle or passements of gold upon the stuff of a Princely garment',[7] but this is writing for effect; Southwell 'is writing the body with a vengeance'.[8] In offering this trope of costly human material torn by frenzied attack, and the immense patience of God as he embroiders over the rents with better motifs of his own, Southwell is using the imagery of creativity and art to neutralise the effects of the State's attempts to control it and the bodies of its members. The remaining 'whole parts', the heads on Tower Bridge, the leg or arm displayed around the city, are not shamefully disjointed non-humans in Southwell's new scenario; they are joined by the invisible lacework of God into a whole better than before, when it was merely the fleshly product of human procreation. Readers of Donne will recognise 'Batter my heart, three-person'd God' in Chrysostom, but not in Southwell's elaboration of him. What Southwell imported as a generalised articulation of the suffering self can later be seen working at the level of the individual self in Donne, an illustration of how Southwell's proposed ideal vision of self was adopted and absorbed by individual authors into their poetry after him.

It also suggests why the verses might have provided a potent pattern for religious poets such as Donne and Herbert. After Southwell's martyrdom, his verses became sacred items in themselves, connected through his connection to the Word. In dying for the 'soul rights' of his readership, and explicitly involving his poetry in that fight for integrity, he sacralised both reader and author in a way not fully possible before in poetry, involving both in a spiritual process that conjoined earth and heaven, evoking rather Thomas More than Thomas Becket, and importing that sacred, literary dignity into the hitherto unlikely realms of the English lyric.

In Southwell's poetry the sympathetic magic of the relic meets the poetics of individual resistance, which in the act of self-sacrifice becomes the poetics of total closure, a result impossible, he might have argued, for a Petrarchan love-poetic such as Sidney's, at least for more than a blissful moment or two; the love-coupling described in Southwell's poetry and exemplified by his death lasted for eternity. His martyrdom was in part an *artistic* act designed around his experience of the martyrdom of his friends and fellows, the poetry a prolepsis, a means of back-referencing the reader to the real act with his own ideological additions, both preparing for and preceding the real, so that demon-images could not be pre-created for it by the State, and thereby reduce its value in the harvesting of English souls.[19] The poetry therefore both superscripted the past martyrdoms of his fellows and pre-scripted that of himself, a web of pre- and post-modifiers.

At the centre of that glamourising network was the dreadful fact of the traitor's death itself. It is the existence of this fact that converts his poetry from a simple mirror of God's creative greatness to something that participates in it, and that draws the reader deeper into Southwell's own spiritual arena. That was why Southwell wrote about the tormented body so much in his lyrics: not to reflect his own miseries in the art, in that confessional or complaint model proposed by many of his past editors, but to have the miseries reflect the art that was the central truth, the Word made flesh, self-sacrificed, and now metaphorically mingled with its imitator, Southwell's martyrdom. The poetry was the invisible lace-work that linked and embroidered over the two, joining it to the Roman martyr cycles and their progression or pilgrimage towards perfection. The gory celebration of the details of martyrdom might seem self-defeatingly off-putting unless one holds, with Baudrillard, that the created of itself recreates 'reality', that:

> the image is interesting not only in its role as reflection, mirror, [...] but also when it begins to contaminate reality and to model it, ... the better to distort it, or better still: when it appropriates reality for its own ends, when it anticipates to the point that the real no longer has time to be produced as such [...] Continuation of war by other means.[20]

Baudrillard cites Francis Ford Coppola's version of the Vietnam War, *Apocalypse Now*, as having become the 'real' Vietnam, the cause after the event. Southwell understood this anticipatory aspect of imagery perfectly, it seems. His martyrological poetic could be said to have made the man in retrospect, activated at and by his death. The State's attempts to dehumanise through the crude pantomime of dismemberment was undermined by Southwell; his thoroughness in preparing his own martyrdom 'not only rendered the normal instruments of power useless: it forced the government to participate in a pageant enacting its own illegitimacy and impotence'.[21]

The production of a priest's heart at his execution had already been appropriated by Southwell's cause, through traditional iconographies and now through his own rhetorical imagery on the scaffold. Continental Catholicism, the Jesuits especially, had revived the medieval symbolism of the burning, wounded Sacred Heart of Jesus, and Southwell's writing is infused with its mystic implications.[22] His poetry had taught the crowd what to see when the heart was held up to them: not a disembodied organ from a dismembered body but a holy completion of Christ's example, the worse the treatment, the closer to Christ's physical experience and to the meaning of the Sacred Heart itself, symbol less of physical anguish than of the transcendence of Christ's love for humanity. Details of Christ's actual passion, 'the whips, the thornes, the nailes, the speare, and roode' ('Christ's Bloody Sweat' (p. 18, l. 6) appear little in Southwell. Instead, he converts the old Passion into a contemporary register of martyrdom as he had seen it performed in the acts of gore and burning that was the death of any one of his companions, and, ultimately, in anticipation of his own. One senses a struggle within these dreadful images to reconcile such horrors to the idea of a merciful and self-sacrificial God, but in working it through in his metaphors, glossing the realities as metaphysical ideals, he was pre-scripting it for other observers, all aware of the significance of the phoenix and the pelican as models of self-sacrifice through fire and blood. Southwell's death completed the reconciliation of the two, in turn altering the quality of the actual words in retrospect. In short, Southwell's many metaphoric uses of the word 'heart' had become symbols, real signs of Christ's heart, upon Southwell's own death.

The 'real' execution stood little chance of being experienced neutrally in such a highly prescribed atmosphere. 'O sacred Fire come shewe thy force on me | That sacrifice to Christe I may retorne', he begs, making the transferral of his into Christ's death near-explicit (l. 20); he is performing the same trick as he did in 'Decease release', converting the real elements of death and disgrace into aspects of the martyr's value. The State would have him see his own bowels burned 'before his face', in the words of the court; so the author rescripts their fire into that of a fiercely loving God, stripping away his impurities like some supernatural blast furnace: Magdalen has been left behind – 'Love is the fire' now, not just the mode of expression and feeling, bringing us closer than in any other poem to the fiery core of 'The burning Babe'. Closer than ever to his own immolation, he finds common ground between violence and God's purposes.

Where a Magdalen could suffer the fires of love without really understanding what was required of her if she were to become as one with the Object of her devotion, the author-martyr's only possible expression of love is to go knowingly through real fire. 'To live where best I love, death I desire' he says in 'What joy to live?' (p. 53, l. 120), in which the word 'love' occurs seven times; he had created in Peter a persona to regret its lack of love, one in Magdalen to regret the loss of its loved one; now he creates the lover who has to die to himself consummate that love:

O Christian, saith S. Augustine. *Ama amorem illius, qui amore tui amoris, descendit in uterum Virginis, ut ibi amorem suum amori tuo copularet.* Love the love of him, that for love of thy love, descended into the womb of a Virgin, and afterward ascended to the ignominy of the Cross, that there he might couple his love, and thy love together. (*Epistle*, pp. 38–38v)

The old teaching was founded on love as a means of gaining access to the divine; Southwell's Magdalen is its personification. But in its Ignatian version it becomes a paradox reconcilable only by an imitation of the Crucifixion as Southwell interprets it for himself. 'Lifes death loves life' (p. 54) weaves this theme into the idea of the conventional lover 'Who lives in love' and who 'long delaies doth rue' (lines 1–2). 'Where love is hot, life hateful is, | Their groundes doe not agree' (lines 13–14); the consummation is with 'him he love by whom he lives': Christ, 'To whom all love is due' (lines 3–4):

> Let us in life, yea with our life,
>   Requite his living love: 10
> For best we live when least we live,
>   If love our life remove.
> [...]
> Mourne therefore no true lovers death:
>   Life onely him annoyes. 30
> And when he taketh leave of life,
>   Then love beginnes his joyes.

This is not about Magdalen, although it repeats the Magdalenic theme of ardent attachment; it is explicitly about the necessary death of a true lover in order to perfect his love; it is an attempt to produce the perfect, the Platonic Poem.

In 'St Peters Complaint' Southwell also offers the image of the less successful lover, this time as a sort of alchemist whose tears are the 'quintessence' produced in 'the limbeck of [his] doelfull breast', the product of the distillation of the fruits of his sins, the lines prefiguring those of 'The burning Babe'. 'For fuel, selfe accusing thoughtes be best, | Use feare, as fire, the coales let penance blow', Peter tells himself (p. 89, lines 457–62). There is another 'Limbecke of thy heart' in 'A vale of teares' (p. 41, l. 70), but 'Lifes death' is the real love-limbeck amongst all his other poems – love decimates the artificial world of words: there is almost one 'love' for every ten words of this lyric; 'lover' appears once, and it is quite unambiguous in its message: death of self is the only proper expression of his love. It is by the models of this and 'Christs bloody sweat' that the 'burning Babe' can perhaps best be understood.

THE BURNING BABE

This book seems to have travelled full circle. Jonson's comment singles out Southwell's 'The burning Babe' for praise, and all we seem to have discovered about it is that it is Southwell's oddest poem. There are so many things it is not. Like 'Christs bloody sweat', it is not one of the poems published in the earliest editions, not appearing until Cawood's 'newlie augmented' 1602 edition.²³ It is not a hymn, a parody, a moral, a complaint, a reproof, a sermon. It is not, fundamentally, about Christmas-tide either, despite Cawood's (or his manuscript source's) placement of it alongside two Nativity poems. It is not even a poeticised spiritual exercise in the style of his longer work. It could be an imitation of an ecstatic state, the *incendium amoris* or fire of love,²⁴ but neither the Babe nor the 'I' is in a state of ecstasy. To add to the commonplace notion of a fiery love which enthuses, though, we have Southwell's own paradoxical version, a 'sacred Fire' which burns as real fire, painfully and consumingly, 'yf fleshe and blood will burne' ('Christs bloody sweat', p. 18, l. 19). This echoes and problematizes more conventional metalworking heat-quench imagery, in Lodge's 'Love guards the roses of thy lips' (1593), for instance, where 'Love works thy heart within his fire, | And in my tears doth firm the same'.²⁵

We have, too, in the furnace-breast of the Babe, the image of the Limbeck of the heart from 'Vale of teares' (p. 41) where grief distils the Christian's sorrows and 'former faults be fuell to the fire', stoking the agony in obedience to the laws of God's justice (lines 69–72). Even the anguish of Southwell's college diaries, his fear of mortal sin and his idea that martyrdom's baptism of fire might save him from it, is there. The fire in 'The burning Babe' struggles to contain all the possible meanings; all the various preoccupations of Southwell's lyrics and writings explored in this book are distilled into this one lambent image, as if a glimpse through a crack into a wider cosmos. 'The burning Babe' is, I would argue, the final and complete poetic expression of Southwell's sense of God's action through his own ministry.

It is the encouragement inherent in the *Exercises* to feel as realistically as possible that excites fiery fervours in response to the loving action of grace, but it is the scholarly response peculiar to Southwell at this time that allows him to translate such fervours into metaphysical poetry. He is importing pictures, more than ideologies, the astounding, surreal images of his Roman days; and more, he is importing those open spaces between image and observer where the effects of the imagery crystallise into feeling and understanding, those spaces that contain multiple layers of nested imagery the untangling of which will lead to enlightenment. Jonson knew the power of the picture, and no doubt recognised its potency in Southwell's little poem. 'Picture is the invention of Heaven, the most ancient, and most a kinne to Nature', he observed in 'De Pictura'; 'being done by an excellent Artificer', it can so penetrate 'the inmost affection [...] as sometimes it orecomes the power of speech and oratory'.²⁶ Quite so. And has Jonson recognised in 'The burning Babe' Southwell's new use of the word-picture? Southwell plays with his imagery almost as Hieronymus Bosch might: the excoriating example of the innocent martyr himself is turned into a metaphysical oddity, the Limbeck or fiery furnace wherein God works the souls of men:

> My faultlesse breast the furnace is,
>   The fuell wounding thornes:
> Love is the fire, and sighs the smoake,
>   The ashes, shames and scornes;   20
>
> The fewell Justice layeth on,
>   And Mercie blowes the coales,
> The metall in this furnace wrought,
>   Are mens defiled soules

The surface layer of the painting peels back to reveal the Southwellian substrata. We are in the company of St Chrysostom again: only in the destructive violence of the metalworker's furnace can anything approaching a real response to God be felt because only in such violence can a real change be wrought on such cold resistant material. As I noted earlier, one immediately calls to mind Donne's 'Holy Sonnet 10' (probably written in 1609, according to Helen Gardner):[27]

> Batter my heart, three person'd God; for, you
> As yet but knocke, breathe, shine, and seeke to mend;
> That I may rise, and stand, o'erthrow mee, 'and bend
> Your force, to breake, blowe, burn and make me new;

Is Donne, in accusing God of acting merely as a pot-mender when he could be a full-blown iron-worker, using Southwell's own lambent imagery to expose a coolness at the heart of the Calvinised new theology, or at least, after all the changes, at the heart of Donne himself? Alexander Grosart's assessment of the potentiality of Southwell's poetry is surely annealed or crystallised here,[28] and Martz's attempt to trace the foundation of metaphysical poetry to the Exercises, too – not their process, but their emotional potential, and their effects upon the imagination and conscience. I would not argue that the metaphysical concept is a direct result of the Exercises, but is it not in a clear line of descent, via their habit of expression as imagery and emblem? Jonson, too, asks God for violence as a sign of his mercy in 'A Hymne to God the Father' (*Metaphysical Poets*, p. 93). And in Donne's sonnet endings: 'Take mee to you, imprison mee' ('Holy Sonnet 10', l. 12), we see the same patterning of concluding prayer as in Southwell's holy poetry; it was the imaginative impulse plus the 'Performing Deed' that combined in both poets' work to create the potent message.

Southwell's authority and his authorship were virtually the same thing, founded on Southwell's belief in, and living of, the principle of sacrifice through love. As I suggested in the discussion of Southwell's reconciliation of extremes, the idea of sacrifice is both a giving-up of the self and an insistence upon one's individual value: a worthless sacrifice is not a sacrifice. Southwell's value as a sacrifice lay both in his authoritative position amongst his congregation and in his own ability to define the value of self-sacrifice to that congregation in his written works. His need to establish a pre-value for what would certainly be a degrading death necessitated a change in his attitude to himself as that death became more and more inevitable, from unworthy sinner towards spotless lamb. Garnet's anxiety about his friend's spiritual state in captivity, bereft as he was of the sacraments, is part of the same process of purification.

Southwell had worried about the extent to which he could be considered spotless even at the last, and even in terms of his physical appearance; the public statement of his martyrdom was to be as carefully worded, and presented with as proper a *punctilio*, as was his poetry. He had had plenty time to plan the best exit, yet he had seemed, once committed to his final public performance, more anxious to defend his *bella figura* than to sermonise. The death itself was the communication, and, as the channel for it, he must look and act his best, in the noble tradition of the Society that had procured the best artists it could afford to demonstrate and realise its way of proceeding. In an act of restoration surpassing, in its way, those mighty works in Rome, the injured, exhausted man had taken pains to clean the filth of the streets off his face as he stood by the gallows; in the same spirit he was almost apologetic about the apparent disgrace of his death, according to one account of his execution. His words as reported have a slightly odd ring to them:

> And this I humbly desire almightie God that it would please his goodness, to take and excepte this my death, the laste farewell to this miserable and infortunate lyfe (althoghe in this moste happy and fortunate) in full satisfaction for all my sinnes and offences, and for the Comfort of many others; which albeit that it seeme here disgracefull, yet I hope that in tyme to come it will be to my eternall glory.[29]

The interval between Southwell's 'disgracefull'-seeming death and his 'eternal glory' is a metaphysical oddity. He knew as well that the martyr by-passes Purgatory and goes straight to heaven; he enlarged upon that theme in 'Decease release'. He surely cannot be referring to the actual progress of his own soul here, proper humility aside. It is as if he was still in the realms of reader-response – pre-scripting what the audience thought of him and his death. Where they saw a crude, dehumanising spectacle reserved for traitors and criminals, he is reassuring them (and himself) that in time to come they will see him translated into a hero for his faith, both in memory, and as an author.

Southwell's own private devotional writings, begun in such a stilted, painful way in his novitiate, had long since placed the Jesuit priest not alongside Christ but physically part of His body, in a mystic self-identification that seems to go beyond a mere sense of holy community and to express itself readily as metaphor – almost a sort of mystic shorthand. We return, with Southwell's martyrdom, to entry no. 8 and its internalised, almost visceralised communication of Truth:

Conclusion

The Son, the Word in the Mind of God: 'My heart hath uttered a good word.' The uttered word: 'I speak my words to the king.' The written word: 'My tongue is the pen of a scrivener that writeth swiftly.'[30]

The references are to Psalms 44.1 (45 in the Authorised Version): 'My heart is inditing a good matter: I speak of the things which I have made touching the king: my tongue is the pen of a ready writer' – it is a 'song of loves'; and 66.6–7 (67): 'Then shall the earth yield her increase; and God, even our own God, shall bless us. God shall bless us; and all the ends of the earth shall fear him.' Southwell was synopsising the Biblical precedent for his own ministry of words, the ministry that brought us the fusion of idea and event of 'The burning Babe'.

This book has attempted to show the reach and impact of Southwell's English poetry, as well as the movement between acolyte and author made by Southwell in the peculiar circumstances of the English mission. His translation into something other than himself began almost before his death. Southwell's work has clearly been 'potential', as Alexander Grosart put it, in English letters, if the various exertions of his sympathisers, editors, publishers, and even detractors are taken into account. Jonson, acknowledged an influential man of letters, admired Southwell's restrained, powerful lines, at least in 'The burning Babe'; poets such as Donne and Herbert seem to have adopted much of Southwell's innovation, his *anthropopathia*, his cleanly expressed, pared-down paradoxes, his elegant moral certainties. Milton, who evidently preferred Southwell's to Spenser's rhetorical vision, borrowed his early baroque imaginative universe-scape. In his visually rich portrayal of Biblical figures in a drama of his own devising, Milton was inheriting from Southwell's rhetoric the pedagogic imagery of the Roman churches, not Spenser's anxiously non-idolatrous allegories.[31] Southwell, true to his training in controversy, confronts such forms head-on in his burlesques or revisions of other poets, and it is this insistent authorial integrity that wins through into seventeenth-century poetics, Protestant or otherwise. Milton's God is ventriloquised, as was Southwell's (albeit in Latin), and his Satan engages us as does Southwell's in a debate over what constitutes 'good' in art. Milton finds Sidney's estimation of 'good' as 'good quality' to be lacking in moral integrity: beauty is *not* always truth, although truth is always beauty, as Southwell worked so hard to prove by his lyrics, and neither can be reduced to a mere confession of strong feeling. Southwell was one of the first to insist that the poet reaches deeper, works harder for his effects than at the surface alone.

The 'personation', engagement, affection that illuminate Shakespeare's work all appear first as comprehensive features in Southwell's poetry: he is one of the first in English poetry to show not tell, demonstrating the difference between a realistic portrayal of someone weeping and a portrayal of psychological distress that makes the reader weep. The literary concept of a created but realistically developing or disintegrating psychology begins with Magdalen or Peter and is only later seen perfected in Hamlet or Lear: thus shorn of its religious implications it has become perhaps more generally useful, though no less indebted to Southwell's Jesuit-informed model, I would argue. The influential Bacon admired not only Southwell, but was flexible-minded enough to admire aspects of Jesuit methods and see their potential value. A sort of historical myopia has caused a dislocation in the account of Southwell's poetic production; Southwell is either just a poet, and a less than brilliant one by modern aesthetically informed standards, or he is a Jesuit, and somehow beyond the pales of literary discussion. That his Jesuitism *was* his poetry (and vice versa) has seldom been able to be discussed; in the standard account of English history, a Jesuit appears only in slapstick recreation as part of the *Henry VI*-type playscript, not as a real man on the leading edge of early modern thought. As such, Southwell could never have been acknowledged part of the poetic movement that brought us Jonson, Shakespeare, Herbert or Milton. Especially Milton.

This false identification through omission has altered impacts and implications alongside realities, and helped to sideline Southwell. Southwell's only 'other' attribute than his Jesuitism was his poetry: commentators in the tradition of omission mentioned above have therefore felt themselves constrained to address his poetry in isolation from his activities. Isolated from its rhetorical strategies and spiritual stratas, as I hope I have demonstrated, it seems, with a few exceptions, sententious and derivative, allowing the bulk of his editors, biographers, critics to have described him as a poet who 'left prosodical craftsmanship [...] exactly where he had found it', but who none the less had a 'talent for description', a 'command of words', a 'spiritual quality', a quality of 'Englishness' which cannot be fully explored without acknowledging his Jesuitism as also part of that 'Englishness'.[32]

Thus divorced by most of his earlier commentators from its wider contexts, Southwell's work is just decent Englished Catholic baroque poetry founded on moral optimism, a Christianised neo-Platonism with some interesting humanist approaches to the Holy Family and to his readership. Janelle allows that Southwell is subject to the odd 'dumpish mood', and expresses it poetically ('Davids Peccavi', p. 35, l. 9; 'A vale of teares', p. 41, l. 34), a generously confessional reading that has, paradoxically, contributed to the continuing tendency to overlook Southwell: to assume that he writes, like a modern poet might prefer to do, solely from the heart of himself, is to miss not only the point of his poetry, but his skill as a rhetorician and the potential influence of his poetry on that of his contemporaries. He was, I would argue, showing poets *how* to reach into the heart to write (for the improvement of others), rather than merely doing so to express himself. His heart was a secret only to be revealed at the place of martyrdom. Any reading of 'The burning Babe', for instance, that is based on a supposed confessional function therefore misses its central rhetorical point altogether; and it is more likely to have been its rhetorical, rather than any mere affective, significance, that attracted the interest of a man like Ben Jonson.

From his very first editions, then, the myth that his work was just 'from the heart', and not of the best either, has been created. One could view such childlike works as 'The burning Babe' as a stumbling step forward in English holy poetry, as florid and sentimental as the rest of the early Catholic English baroque, if plainer, leading only to the cul-de-sac of Crashavian excess. Or one could understand Southwell as the nexus of much of the most profound thought of his age, and a lyric like 'The burning Babe' as the full expression of that, leading to Donne, to Herbert, to Milton, to Shelley and beyond.[33]

Southwell had moved from a ministry based on a theory of proper subjection, an interpellee-hood, so to speak, as seen in a work such as *Epistle of Comfort*, produced early in his mission, to theories of individual subject-status and the proper relationships between the subject and the authority, as in *Humble Supplication*. His poetry reflects both these positions and more, always in a subtly informed manner calculated to appeal to the widest community of English readers, all, that is, apart from the wilfully ungodly. The movement of his attitudes was part of his trained response to his readership, that Jesuit flexibility and need to match the rhetoric to the situation, whatever it may be. After the printing of his works, the young priest's authorship was, as his recent biographers have noted, an 'open secret'.[34] During his lifetime, though, this was not necessarily the case, and his lyrics are constructed with an insinuating skill to allow access to the priest almost without the reader's being aware, sliding his authority imperceptibly into the priest-hole of the reader's heart. After his death there was that added value: the poems, when offered by a priest, were almost sacraments in themselves; offered by a martyr in the mould of Campion they were relics. As a martyr went direct to heaven, to read and inwardly digest the full import of these works was almost to realise the living Presence of God inside the individual reader, strung out on that bright connection between what the martyr imagined and touched and where he is now. William Barret, publisher of a 1620 edition of Southwell, makes this explicit in calling the works 'dismembred parcels', resurrected by reading.[35]

I would argue that Southwell was very aware of the transferable value of his priestly authority to cultural activities outside the doctrinal or religious, a sideways movement from doctrine into art apparently appropriated by other non-religious writers very quickly after this date.[36] What might it have meant to these new writers, like Jonson, insisting that their work be taken seriously as both an important skill and an almost magical way of altering states, to have read 'Men must with sounde and silent faith receive | More then they can by sence or reason lerne'; or 'A body is endew'd with ghostly rightes, | A natures worke from natures law is free' ('Sacrament', lines 52–3, 56–7). This, although arguing that Soul gives humanity access to things other than the natural and earthly, allowing it to transcend their laws, is also pleading implicitly for an individual's rights of conscience over an earthly ruler's claims on the loyalty of that individual. As it is not specifically identified with any ruler or regime, or even any single doctrine, however, its message, detached from doctrinal specificity, becomes universal. Southwell, having pleaded for the realms of magic inside the human mind, finishes, with a magician's flourish, on the Old and New Testaments' major transubstantiations: Moses' of his wand into a snake, and Christ's of water into wine. What is this but a claim for the supernatural, transformative faculties of the inspired imagination?

Southwell was more than a copyable poet in the way that the form or style or phrasing of a Surrey or a Sidney could be copied: his status as both priest and martyr turned the actual process of creativity around from upthrusting creative ambition to an authoritative interpretation of the Divine creativity as it descends humanwards. Where the secular poet can, as Milton said in his version of the Nativity, use his 'sacred vein' to 'afford a present *to* the Infant God' ('Ode on the morning of Christ's Nativity', lines 15–16; my emphasis), a poetic priest can offer us a Christmas present *from* God. Clifford Davidson describes 'The burning Babe' as a poetic evocation of the 'emotional response to God's love always central in Southwell's theology', a reading based on the confessional model; but he also calls it a use by Southwell of a 'highly disciplined imagination to create in words a visible depiction of the Saviour'[37]. Neither of these descriptions is, in my view, strictly accurate, but I doubt that Southwell would have objected to them. Southwell's vocation and imaginative flair are certainly evident in this poem, but I hope that the previous chapters of this book have alerted a reader to the likelihood that Southwell had invested more levels of significance than that in it. The lyric simplicity of its message and language is, I would argue, deceptive, although it is, in itself, new, poetically speaking, for its time. It is a more complex piece than its brevity and simple register might suggest.

After all, what has the winter traveller of 'The burning Babe' seen in the fiery sky? It is more than a simple depiction of the Christmas Babe, despite the seemingly obvious tracks that Southwell has left in the snow for us. An inquisitive reader will notice that although the Babe has all the vivifying, improving effects that Ignatian discernment identifies as proper to the action of a good spirit upon the observer, it is never actively identified, certainly not described anywhere as the Christ-child. There are insinuations in the 'newborn' appearing on Christmas Day, but the puzzling vortices of meaning around the seemingly destructive acts of 'justice' and 'mercy' in the centre of the poem actually conflate the Babe with those subjected to the unrelenting action of legal authority as much as with Christ. God's righteous justice, acting through (though not necessarily in sympathy with) this harsh authority, is purging humanity's sins as well; the moments-old heart, offered as the site of redemption, is already being seared by the force of the love it embodies, it seems clear, the flaming 'thorns' there to prefigure the crucifixion.

But, as in so many other poems, Southwell is offering his reader layers of understanding to ascend through, the seemingly unambiguous emblems of Christ's Passion seeming to melt into something else when focused upon. The Babe himself melts, through the consuming heat of the fire, into the blood of the Sacrament later in the poem, in a graceful metaphor which conflates the act (the Crucifixion) with the result (the Mass) of Christ's self-sacrifice, while never quite identifying them. They exist, as did the disguised, hunted priest himself, in the centre of a vortex of punishing or purging fires, never fixed to any one aspect of the action of justice or the access of grace, that Southwellian metaphoric sky-space into which the reader can pour his or her own identification of the relationship between the self and the core Christian truth. The deeper their meditation and comprehension, the deeper and more personally relevant the 'truths' apprehended. The 'wounding thornes', although suggesting Christ's Crown of Thorns as anticipated in 'Christs bloody sweat' (p. 18), are more like the 'selfe accusing thoughtes' used as fuel in the long 'St Peters Complaint' mentioned earlier; there, though, the coals are blown by penance – sighs – not 'Mercie' (lines 459–60). But how could it be mercy that stokes up the fire that hurts this innocent, eloquent 'I'? The thorns here seem closer to the thorns of remembered sins, those 'former faults' that are to be 'fuell to the fire' in 'Vale', or those metaphorised in 'A Phansie turned to a sinners complaint' (p. 36), where the persona's regretful 'phansies are like thornes' (l. 33). They represent the body of the sinner, that 'withered wood [that] for fuell fittest bee' in 'Christs bloody sweat' (l. 21), or the sere pricks of conscience that burn the heart into remorse, which it was a primary purpose of the *Exercises* to stimulate, after all, seen metaphorised in 'Saint Peters Complaynte', where 'deepe remorse' and 'teares' temper God's 'deserved hate' (p. 29, lines 68–70).

That closing negotiation for grace, seen in so many of Southwell's poems, is oddly absent from 'The burning Babe', in which the grace is accessed via the violence at the centre of Southwell's sudden metaphoric understanding of becoming Christ. In it the violence of justice comes both from God and from lawful authority, the tears from both the remorseful supplicant and from a wounded Christ.

The violence is tempered with hints of passivity and silent acceptance too – it is not a war-cry or a howl of rage. The weeping Babe repeats the motif of the sinner as Orphan, whose 'heavenly kinne' have become 'dead to [his] reliefe', and who, 'Forlorne and left like Orphan child' feeds his grief with sighs ('S. Peters afflicted minde', p. 31, lines 13–16). A similar Orphan addresses himself or herself in 'I dye without desert', hoping that 'some tender eares | Will rue my orphane state and feeble teares' (lines 5–6). Like the burning Babe, this Orphan too has 'onely sighes and teares' to plead his or her case (l. 14), conflating the subject, as I have argued earlier, with the hapless Innocents of the Gospel, the willing martyrs, and Christ. In his journeying or witness of the deaths of friends, was Southwell asked why God was allowing such relentless punishment of the good? This is his answer: the Gospel story of the slaughter of the Innocents shows us that God's will is also worked out through the cruellest imaginable acts in the Bible; a godless tyrant may be doing the slaughtering, but God's will is nonetheless being done. The burning Babe is both Christ-Child anticipating, in the moment of his birth, his later suffering, and the martyrs suffering in his place.

As the limbeck-heart he is also the remorseful exercisant; 'justice' insists that he recall his sins honestly, thereby laying on the thorny fuel even more thickly. 'Mercie' is blowing the furnace's coals harder, the more utterly to transform his tinpot soul, after the imagery of Chrysostom, borrowed by both Donne and Jonson. It is the back-to-front mercy of the martyr, the deconstructive mercy asked of Jesus by Southwell in his college diary, where he begs 'to be dissolved'.[38]

Even the mention of Christmas that has transfixed the poem's interpretation since its first appearance in 1602 cannot quite fix the meaning.[39] As the homely, earthly model for the transubstantiation of the body of Christ in the Mass, the conception and birth of Christ into mortal flesh and human affairs, 'Christmas' acts not as a limiting identifier but as a sign of divine approval of their suffering, perfecting and admitting it into the sacrifice of Christ, as Southwell believed he was to be admitted by his own sacrifice.

Written, it seems very likely, in the wintry travels Southwell made immediately after the dreadful executions of so many friends in 1588, it is his way of reconciling the violence of their deaths with God's providence and mercy, just as he did in anticipation of his own. It is an act of supreme intellectual acuity and philosophical vision, combined with a faith that was occasionally floundering – 'an inveigled zeale', perhaps, but never blind; 'a zeale notwithstanding, and a faithe yt was'.[40] It is Southwell himself who, while tramping frozen and gloomy in the snow, at extreme risk from the thing he feared above all, the self-annihilation of mortal sin, 'that winter in the soul, which we must at all costs avoid' – perhaps dreaming of a warm fire ahead whilst feeling guilty for surviving those left behind in London – Southwell himself who is surprised by a sudden insight centred upon the cleansing image of fire itself.[41] He has found in the burning Babe the locus for all that takes his friends and himself to the fire both of love and of punishment, an image that reconciles remorse, suffering, violence, ardour, and sacrifice, and locates it in the person of the martyr, whether Christ, Campion, Gunter, or Southwell. As I have noted before, it takes longer to explain than to absorb poetically, through Southwell's compact, illuminating genius.

And this is the core of my argument: one must unwrap Southwell's poetic packages completely to find their value. Read superficially, via Puttenham, or carelessly, via the English national project, 'The burning Babe' is a decent little moral diversion about Christmas. Read more widely, and fully, via great thought-changers like Chrysostom, Ignatius, or Suárez, via, most of all, the bloody crucible of Southwell's English mission, 'The burning Babe' becomes a gem-perfect, coruscating exercise in the faceting of Self upon the adamantine authority of the Cosmos:

> As I in hoarie Winters night
>   Stoode shivering in the snow,
> Surpris'd I was with sodaine heate,
>   Which made my hart to glow;
>
> And lifting up a fearefull eye
>   To view what fire was neare,
> A pretty Babe all burning bright
>   Did in the ayre appeare;
>
> Who scorched with excessive heate,
>   Such floods of teares did shed,
> As though his floods should quench his flames,
>   Which with his teares were fed:
>
> Alas (quoth he) but newly borne,
>   In fiery heates I frie,
> Yet none approach to warme their harts,
>   Or feele my fire, but I;
>
> My faultlesse breast the furnace is,
>   The fuell wounding thornes:
> Love is the fire, and sighs the smoake,
>   The ashes, shames and scornes;
>
> The fewell Justice layeth on,
>   And Mercie blowes the coales,
> The metall in this furnace wrought,
>   Are mens defiled soules:
>
> For which, as now on fire I am
>   To worke them to their good,
> So will I melt into a bath,
>   To wash them in my blood.
>
> With this he vanisht out of sight,
>   And swiftly shrunk away,
> And straight I called unto minde,
>   That it was Christmasse day.

NOTES

1. Fr Henry Garnet, letter to his father general, Claudio Acquaviva, on the death of Fr Robert Southwell, S.J., 22 February 1595, in Henry Foley, *Jesuits in Conflict* (London: Burns and Oates, 1873), p. 376; see Scott Pilarz, S.J., *Robert Southwell and the Mission of Literature 1561–1595: Writing Reconciliation* (Aldershot: Ashgate, 2004), p. xvii.
2. From Southwell's letter to Robert Cecil of 6 April 1593, l. 82, quoted in Pilarz, p. 276; see Nancy Pollard Brown (ed.), *Robert Southwell, S.J.: Two Letters and Short Rules of a Good Life* (Charlottesville: University Press of Virginia, for the Folger Shakespeare Library, 1973), p. lxii; hereafter *Two Letters*; see Pilarz's discussion of the letter, pp. 271–6.
3. See a discussion of this in F. W. Brownlow, *Robert Southwell*, Twayne's English Authors Series, 516 (New York: Simon & Schuster Macmillan, 1996), pp. 8, 24–5, 30–33; also see Christopher Devlin, *The Life of Robert Southwell Poet and Martyr* (London: Longmans, Green, 1956), p. 85; both hereafter cited in the text.
4. Southwell to Robert Cecil, 6 April 1593, l. 243, quoted in Pilarz, p. 272.
5. Pilarz, pp. 273, 276.
6. Robert Southwell, *A Short Rule of Good Life*, with the letter to his father, printed by Garnet's secret press in 1596–97, in M&B, p. xxiv, quoted in Brownlow, p. 138, n. 3. See also Brown (ed.), *Two Letters*, p. 90.
7. Brownlow, pp. 8, 24.
8. 'Of the Blessed Sacrament of the Aulter', pp. 26–9, lines 4, 7–9.
9. Hélène Cixous, 'Laugh of the Medusa', in Robyn R. Warhol and D. P. Herndl (eds), *Feminisms: An Anthology of Literary Theory and Criticism* (New Brunswick: Rutgers University Press, 1991), pp. 335–49 (p. 337); hereafter cited in the text; see also Frances Barker, *The Tremulous Private Body: Essays on Subjection* (London: Methuen, 1984).
10. *Spiritual Exercises and Devotions*, ed. J. M. de Buck and trans. P. E. Hallett (London: Sheet and Ward, 1931), 20.4, p. 29; hereafter *SE&D*; see also Brownlow, p. 27.
11. *An Epistle of Comfort*, (London: secretly printed, 1587); repr. ed. D. M. Rogers, *English Recusant Literature, 1538–1640* (London: Scolar Press, 1974), vol. 211, p. 32; hereafter *Epistle*.
12. This inevitably raises the spectre of the suicide bomber; it may seem to have hovered over the pages of this book from the beginning. Lessons may be learned from history about the instilling of severe attitudes in the young, perhaps, and about the results of a polarising over-identification with the glorious dead, but, although fundamental in their response to God, the Jesuits were too sensitive to the changeful world to ever be accused of fundamentalism in its modern sense: Southwell's 'violence' was not a blow in the face of society born out of frustration and a sense of weakness but a sacrament reserved solely for himself, as the companion of a suffering Christ.
13. Brownlow, p. 34.
14. See *SE&D*, 63, pp. 72–6; see also Brownlow, pp. 24–5; Devlin, p. 72; C. S. Lewis, *English Literature in the Sixteenth Century Excluding Drama* (Oxford: Clarendon Press, 1944), pp. 545–6.
15. *Epistle*, p. 28.
16. *SE&D*, 31 'Natural Affection and the Wounds of Christ', p. 41.

17 *The Arte of English Poesie*, ed. Gladys Doidge Willcock and Alice Walker (London: R. Field, 1589; repr. London: Cambridge University Press, 1970), pp. 137–8.

18 Brownlow, p. 32.

19 In its power to recreate or simulate realities, to manipulate images inside its reader's head, poetry can be related to Jean Baudrillard's view of the perverse relationship between the image and 'its referent, the supposed real'; it is not 'true', argues Baudrillard, this 'strategy by means of which [images] always appear to refer to a real world ... anterior to themselves. None of this is true. As simulacra, images precede the real'; to read a poem is to be temporarily possessed by imagery released from normal physical constraint by the artificiality of the form; Jean Baudrillard, 'The Evil Demon of Images', Mari Kuttna Memorial Lecture Series, 1 (Sydney: University of Sydney, Power Institute of Fine Arts, 1987), p. 13.

20 Baudrillard, p. 16.

21 Brownlow, p. 33.

22 Lady Mary Percy, daughter of the Catholic martyr Sir Thomas Percy and the unfortunate Anne Somerset who had fled England after the rising of the Catholic lords of the North, had the Sacred Heart set above the door of the Benedictine Abbey she founded at Brussels a year after Southwell's death, in 1596. See Sir Cuthbert Sharp (ed.), *The Rising in the North: The 1569 rebellion, being a reprint of the 'Memorials of the rebellion of the Earls of Northumberland and Westmoreland'* (1840), foreword Robert Wood (Durham: J. Shotton, 1975; facsimile repr.).

23 STC 22960a in A. F. Pollard and G. R. Redgrave (eds), *A Short-title Catalogue of Books Printed in England, Scotland, and Ireland, and of English Books Printed Abroad, 1475–1640* (London: Bibliographical Society, 1926); hereafter *STC*; Cawood had found extra pieces from manuscripts, it seems. Later in 1602 Cawood died and his printing rights were assigned to William Leake; M&B, p. lxv.

24 Brownlow, pp. 119–20.

25 Thomas Lodge, 'Love guards the roses of thy lips', in Emrys Jones (ed.), *The Oxford Book of Sixteenth Century Verse* (Oxford: Oxford University Press, 1991), p. 434.

26 In *Timber; Or Discoveries*, 'De Pictura', lines 1523–28; in C. H. Herford and P. and E. Simpson (eds), *Ben Jonson: Works*, 8 vols (Oxford: Clarendon Press, 1925–1952), VIII (1947), p. 610.

27 Helen Gardner (ed.), *John Donne: The Divine Poems* (Oxford: Clarendon Press, 1952), p. 11.

28 Alexander B. Grosart (ed.), *The Complete Poems of Robert Southwell, S.J.* (London: Robson, Fuller Worthies' Library, 1872), p. lxxxi; hereafter cited in the text.

29 From *A Brefe Discourse of the condemnation and execution of Mr Robert Southwell*, by an unknown witness, Stonyhurst, MS Anglia II, 1, printed by Henry Foley, S.J., *Records of the English Province of the Society of Jesus*, 7 vols (London: Burns and Oates, 1877), III, pp. 164–75; see Janelle, p. 89.

30 *SE&D*, 8, p. 7.

31 Alison Shell discusses the extent to which Southwell forced Spenser to readdress his rhetorical strategies of allegory (which looked more and more like self-distancing than an honest artistic tool when compared with Southwell's in 1595) in *Catholicism, Controversy and the English Literary Imagination 1558–1660* (Cambridge: Cambridge University Press, 1999), pp. 72–7.

32 Janelle, pp. 286–7.

33 See Geoffrey Hill, 'Tenebrae', *Collected Poems*, Penguin International Poets Series (Harmondsworth; Penguin, 1990).

34 Brownlow, p. 74.

35 They were primarily reanimated by the sunshine of Richard, Earl of Dorset's favour; see Grosart, p. xxi.

36 Stephen Greenblatt, though avoiding discussion within the sacred arena, identifies the wider borrowing of such symbolic value by the Elizabethan theatre, noting for instance the transforming of Catholic marriage ritual into fairy blessings in *A Midsummer Night's Dream*; see *Shakespearean Negotiations: The Circulation of Social Energy in Renaissance England* (Oxford: Clarendon Press, 1988), pp. 10–11.

37 Clifford Davidson, 'Robert Southwell: Lyric Poetry, the Restoration of Images, and Martyrdom', *Ben Jonson Journal*, 7 (2000), 157–86 (p. 159).

38 SE&D, 63, p. 74; see Devlin, p. 72.

39 It appeared in Cawood's augmented edition of *St Peters Complaint* (STC 22960a), along with other new poems: the Dyer parody 'A Phancie turned to a sinners complaint', 'David's peccavi', 'sinnes heavie loade' and four 'Nativity' poems: 'Joseph's Amazement', 'New Prince, newe pompe', 'The burning Babe', and 'New heaven, new warre', all of which share those deceptively simple, multi-layered aspects that characterise, in my view, Southwell's most telling work. See M&B, pp. lxii–lxv; the chapter on 'The Editions' contains an exhaustive discussion on the subject.

40 Letter to Sir Robert Cecil, quoted in Nancy Pollard Brown, 'Robert Southwell: The Mission of the Written Word', in Thomas M. McCoog, S.J. (ed.), *The Reckoned Expense: Edmund Campion and the Early English Jesuits* (Woodbridge: Boydell, 1996), pp. 193–214 (p. 197); there is a modern spelling version in Brown (ed.), *Two Letters*, p. 81. A decade earlier, Southwell had written to Persons in the same vein in the unhappy aftermath of the Campion mission; in John Hungerford Pollen, S.J. (ed.), *Unpublished Documents Relating to the English Martyrs*, I (1584–1603), Publications of the Catholic Record Society Series, 5 (1903) ([London?]: Catholic Record Society, 1908), pp. 293–333 (pp. 301–3); also see Pilarz, pp. 2–4.

41 Southwell to Acquaviva, 21 and 29 December 1588, in Devlin, p. 180.

Bibliography

SOURCES AND EDITIONS OF SOUTHWELL'S WORK

The following information is largely taken from James H. McDonald and Nancy Pollard Brown (eds), *The Poems of Robert Southwell, S.J.* (Oxford: Clarendon Press, 1967). For information on the manuscripts the reader is recommended to see this edition or Peter Davidson and Anne Sweeney (ed. and intro.), *The Collected Poems of S. Robert Southwell S.J.* (Manchester: Carcanet, forthcoming).

Editions

Saint Peters Complaint, With other Poemes

Wolfe, 1595a *STC* 22957 (March)
Wolfe, 1595b *STC* 22957 (by 5 April)
Cawood, 1595 *STC* 22956 (entered on *Stationers' Register* 5 April)
Cawood, 1597 *STC* 22958 (based on Cawood, 1595)
Cawood, 1599 *STC* 22959 (based on Cawood, 1597)
Waldegrave, ?1599 *STC* 22960 (Scotland; based on Wolfe, 1595b)
Cawood, 1602 *STC* 22960a (some new material, based on Cawood, 1599)
Leake, ?1608 *STC* 22961 (corr., based on Cawood, 1602)
Barrett, 1615 *STC* 22962
Wreittoun, 1634 *STC* 22967 (Scotland; based on Barrett, 1615)

Moeoniae

(Busby, 1595a; and Busby, 1595b) *STC* 22955 (augmented from Folger MS)
(Busby, 1595c) *STC* 22954 (augmented from Folger MS)

'Collected' works

St Omer, 1616 *STC* 22963 (some new material ('WS', 'cosen', etc.); based on Cawood, 1602)
St Omer, 1620 *STC* 22964 (revsd.; first full identification of Southwell, S.J.)
Barrett, 1620 *STC* 22965 (Anglicanised; first 'complete' works)
Haviland, 1630 *STC* 22966 (2nd edn. of Barrett, 1620)
Haviland, 1634–36 *STC* 22968 (as Haviland, 1630)

Prose works

The Triumphs over Death (Busby, London, 1595) *STC* 22971
An Epistle of Comfort (printed secretly in England, 1587–88) *STC* 22946
Marie Magdalens Funeral Teares (Cawood, London, 1591) *STC* 29950

Bibliography

More recent editions

Poetry

Alexander B. Grosart (ed.), *The Complete Poems of Robert Southwell, S.J.* (London: Robson, Fuller Worthies' Library, 1872)

James H. McDonald, and Nancy Pollard Brown (eds), *The Poems of Robert Southwell, S.J.* (Oxford: Clarendon Press, 1967)

Peter Davidson and Anne Sweeney (ed. and intro.), *The Collected Poems of S. Robert Southwell S.J.* (Manchester: Carcanet, forthcoming)

Prose

An Epistle of Comfort (London: secretly printed, 1587); repr., ed. D. M. Rogers, *English Recusant Literature, 1538–1640* (London: Scolar Press, 1974), vol. 211

'An Epistle of Robert Southwell unto His Father' (1589), in *Two Letters and Short Rules of a Good Life*, ed. Nancy Pollard Brown (Charlottesville: University Press of Virginia, for the Folger Shakespeare Library, 1973)

An Humble Supplication to Her Majestie, ed. R. C. Bald (Cambridge: Cambridge University Press, 1953)

Marie Magdalens Funeral Teares (London: Gabriel Cawood, 1591); repr., ed. Vincent B. Leitch (New York: Delmar, 1975)

Spiritual Exercises and Devotions, ed. J. M. de Buck and trans. P. E. Hallett (London: Sheed and Ward, 1931)

The Triumphs over Death, ed. J. W. Trotman (London: Manresa Press, 1914)

Southwell's letters

Sources

The Jesuit Archives, Rome (Fondo Gesuitico, 651); Annual Letters of the English College, Rome

Editions and collections

Nancy Pollard Brown (ed.), *Robert Southwell, S.J.: Two Letters and Short Rules of a Good Life* (Charlottesville: University Press of Virginia, for the Folger Shakespeare Library, 1973)

Henry Foley, S.J., *Records of the English Province of the Society of Jesus*, 7 vols (London: Burns and Oates, 1877), I, 301–87

Thomas M. McCoog, S.J., *English and Welsh Jesuits, 1555–1650*, Publications of the Catholic Record Society Series, 74–75 ([London]: Catholic Record Society, 1994–95)

Anthony G. Petti (ed.), *The Letters and Dispatches of Richard Verstegan, c.1550–1640*, Publications of the Catholic Record Society Series, 52 (London: Catholic Record Society, 1959)

John Hungerford Pollen, S.J. (ed.), *Unpublished Documents Relating to the English Martyrs*, 1 (1584–1603), Publications of the Catholic Record Society Series, 5 (1903) ([London]: Catholic Record Society, 1908), pp. 293–333

OTHER PRINTED SOURCES

Alabaster, William, *Sonnets*, ed. G. M. Story and Helen Gardner (Oxford: Oxford University Press, 1959)

Allison, Anthony, and D. M. Rogers, *The Contemporary Printed Literature of the English Counter-Reformation Between 1558 and 1640*, 2 vols (Aldershot: Scolar Press, 1989–94)

Alpers, Paul, 'Spenser's Domain of Lyric', in Hugh Maclean and Anne Lake Prescott (eds), *Edmund Spenser's Poetry*, 3rd edn (New York: Norton, 1968), pp. 787–96

Althusser, Louis, 'Ideology and the State', in *Lenin and Philosophy and Other Essays*, trans. B. Brewster (London: New Left Books, 1977)

Arber, Edward (ed.), *A Transcript of the Registers of the Company of Stationers of London 1554–1640 AD*, 5 vols (London: privately printed, 1875–94)

Ault, Norman (ed.) *Elizabethan Lyrics* (New York: Capricorn, 1960)

Bacon, Francis, *Major Works*, ed. Brian Vickers (Oxford: Oxford University Press, 1996)

Bailey, Gauvin Alexander, *Between Renaissance and Baroque: Jesuit Art in Rome, 1565–1610* (Toronto: University of Toronto Press, 2003)

—— '"Le style jésuite n'existe pas": Jesuit Corporate Culture and the Visual Arts', in John W. O'Malley, S.J., Gauvin Alexander Bailey, et al., *The Jesuits: Cultures, Sciences, and the Arts 1540–1773* (Toronto: University of Toronto Press, 1999), pp. 38–89

—— 'The Truth-Showing Mirror: Jesuit Catechism and the Arts in Mughal India', in John W. O'Malley, S.J., Gauvin Alexander Bailey, et al., *The Jesuits: Cultures, Sciences, and the Arts 1540–1773* (Toronto: University of Toronto Press, 1999), pp. 380–401

Bakhtin, Mikhail, *Rabelais and His World*, trans. Hélène Iswolsky (Cambridge, MA: MIT Press, 1968)

Baldwin, T. W., *William Shakespeare Adapts a Hanging* (Princeton, NJ: Princeton University Press, 1931)

—— *William Shakespeare's Small Latine and Lesse Greeke* (Urbana: University of Illinois Press, 1944)

Barker, Frances, *The Tremulous Private Body: Essays on Subjection* (London: Methuen, 1984)

—— and Jay Bernstein, et al. (eds), *1642: Literature and Power in the Seventeenth Century* (Colchester: University of Essex, 1981)

Barroll, Leeds, *Politics, Plague and Shakespeare's Theatre* (Ithaca, NY: Cornell University Press, 1991)

Bate, Jonathan, *Shakespeare and Ovid* (Oxford: Clarendon Press, 1993)

Bath, Michael, *Speaking Pictures: English Emblem Books and Renaissance Culture* (London: Longman, 1994)

Batley, Karen, *The Genius of Shakespeare* (London: Picador, 1997)

—— 'Southwell's "New Heaven, New Warre"', *Explicator*, 53 (Fall, 1994), 7–10

Baudrillard, Jean, 'The Evil Demon of Images', Mari Kuttna Memorial Lecture Series, 1 (Sydney: University of Sydney, Power Institute of Fine Arts, 1987)

Beal, Peter, *Index of English Literary Manuscripts*, 2 vols (London: Mansel, 1980–93), 1 (1450–1623) (1980)

Bibliography

Bellarmine, St Roberto, Cardinal, S.J., *De gemitu columbae, sive, De bono lacrymarum*, 3 vols (Antwerp: Ex Officina Plantiniana; Moretos, 1617)

Du Bellay, Joachim, *La Defence, et illustration de la Langue Francoyse* (Angevin: 1549)

Belsey, Catherine, *The Subject of Tragedy* (London: Routledge, 1985)

Berry, Philippa, *Shakespeare's Feminine Endings: Disfiguring Death in the Tragedies* (London: Routledge, 1999)

Bevington, David M., *From Mankind to Marlowe* (Cambridge, MA: Harvard University Press, 1962)

Black, J. B., *The Reign of Elizabeth, 1558–1603*, Oxford History of England Series (Oxford: Clarendon Press, 1959)

Bossy, John, *The English Catholic Community 1570–1850* (London: Darton, Longman & Todd, 1975)

—— 'The Heart of Robert Persons', in Thomas M. McCoog, S.J. (ed.), *The Reckoned Expense: Edmund Campion and the Early English Jesuits* (Woodbridge: Boydell, 1996), pp. 141–58

—— 'The Society of Jesus in the Wars of Religion', in Judith Loades (ed.) *Monastic Studies: The Continuity of Tradition* (Bangor: Headstart History, 1990), pp. 229–44

Van den Broecke, Marcel P. R., *Ortelius Atlas Maps: An Illustrated Guide* ('t Goy: HES Publishers, 1996)

Brown, Cedric C. (ed.), *Patronage, Politics, and Literary Traditions in England 1558–1658* (Detroit: Wayne State University Press, 1993)

—— and Arthur F. Marotti (eds), *Text and Cultural Change in Early Modern England* (Basingstoke: Macmillan, 1997)

Brown, John (ed.), *John Bunyan: Grace Abounding to the Chief of Sinners* (Cambridge: Cambridge University Press, 1907)

Brown, Nancy Pollard, 'Robert Southwell: the Mission of the Written Word', in Thomas M. McCoog, S.J. (ed.), *The Reckoned Expense: Edmund Campion and the Early English Jesuits* (Woodbridge: Boydell, 1996), pp. 193–214

—— (ed.), *Robert Southwell, S.J.: Two Letters and Short Rules of a Good Life*, (Charlottesville: University Press of Virginia, for the Folger Shakespeare Library, 1973)

Brown, Rawdon (ed.), *Calendar of State Papers and Manuscripts Relating to English Affairs, Venetian, 1202–* [1675] (London: Longmans, 1864–1947)

Brownlow, F. W., 'Richard Topcliffe: Elizabeth's Enforcer and the Representation of Power in *King Lear*', in Richard Dutton, Alison Findlay, and Richard Wilson (eds), *Lancastrian Shakespeare: Theatre and Religion* (Manchester: Manchester University Press, 2003), pp. 161–78

—— *Robert Southwell*, Twayne's English Authors Series, 516 (New York: Simon & Schuster Macmillan, 1996)

Bruno, Giordano, *The Heroic Frenzies*, trans. Paul Eugene Memmo, University of North Carolina Studies in Romance Languages and Literatures Series, 50 (Chapel Hill; Valencia printed: University of North Carolina Press, 1964)

Bulfinch, Thomas, *Mythology* (New York: Avenel, 1978)

Bullough, Geoffrey (ed.), *Narrative and Dramatic Sources of Shakespeare*, 8 vols (London: Routledge and Kegan Paul, 1957–75)

Byrd, William, *Collected Works: Psalms, Sonnets and Songs* (1588), ed. Edmund H. Fellowes (London: Stainer & Bell, 1965)

Calvin, John, *Institutes of the Christian Religion*, trans. Henry Beveridge, 3 vols (Edinburgh: Calvin Translation Society, 1845–46; repr. Grand Rapids: Eerdmans, 1983)

Campbell, Roy, *The Poems of St John of the Cross* (Harmondsworth: Penguin, 1960)

Caraman, Philip, S.J., *A Study in Friendship: Saint Robert Southwell and Henry Garnet* (Saint Louis, MO: The Institute of Jesuit Sources, 1995)

—— ed., and trans., *John Gerard, S.J.: The Autobiography of an Elizabethan* (London: Longmans, Green, 1951)

Carey, John, ed., *John Donne* (Oxford: Oxford University Press, 1990)

Carroll, Michael P., *Catholic Cults and Devotions: A Psychological Enquiry* (Kingston, Montreal: McGill-Queen's University, 1989)

Cavalli, Vittorio F., 'St Robert Southwell, S.J.: a Selective Bibliographic Supplement to the Studies of Pierre Janelle and James H. McDonald', *Renaissance History*, 21.3 (1993), 297–304

Cheney, Patrick, *Spenser's Famous Flight: A Renaissance Idea of a Literary Career* (Toronto: University of Toronto Press, 1993)

Cixous, Hélène, 'Laugh of the Medusa', in Robyn R. Warhol and D. P. Herndl (eds), *Feminisms: An Anthology of Literary Theory and Criticism* (New Brunswick: Rutgers University Press, 1991), 335–49

Cleri, Bonita (ed.), *Federico Zuccari: le idée, gli scritti: atti del convegno di Sant'Angelo in Vado* (Milan: Electa (Pesaro), Provincia di Pesaro e Urbino, 1997)

Collinson, Patrick, *The Elizabethan Puritan Movement* (London: Cape, 1967)

Corthell, Ronald, 'Robert Persons and the Writer's Mission', in Arthur F. Marotti (ed.), *Catholicism and Anti-Catholicism* (London: Macmillan, 1999), pp. 35–62

Craik, T. W. (ed.), *Sir Philip Sidney, Selected Poetry and Prose* (London: Methuen, 1965)

Cressy, David, *Education in Tudor and Stuart England* (London: Edward Arnold, 1975)

Croft, P. J., *Autograph Poetry in the English Language: Facsimiles of Original Manuscripts from the Fourteenth to the Twentieth Century*, 2 vols (London: Cassell, 1973)

Cust, Richard, and Ann Hughes (eds), *Conflict in Early Stuart England: Studies in Religion and Politics 1603–1642* (Harlow: Longmans, 1989)

Davidson, Clifford, 'Robert Southwell: Lyric Poetry, the Restoration of Images, and Martyrdom', *Ben Jonson Journal*, 7 (2000), 157–86

Davidson, Peter, 'Archives of the British Province of the Society of Jesus', unpublished conference paper, *Recusant Archives and Remains from the Three Kingdoms 1560–1789: Catholics in Exile at Home and Abroad* (Downside Abbey, 2004)

—— 'Emblems for the Vulnerata, Valladolid, September 1600' (unpublished conference paper, 2003)

Davidson, Peter et al., 'Festivals of the New World: the viceroyalties of Mexico and Peru', in J. R. Mulryne, Helen Watanabe-O'Kelly, and Margaret Shewring (eds), *Europa Triumphans, Court and Civic Festivals in Early Modern Europe* (Aldershot: MHRA in association with Ashgate, 2004), II, pp. 345–9.

Devlin, Christopher, *Hamlet's Divinity and Other Essays* (London: Hart-Davis, 1963)

—— *The Life of Robert Southwell Poet and Martyr* (London: Longmans, Green, 1956)

Bibliography

Dillon, Anne, *The Constitution of Martyrdom in the English Catholic Community, 1535–1603* (Aldershot: Ashgate, c.2002)

—— 'Praying by Number: the Confraternity of the Rosary and the English Catholic Community, c.1580–1700', *History*, 88 (July 2003), 451–71

Dollimore, Jonathan, *Radical Tragedy: Religion, Ideology and Poetry in the Drama of Shakespeare and his Contemporaries*, 2nd edn (Brighton: Harvester Wheatsheaf, 1989)

Donne, John, *Pseudo-Martyr* (London, 1610)

Douay, English College, *The First and Second Diaries of the English College, Douay*, trans. Thomas Francis Knox (London: Nutt, 1878; repr. Farnborough: Gregg, 1969)

Duffy, Eamon, 'Bare Ruined Choirs: Remembering Catholicism in Shakespeare's England', in Richard Dutton, Alison Findlay, and Richard Wilson (eds), *Lancastrian Shakespeare: Theatre and Religion* (Manchester: Manchester University Press, 2003), pp. 40–57

—— *The Stripping of the Altars: Traditional Religion in England c.1400–1580* (New Haven: Yale University Press, 1992)

Duncan-Jones, Katherine, *Shakespeare's Sonnets* (London: Arden Shakespeare, 1997)

—— 'Sir Philip Sidney's Debt to Edmund Campion', in Thomas M. McCoog, S.J. (ed.), *The Reckoned Expense: Edmund Campion and the Early English Jesuits* (Woodbridge: Boydell, 1996), pp. 85–102

—— (ed.), *Sir Philip Sidney* (Oxford: Oxford University Press, 1989)

Dutton, Richard, 'Licensing and Censorship', in David Scott Kastan (ed.), *A Companion to Shakespeare* (Oxford: Blackwell, 1999), pp. 377–91

—— *Mastering the Revels: The Regulation and Censorship of English Renaissance Drama* (Iowa City: University of Iowa Press, 1991)

—— *William Shakespeare* (London: Macmillan, 1989)

—— (ed.), *Ben Jonson*, Longman Critical Reader Series (Harlow: Pearson, 2000)

—— and Jean E. Howard (eds), *A Companion to Shakespeare's Works*, ii (Oxford: Blackwell, 2003)

Elizabeth I, *Collected Works*, ed. Leah S. Marcus, Janel Mueller, and Mary Beth Rose (Chicago, IL: University of Chicago Press, 2000)

Elton, G. R. (ed.), *The Tudor Constitution: Documents and Commentary*, 2nd edn (Cambridge: Cambridge University Press, 1982)

Fenlon, Dermot, *Heresy and Obedience in Tridentine Italy: Cardinal Pole and the Counter-Reformation* (Cambridge: Cambridge University Press, 1972)

Finch, M. E., 'The Wealth of Five Northamptonshire Families', *Northamptonshire Record Society*, 19 (1956) [no page nos]

Flynn, Dennis, '"Out of Step": Six Supplementary Notes on Jasper Heywood', in Thomas M. McCoog, S.J. (ed.), *The Reckoned Expense: Edmund Campion and the Early English Jesuits* (Woodbridge: Boydell, 1996), pp. 179–92

Foley, Henry, S.J., *Records of the English Province of the Society of Jesus*, 7 vols (London: Burns and Oates, 1877)

Fraser, Antonia, *Mary Queen of Scots* (London: Panther, 1970)

Ganss, George E., *Saint Ignatius' Idea of a Jesuit University*, 2nd edn (Milwaukee: Marquette University Press, 1956)

Gardner, Helen, *The Metaphysical Poets*, 2nd rev. edn (Harmondsworth: Penguin, 1985)

—— (ed.), *John Donne: The Divine Poems* (Oxford: Clarendon Press, 1952)
Garnet, Henry, *The Societie of the Rosary, wherein is conteined the beginning, increase & profit of the same. Also the orders and manifold graces annexed unto it, with divers other things thereunto appertaining* (n.p.d. [London, 1593–94])
Gerard, John, S.J., *The Autobiography of an Elizabethan*, trans. and ed. Philip Caraman, S.J. (London: Longmans, Green, 1951)
Gerard, John, *Catalogus arborum* (London: *exofficina Arnoldii Hatfield, impensis Ioannis Norton*, 1599)
Gibson, T. E., *Crosby Records* (Manchester: Chetham Society, 1887)
Green, Mary Anne Everett (ed.), *Calendar of State Papers, Domestic Series, of the Reign of Elizabeth, 1581–1590* (London: Longmans, 1865)
—— *Calendar of State Papers, Domestic Series, of the Reign of Elizabeth, 1591–1594* (London: HMSO, 1867; repr. Liechtenstein: Kraus, 1967)
Greenblatt, Stephen, *Hamlet in Purgatory* (Princeton, NJ: Princeton University Press, 2001)
—— *Renaissance Self-Fashioning: From More to Shakespeare* (Chicago: University of Chicago Press, 1980)
—— *Shakespearean Negotiations: The Circulation of Social Energy in Renaissance England* (Oxford: Clarendon Press, 1997)
Greg, W. W., *Some Aspects and Problems of London Publishing* (Oxford: Oxford Clarendon Press, 1956)
Gregerson, Linda, *The Reformation of the Subject: Spenser, Milton, and the English Protestant Epic* (Cambridge: Cambridge University Press, 1997)
Grosart, Alexander B., *A Bower of Delights; being interwoven Verse and Prose from the works of Nicholas Breton* (London: Elliot Stock, 1893)
—— *Complete Works in Verse and Prose of Samuel Daniel*, 5 vols (New York: Russell & Russell, 1963)
—— (ed.), *The Complete Poems of Robert Southwell, S.J.* (London: Robson, Fuller Worthies' Library, 1872)
Guy, John, *My Heart Is My Own: The Life of Mary Queen of Scots* (London: Harper Collins, 2004)
Hackett, Helen, *Virgin Mother, Maiden Queen: Elizabeth I and the Cult of the Virgin Mary* (Basingstoke: Macmillan, 1995)
Hadfield, Andrew, *The English Renaissance 1500–1620* (Oxford: Blackwell, 2001)
Haigh, Christopher, 'The Continuity of Catholicism in the English Reformation', in Christopher Haigh (ed.), *The English Reformation Revised* (Cambridge: Cambridge University Press, 1987), pp. 176–215
—— *English Reformations: Religion, Politics and Society under the Tudors* (Oxford: Clarendon Press, 1993)
Hamilton, Bernice, *Political Thought in Sixteenth Century Spain: A Study of the Political Ideas of Vitoria, De Solo, Suárez and Molina* (Oxford: Clarendon Press, 1963)
Hanson, Elizabeth, *Discovering the Subject in Renaissance England* (Cambridge: Cambridge University Press, 1998)
Happold, F. C., *Mysticism: A Study and an Anthology* (Harmondsworth: Penguin, 1990)
Headlam-Wells, Robin, *Spenser's Faerie Queene and the Cult of Elizabeth* (London: Croom Helm, 1983)

Hedley, Jane, *Power in Verse: Metaphor and Metonymy in the Renaissance Lyric* (University Park; London: Pennsylvania State University Press, 1988)

Helgerson, Richard, 'Shakespeare and Contemporary Dramatists of History', in Richard Dutton and Jean E. Howard (eds), *A Companion to Shakespeare's Works*, 4 vols (Oxford: Blackwell, 2003), II, pp. 26–47

Heninger, S. K., Jr, *Touches of Sweet Harmony: Pythagorean Cosmology and Renaissance Poetics* (San Marino, CA: Huntington Library, 1974)

Hermann-Fiore, Kristina, 'Gli angeli, nella teoria e nella pittura di Federico Zuccari', in Bonita Cleri (ed.), *Federico Zuccari: le idée, gli scritti: atti del convegno di Sant'Angelo in Vado* (Milan: Electa (Pesaro), Provincia di Pesaro e Urbino, 1997), pp. 90–107

Hertz, Alexandra, 'Imitators of Christ: The Martyr-Cycles of Late Sixteenth Century Rome Seen in Context', *Storia dell'Arte*, 62 (1988), 53–70

Hill, Geoffrey, 'The Absolute Reasonableness of Robert Southwell', in *The Lords of Limit* (New York: Oxford University Press, 1984)

—— 'Tenebrae', *Collected Poems*, Penguin International Poets Series (Harmondsworth; Penguin, 1990)

Hirn, Yrjö, *The Sacred Shrine: A Study of the Poetry and Art of the Catholic Church*, 2nd edn, rev. C. H. Talbot (London: Faber & Faber, 1958)

Höltgen, Karl Josef, 'Henry Hawkins: A Jesuit Writer and Emblematist in Stuart England', in John W. O'Malley, S.J., Gauvin Alexander Bailey, et al., *The Jesuits: Cultures, Sciences, and the Arts 1540–1773* (Toronto: University of Toronto Press, 1999) pp. 601–26

Honan, Park, *Shakespeare, a Life* (Oxford: Oxford University Press, 1998)

Honigmann, E. A. J., *Shakespeare: The 'Lost Years'*, 2nd edn (Manchester: Manchester University Press, 1998)

Hood, Christobel M., *The Book of Robert Southwell* (Oxford: Blackwell, 1926)

Houliston, Victor, '*Brevis Dialogismus*: An Anonymous Becket Play from the Jesuit Seminary at St Omer', *English Literary Renaissance*, 23 (1993), 382–427

—— 'Why Robert Persons Would Not Be Pacified: Edmund Bunny's Theft of *The Book of Resolution*', in Thomas M. McCoog, S.J. (ed.), *The Reckoned Expense: Edmund Campion and the Early English Jesuits* (Woodbridge: Boydell, 1996), pp. 159–78

Huffman, Clifford Chalmers, *Elizabethan Impressions: John Wolfe and his Press*, AMS Studies in the Renaissance Series, 21 (New York: AMS, 1988)

Hughes, Gerard W., S.J., *In Search of a Way: Two Journeys of Spiritual Discovery* (London: Darton Longman & Todd, 1998)

Hughes, Philip, *The Reformation of England*, rev. 5th edn, 3 vols (New York: Macmillan, 1963)

Hughes, Thomas, S.J., *The Educational System of the Jesuits* (London: Heinemann, 1904)

Hutchison, F. E. (ed.), *George Herbert: Works* (Oxford: Clarendon Press, 1941)

Ignatius of Loyola, S.J., St, *The Autobiography: With Related Documents*, ed., intro. and notes John C. Olin, trans. Joseph F. O'Callaghan (London: Harper and Row, 1974)

—— *Letters*, selected and trans. William J. Young, S.J. (Chicago, IL: Loyola University Press, 1959)

—— *The Spiritual Exercises and Selected Works*, ed. George E. Ganss (New York: Paulist Press, c.1991)

Ingleby, C. M., et al., *The Shakespeare Allusion-Book*, 2 vols (London: Oxford University Press, 1932)
Isham, Sir Gyles, *Sir Thomas Tresham and his Buildings*, Northamptonshire Antiquarian Society, Reports and Papers Series (Northampton: Northamptonshire Antiquarian Society, 1966), vol. 65 (1964, 1965), Part 2 [no page nos]
Janelle, Pierre, *Robert Southwell the Writer: A Study in Religious Inspiration* (London: Sheed and Ward, 1935)
Jones, Emrys (ed.), *The New Oxford Book of Sixteenth Century Verse* (Oxford: Oxford University Press, 1991)
Jonsen, Albert R., and Stephen Toulmin, *The Abuses of Casuistry: A History of Moral Theology* (Berkeley and Los Angeles: University of California Press, 1988)
Jonson, Ben, *Works*, ed. C. H. Herford, and P. and E. Simpson, 8 vols (Oxford: Clarendon Press, 1925–52)
Kastan, David Scott (ed.), *A Companion to Shakespeare* (Oxford: Blackwell, 1999)
Keene, Dennis (ed.), *Henry Howard, Earl of Surrey: Selected Poems* (Manchester: Carcanet, 1985)
Kerman, Joseph, *The Masses and Motets of William Byrd* (London: Faber & Faber, 1981)
Kermode, Frank, *Shakespeare's Language* (Harmondsworth: Penguin, 2000)
King, John N., *English Reformation Literature: The Tudor Origins of the Protestant Tradition* (Princeton, NJ: Princeton University Press, 1982)
Klebanoff, Randi, 'The *Vita* and the *Morte*: Making the Sacred in Renaissance Bologna'; paper delivered at the Sixteenth Century Studies Conference (Toronto, 24 October 1998)
Knox, R. A., *Enthusiasm: A Chapter in the History of Religion* (Oxford: Clarendon Press, 1950)
Knox, Thomas Francis, trans., *The First and Second Diaries of the English College, Douay* (London: Nutt, 1878; repr. Farnborough: Gregg, 1969)
Kuchar, Gary, 'Southwell's "A vale of teares": A Psychoanalysis of Form', *Mosaic*, 34.1 (2001), 107–20
Lake, Peter, 'Religious Identities in Shakespeare's England', in David Scott Kastan (ed.), *A Companion to Shakespeare* (Oxford: Blackwell, 1999), pp. 57–84
Larocca, John J., S.J., 'Popery and Pounds: The Effect of the Jesuit Mission on Penal Legislation', in Thomas M. McCoog, S.J. (ed.), *The Reckoned Expense: Edmund Campion and the Early English Jesuits* (Woodbridge: Boydell, 1996), pp. 249–64
Lewalski, Barbara Kiefer, *Protestant Poetics and the Seventeenth Century Religious Lyric* (Princeton, NJ: Princeton University Press, 1979)
Lewis, C. S., *Allegory of Love* (Oxford: Oxford University Press, 1936)
—— *English Literature in the Sixteenth Century excluding Drama* (Oxford: Clarendon Press, 1944)
—— *Studies in Medieval and Renaissance Literature*, coll. Walter Hooper (Cambridge: Cambridge University Press, 1966)
Loades, David, 'The Spirituality of the Restored Catholic Church (1553–1558) in the Context of the Counter Reformation', in Thomas M. McCoog, S.J. (ed.), *The Reckoned Expense: Edmund Campion and the Early English Jesuits* (Woodbridge: Boydell, 1996), pp. 3–20
Lodge, David, and Nigel Wood (eds), *Modern Criticism and Theory: A Reader*, 2nd edn (Harlow: Pearson Educational, 1988)

Lynch, Michael, *Mary Stuart: Queen in Three Kingdoms* (Oxford: Blackwell, 1988)

MacCulloch, Diarmaid, *Thomas Cranmer: A Life* (New Haven: Yale University Press, 1996)

MacGrath, Patrick, and Joy Rowe, 'Anstruther Analysed: The Elizabethan Seminary Priests', *Recusant History*, 18.1 (May 1986), 1–13

Maclean, Hugh, and Anne Lake Prescott (eds), *Edmund Spenser's Poetry*, 3rd edn (New York: Norton, 1968)

Maritain, Jacques, *An Introduction to Philosophy*, trans. E. I. Watkins (London: Sheed and Ward, 1979)

Marotti, Arthur F., (ed.), *Catholicism and Anti-Catholicism in Early Modern English Texts* (Basingstoke: Macmillan, 1999)

—— *Manuscript, Print and the English Renaissance Lyric* (Ithaca: Cornell University Press, 1995)

Martin, Patrick H., and John Finnis, 'Thomas Thorpe, "W.S.," and the Catholic Intelligencers', *English Literary Renaissance*, 33 (2003), 3–43

Martz, Louis L., *The Poetry of Meditation* (New Haven: Yale University Press, 1954)

Mayer, Thomas F., 'A Test of Wills: Cardinal Pole, Ignatius Loyola, and the Jesuits in England', in Thomas M. McCoog, S.J. (ed.), *The Reckoned Expense: Edmund Campion and the Early English Jesuits* (Woodbridge: Boydell, 1996), pp. 21–38

McConica, James, 'The Catholic Experience in Tudor Oxford', in Thomas M. McCoog, S.J. (ed.), *The Reckoned Expense: Edmund Campion and the Early English Jesuits* (Woodbridge: Boydell, 1996), pp. 39–66

McCoog, Thomas M., S.J. (ed), *The Mercurian Project: Forming Jesuit Culture 1572–1580* (Rome: Institutum Historicum Societatis Iesu, 2004)

—— '"Playing the Champion": The Role of Disputation in the Jesuit Mission', in Thomas M. McCoog, S.J. (ed.), *The Reckoned Expense: Edmund Campion and the Early English Jesuits* (Woodbridge: Boydell, 1996), pp. 119–41

—— (ed.), *The Reckoned Expense: Edmund Campion and the Early English Jesuits* (Woodbridge: Boydell, 1996)

McDonald, James H., and Nancy Pollard Brown (eds), *The Poems of Robert Southwell, S.J.* (Oxford: Clarendon Press, 1967)

McEachern, Claire, *The Poetics of English Nationhood 1590–1612* (Cambridge: Cambridge University Press, 1996)

McInerny, Ralph, *Art and Prudence: Studies in the Thought of Jacques Maritain*, Publications of the Jacques Maritain Center Series, 1 ([n.p.]: University of Notre Dame Press, c.1988)

Medina, Francisco de Borja, S.J., 'Intrigues of a Scottish Jesuit at the Spanish Court: Unpublished Letters of William Crichton to Claudio Acquaviva (Madrid 1590–1592)', in Thomas M. McCoog, S.J. (ed.), *The Reckoned Expense: Edmund Campion and the Early English Jesuits* (Woodbridge: Boydell, 1996), pp. 215–98

Meissner, W. W., *Ignatius of Loyola: The Psychology of a Saint* (New Haven: Yale University Press, 1992)

Melchiori, Giorgio, *Shakespeare's Dramatic Meditations: An Experiment in Criticism* (Oxford: Clarendon Press, 1976)

Meyer, A. O., *England und die katholische Kirche unter Elisabeth*, Bibliothek des Kgl. Preussischen Historischen Instituts in Rom Series, 6, 2 vols (Rome: Loescher, 1911)

Milward, Peter, S.J., 'Shakespeare's Jesuit Schoolmasters', in Richard Dutton,

Alison Findlay, and Richard Wilson (eds), *Lancastrian Shakespeare: Theatre and Religion* (Manchester: Manchester University Press, 2003), pp. 58–70
—— *Shakespeare's Religious Background* (London: Sidgwick and Jackson, 1973)
Milton, Anthony, 'Qualified Intolerance: The Limits and Ambiguities of Early Stuart Anti-Catholicism', in Arthur F. Marotti (ed.), *Catholicism and Anti-Catholicism in Early Modern English texts* (Basingstoke: Macmillan, 1999), pp. 85–109
Montrose, Louis A., 'Of Gentlemen and Shepherds: The Politics of Elizabethan Pastoral Form', *Elizabethan Literary History*, 50 (1983), 415–60
More, Henry, *Historia Missionis Anglicanae Societatis Jesu* (St Omer, 1660)
Morris, J., *Troubles of Our Catholic Forefathers*, 3 vols (Farnborough: Gregg, 1970)
Muir, Kenneth, *The Sources of Shakespeare's Plays* (London: Methuen, 1977)
Munday, Anthony, *The English Roman Life*, ed. Philip Ayres (Oxford: Clarendon Press, 1980)
Murdin, William (ed.), *A Collection of State Papers relating to Affairs in the Reign of Elizabeth, 1571–1596, transcribed from original papers and other authentic memorials left by W. Cecill Lord Burghley, and reposited in the Library at Hatfield House* (London: William Bowyer, 1759)
Murphy, Andrew (ed.), *The Renaissance Text: Theory, Editing, Textuality* (Manchester: Manchester University Press, 2000)
Neill, Michael, *Issues of Death: Mortality and Identity in English Renaissance Tragedy* (Oxford: Clarendon Press, 1997)
De Nicolás, Antonio T., *Ignatius de Loyola: Powers of Imagining* (Albany: State University of New York Press, 1986)
Nicoll, Allardyce (ed.), *Shakespeare in his own Age* (Cambridge: Cambridge University Press, 1976)
Norbrook, David, *Poetry and Politics in the English Renaissance* (London: Routledge and Kegan Paul, 1984)
O'Callaghan, Michelle, *The 'Shepheards Nation': Jacobean Spenserians and Early Stuart Political Culture, 1612–1625* (Oxford: Clarendon Press, 2000)
O'Connell, Robert J., *Art and the Christian Intelligence in St Augustine* (Oxford: Blackwell, 1978)
O'Malley, John W., *The First Jesuits* (Cambridge, MA: Harvard University Press, 1993)
—— S.J., and Gauvin Alexander Bailey, et al., *The Jesuits: Cultures, Sciences, and the Arts 1540–1773* (Toronto: University of Toronto Press, 1999)
Ong, Walter, *Fighting for Life: Contest, Sexuality and Consciousness* (Ithaca: Cornell University Press, 1981)
Ousby, Ian (ed.), *Cambridge Guide to Literature in English* (Cambridge: Cambridge University Press, 1988)
Oxley, Brian, 'The Relation between Robert Southwell's Neo-Latin and English Poetry', *Recusant History* 17.3 (May 1985), 201–7
Palgrave, Francis T., *The Golden Treasury: Selected from the Best Songs and Lyrical Poems in the English Language and Arranged with Notes, with a Supplementary Fifth Book Selected, Arranged, and Annotated by Laurence Binyon*, 3rd edn (London: Macmillan, 1939)
Palmer, Alan and Veronica, *Who's Who in Shakespeare's England* (London: Methuen, 1999)
Partridge, A. C. (ed.), *The Tribe of Ben: Pre-Augustan Classical Verse in English* (Columbia: University of South Carolina Press, 1970)

Patrides, C. A. (ed.), *Sir Thomas Browne: The Major Works* (Harmondsworth: Penguin, 1977)

Patterson, Annabel M., *Censorship and Interpretation: The Conditions of Writing and Reading in Early Modern England* (Madison, WI: University of Wisconsin Press, 1984)

Peers, E. Allison, trans. and ed., *The Complete Works of St Teresa of Jesus*, 3 vols (London: Sheed and Ward, 1946)

Petti, Anthony G., *The Letters and Dispatches of Richard Verstegan*, Publications of the Catholic Record Society Series, 52 (London: Catholic Record Society, 1959)

Pieper, Josef, *Only the Lover Sings: Art and Contemplation*, trans. Lothar Krauth (San Francisco: Ignatius Press, 1990)

Pilarz, Scott, S.J., *Robert Southwell and the Mission of Literature 1561–1595: Writing Reconciliation* (Aldershot: Ashgate, 2004)

Pincombe, Mike (ed.), *The Anatomy of Tudor Literature: Proceedings of the First International Conference of the Tudor Symposium (1998)* (Aldershot: Ashgate, 2001)

Pollard, A. F., and G. R. Redgrave (eds), *A Short-title Catalogue of Books Printed in England, Scotland, and Ireland, and of English Books Printed Abroad, 1475–1640* (London: Bibliographical Society, 1926)

Pollen, John Hungerford, S.J., *Acts of the English Martyrs hitherto unpublished* (London: Burns and Oates, 1891)

—— *Unpublished Documents Relating to the English Martyrs*, Publications of the Catholic Record Society Series, 5 (London: Catholic Record Society, 1908)

—— 'Father Robert Southwell and the Babington Plot', *The Month* 119 (1911), 302–4

—— 'Religious Terrorism under Queen Elizabeth', *The Month*, 105.489 (March 1905), 271–87

Porges-Watson, Elizabeth (ed.), *Sir Philip Sidney: Defence of Poesie, Astrophil and Stella, and Other Writings* (London: Dent, 1997)

Praz, Mario, 'Baroque in England', *Modern Philology*, 61 (1963/4), 169–79

—— 'Robert Southwell's "Saint Peters Complaint" and its Italian source', *Modern Language Review*, 3 (July, 1924), 273–90

Pritchard, Arnold, *Catholic Loyalism in Elizabethan England* (Chapel Hill: University of North Carolina Press, c.1979)

Puppi, Lionello, *Torment in Art: Pain, Violence and Martyrdom* (New York: Rizzoli, 1991)

Puttenham, George, *The Arte of English Poesie*, ed. Gladys Doidge Willcock, and Alice Walker (London: R. Field, 1589; repr. London: Cambridge University Press, 1970)

Questier, Michael, *Conversion, Politics and Religion in England, 1580–1625* (Cambridge: Cambridge University Press, 1996)

—— '"Like Locusts over all the World": Conversion, Indoctrination and the Society of Jesus in Late Elizabethan and Jacobean England', in Thomas M. McCoog, S.J. (ed.), *The Reckoned Expense: Edmund Campion and the Early English Jesuits* (Woodbridge: Boydell, 1996), pp. 265–84

Raspa, Anthony, *The Emotive Image: Jesuit Poetics in the English Renaissance* (Fort Worth: Texas Christian University Press, 1983)

Reynolds, E. E., *Campion and Parsons: The Jesuit Mission of 1580* (London: Sheed and Ward, 1980)

Rice, Louise, 'Jesuit Thesis Prints and the Festive Academic Defence at the Collegio Romano', in John W. O'Malley, S.J., Gauvin Alexander Bailey, et al., (eds), *The*

Jesuits: Cultures, Sciences, and the Arts 1540–1773 (Toronto: University of Toronto Press, 1999), pp. 148–69

Richeôme, Louis, *La peinture spirituelle* (Lyon, 1611)

Robertson, Jean (ed.), *Nicholas Breton: Poems Not Hitherto Printed* (Liverpool: Liverpool University Press, 1967, first published 1952)

Rogers, D. M. (ed.), *English Recusant Literature, 1558–1640* (London: Scolar Press, 1974)

Ross, Andrew C., 'Alessandro Valignano: The Jesuits and Culture in the East', in John W. O'Malley, S.J., Gauvin Alexander Bailey, et al., (eds), *The Jesuits: Cultures, Sciences, and the Arts 1540–1773* (Toronto: University of Toronto Press, 1999), pp. 336–51

Rowe, Katherine, *Dead Hands: Fictions of Agency, Renaissance to Modern* (Stanford, CA: Stanford University Press, 1999)

Rowse, A. L., *The Elizabethan Renaissance: The Life of the Society* (Harmondsworth: Penguin, 2000)

Ruff, Lilian M., and Arnold Wilson, 'The Madrigal, the Lute Song and Elizabethan Politics', *Past & Present*, 44 (1969), 3–51

Sams, Eric, *The Real Shakespeare: Retrieving the Early Years 1564–1594* (New Haven: Yale University Press, 1995)

Saward, John, *The Beauty of Holiness and the Holiness of Beauty: Art, Sanctity and the Truth of Catholicism* (San Francisco: Ignatius Press, 1997)

Scallon, Joseph D., *The Poetry of Robert Southwell, S.J.* (Salzburg: Institut für Englische Sprache und Literatur, 1975)

Schoenfeldt, Michael C., *Bodies and Selves in Early Modern England*, Cambridge Studies in Renaissance Literature and Culture Series, 34 (Cambridge: Cambridge University Press, 1999)

Schroeder, H. J. (trans.), *Canons and Decrees of the Council of Trent* (Rockford, IL: Tan Books, 1982)

Sharp, Sir Cuthbert (ed.), *The Rising in the North: The 1569 rebellion, being a reprint of the 'Memorials of the rebellion of the Earls of Northumberland and Westmoreland'* (1840), with a new foreword by Robert Wood (Durham: J. Shotton, 1975; facsimile repr.)

Sheavyn, Phoebe, *The Literary Profession in the Elizabethan Age*; 2nd edn, rev. J. W. Saunders (Manchester: Manchester University Press, 1967)

Shell, Alison, *Catholicism, Controversy and the English Literary Imagination 1558–1660* (Cambridge: Cambridge University Press, 1999)

—— 'Sources for the Study of Recusant Literary Culture', unpublished conference paper, *Recusant Archives and Remains from the Three Kingdoms 1560–1789: Catholics in Exile at Home and Abroad* (Downside Abbey, 2004)

—— '"We are Made a Spectacle": Campion's Dramas', in Thomas M. McCoog, S.J. (ed.), *The Reckoned Expense: Edmund Campion and the Early English Jesuits* (Woodbridge: Boydell, 1996), pp. 103–18

Shuger, Debora, *Habits of Thought in the English Renaissance: Religion, Politics and the Dominant Culture* (Berkeley: University of California Press, 1990)

—— *Renaissance Bible: Scholarship, Sacrifice and Subjectivity* (Berkeley: University of California Press, 1999)

Simon, Joan, *Education and Society in Tudor England* (Cambridge: Cambridge University Press, 1967)

Bibliography

Sinfield, Alan, *Literature in Protestant England 1560–1660* (Beckenham: Croom Helm, 1983)

Smialkowska, Monika, 'Skipping Sports and Solemn Rites: Popular and High Culture in the Early Stuart Court Masque', unpublished doctoral thesis (University of Gloucester, 2001)

Smith, Bruce, *Homosexual Desire in Shakespeare's England* (Chicago: University of Chicago Press, 1991)

Smith, Jeffrey Chipps, 'The Art of Salvation in Bavaria', in John W. O'Malley, S.J., and Gauvin Alexander Bailey, et al., *The Jesuits: Cultures, Sciences, and the Arts 1540–1773* (Toronto: University of Toronto Press, 1999), pp. 568–99

—— *Sensuous Worship: Jesuits and the Art of the Early Catholic Reformation in Germany* (Princeton, NJ: Princeton University Press, 2002)

Smith, Lacey Baldwin, *Elizabeth Tudor: Portrait of a Queen* (London: Hutchinson, 1976)

Stone, Lawrence, *Crisis in the Aristocracy 1558–1641* (Oxford: Oxford University Press, 1967)

Strong, Roy, *The Cult of Elizabeth: Elizabethan Portraiture and Pageantry* (London: Pimlico, 1999)

—— *Gloriana: The Portraits of Queen Elizabeth I* (London: Pimlico, 2003)

—— *The Spirit of Britain: A Narrative History of the Arts* (London: Pimlico, 1999)

Stukenbrock, Christiane, and Barbara Töpper (eds), *1000 Masterpieces of European Painting from 1300 to 1850* (Cologne: Könemann, 2000)

Suárez, Francisco, *Of Laws and God the Lawgiver (De legibus ac deo legislatore)* (New York: Wiley, 1964)

Sutton, Dana F. (ed.), *Unpublished Works by William Alabaster*, Salzburg Studies in English Literature Series: Elizabethan and Renaissance Studies, 126 (Salzburg: University of Salzburg, 1997)

Swain, Margaret, *Needlework of Mary Queen of Scots* (New York: Van Nostrand-Reinhold, 1973)

Sweeney, Anne, 'Robert Southwell's English Lyrics: Authorial Integrity on the Mission to Elizabethan England (1580–1595)', unpublished doctoral thesis (Lancaster University, 2004)

Teresa of Jesus, St, *Obres de Sta Teresa de Jesús*, ed. el p. Silverio de Santa Teresa, Biblioteca Mistica Carmelitana Seriès, 1 (Burgos: Tip. de 'El Monte Carmelo', 1915–24)

Thomas, Paul, *Authority and Disorder in Tudor Times 1485–1603* (Cambridge: Cambridge University Press, 1999)

Thorne, Alison, *Vision and Rhetoric in Shakespeare: Looking through Language* (Basingstoke: Macmillan, 2000)

Tottel, Richard (ed.), *Tottel's Miscellany 1557: Songs and Sonnets* (London: 1557; repr. London and Menston: Scolar Press, 1970)

Turnbull, W. B. (ed.), *Rev. Robert Southwell: The Poetical Works* (British Library 2340.a.2. in 'Old Authors, 1856, etc.')

Tuve, Rosamund, 'Sacred "Parody" of Love Poetry, and Herbert', *Studies in the Renaissance*, 8 (1961), 250

Valone, Carolyn, 'Women on the Quirinal Hill: Patronage in Rome, 1560–1630', *Art Bulletin*, 36 (1994), 129–46

Vickers, Brian (ed.), *Francis Bacon* (Oxford: Oxford University Press, 1996)

Waller, Gary, *English Poetry of the Sixteenth Century* (Harlow: Longman, 1986)
Wallerstein, Ruth, *Studies in Seventeenth Century Poetic* (Madison: University of Wisconsin Press, 1965)
Walsham, Alexandra, *Church Papists: Catholicism, Conformity and Confessional Polemic in Early Modern England* (Woodbridge: Boydell, 1993)
—— 'Miracles and the Counter-Reformation Mission to England', *The Humanities Journal*, 46 (2003), 779–815
Warhol, Robyn R., and Diane Price Herndl (eds), *Feminisms: An Anthology of Literary Theory and Criticism* (New Brunswick: Rutgers University Press, 1991)
Warnlop, Jessica Jean, 'The Influence of Giordano Bruno on the Writings of Sir Philip Sidney' (unpublished dissertation, Texas A&M University, August 1973)
Watts, V. E., trans., *Boethius: The Consolation of Philosophy* (Harmondsworth: Penguin, 1969)
Waugh, Evelyn, *Edmund Campion: Scholar, Priest, Hero, and Martyr* (Oxford: Oxford University Press, 1980)
Wells, Robin Headlam, *Spenser's Faerie Queene and the Cult of Elizabeth* (Beckenham: Croom Helm, 1983)
Wells, Stanley (ed.), *Shakespeare: A Bibliographical Guide* (Oxford: Clarendon Press, 1990)
—— and Gary Taylor (eds), *The Oxford Shakespeare Complete Works* (Oxford: Clarendon Press, 1988)
White, Helen C., *Tudor Books of Saints and Martyrs* (Madison: University of Wisconsin Press, 1963)
—— 'Southwell – Metaphysical and Baroque', *Modern Philology*, 61 (1963/4), 159–68
Willcock, Gladys Doidge, and Alice Walker (eds), *George Puttenham: The Arte of English Poesie* (London: R. Field, 1589; repr. London: Cambridge University Press, 1970)
Williams, Michael E., 'Campion and the English Continental Seminaries', in Thomas M. McCoog, S.J. (ed.), *The Reckoned Expense: Edmund Campion and the Early English Jesuits* (Woodbridge: Boydell, 1996), pp. 285–99
—— *The Venerable English College Rome: A History 1579–1979* (London: Associated Catholic Publications (on behalf of the College), 1979)
Williamson, Claude, *Letters from the Saints: Early Renaissance and Reformation Periods from St. Thomas Aquinas to Bl. Robert Southwell* (London: Rockliff, 1958)
Wilson, Richard, 'A Bloody Question: The Politics of Venus and Adonis' (unpublished lecture, Sorbonne, 1998)
—— *Secret Shakespeare: Studies in Theatre, Religion and Resistance* (Manchester: Manchester University Press, 2004)
—— 'Shakespeare and the Jesuits', *Times Literary Supplement*, 19 December 1997, 11–13
—— *Will Power: Essays on Shakespearean Authority* (London: Harvester Wheatsheaf, 1993)
Wilson, Scott, 'The Struggle for Sovereignty in *Astrophil and Stella*', *Criticism*, 33.3 (Summer 1991), 309–32
Wormald, Jenny, *Mary Queen of Scots: Politics, Passion and a Kingdom Lost*, rev. edn (London: Taurus Parke, 2001)
—— *Mary Queen of Scots: A Study in Failure* (London: Collins & Brown, 1991)
Woudhuysen, H. R., *Sir Philip Sidney and the Circulation of Manuscripts, 1558–1640* (Oxford: Clarendon Press, 1996)

Bibliography

—— (ed.), *The Penguin Book of Renaissance Verse 1509–1659* (Harmondsworth: Penguin, 1993)

Yates, Frances, *The Occult Philosophy in the Elizabethan Age* (London: Routledge & Kegan Paul, 1979)

—— *Giordano Bruno and the Hermetic Tradition* (London: Routledge & Kegan Paul, 1971)

de Yepes, Diego, *Historia particular de la persecution de Inglaterre* (Madrid, 1599), ed. D. M. Rogers (Farnborough: Gregg, 1971)

Young, William J., S.J. (ed. and trans.), *St Ignatius of Loyola: Letters* (Chicago, IL: Loyola University Press, 1959)

Zeri, Federico, *Pittura e controriforma: l'arte senza tempo di Scipione da Gaeta*, repr. (Vicenza: Neri Pozzone, c.1997)

INTERNET SOURCES

http://apm.brookes.ac.uk/publishing/contexts/elizabet/mechanis.htm
www.catholic-forum.com/saints/pray0055.htm
www.ccel.org/ccel/calvin/calcom.html
www.cuencanet.com/ortiz/chinchona.htm
www.eebo.chadwyck.com/home
www.faculty.fairfield.edu/jmac/nadal/nadalintro.htm
www.jesuit.org
www.nationaltrust.org.uk/places/lyvedennewbield/history_papers.html
www.newadvent.org/cathen.htm
www.noosphere.cc/flandersScientists.html
www.philological.bham.ac.uk/minutum/intro.html
www.rembert-dodoens.biography.ms
www.sjweb.info/articles/rometour_all.cfm
www.tudorplace.com.htm
www.walsingham.org

Index

Abbreviations: RS = Robert Southwell

Note: Literary works can be found under authors' names
'n.' after a page reference indicates the number of a note on that page

Acquaviva, Claudio 23, 25, 37n.100, 42–5, 62, 65n.19, 69n.90, 86–8, 93–4, 104, 106, 111, 112, 165, 192n.42, 194–5, 259
Agazzari, Alfonsus (Rector of the English College, Rome) 54, 55, 63, 94–5, 101
Allen, William, Cardinal 4–7, 24, 30, 54, 59–62 passim, 85–8, 97, 197, 210–11
alter Christus, RS as 114, 229, 234, 236, 260, 262, 270, 277–8, 282
angels 4, 16, 38–9, 40, 47, 49, 52–3, 71–4, 83, 114–15, 123–9, 134, 141–2, 157, 232, 243, 260
   Gabriel 16, 24, 39, 47, 71–3, 94, 123–4, 175, 246–7
   Protestantism, and 71, 123–4, 128–9, 133, 157
   Raphael 16, 73, 123
apostasy 79, 100, 126, 144, 147, 150, 153
Armada Crisis, the 97–8, 105, 194, 196–7, 203, 213, 219, 221–2

Babington, Anthony 106–7, 111, 198–201, 254
baroque style, the, influence on RS of 9–12, 25–6, 34n.43, 40, 115, 156, 165, 270, 284–5
du Bartas, Guillaume de Salluste 18
Bellamy, Anne 248, 257
Bellarmine, Robert, Cardinal 55, 88, 96–7, 103–4, 107, 123–4, 127, 149, 165, 174, 184, 206, 211
   Controversies (1586) 92n.48, 97
   De Gemitu columbae 79
   on image and visual integrity 42, 49, 81, 165, 174, 184, 206
   on the relationship between papal and secular power 104, 254
   on the Virgin as active Mediatrix 124, 149, 247
Bethany 138–9, 155, 156–7, 168, 185
biblical texts 15, 16, 42, 46, 49, 53, 83–4, 147, 151, 156–7, 173, 185, 212–13, 217, 221–2, 248–9, 275, 283
Breton, Nicholas 146, 151, 171, 186, 188–9
Brown, Nancy Pollard 35n.59, 36n.84, 36n.87, 118n.25, 119n.33, 161n.42, 219, 223n.6, 241
Brownlow, F. W. 32n.27, 35n.59, 70n.102, 78, 118n.25, 119n.33, 151, 161n.48, 196, 203, 223n.7, 224n.22, 226n.55, 226n.57, 246, 254, 266n.49, 267n.61, 274
Bruegel, Peter 23–4,
   Census of Bethlehem 165
Burghley see Cecil, Robert, or Cecil, William
burlesques (in RS's writing) 16, 20, 73, 128, 171–2, 211–18, 283
Byrd, William 105–6, 124, 168, 181–8 passim, 217, 221, 235, 256–7

Campion, Edmund 4, 6, 15, 56–62 passim, 86, 97, 204, 238, 258
casuistry 52–3, 85, 99, 108
catechesis
   English mission and 97
   RS's poetry and 27–9, 37n.98, 79, 103

Index

Catholicism in England 6, 15, 18, 22,
    54–5, 86, 88, 97, 105, 108, 110,
    112, 138–9, 143, 169, 176, 195, 197,
    210–12, 221–2, 253
  acts and laws against 85–6, 130, 140,
    171, 195–7, 202, 204–5, 222, 275
  coteries 3, 50, 103, 105–6, 111–12, 124,
    140, 151, 169
  exiles 4–5, 10, 11–14, 22, 54, 57, 62,
    97, 109, 130, 135, 199
  nostalgia for old ways 2–3, 107, 124,
    135, 142, 156–7, 201, 248
  persistence of 3, 4, 18, 22, 105, 142,
    256
  recusancy and resistance 3, 4, 18,
    20, 22, 51, 103, 106–9, 110–12,
    114, 131–3, 142–3, 155, 197, 212–14,
    221–2, 248, 255–6
Cecil, Robert 6, 14, 119–20n.55, 196,
    257–8, 269–70
Cecil, William, Lord Burghley 3, 57, 85,
    96, 110, 130, 140, 171, 176, 196,
    198, 204
  'Bloody Question', the 197, 224n.16,
    222
  'Proclamation' (1591) 254, 266n.49,
    RS's criticism of 254–5, 266n.51
Chrysostom, St 275–6, 281, 288–9
complaint poetry 44, 124–5, 128, 135,
    140, 154–5, 182, 189, 200, 257
  interrogated by RS 152
confession
  influence on RS's writing 7–8, 20,
    44, 50–3, 76–7, 79, 125–6, 188,
    283–6
Constable, Henry 146, 148
  'To St Mary Magdalene' 150–1
contemporaneity 17, 19–20, 59–60, 62,
    75, 80–3, 95, 145, 171, 212, 215,
    217, 230, 253, 275, 278, 284
controversialism 5, 15, 20, 50, 54–5,
    59, 73, 97, 100–1, 103, 150, 174,
    196–7, 283
Copley, Anthony 3, 63–4
  A Fig for Fortune 64, 70n.102
Copley, Bridget (mother) 3
Cotton family 3, 4, 14, 21, 109–11, 256
Crashaw, Richard 9, 11, 79, 285

  'The Weeper' 79

Dacres, Anne (Countess of Arundel)
    113, 208, 210
Deckers, John 7, 44
disguise (RS's uses of) 109, 138–9, 185,
    196, 207–9, 213–4, 217, 251–2,
    285
  hiding 111–12, 139, 257
Dillon, Anne 107–9
Donne, John 85–6, 283, 288
  Holy Sonnet 2 'Show me Dear
    Christ' 144, 206
  Holy Sonnet 10 'Batter my heart'
    276, 281
Dyer, Sir Edward 5, 164, 168–9, 172–4,
    179
  'My Mind to Me a Kingdom is' ('In
    Praise of a Contented Mind')
    168, 174, 179
  'Dyer's Phancie' 5, 172

Elizabeth I (Queen of England) 3, 4, 6,
    11, 56, 68n.66, 87, 106, 130, 135,
    174, 176–7, 196–9, 202–4, 205–7,
    210, 217–8, 224n.22, 227,n.64,
    227n.66, 242, 257–8, 267n.61
  compromises of English Catholics
    with 15, 54, 68n.66, 86–8, 106,
    169, 197
  cult of 206, 214–5, 242, 255
  her government and favourites 5,
    20, 91n.38, 95–6, 139, 164–79,
    182, 188–9, 195, 198–9, 202–7,
    209–10, 212, 215, 218–9, 254–5
  metaphorised as Fortuna/Love by
    RS 205–7, 213, 215–8, 228
  nationalising agendas 10–11, 17, 19,
    164–8, 174–5, 178–9, 184, 197,
    203–5, 207, 214–5, 260
  temporal power 10–11, 15, 20, 56,
    104, 130–2, 167, 185, 196–7, 202,
    204, 209, 210, 221, 228, 248–9
emotional expressivity 7, 8, 30, 44, 58,
    77, 101, 115, 152, 286
English College (Venerabile), Rome
    39–40, 54–7, 61–4, 81, 85, 87,
    99, 101, 137, 232

Index

English language (RS's use of) 4–5, 7–9, 11–12, 21, 23, 26, 39, 45, 49, 55, 68–9n.86, 72, 77–8, 98–104, 110, 115–16, 119n.33, 152–3, 168, 174, 184, 206–7, 211–12, 216–8, 222, 255, 272, 284–5
English missions 6, 23, 54–5, 86, 97, 105, 112, 256–7
  compromises or conciliations on 15, 21, 32n.27, 52, 54, 86, 98–9, 104, 106, 107–8, 135, 139–40, 255, 285
  conflicts 54, 85–7, 97, 104, 106, 194–5, 214
  Edmund Campion and Robert Persons, of 54–7, 60–1, 63, 85–7
  printing of books on 97–8, 107
  RS's travels during 24, 104–6, 111–12, 151, 176, 184, 205, 256–7, 288
  RS's writing during 16, 22, 23, 26–7, 29, 48, 51, 71–3, 93–4, 96, 97–104, 109, 112, 114–5, 136, 142, 156, 170, 183, 185, 194
  rosary, introduction and uses of during 107–9, 260
  virtual church, creation of 48, 96–8, 102–3, 105–6, 109, 132, 134, 243
equivocation 120n.65, 272

female models 3, 10, 22, 138–9, 144–57, 178, 205–19, 248–9, 265–6n.38
  anti-female 215–6, 248
Foxe, John
  Acts and Monuments of These Latter and Perilous Days (1563) 61, 69n.88, 274
free will *see* grace and free will

Garnet, Henry 15, 86–8, 94–5, 98, 104, 105–7, 171, 175–6, 194, 222, 242, 248, 256–60, 271
  closeness to RS 98–9, 194, 258–62
  on the English mission 4–6, 15, 19, 20–2, 23, 25, 42, 51, 57–60, 86–8, 93–7, 103–8, 150, 176, 194–5
  letters 29, 98–9, 104, 105, 111, 112, 116n.6, 118n.27, 138, 170, 194, 256, 258–62

printing 97–8, 114, 117n.13
RS's writing, and 98–9, 103–4, 107, 120n.65, 156, 170, 242, 246, 271
rosary, re-introduction to England of 86, 107–8, 246
Gerard, John 109, 163n.74, 258
grace and free will 4, 20, 25–7, 44–5, 72, 76, 108–9, 123–6, 133–4, 143–4, 149, 155, 228–32, 245–51, 271, 273, 280, 287
  'cross-action' of grace 134, 230–1, 241–2, 244–5, 251
Gregory XIII (Pope) 6, 55–6, 63, 87
  'Bull of Foundation of the Venerable English College in the City' (1579) 55–6

Herbert, George 100, 184, 235, 276, 283–5
  'Jordan (1)' 184
  'Prayer' 115–16
Heywood, Jasper 130
  differences with Robert Persons 54, 85–7, 112
  poetry 151–4, 156
Howard, Henry (Earl of Surrey) 24, 112–13, 121n.74, 164, 167
Howard, Philip (Earl of Arundel) 88, 112–13

iconoclasm 79, 133, 140, 156, 174–5, 183
identity 6–7, 14–15, 17, 21–2, 30, 53–4, 57–8, 62, 73–4, 87, 98, 104, 109–11, 137–9, 229–36, 258, 260, 269–70, 282, 284
Ignatius of Loyola, St 8, 13, 27, 41, 49, 75–8, 83–4, 92n.52, 175–6, 273
innovation 7–11, 13, 15, 24, 27, 30, 44, 46, 50, 53, 71–8, 82, 102, 115–16, 145, 153, 184, 229, 230, 241, 256, 280–1, 286

Jerusalem, England as a divided 138–40, 156, 164
Jesuits
  artistic initiatives and innovations 9, 25–6, 40–7, 49, 57, 59, 62, 75–6, 80–1, 96, 102–3, 176–7

311

Index

arts 4–11, 24–6, 41–5, 48–9, 57, 62, 75–6, 102, 105–6, 107–8, 115, 177–8, 209, 244, 277
confession 20, 43–4, 50–3, 75–9, 85, 106, 126, 277
consolation, ideal of 13–14, 62, 79, 112, 125, 143–7, 154, 243, 260
drama and college theatricals 8–12, 24, 29, 33n.39, 42, 44–5, 71, 76, 82, 101, 116n.7, 118n.22, 128, 145–6, 152–4, 213, 283
martyrdom 41, 48–9, 56–7, 62, 69n.90, 81, 87, 94–5, 165, 270
status on English missions 15, 23, 96–7, 117n.19, 139, 156, 176, 183, 270
Jonson, Ben 2, 16–17, 21, 49, 100, 270, 280–5, 288
'A Hymne to God the Father' 281
De Pictura 280

Kermode, Frank 17, 81, 154, 162n.69, 163n.73
Kuchar, Gary 165–8, 186, 225n.40, 241

Latin (RS's uses of) 4–5, 10–11, 14, 24, 30–1n.2, 32n.23, 38–9, 45, 47, 63, 88, 90n.19, 99–101, 115, 118n.25, 178, 223n.12, 246, 253, 261
law 3, 11, 14, 22, 61, 85–6, 128–31, 141–2, 156, 202, 207, 248–9, 254–5, 259, 272, 286
Lessius, Leonard 4, 24–5, 229

Magdalen, Mary 9, 13–15, 28, 55, 106, 148–9, 155–6
English Catholic exemplar 14–15, 26, 44, 55, 79, 106, 114, 125, 138, 140–50, 152–7, 168, 185, 203, 211, 245, 273, 279
female exemplar 151–5
lover not weeper, as 147–50, 153, 155, 278–9
manuscript dissemination 17, 18, 76, 98–9, 103–4, 112, 114, 119n.33, 120n.65, 122n.85, 123–4, 125, 130–1, 161n.42, 162n.69, 169, 200, 203, 207, 217, 219, 230–1, 235, 243, 248, 251–2, 256, 260, 279–80
Mariology 2, 16, 28–9, 38–9, 46–8, 74, 106–7, 124, 129, 147, 149, 175–7, 206, 245–7, 256
Elizabeth I, and 214–15, 255
hortus conclusus 175–7
'Salve Regina' 16–17
Vulnerata, the 209
martyr cycles and frescos in Rome 41, 45, 48–9, 55–62, 81, 87, 94–6, 137, 165, 199, 261, 274, 277
Martyrdom (RS's attitudes to) 43, 48–9, 57–63, 87–8, 94–7, 132, 170, 181, 194, 199–203, 229–32, 236, 240–1, 246, 253–7, 269–86, 288
martyrology 27, 30, 45, 55–63, 87, 94–6, 124, 209–10, 232, 262, 274, 282, 284–5
Martz, Louis 89n.13, 115, 145, 153, 219, 246, 281
Mary (Queen of Scots) 106, 143, 196–7
and RS's poetry 122n.85, 204, 207–10, 272–3, 278, 282
Milton, John 11–12, 39, 157, 185, 283–6
'Ode on the morning of Christ's Nativity' 286
Paradise Lost 11, 39, 157, 250, 283
de Molina, Luis 25, 123
music (RS's uses of) 8, 48–9, 105–7, 124, 168, 181, 187–8, 221, 234–5, 242–3, 256–7

Nadal, Jerome 25, 30, 45, 49, 80–1, 143
Neoplatonism 75–6, 169, 230–5, 239–40, 246, 248–51

Paintings discussed
Annunciation (Giuseppe Valeriano) 46
Assumption of the Virgin (Giuseppe Valeriano) 46
Birth of the Virgin (Giuseppe Valeriano) 46
Crucifixion (Taddeo Gaddi) 148
Descent from the Cross (Rogier van der Weyden) 149
Ignatius's Vision at La Storta 13

Heavenly Celebration of the Birth of Christ (Niccolò Circignani) 40
Holy Trinity with St Edmund and St Thomas of Canterbury (Durante Alberti) 81, 232
Madonna of the Seven Sorrows (Antonio Tempesta) 46
Marriage of the Virgin (Giuseppe Valeriano) 46
Presentation of Christ at the Temple (Niccolò Circignani) 46
Presentation of the Virgin (Giuseppe Valeriano) 46
St Andrew Altarpiece (Durante Alberti) 41
The Immaculate Conception (Giuseppe Valeriano) 46
Visitation (Giuseppe Valeriano) 46
parody 20, 29, 75, 168, 201, 213, 226n.55
pastoral poetry 16, 112, 164–9, 183–5
patronage 88, 111–14, 121n.80, 150–1, 175, 197, 256, 262
'performing deed' 18–20, 81, 229, 236–8, 241, 250, 253, 257, 271, 281
personation and ventriloquism 9, 44, 55, 75, 78–84, 99, 127–8, 138, 141, 146, 152–4, 157, 162n.69, 212, 230, 283–4
Persons, Robert 7, 15, 40, 53–4, 57, 59, 60–2, 68–9n.85, 69n.90, 85–8, 97–8, 104, 108, 194–5, 197, 206, 209, 257
  missionary oath 6, 56, 87
Petrarchanism 15, 20, 112, 125, 149, 168–9, 186–8, 200–1, 218, 233, 239–41, 247–8, 276
Philip II (King of Spain) 197, 203, 209–10, 254
Pilarz, Scott, S.J. 22, 31n.11, 32n.27, 33n.33, 35n.59, 36n.84, 44, 64n.3, 68n.66, 70n.99, 89n.13, 91n.38, 219, 270
popularity (of RS's poetry) 17–18, 21, 114, 122n.85
power, papal and secular 143, 254–5, 272–3, 286
priest-poet (RS as) 242–4, 246–8, 251, 253, 269–70, 277–8, 280–3, 285
Protestantism or Calvinism 22–3, 26, 61–2, 71, 79, 82, 89n.13, 109–10, 123, 134, 140, 144, 154, 174, 180, 204–5, 215, 229, 237
  RS's criticism of 11–13, 15, 18, 20, 26–7, 30, 38, 42–3, 54–6, 97, 103, 124–5, 128–9, 131–4, 150, 157, 179–80, 184, 196–7, 205–13, 228–9, 238, 243, 247, 281, 283
psychological insights in RS's writing 72–3, 77–81, 115, 131–2, 146–7, 152–3, 284
pursuivants 106, 108, 111, 139, 184, 219, 256–7
Puttenham, George 17
  The Arte of English Poesie (1589) 154, 168, 184–5, 203, 207, 237, 240, 276, 289
Pythagorean patterning 108, 234–5, 243–6

Ralegh, Sir Walter 36n.87, 167–8, 175, 179, 210, 214–15, 217–18, 227n.64, 227n.66
  Discourse of War 210
reader or audience management 10–12, 19–20, 24, 27–9, 41, 72–84, 94, 96–7, 101–2, 109, 113–15, 118n.22, 123–37, 141–5, 151–2, 156, 166, 169, 174–5, 178–82, 203–4, 206–7, 213, 216–17, 219–21, 230–6, 240–6, 249, 251–2, 260–2, 270–8, 281–5, 287
Real Presence
  perceived loss of in England 141–3, 157, 196–7
  RS's poetry and 230, 232, 236–7, 241–6, 252–3
Richeôme, Louis 45, 62, 66n.31
Roman College (Collegio Romano) 25, 41–2, 45, 55, 99, 175

satire in RS's work *see burlesques*
Shakespeare, William 187, 242
  Catholicism, and 36n.76, 63, 110, 263–4n.11, 292n.36

new realism in characterisation, and 11, 16–17, 81, 146, 152–4, 162n.69, 283–4
poetry 20, 102–3, 160–1n.41, 161n.42
Venus and Adonis 145, 150, 154, 170, 211
Shell, Alison 10–11, 17–18, 33–4n.40, 34n.41, 35n.59, 64, 70n.102, 90n.27, 90n.30, 139, 160–1n.41, 219, 291n.31
Sidney, Sir Philip 16–18, 81, 102–3, 145, 150–3, 166–9, 175, 179–85, 189, 213, 228–9, 235–42, 244–5, 249–51, 256–7, 276, 283, 286
Astrophil and Stella (1591) 145, 168, 238–9, 245
Defence of Poesie (1595) 18, 237–8
Society of Jesus
conflicted agendas 53–5, 62, 69n.90, 85, 87, 97–9, 104, 108, 139, 170, 194–5, 209, 257
international outlook 30, 45, 84–5, 99, 117n.19, 177, 205
missions 27, 30, 41, 45, 60, 102, 117n.19, 270
RS's poetry, and 72, 77, 80–3, 89n.13, 98–9, 102–3, 115, 126, 131–2, 137, 141, 144–7, 151–153, 156, 162n.68, 163n.74, 230, 262–3n.2, 281, 287
training for ministry 18, 29–30, 50–2, 82
RS's writing, effect on 13, 18, 20, 24, 29, 43–4, 46, 51–4, 61, 72, 75–80, 97–103, 232, 234, 237
Sodality of the Blessed Virgin 38, 46, 64n.3
'soul rights' 20, 25–6, 130–2, 139, 145, 156, 179, 182–3, 199, 221, 229, 243, 249, 259, 272, 276, 285–6
Southwell, Sir Richard (grandfather) 31n.12, 121n.74
Southwell, Richard (father) 3, 4, 5, 195–7, 254
RS's reproof of 5, 136, 195–8
Southwell, St Robert
appearance of 21, 110–11
capture and death of 248, 257–61

desire to return to England 56–7, 60, 63, 85, 87, 93–4
Douai, and early schooling 4–7, 10–11, 23–4, 30, 99
early life 2–3, 22
family 3–4, 6, 30, 44, 60–1
connections 3, 14, 16, 39, 64, 96, 111, 166, 193n.52, 207, 214, 255
problems with 3, 5–6, 39–40, 60, 139, 172, 195–8, 254
hidden or stratified meanings in RS's poetry 10–11, 15–19, 50, 61, 71–5, 84, 98, 100, 105, 213, 217, 235, 248, 286
immaturity 7, 33n.33, 40, 44, 64
last words 88, 261
letters 7, 17, 29, 57, 93–4, 194–5
in England 3, 6, 14, 29, 93–4, 101, 106, 111–12, 139, 192n.42, 195–7, 210, 222, 254–5, 258, 269–70
in Rome 55, 57, 60–1, 86–7
novitiate 8–9, 13, 27–30, 38–45, 50–3, 57, 60–2, 72–3, 80, 99, 143–4, 157, 165, 169, 171, 177–8, 234, 282–3
ordination 15
RS's poems
'At home in Heaven' 26–7, 29, 231–2, 234, 246–7
'The burning Babe' 2, 12–13, 24, 50, 132, 184, 189, 256, 279–89
'A childe my Choyce' 73, 147–9, 236, 265n.37
'Christs bloody sweat' 108, 236, 251–3, 271, 278–80, 287
'Christs sleeping friends' 103, 136–7, 172, 220
'Content and rich' 168, 179
'Davids Peccavi' 52–3, 170, 200, 284
'Decease release' 122n.85, 203–4, 207–10, 272, 278, 282
'Elegia VIII' 246
'Fortunes Falsehoode' 140, 206–7, 216–17
'From Fortunes reach' 19–20, 99, 249
'A holy Hymne' 236, 241–2
'I die alive' 29, 201–2, 231

Index

'I dye without desert' 199–200, 203, 287–8
'Josephs Amazement' 29, 123, 125–31, 141–3, 152–3, 157, 196–7
'Lewd Love is Losse' 99, 231
'Life is but Losse' 29, 99
'Lifes death loves life' 279
'Looke home' 26, 99, 234, 237, 248–50
'Losse in Delaies' 184, 219–22
'Loves Garden Griefe' 171–2, 178, 182
'Loves servile lot' 164–5, 217–18
'Mans civill warre' 43, 125, 143, 275
'Man to the wound in Christs side' 93–4, 253, 273
'Marie Magdalens complaint at Christs death' 125–6, 143, 149
'Mary Magdalens blush' 26, 78, 153, 244–5
'New heaven new warre' 16, 24, 73, 123–5, 184
'New Prince, new pompe' 24, 125, 184, 236
'Of the Blessed Sacrament of the Aulter' 23, 26, 71–2, 115, 127, 233, 237, 241–3, 248, 271
'Peeter Playnt' 34n.43, 55, 100–1
'A Phansie turned to a sinners complaint' 5, 29, 172–4, 198, 287, 292n.39
'Poema de Assumptione B.V.M.' 11–12, 24, 38, 47, 56, 71–2, 177–8, 246
'The prodigall childs soule wracke' 7, 76, 113, 125, 127, 175
Querimonia 7–8, 33n.33, 55
Saint Peters Complaint and Other Poems 18, 73, 114, 122n.85, 147, 212
'Saint Peters Complaint' (long) 12, 17, 27–9, 38, 79–80, 83, 99, 100, 121n.74, 126, 152–3, 161n.42, 185, 211–12, 222, 279, 287
'Saint Peters Complaynte' (short) 5, 78–9, 152, 211–12, 237–8, 287
'Scorne not the Least' 99, 142–3, 165, 204, 212–13, 219, 221

'Seeke flowers of heaven' 9–10, 174–5, 246–7, 265n.37
'Sinnes heavie loade' 81–2, 132–4, 236, 292n.39
'S. Peters afflicted minde' 78, 287
'S. Peters remorse' 78
'A vale of teares' 16–17, 84, 165–7, 171, 178–9, 180–1, 184, 186–8, 219, 279–80, 284
'The virgin Mary to Christ on the Crosse' 49, 94, 124
'Virgin Sequence' poems *also see individual entries below* 28, 46, 48, 74, 106, 129, 147, 182, 198, 234–5, 245
'What joy to live?' 29, 125, 201, 278
Virgin Sequence
  'The Assumption of our Lady' 46–7
  'Christs Childhoode' 47, 265n.37
  'Christs returne out of Egypt' 47, 176
  'The death of our Ladie' 47
  'The Epiphanie' 47
  'The flight into Egypt' 47, 48, 198–9, 210
  'Her Nativity' 47, 176
  'Her Spousals' 47, 176
  'His circumcision' 46, 47, 74
  'Nativitie of Christ' 47, 265n.37
  'The Presentation' 46–7
  'The Virgine Maries Conception' 47, 176
  'The Virgins Salutation' (VS) 47, 107, 176, 246
  'The Visitation' (VS) 47, 129
Works
  'The Author to his loving Cosen' 77, 147, 226n.55, 238, 241
  An Epistle of Comfort 138, 213, 215–19, 222, 254, 256, 269, 273–9, 285
  Epistle unto His Father 136
  An Humble Supplication to her Majesty 20, 104, 122n.85, 198, 254–5, 256, 285
  A Hundred Meditations on the Love of God 82
  Marie Magdalens Funeral Teares 44, 103, 114, 125, 138, 141–7, 150, 152,

315

156, 161n.48, 162n.67, 168, 185
Moeoniae 49, 94, 127, 253
A Short Rule of Good Life 89n.13, 256, 271
Spiritual Exercises and Devotions 22, 43–4, 50–2, 57–60, 63, 67n.49, 85–6, 88, 147, 169–70, 172, 230–2, 257, 261, 273–5, 283, 288
The Triumphs over Death 122n.85, 256

RS's English poetic projects
active readership 151–2, 231–2, 287
dating 7, 14–15, 46–8, 66n.40, 106, 141, 147, 198–200, 202–3, 219
pattern for English poets 147, 149, 231, 233, 235, 238, 245–51, 253, 274–7, 282–5
poems
as prayer 134, 232–3
as sacraments 27, 48, 230–6, 240–8, 260, 262, 269, 271–2, 281–3, 285–7
as relics 41, 48, 230–1, 235, 240, 262, 276–8, 285
poetic agendas 15–20, 24, 27–8, 49–51, 72, 76, 83, 98, 100, 102–5, 174, 183–4, 197–9, 203–4, 210–11, 213, 217, 232, 237, 254–5, 259–60, 271–3, 274–8, 284

Spenser, Edmund 174, 283
The Faerie Queene 70n.102, 168, 215, 263n.9
'Muiopotmos' 174–5
Spiritual Excercises of Ignatius, The 19, 26–8, 41–2, 44, 49, 51, 72–85, 88, 90n.27, 93, 109, 115, 262–3n.2

Suárez, Francisco 25–6, 37n.95, 107–9 *passim*, 123, 211
influence on RS 27, 29, 45, 97, 123, 150, 228, 262n.2, 289

Tansillo, Luigi, *Le Lagrime di San Pietro* 34n.43, 55, 100
Topcliffe, Richard 63, 122n.85, 224n.22, 248, 256–7, 269
torture of RS, and 258, 267n.61, 269
transubstantiation addressed in RS's poetry 72, 131, 134, 196–7, 229–37, 241–2, 246, 248–9, 252–3, 271, 281, 286, 288
Trent, Council of 4, 26, 36, 37n.96, 51, 174
artistic theories, and 12, 18, 23–4, 37n.89, 115, 123, 238
RS's poetry and 12, 23, 27, 123, 125, 130, 149, 156
Tresham, Sir Thomas 3, 143, 171–2, 183

Verstegan, Richard 68–9n.86, 113, 195, 257–8
Violence (RS's attitudes to) 50–1, 55, 59, 62, 275–6, 277–9
'visualisation' 8–13, 19, 39–42, 45–9, 72, 75, 80–2, 101–2, 109, 115, 175, 180–1, 229–30, 241, 244, 283

Weston, Willam 85–6, 91n.45, 97, 104–7, 114, 259
Whitgift, John (Archbishop of Canterbury) 130, 205, 212

EU authorised representative for GPSR:
Easy Access System Europe, Mustamäe tee 50,
10621 Tallinn, Estonia
gpsr.requests@easproject.com

www.ingramcontent.com/pod-product-compliance
Lightning Source LLC
Chambersburg PA
CBHW070935230426
43666CB00011B/2447